The Epistle to Diognetus

Classic Studies on the Apostolic Fathers

Edited by Jeremiah Bailey, George Kalantzis, and Jacob N. Cerone

Volume 4

Classic Studies on the Apostolic Fathers publishes works which have had a significant impact on Apostolic Fathers scholarship but are not easily accessible. The series primarily consists of original translations of works which have never appeared in English and new publications of works in English which have gone out of print or are otherwise difficult to acquire. The series exists to make scholarship on the Apostolic Fathers accessible to the widest audience possible.

The Epistle to Diognetus
The Greek Text with Introduction, Translation, and Notes

Henry G. Meecham

Edited and Lightly Revised by
Jacob N. Cerone

Foreword by
Michael F. Bird

PICKWICK *Publications* • Eugene, Oregon

THE EPISTLE TO DIOGNETUS
The Greek Text with Introduction, Translation, and Notes

Classic Studies on the Apostolic Fathers 4

Copyright © 2024 Jacob N. Cerone. All rights reserved. Except for brief quotations in critical publications or reviews, no part of this book may be reproduced in any manner without prior written permission from the publisher. Write: Permissions, Wipf and Stock Publishers, 199 W. 8th Ave., Suite 3, Eugene, OR 97401.

Original edition published by Manchester University Press, 1949

Pickwick Publications
An Imprint of Wipf and Stock Publishers
199 W. 8th Ave., Suite 3
Eugene, OR 97401

www.wipfandstock.com

PAPERBACK ISBN: 978-1-6667-6150-4
HARDCOVER ISBN: 978-1-6667-6151-1
EBOOK ISBN: 978-1-6667-6152-8

Cataloguing-in-Publication data:

Names: Meecham, Henry George, 1886–1955 [author]. | Cerone, Jacob N. [editor]. | Bird, Michael F. [foreword writer].

Title: The Epistle to Diognetus : the Greek text with introduction, translation, and notes / Henry G. Meecham, edited and lightly revised by Jacob N. Cerone.

Description: Eugene, OR: Pickwick Publications, 2024 | Series: Classic Studies on the Apostolic Fathers 4 | Includes bibliographical references and index.

Identifiers: ISBN 978-1-6667-6150-4 (paperback) | ISBN 978-1-6667-6151-1 (hardcover) | ISBN 978-1-6667-6152-8 (ebook)

Subjects: LCSH: Epistle to Diognetus. | Diognetus. | Apologetics—History—Early church, ca 30–600.

Classification: BR65.E666 M44 2024 (paperback) | BR65.E666 (ebook)

VERSION NUMBER 02/20/24

To
A. G. M.
And
P. H. M.

Contents

Series Foreword: Classic Studies on the Apostolic Fathers | ix
Editor's Preface | Jacob N. Cerone | xi
Foreword | Michael F. Bird | xiii
Author's Preface | Henry G. Meecham | xvii

I. Introduction | 1
   1. Apologetic Class and Aim | 1
   2. Title and Plan | 5
   3. Literary Form | 6
   4. Vocabulary, Grammar, and Style | 9
   5. Authorship and Date | 15
   6. Teaching | 19
      i. Chapters 1–10 | 19
         a. God | 20
         b. Son | 25
         c. Man and the Christian Community | 28
         d. Pagan Idolatry and Philosophy | 30
         e. Jewish Worship | 34
         f. Persecution of the Christians | 37
         g. Moral and Religious Values | 39
         h. Eschatology | 40
         i. Relation to Current Thought | 42
         j. Summary | 47
      ii. Chapters 11–12 | 49

7. Literary Relationships | 52
   a. Old Testament (LXX) | 52
   b. New Testament | 53
   c. The Apologists | 56
8. Integrity | 63
9. History of the Text | 67
10. Select Bibliography | 68

II. Text | 76   **II. Translation** | 77

Notes | 95

Additional Notes | 170
   A. The Imitation of God (10:4–6) | 170
   B. The Deification of Man | 171
   C. The Sonship of the Logos | 173
   D. Guarded Tradition | 174
   E. Diognetus and the Apology of Quadratus | 176

Bibliography | 181
Index of Subjects | 191
Index of Authors | 195
Index of Sources | 199

Series Foreword
Classic Studies on the Apostolic Fathers

THE LATE SCHOLAR OF early Christianity Larry Hurtado described the second century as "the Cinderella century," because it occupies the liminal space between the apostolic period of the New Testament and the world of the apologists at the end of the second century and beginning of the third. The post-apostolic era was a vibrant period of development as early Christians struggled to narrate their beliefs about the person of Jesus, decide the structure of their assemblies, find their place in the vastness that was the Roman Empire, and tackle the social issues that arose when a Jewish sect took on a massive influx of gentiles.

Some of the earliest voices of this period are found in the grouping of texts that is commonly called "The Apostolic Fathers." These texts are a record of early Christian self-expression composed without the limits of later creeds and bear witness to the hard work of identifying one's own theological boundaries or rejecting the boundaries that others have created. The presentation of these texts as a collection, however, is an artificial construct of scholarship, which is reflected in the variety of genres found within: the corpus includes epistolary material (both corporate and individual; both pseudepigraphic and genuine), a sermon, an apology, and an apocalypse. In many respects, it is precisely this variety that makes the Apostolic Fathers an excellent entry point to the broader second century.

Even though in the last few decades there has been an increase in interest in the Apostolic Fathers, the volume of scholarship remains small. There are likely many causes for this neglect, but two seem particularly prominent. First is the inherent difficulty of any transitional period to fit comfortably within the delineations of historical scholarship. To those who were trained in New Testament studies, the boundaries of that corpus have more recently tended to exclude the post-apostolic writings, while those trained in Patristics or Late Antiquity sometimes gloss over the second century in favor of the action-packed third and fourth centuries. Hurtado argued (and we agree), however, that the study of the second century makes the scholars working on either side of that century better. When we skip over these texts, we erase important strata of early Christian theological development.

Another significant cause of this neglect is access to scholarship. The student who wishes to study these texts closely is already faced with the challenge of greatly expanding their Koine vocabulary and, if they desire to engage in textual criticism, acquiring Latin, Coptic, and Syriac. Having accomplished these things, the would-be student of the Apostolic Fathers is then confronted by the reality that most of the secondary literature is in German, French, or Italian. In addition, much of the important English language scholarship is out-of-print and/or prohibitively expensive to acquire. Studying these texts beyond a surface level might, therefore, seem quite daunting.

The goal of *Classic Studies on the Apostolic Fathers* is to bridge this gap by bringing back to print some of the most important but hard-to-find resources in English and by providing translations of important works of scholarship on the Apostolic Fathers into English for the very first time. It is our hope that *Classic Studies on the Apostolic Fathers* will allow students and scholars to see for themselves the promise of these texts and engage this vital period anew.

—Jeremiah Bailey,
George Kalantzis, and
Jacob N. Cerone

Editor's Preface

Jacob N. Cerone

In this edition of Meecham's work on Diognetus, I have attempted to present a lightly revised version of this classic work. The contents of the work and Meecham's positions and views remain intact and unchanged. However, I have taken certain liberties to make the text more accessible for a contemporary audience. First, all the French and German citations within the original work have been translated into English. Second, I have updated Meecham's somewhat antiquated language by removing thee and thou and other vestiges of a former era. Third, since the original version of Meecham's work only cited the author's last night, abbreviated title, and year of publication, I have filled supplied the missing bibliographical information, at great effort. I am thankful to Jeremiah Bailey for tracking down some of the information I was missing. Finally, the volume has been typeset anew instead of reproducing a facsimile copy of the book. My thanks to the kind and professional staff at Wipf and Stock for the tedious work of copy-editing and typesetting this volume. I am especially grateful to Elisabeth Rickard, who caught many inconsistencies in the manuscript and also translated several French quotations which I had overlooked, to the typesetter for the difficult task of typesetting this volume, especially since it involved the complicated work of formatting Meecham's diglot Greek-English version of Diogentus, and to Robin Parry for all his work shepherding the volume through to publication. Additional thanks are owed to Michael Bird for his foreword which places Meecham's work in its historical context and expounds upon its significance and continuing relevance to the field.

Foreword

Michael Bird

HENRY G. MEECHAM (1886–1955) was a Methodist clergyman and biblical scholar whose commentary on *The Epistle to Diognetus* first appeared in 1949, published by the University of Manchester Press. For a very long time, Meecham's commentary on Diognetus was the only one of its kind available in English. L. B. Radford produced a translation and notes on Diognetus in 1908, but that work was a very modest venture, almost a pamphlet, and offered very little analysis of the actual contents of the text or exploration of its many interpretive problems. Otherwise, beyond Meecham's volume, one had to consult the French commentary by H. I. Marrou (1997) and in German that of H. E. Lona (2001) to find thorough explorations of Diognetus. Consequently, for many years, Meecham's volume was the only comprehensive analysis of this notoriously obscure and neglected letter in the English-speaking world. To be honest, Meecham's volume is now somewhat dated and supplanted by the erudite commentary by Clayton N. Jefford with his *The Epistle to Diognetus (with the Fragment of Quadratus): Introduction, Text, and Commentary*, Oxford Apostolic Fathers (Oxford: Oxford University Press, 2013). However, Meecham's commentary remains something of a watershed in the study of Diognetus as he brought his skills as a New Testament scholar and his vast knowledge of the patristic era and of theological *topoi* to the study of the letter.

Concerning Diognetus itself, the work is most probably a second century apologetic-protreptic treatise with a homiletical addition spliced on at the end. The letter is ordinarily dated to 150–200 CE, although the homiletical section may be dated considerably later and may not even be by the same author. Speaking of the author, we know next to nothing about them apart from what we glean from the letter. They are someone learned in Greek philosophy and Christian Scripture (especially the apostle Paul's letters), and seek to promote Christianity as an alternative to both Judaism and Greco-Roman religion. The designated addressee is one "Diognetus," who could be a real person or else comprise a literary fiction ("Diognetus" means literally "son of Zeus"). While Diognetus has a great deal of literary artistry, religious rhetoric, and theological poignancy, the letter is never once mentioned by authors of the patristic and medieval periods, so we are at a complete loss as to its origins. There remains an outside chance that the letter could in fact be a renaissance forgery! What we do know is that a manuscript containing Diognetus was allegedly discovered in a fishmonger's shop in Constantinople in 1436. The text of Diognetus was found in a manuscript labeled as *Codex Argentoratensis Graecus* ix, dated to the thirteenth to fourteenth centuries, and in that manuscript Diognetus was located at the end of a series of works by Justin Martyr (which led many to initially surmise that Justin was the author, although that view has since been long abandoned on stylistic grounds). The manuscript was first published in 1592 by Henri Estienne (aka Henricus Stephanus). Unfortunately, the codex containing Diognetus was destroyed in the nineteenth century during the Franco-Prussian war of 1870. The Greek text is now preserved only in transcriptions made by several scholars who had seen and studied the letter. Using those transcriptions, the most recent translations are those by Michael Holmes, Rick Brannan, and Bart Ehrman in their respective volumes on the Apostolic Fathers.

There is much about Diognetus that is misunderstood. For a start, it is not actually an epistle. It is more properly an apologetic-protreptic treatise with an epistolary opening and a homiletical appendix. As such, it belongs more to the second century apologists than it does among the Apostolic Fathers (even then the Apostolic Fathers are an artificial and elastic literary collection!). It was the Italian patristic scholar Andrea Gallandi (1709–1779) who first included Diognetus in his 1765 edition of the Apostolic Fathers based on his speculative inference that the work was written by Paul's missionary companion Apollos. While Gallandi's authorial conjecture never acquired support in subsequent scholarship, nonetheless, the inclusion of Diognetus among the Apostolic Fathers has become something of an accepted custom for the collection ever since.

The apology for Christianity made to "Diognetus" breaks down into several distinct parts. First, there is the prologue (Diogn. 1:1–2) which sets forth the three questions that are addressed in the document: (1) What god do the Christians believe in and worship? (2) What is the nature of their love for each other? and (3) Why has this new people with their peculiar way of life suddenly appeared now? Second, the author next turns to a dual critique of pagan idol worship as well as the Jerusalem *cultus* and Jewish ceremonial laws (Diogn. 2–4). Third, the author constructs an artful encomium to Christians for their exemplary way of life and positive impact upon the world as upright citizens (Diogn. 5–6). Fourth, there is a section on God's providence and purposes surrounding the divine Word/child who is sent to save the powerless and unrighteous, which is one of the finest christological pieces prior to Nicaea for my mind (Diogn. 7–9). Fifth, the author argues that faith leads to knowledge, which leads in turn to love, and love is an imitation of God's very own goodness (Diogn. 10). Finally, there is the closing section known as the homily, which was probably not organic to the work, perhaps even written by a subsequent author, but is nonetheless attached here. The homily offers an exposition of the incarnation of the Logos and allegorical reflections on the two trees planted in the garden of Eden (Diogn. 11–12).

As for Meecham himself, he authored several earlier works including *Light from Ancient Letters* about the Oxyrhynchus papyri (1923), *The Oldest Version of the Bible* (1932), and *The Letter of Aristeas* (1935) concerning Jewish and Christian apologetics about the origins of their Scriptures, and finally his magisterial and celebrated commentary on *The Epistle of Diognetus* (1949). In retirement, Meecham also revised J. H. Moulton's *Introduction to the Study of New Testament Greek* for its fifth edition (1955). Meecham's Methodism meant that he inherited something of an "evangelical" ethos, albeit one that sometimes sailed in the direction of the British liberal tradition.

For example, Meecham eschewed substitutionary atonement in favor of moral influence theory. He wrote in an article prior to the publication of his commentary that "it is clear that in the main *Diognetus* conceives the Atonement from the point of view of 'moral influence' . . . while the moral theory of the Atonement predominates in our author's thought, it is not exclusive of other elements which later developed into the vicarious penal and substitutionary theories."[1] In the commentary itself, when explaining Diogn. 9:5 about the "sweet exchange," Meecham earnestly asserted that "the context suggests that the 'exchange' is one of *state* rather than *person*, of wickedness for justification, not the substitution of Christ for me" (see p. 151). Concerning the incarnation, Meecham recognized that the letter does describe the beloved divine Son with angelic characteristics, yet he observed that "God sent no minister to men whether we call him angel or ruler, an earthly governor or a heavenly ruler. But the general sense of the passage is clear. The one sent did not belong in any subordinate order of celestial beings; he was the very 'Artificer and Maker of the universe'" (see p. 134). Meecham was we could say, in theological terms, very much his own man,

---

1. Meecham, "Theology of the Epistle to Diognetus," 99–100.

and not given to tethering himself to the theological proclivities of one particular school or any single tribe of the Christian tradition.

Meecham's commentary had the ambitious aim to discuss the text's "aim, authorship, date, and integrity; to estimate its literary character in form, language, and style; to explore the content of its thought; to determine its relation to the Greek Bible and early Christian writings; finally to provide a translation and a commentary" (see p. xvii). It was the first major critical study of the letter, and Meecham's work remains to this day an intelligent, learned, and robust analysis of the major questions that the letter creates and offers a close reading of the Greek text. Meecham was undoubtedly at his best as a historian of ancient texts, a reader of Hellenistic Jewish and patristic literature, and as a lexicographical and linguistic explorer of ancient Greek. His analysis of the Greek of Diognetus is dense and detailed and remains peerless to this day. His prior works in Greek papyri, Hellenistic Jewish texts, and the patristic corpus made him particularly fit to write his commentary on Diognetus. Meecham was rightly awarded a British Doctor of Divinity by Manchester University for his commentary given its attention to analytical detail, reasoned judgments, sober conclusions on contested matters, and grasp of the theological atmospherics of the letter. Meecham's commentary on Diognetus continues to be the main starting point for the study of this letter, and scholars continue to approvingly cite his work in recent research of the letter even though many changes have taken place in the study of early Christianity in general and of the second century Christian apologists in particular. It is partly because of the paucity of publications on this text that Meecham's commentary remains important, but I believe it is primarily due to the eruditeness of Meecham's scholarship that his commentary remains inherently useful even into the present day.

Accordingly, the republication of Meecham's volume by Wipf and Stock under the editorial oversight of Jacob Cerone, George Kalantzis, and Jeremiah Bailey is to be celebrated. It makes this invaluable commentary of this neglected Christian text available for a new generation of readers and researchers of Diognetus. I do not doubt that Meecham would be most pleased for more students to embark upon the study of early Christianity and find enjoyment and refreshment from the study of texts like the Epistle to Diognetus for which he labored so profitably and so enabled us to better understand the shape and sound of Christianity in antiquity.

Author's Preface

Henry G. Meecham

In this book an attempt is made to present a comprehensive study of the Epistle to Diognetus. I have sought to discuss its aim, authorship, date, and integrity; to estimate its literary character in form, language, and style; to explore the content of its thought; to determine its relation to the Greek Bible and early Christian writings; finally to provide a translation and a commentary. The whole rests on a detailed examination of the Greek text.

The Epistle to Diognetus is of limited scope. Its value, however, is commensurate with its size. This tractate with its stress on the divine initiative in the redemption of impotent man, its picture of the Christians as "the soul of the world," and its plea for the imitation of God in love and beneficence makes its own timely appeal. Moreover, the investigation of the *Diognetus* may assist in some degree a wider inquiry, namely, how far the teaching of early Christian writers adequately interprets and restates New Testament thought.

Here and there the text of the epistle is corrupt and its Greek obscure. It is hoped that the *apparatus criticus* may furnish a sufficient guide to the meaning. An effort has been made to mark in the Notes every important variant and conjectural emendation. In the English translation words in italics are added where necessary as an aid to clarity; a series of dots denotes lacunae in the text.

This book, along with subsidiary work, was approved as a thesis for the degree Doctor of Divinity in the University of Manchester. I have taken advantage of the interval before publication to make some rearrangements in the Introduction and to bring in a small amount of additional matter.

To the Rev. Professor T. W. Manson I am deeply indebted for his kindly interest and expert counsel. The Rev. Dr. W. F. Howard and the Rev. Dr. H. McLachlan have laid me under further obligation. Both read the original typescript and made valuable suggestions. I record with gratitude the generous help I have received from the Rev. A. Raymond George, who carefully read the proofs. To the editors and publishers of the *Expository Times* I am grateful for their kindness in permitting me to incorporate the substance of an article on the theology of the Epistle to Diognetus which appeared in that Journal.[1] Lastly, my thanks are due to Mr. H. M. McKechnie for his unfailing consideration and his skill in seeing the book through the press.

—H. G. Meecham

---

1. Meecham, "Theology of the Epistle to Diognetus."

I. Introduction

1. Apologetic Class and Aim

It has become an axiom that no religious movement can be adequately interpreted apart from its historic setting. Hence biblical research tends more and more to stress the contact of Christianity with the age in which it arose. This emphasis does not imply that Christianity was a product of its own time. But it does recognize that what environment fails to account for it may serve to illuminate. The New Testament writings, therefore, as the classical documents of the faith, cannot stand in isolation. Their whole context is significant. As earlier and contemporary Jewish literature is indispensable for the interpretation of the New Testament, so too some at least of the second century Christian writings have considerable value in this regard. The works of the Apostolic Fathers (ca. 96–150 CE) and the Apologists (ca. 150–200)[1] form a vital link in the continuity of New Testament teaching. It is not without significance that of the former writings four were included as supplements to the canon in the codices Sinaiticus and Alexandrinus of the fourth and early fifth centuries respectively.[2]

In the age of the apologists literary activity was both considerable and varied.[3] It is no part of our purpose to discuss the genesis and development of early Christian apologetic. It must suffice here to point out its historic precedents. The Hellenistic age provides a convenient starting point. The first vital contact of Jew and Greek (about the time of Alexander the Great) set in motion incalculable forces. The Jew of the dispersion now found himself in a new intellectual world, and a measure of accommodation to

---

1. These dates are approximate. The apologists Quadratus and Aristides were somewhat earlier, while apologetic writings appeared during the early fourth century.

2. The Epistle of Barnabas and the Shepherd of Hermas in Codex Sinaiticus; 1 and 2 Clement in Codex Alexandrinus.

3. A list of Christian apologetic writings is conveniently given in Cadoux, *Early Church*, 202ff. See also Krüger, *Early Christian Literature*, 100ff.

Hellenistic life and thought became inevitable. The Alexandrian Jew in particular was faced with the problem of harmonizing his traditional faith with what was for him a new and pervasive culture. There must be shown to exist an affinity between Greek philosophy and Jewish wisdom.

Moreover, attacks by anti-Semitic Greek writers like Posidonius and Apollonius Molon made some kind of literary defense imperative.[4] The heathen world must be impressed by the story of Israel's sacred past, by the greatness of her religious life and institutions. The type and method of such apologetic are clearly seen, for example, in the Letter of Aristeas with its appeal to reason, its combination of religious liberalism with loyalty to fundamental Jewish beliefs, and its subtle plea for the political toleration of the Jews.[5] How far a conscious apologetic purpose lies behind the Septuagint itself is still a matter in debate. That it not only attests Jewish reaction to a changed cultural environment but also actually furthered apologetic and missionary ends is plain. While made principally to meet the religious needs of Greek-speaking Jews, it served also as the chief instrument to bring the Greek world into the Jewish faith. Philo[6] early in the first century CE and Josephus[7] towards its close show the apologetic aim on a far wider scale. The main purpose of all such literary activity was to magnify Judaism in the eyes of the pagan world and to win the outsider to the Jewish faith.

During the first century CE, while Christianity was rapidly spreading, Christian missionaries were largely occupied with the instruction of converts. Christians themselves lived in the glow of a new religious experience and were thrilled by the fervent hope of the second coming of Christ. Therefore relatively little attention was paid to countering pagan attacks upon the new religion. But towards the end of the century, when the "first fine careless rapture" was apt to die down,[8] and heresies began to wean some from the faith, and to the hostility of the Jew was added incipient persecution by the State, the need for explicit apologetic plainly arose.[9] This was the

---

4. Some earlier Greek writers had given a favorable view of the Jews. For example, Hecataeus of Abdera (*floruit*, ca. 332 BCE) appreciated the wise principles of Jewish theocracy (see Josephus, *C. Ap.* 1.183–205; 2.43). Manetho, however, an Egyptian historian of the third century BCE, gave new currency to a scurrilous story of Jewish origins (see *C. Ap.* 1.73ff., 227ff.). The worst outbursts of Greek contempt for the Jews occurred after the Maccabean revolt. For a review of the early stages of anti-Semitism see Herzog, "Outlook," 49–60. See Schürer, *History*, 2.3:302ff., 249ff.

5. The writings of Demetrius, Eupolemus, and Artapanus (preserved by Alexander Polyhistor ca. 50 BCE) represent a feebler type of Jewish literary propaganda.

6. See especially *Flacc.* and *Legat.*

7. Cf. *C. Ap.* 1.1.

8. Cf. the seer's lament: "you left your first love" (Rev 2:4).

9. It is clear that a more general apologetic interest pervades the NT itself. See Scott, *Apologetic*.

more necessary in that there was widespread ignorance of the new faith. Many apologists plead that Christians should not be condemned unheard.[10] The case for Christians had now to be stated before the wider cultural world.

For such a role Christian writers had ready at hand in the Hellenistic-Jewish apologies a precedent and to some extent material for their task. Not infrequently similar calumnies confronted both defenders of their respective faiths. Jew and Christians alike were charged with "atheism," hatred of the human race, and immorality. Hence the literary defense of the one prepared the way for that of the other. The influence of Philo especially is traceable in the Alexandrian Christian apologists.[11]

Among the comparatively few surviving works of the apologetic age Diognetus holds an honorable place. The interest and charm of the epistle are undeniable. Its rare elevation of thought is clothed in language at once simple and stately and warmed by "intensity of conviction." Many older scholars disregarded Diognetus as an addendum to the works of Justin Martyr. But nearly all who have given it attention accord it high praise. Neander ranks it "among the finest remains of Christian antiquity."[12] Bunsen says that it "is indisputably, after Scripture, the finest monument we know of sound Christian feeling, noble courage, and manly eloquence,"[13] while Lightfoot characterizes it as "the nobles of early Christian writings."[14]

There is, however, an air of mystery about this little document. Not only is it of unknown authorship and provenance, uncertain in date and composite in character, but, strangely enough, it is known neither to Eusebius nor to Photius nor indeed to any ancient or medieval writer.[15] Moreover, its sole textual source is a single medieval manuscript, which has itself perished.

10. Cf. Athenagoras, *Suppl.* 2 (*sub fin.*), and see note on 5:12, below.

11. Reagan, *Preaching of Peter*, 54, suggests that the picture of the Christian life in Aristides, Athenagoras, and Diognetus is modelled on Philo's portrayal of the Therapeutae (*Contempl. Life*).

12. Neander, *General History*, 2:425.

13. Bunsen, *Christianity and Mankind*, 1:170f.

14. Lightfoot, *Commentary on Colossians*, 154ff.

15. It is certainly a striking fact that no ancient writer quotes or even alludes to Diognetus. How may we account for this unbroken silence? By the generation more or less contemporary with Diognetus it may have been viewed with disfavor as remote from the facts of Christ's life and ministry, a piece of mere moralizing on the virtues of the Christian life. Writers of a later period may well have discarded it on the ground that it was too vague in doctrine and lacked dogmatic fullness and precision. The fact too that the NT canon was then closed would tend to the relative neglect of those writings of the first and second centuries which found no place therein. Bunsen (*Hippolytus and His Age*, 1:170–73) thought that the silence respecting Diognetus might be explained on the supposition that it was regarded with suspicion as the work of a heretical writer (Marcion). But the Marcionite authorship of Diognetus is quite improbable. See p. 16.

Often classed with the writings of the Apostolic Fathers, Diognetus belongs rather to those of the Apologists. Or perhaps we may say that it forms a literary nexus between the practical exhortations of the Fathers and the more formal apologies of Justin and his successors. The relation of Diognetus to the apologetic class may be more closely defined. Its theology, inchoate as it is, anticipates the Eastern rather than the Western type of Christian thought.[16] That aspect of thought, primarily christological, which was to appear clearly in Athanasius, is here foreshadowed. Further, Diognetus ranks itself with those didactic and apologetic tracts which sought especially to commend Christianity to educated readers of the time.[17] A twofold aim underlies the apologetic literature: first, to emphasize the truth and excellence of Christian teaching, to show its rational basis and relate it to the philosophic thought of the age; secondly, to justify, by affirming the blameless conduct of Christians, the place of the faith in society and thus secure its toleration in the Empire.

Included in this twofold purpose was a polemic of varying intensity directed against both pagan idolatry and Jewish superstition. This served more or less as an offset to the apologetic appeal. The author of Diognetus is not indifferent to the second aim,[18] but it is not his primary concern, and, while his polemic against pagan and Jewish worship is vigorous (if flat and unoriginal), it is ancillary to his main object, namely, to show the reasonableness of the Christian faith and its appeal as a way of life.[19] He does not specifically refute the gross calumnies current about Christians. He is content to allow his picture of the Christian manner of life to give them the lie. Moreover, our author is to be classed with Tatian and Theophilus in making a strong contrast between Christianity and antecedent faiths, heathen and Jewish alike. Some apologists, for example Athenagoras, recognize that there had been a progressive revelation of God in human history; hence Christianity was the fulfillment of good already present in the pre-Christian world, a view well marked in Clement of Alexandria. It is not so in this epistle. Here the Christian religion is conceived as a wholly new moral power rescuing men darkened in mind and doomed under sin.[20] Again, the author puts the

---

16. See Scullard, *Early Christian Ethics*, 8ff.; Allen, *Continuity*, 103.

17. Diognetus and the Octavius of Minucius Felix are the two best examples of this type. Each, addressed to a private person, has in view a wider circle.

18. See below, p. 38.

19. Harnack's strictures (*Geschichte*, 2.1:515) on the feeble apologetic of the early chapters may be admitted. But the strength of Diognetus lies in its positive account of the Christian way of life.

20. See below, pp. 22–23. Note the contrasted ὁ τῆς ἀδικίας καιρός and ὁ νῦν τῆς δικαιοσύνης (καιρός), 9:1.

apologetic emphasis in the surest place. He has nothing to say of miracles or even of the argument from prophecy. For him the Christian life itself is the unanswerable proof. True, other apologists make much of this plea;[21] but for him it seems almost the whole of his positive case. Theologically, the most striking differentia of Diognetus from the apologists generally is the insistence upon the redemptive function of the Son.[22]

2. Title and Plan

Codex Argentoratensis Graec. 9 contained five treatises ascribed to Justin Martyr (τοῦ ἁγίου Ἰουστίνου φιλοσόφου καὶ μάρτυρος).[23] Of these our epistle was the last, though it was followed in the MS by several other writings, some by a later hand. It bore the heading: τοῦ αὐτοῦ πρὸς Διόγνητον. It is printed variously by editors as ΕΠΙΣΤΟΛΗ ΠΡΟΣ ΔΙΟΓΝΗΤΟΝ, ΠΡΟΣ ΔΙΟΓΝΗΤΟΝ ΕΠΙΣΤΟΛΗ, ΠΡΟΣ ΔΙΟΓΝΗΤΟΝ, and *Epistola (Epistula) ad Diognetum*.

The contents and plan may be briefly indicated. Ostensibly the epistle is written to answer an inquiry made by a certain Diognetus[24] about the character of the Christian faith. Diognetus asks three pointed questions:

1. Who is the God the Christians trust in, and what is the nature of the worship they offer him, that they are all led to disregard the world and despise death, to deny those to be gods whom the Greeks consider as such, and to refrain from the superstition of the Jews?
2. What kind of affection is this that the Christians have for one another?
3. Why has this new race or practice entered the world now and not formerly?

The body of the epistle enlarges upon these questions. First, it discourses on the variety and material nature of heathen gods and the folly of worshiping them. Then follows a severe condemnation of Jewish sacrifices, rites, and customs. This leads to a delightful picture of early Christian life and a quasi-theological interpretation of the Son of God as revealer of the true knowledge of the Father and agent of man's salvation. After the manner of an epilogue the closing chapter commends the character and fruits of the faith as an *imitatio Dei*. Chapters 11 and 12 form an appendix by a

---

21. See Aristides, *Apol.* 15–17 (Syr.); Justin Martyr, *1 Apol.* 14.
22. See below, pp. 23, 26–27.
23. See below, p. 67.
24. See note on κράτιστε Διόγνητε (1:1).

later hand,[25] the one chapter being a short summary of Apostolic teaching and practice, the other a little homily enforcing on the basis of the garden of Eden story the union of knowledge and life. The plan of the epistle is not explicitly stated. But the author follows the historical and logical order (cf. ἑξῆς, 3:1). Heathen and Jewish worship having been satirized, the main part of the epistle is devoted to an exposition of Christian faith and conduct. In these chapters (5–10) the sequence is significant: first the picture of the Christian life in the world, then a theological treatise on the Son of God, and finally a return to the appeal of the Christian life. It is interesting to see how skillfully the author rearranges the order of Diognetus's questions.[26] Twice he touches briefly on a point (4:6; 5:3) which he elaborates later (7:1ff.), but in the main the progress of thought is clearly marked. The transition (4:6) to the chief theme is especially neat.

The outline of the contents is as follows:

ch. 1: Prologue	The questions of Diognetus.
ch. 2: The Heathen	The variety and nature of their gods and the folly of worshiping them.
ch. 3–4: The Jews	(a) Their foolish sacrifices. (b) Their absurd rites and customs.
chs. 5–7: The Christians	(a) The distinctive manner and conditions of their life. (b) They are the soul of the world. (c) Their religion not discovered but revealed; the mode of the revelation.
chs. 8–9: The Son of God	(a) Revealer of the true knowledge of God. (b) Agent of salvation.
ch. 10: Epilogue	The Christian faith as an *imitatio Dei*—its character and fruits.
chs. 11–12: Appendix	The ministry of the Word in the Church and the individual (ch. 11). The indissoluble union of knowledge and life (ch. 12)

3. Literary Form

It is a necessary preliminary in appraising an ancient piece of writing to set it in its proper literary class. As regards Diognetus the general category is clear. It is an epistle, a term which, as we have seen,[27] editors generally add to

---

25. See below, pp. 63–67.
26. See below, p. 95.
27. See above, p. 5.

its original title. We need not here trace the origin and development of the epistolary form.[28] It is more to the point to state the character of an epistle. The term may be interpreted in the light of Deissmann's[29] fundamental distinction between a "letter" and an "epistle," a distinction which, while calling for caution in its application to the letters of the New Testament, remains valid in the main. A letter is a written communication destined for one definite person or group of persons. It is, therefore, private in content and aim and instinct with personal feeling. Anything in the nature of elaboration or artifice is foreign to its purpose, namely, the maintenance of intimate communication.[30] The aim of an epistle, on the other hand, is avowedly general. The wider its circulation, the more fully is its purpose met. Hence an epistle is usually restrained and impersonal. It casts little, if any, direct light upon the personality of its author. Written with an eye upon a public circle, it has necessarily something of a studied character. It is, in Deissmann's words, "a product of literary art."

Certainly Diognetus is not a true letter after the Pauline type (Romans and Ephesians excepted) or even in the manner of the writings of Ignatius and Polycarp.[31] These were called forth for the most part by a specific occasion and need and aspire to little or no literary merit. This is not to deny high literary quality, especially in Paul's writings,[32] but to affirm that literary excellence was not their conscious aim. On the other hand, our author, whether answering a genuine inquirer or penning an open letter to an imaginary one,[33] is quite alive to literary effect and states his case with obvious care. He furnishes his "epistle," with an individual address and sets forth in the Prologue his purpose and function.[34] It may well be that, had the Epilogue been complete (10:8),[35] some reference would have appeared to the fulfillment of his task.[36] Despite its individual address, the document is

28. See Meecham, *Oldest Version*, 206ff.

29. Deissmann, *Bible Studies*, 3–59.

30. "The more faithfully it catches the tone of the private conversation, the more of a letter, that is, the better a letter, it is" (Deissmann, *Bible Studies*, 3).

31. Note the absence from our epistle of the familiar formulae of greeting, χαίρειν or χαίρειν καὶ ἐρρῶσθαι, and of valediction, ἔρρωσο (ἔρρωσθε).

32. See Wilamowitz's tribute to Paul as "one of the classicists of Hellenism" (cited in Weiss, *Primitive Christianity*, 399). For an adverse view of Paul's Greek, see Rutherford, *Romans*, xvii.

33. "Undoubtedly a fictional character by the name of Diognetus," Batiffol, *Anciennes Littératures*, 93. But see Molland, "Diognetbriefes," 303.

34. Cf. the Prologue of Sirach; 2 Macc 2:19–32; Polyb. 4:1–2; Luke 1:1–4; Acts 1:1.

35. See below, p. 63.

36. Cf. Let. Aris. 322: "you are now, O Philocrates, in receipt of the full story, as I promised."

obviously intended to reach a wider constituency.[37] Under cover of answering the inquiries of an individual the author seeks to offer to the cultured world a reasoned exposition of the Christian faith. He makes no attempt to maintain the illusion of an "epistle" by the repeated mention of the name of the addressee or by the inclusion of any homely personal touches. The didactic aim and content of our epistle mark it out as an apologetic treatise in epistolary address.[38] Ewald thinks that it is a studied answer to a book written by Diognetus about his failure to understand Christianity.[39] But this is mere surmise.

The question may be raised whether this so-called epistle is not more in the nature of a written discourse. Some phrases favor that view: καὶ τὸ λέγειν καὶ τὸ ἀκούειν (1:1 *sub fin.*), εἰπεῖν οὕτως . . . οὕτωςἀκοῦσαι (*ibid.*), λόγου καινοῦ . . . ἀκροατής (2:1), πολλὰ . . . εἰπεῖν ἔχοιμι . . . τὸ πλείω λέγειν (2:10). See 2 Clem. 15:2, ὁ λέγων καὶ ἀκούων, 1:2, οἱ ἀκούοντες. The rhetorical passages in Diognetus (ch. 2; 7:1f.; 9:3 *al.*), the frequent interrogative form (chs. 2 and 4), and the brief partial arguments may also point in this direction. On the other hand may be set epistolary features in the individual address[40] and the Prologue. Birks thinks that Diognetus "seems rather to be a discourse delivered in a Christian assembly into which the eminent inquirer has found his way."[41] This hypothesis may, as Dr. W. Telfer points out,[42] absolve our author from the charge of inadequacy in statement (e.g., in his discussion of idolatry, ch. 2), since spoken arguments are necessarily short and self-contained. But there is no decisive evidence on the point.[43] We can hardly go further than to describe Diognetus as a tract in epistolary form.

---

37. The dedication to an individual is quite in keeping with an ancient practice that first prevailed in the Hellenistic age. See Cadbury, *Luke-Acts*, 201. Cf. the dedication of the Third Gospel and Acts to Theophilus and that of Josephus to "most excellent Epaphroditus." Several Christian apologies were addressed to Roman emperors. In all such instances the individual is but the single representative of the class to whom the writer wishes to appeal.

38. In this regard Diognetus is like Theophilus's *Autol.* and Cyprian's *Donatum*. So also 2 Clement and the Epistle of Barnabas are "epistles" in form only.

39. Ewald, *History of Israel*, viii and 175.

40. This, however, is not infrequent in *treatises*. Cf. Hippolytus, *Antichr.*, addressed to "my beloved brother, Theophilus."

41. Birks, "Epistle of Diognetus," 257ff.

42. In Telfer, "Review," 224–25.

43. Moffatt, *Introduction*, 47, points out that the epistle and the oral address were of kindred origin. "It is often a real problem to determine whether a given writing is a λόγος or an ἐπιστολή. In many cases the epistolary form is little more than a literary device . . . the epistolary form of composition as the nearest to that of the oration."

I. Introduction

4. Vocabulary, Grammar, and Style

i. Vocabulary

1. Size

Diognetus contains 698 words, excluding proper names, pronouns, and the article. Ninety-three of those which occur in chs. 11–12 are not found in chs. 1–10.

2. Analysis

A careful analysis of the vocabulary yields the following results. The classical words[44] number 664, the post-classical[45] thirty-four. This predominance of the classical strain (95 percent) holds good for the epistle proper (1–10); in the two appended chapters the proportion of post-classical words is higher (2 percent). There appear occasionally a word of Ionic origin[46] and a predilection for semi-poetical.[47]

In relation to the Greek Bible, 580 words of Diognetus are found in both the LXX and the NT, sixty-four in the LXX only, and ten in NT only. Forty-four words do not appear in the Greek Bible. To the influence of the language of the Greek Bible we may trace some forms or words which are rare in Attic prose (e.g., λαός, ἅγιος) or used there in a different sense (e.g., δόξα). Some terms derive directly from their use in the Greek Bible: πάσχα, ἀνεξιχνίαστος, μακρόθυμος (-έω), ὁλοκαύτωμα, περιτομή, ἀμήν.

3. Rare Words

ἀνταλλαγή, ἀπερινόητος, ἐγκαταστηρίζω, εἰκαιότης, λιθοξόος, παντοκτίστης, προαγαπάω, συγχρωτίζομαι, συνετίζω, τεκνογονέω, ὑπερσπουδάζω.

4. Favorite Words (the figures indicate the number of occurrences)

ἐπιγινώσκω (5), θεοσέβεια (5), ἴδιος (8), κολάζω (7), λοιπός (5), παρέχω (7).

---

44. Words found before 322 BCE.
45. Words first found after 322 BCE. Most of these terms are specified in the notes.
46. E.g., καλύπτω (9:3; see note).
47. ἀθέμιστος (4:2 variant), ἄφραστος (8:9).

5. Other Features

Religious and ethical terms naturally predominate. A noticeable feature is the use of apparent synonyms:

προσκυνέω (of the worship of idols, 2:4, 5), θεοσεβέω (of the worship of God, 3:1). σέβω (2:7; 3:2) and θρησκεύω (1:1; 2:8) are used of both idols and God.

θεοσέβεια, λατρεία, θρησκεία (3:2, 3).
νομίζω, οἴομαι, δοκέω, ἡγέομαι, λογίζομαι, φρονέω (4:1, 5 al.).
ὑπομένω, ἀνέχομαι (2:9)
προσάγω, προσφέρω (3:2–3).
ἀφροσύνη, μωρία (3:3).
χορηγέω, παρέχω (3:4).
καταφρονέω, ὑπεροράω (1:1).
ὑπόστασις, ὕλη (2:1, 3).
εἶδος, μορφή (2:1, 3).
ἐπιδείκνυμι, ἀποκαλύπτω, φανερόω (8:5, 6, 11).

Some terms suggest Philonic influence on our author:[48] ἀπερινόητος (7:2). See Philo, *Mut.* 15 (ὁ λόγος). For εἰκαιότης (4:6) see *Det.* 10 (see p. 116), while βελτιοῦσθαι (6:9) is frequently used of the soul in Philo. See also note on χλεύης ἄξιον (4:4).

Terms of a Pauline flavor are frequent: χρηστότης, οἰκονομία, παρεδρεύω, συνήθεια, ἀφθαρσία, ἐκλογή, etc.

The author makes liberal use of compound formations in both verbs[49] (μεταμορφόω, τεκνογονέω, etc.) and nouns (ἀργυροκόπος, etc.). Words in ἀ-privative abound. For other points of vocabulary, see pp. 64–65.

ii. Grammar

1. Orthography

We note πλέον (2:7; 4:5; 10:5), not πλεῖον. Attic Greek often dropped the ι in ει before vowels. Hellenistic Greek almost always shows the diphthong, though the ι is occasionally omitted in Ptolemaic papyri. For the preponderance of πλεῖον in the LXX and the NT see Thackeray, *Grammar*, 1:81; and Westcott and Hort, *New Testament*, Appendix, 158, respectively. See also Moulton and Howard, *Grammar*, 82, and for the Ptolemaic papyri Mayser,

---

48. Cassels, *Supernatural Religion*, 2:358, thinks that the writer of the epistle was "evidently well acquainted" with the works of Philo.

49. Compound verbs number ninety-six in all, among which the formative prepositions διά (eleven times), παρά (ten), πρό (nine), ἀπό predominate.

Grammar, 1:68f. Instances of vowel contraction appear in χρυσοῦς, Diogn. 2:7 (but ἀργυρέους, 2:7, where, however, Otto prints the contracted form), ἀρκούντως (4:6), νουμηνία (4:1, the correct Attic form. The Koine shows νεομηνία and νουμηνία), οἶμαι (3:1), πραΰτης (7:4) for classical πραότης.

Elision takes place usually before pronouns, particles, negatives, and prepositions. For example, ἀλλ᾽αὐτός (7:2), ἀλλ᾽ὥς (5:5), ἀλλ᾽οὐ (5:6 et al.), ἀλλ᾽ἐν (7:4). But no elision occurs before a distinctive or emphatic word. So ἀλλὰ ἄνθρωπος (2:9; cf. 9:2; 11:1), παρὰ ἀνθρώπου (4:6; contrast παρ᾽ἐμοῦ, 4:1). We find διά (11:3 et al.), but δι᾽ (11:5). ἀπό (7:2), ἐπί (12:6), κατά (9:1) are elided. We have ὑφ᾽ ὑμῶν (2:4), ὑπὸ ἀνθρώπων (2:4). Cf. 11:2, ὑπὸ ἀπίστων ... ὑπ᾽ αὐτοῦ. δ᾽ occurs six times (2:2 et al.), but δέ sixteen times (2:2 et al.). τε is not elided (12:5), nor are οὔτε (5:1) and οὐδέ (7:1). But we find ποτ᾽ (8:1), γένοιτ᾽ ἄν (2:3), δύναιτ᾽ ἄν (2:4; 8:3), ἡγοῖντ᾽ ἄν (3:3), ταῦθ᾽ ὑμῶν (2:9; cf. 2:3), τοῦτ᾽ αὐτοῖς (5:3), πάντ᾽ (9:1), πάνθ᾽ (5:5). Only one instance of crasis appears, κἄν (2:10).

As to consonants the spelling σσ is predominant over ττ. Note ἀντιτάσσω (6:5), θάλασσα (7:2), περισσός (2:10), πλάσσω (2:3), φυλάσσω (7:1), κρείσσων (2:2; 10:6), but ἐλάττων (10:6). The Attic ττ (shared only with some two or three other dialects) makes but sporadic appearances in the Koine, which has generally adopted σσ. But exceptions are ἐλάττων, ἥττων, κρείττων (and derivations of the first two), both forms of which appear, e.g., in the books of Maccabees (cf. 2 Macc 5:5; 4:40; 1 Macc 3:59; 13:5). For the Attic ἁρμόττω we have the Hellenistic ἁρμόζω (12:9), as in Let. Aris. 43; Polyb. 3.16; 2 Macc 14:22; 2 Cor 11:2.

The author writes οὕτως before both vowels (7:1) and consonants (10:3), as also in the LXX, NT, and papyri. "Final—ς in οὕτως is practically fixed."[50] μέχρι occurs twice, each time before a consonant (9:1; 10:7). Final -ν is invariably appended to the third person verbal-ending before a vowel or diphthong (εἰσῆλθεν, 1:1).

2. *Inflexion*

Here we note the present forms θέλω, ἐθέλω (10:4, 6) and the augmented forms of δύναμαι and βούλομαι: ἠδυνήθη (9:3), as commonly in later Attic, but ἐβουλόμεθα (9:1), ἐβουλήθη (9:6). So also in the NT the ἐβουλ- form always appears, and prevails in the LXX. The syllabic augment is dropped from the pluperfects πεπλήρωτο and πεφανέρωτο (9:2), as usually in the NT (Mark 14:44 *al.*). In εἴασεν (9:1) we have the Attic augment in εἰ, which the Koine generally retains. The author prefers the classical form of the

---

50. Moulton and Howard, *Grammar*, 2:112.

infinitive χρῆσθαι (7:5; cf. 2 Macc 4:19; 11:31), not the later Attic and Hellenistic χρᾶσθαι.

3. Syntax

The future ἐρεῖτε (2:1) is used for the present tense. See note *ad loc.* A verb of perception is idiomatically followed by accusative and participle (ὁρῶ ... ὑπερεσπουδακότα σε ... πυνθανόμενον, 1:1). The articular infinitive is in frequent use as equivalent to a noun (eleven examples, 4:2 *al.*), and following a preposition (εἰς, 9:6; ἐπί, 10:7; περί, 2:10; 3:1). The simple infinitive expresses purpose (φανερῶσαι, 9:2), and is frequently epexegetic after verbs (μαθεῖν, 1:1; cf. 4:6; καλύψαι, 9:3) and adjectives (εἰσελθεῖν, 9:1; σώζειν, 9:6). It follows κωλύω (4:3; 6:5), πρὶν ἤν (2:3, see note), πρίν (8:1), and is used absolutely in ἁπλῶς δ' εἰπεῖν (6:1). The future infinitive follows μέλλω (8:2), as often in classical Greek. The present participle (κρίνοντα, 7:6) inclines to express purpose (see note). For the imperatival force of ἴδε (accented as in later Greek; Attic ἰδέ) see on 2:1. We note the periphrastic perfect in 5:1, 3, and a fondness for the optative with ἄν (2:3, 4 *al.*). The middle voice occurs fifteen times and is appropriately used; cf. the force of ἐνδείκνυνται (5:4) and ἀπέδοτο (9:2), etc.

Under cases we note the dative of agent (ἑκάστῳ) after the perfect participle pass. (2:3). The prepositions call for little notice. ὑπό, with genitive, is used of an inanimate agent (2:2 *al.*), καθ' ἑαυτούς (9:1) as a periphrasis for the simple genitive. We note the practical equivalence of κατά, with genitive, and κατά, with accusative (6:2). The conjunction ἵνα is found five times in its classical use denoting purpose (2:2 *al.*) and once in the extended sense indicating content (9:5).

Particles, etc., are plentiful and representative. We remark οὕτως ... ὡς (1:1); ἄν, with infinitive (1:1), aorist indicative (8:11), and potential optative (2:3, 4 *al.*). ὡς ἄν occurs with future participle (2:1); οὖν appears always in the second place (2:9; 9:1, 6). ὡς is very frequent (4:2, 3 *al.*); διό (12:4), ἄρα (7:3), καίτοι (8:3), τοίνυν (3:2) occur but once each.

Under the Article we mark its omission with proper names (Ἰουδαῖοι, see below p. 98) and with definite natural phenomena (σελήνη, 4:5; γῆ, θάλασσα, 7:2). The principle seems to be observed that where a genitive is dependent on another noun the article is used with both or neither; cf. τῇ δυνάμει τοῦ θεοῦ (9:1), ἀνομία πολλῶν (9:5), μυστήρια θεοῦ (10:7). The presence or absence of the article with θεός is instructive. It is mostly used with θεός in the nominative (6:10; 7:2 *al.*), except in subordinate clauses (8:1; 9:2; 10:7; 12:3). In the oblique cases it is occasionally inserted (4:2 *al.*), sometimes to effect correlation (9:1, 2, 4) and once (8:2) to distinguish the subject of εἶναι; but more frequently it is omitted (4:3; 8:3 al.). In some instances the absence of the article serves to bring out the characteristic quality of the noun, "one who is God." So 7:9; 10:4, 5, 6 (bis); 12:8. After prepositions the usage varies. Cf. ὑπὸ τοῦ θεοῦ (4:2), ὑπὸ θεοῦ (4:4), παρὰ τοῦ θεοῦ (10:6), παρὰ θεῷ (12:8). See p. 21n101. The relative pronoun as the demonstrative force of the article in ὃς μὲν ... ὃς δέ (= ὁ μὲν ... ὁ δέ), 2:3, al.

In general, the author's syntax is correct and careful. Some laxity, however, is seen in 3:5, where the sentence τῶν μὲν κτλ. is isolated, being either an irregular genitive absolute or a clause loosely attached to the preceding genitive τῶν ... ἐνδεικνυμένων. See note ad loc.

iii. Style

The style throughout is elegant and graceful.[51] It is clear that the author did not share the indifference of some apologists to charm of diction and style.[52] Fitting word and phrase, an abundance of striking contrast, an arrangement orderly and concise, and a tone instinct with vigor and life all stamp the unknown author as a man of high literary skill. Some grandiose phrases create a semi-rhetorical effect,[53] which is enhanced by the frequent use of the rhetorical question (2:2ff.; 4:2ff.) and exclamation (9:2, 5). The epigrammatic element is marked ("they share all things as citizens, and suffer all things as strangers," 5:5, etc.). We find pleonasm (2:9; note ὑπομένω and ἀνέχομαι), paronomasia (κοινὴν ... κοίτην, 5:7),[54] alliteration (5:13; 7:12 [init.]; 8:8), and the use of negative opposites formed by ἀ-privative (ὁρατός ... ἀόρατος 6:4, etc.). The following figures of speech appear (see Notes) zeugma (2:1), chiasmus (4:5), epanastrophe (5:16 κολάζω, 8:5–6 ἐπιδείκνυμι), and litotes (12:3 οὐδὲ ἄσημα). Apart from the elaborate opening period the sentences are mainly short (7:2; 9:6 are exceptions), while sometimes pregnant with meaning; how striking, for example, is the terse statement "free board they provide—but no carnal bed" (5:7). The sentences are often idiomatic and well-balanced (4:2; 5:12), and occasionally take the form of a neat antithesis

---

51. Keim, Rom und das Christenthum, 461, eulogizes "the pure, classical language, the beautiful, correct sentence structure, the rhetorical freshness, the striking antitheses, the witty expression, the logical smoothness" of Diognetus, while E. Norden (Die antike Kunstprosa, 2:513n2) sums up the style as "brilliant" ("The letter of Diognetus ... is among the most brilliant of letters").

52. There is nothing in the epistle to match, for example, the tedious digressions and cumbersome clauses which appear in Justin Martyr.

53. For example, ἡ κατάστασις τῆς ἑαυτῶν πολιτείας (5:4).

54. Cf. Wis 13:11 (εὐμαθῶς ... εὐπρεπῶς); Luke 21:11 (λοιμοὶ καὶ λιμοί).

(9:5; cf. also 7:4–5). It is especially noticeable that in 5:5—6:9 short sentences of almost similar length are of the antithetic type and marked by a kind of rhyme (cf. πᾶσα ξένη πατρίς ἐστιν αὐτῶν, καὶ πᾶσα πατρὶς ξένη, 5:5).[55] Note especially the succession of brief clauses ending in -ται (5:11–12, 14–16).

A certain rhythmical force in three passages suggests that they are excerpts from Christian hymns (see on 7:4; 9:2; 11:3). We note the series of coordinate clauses strung together by καί (5:10–15; 6:2–9; cf. 11:6; 12:9), though asyndeton is not uncommon (2:9; 5:6 γαμοῦσιν . . . τεκνογονοῦσιν, 9:2b, 6). The word order is careful in the main; not infrequently the verb stands at the beginning of the sentence (6:2f.).

The author is especially prone to reiterate the same root words and constructions as a kind of link in the immediate context. The following instances show this marked feature of the style:

> Repetition of προειρημένος (3:2), ζωοποιοῦμαι (5:12, 16), ᾧ πειθαρχεῖ (7:2). See also κολάζω (5:16), ἐπιδείκνυμι (8:5–6) noted above. παρέχει αὐτός follows up πᾶσιν ἡμῖν χορηγῶν (3:4), βία resumes βιαζόμενος (7:4), ἀποδεκτός answers to ἀποδέχῃ (8:2–3), and κρίνοντα follows κρίνων (7:5, 6).[56] In this connection note 7:4–6 (πέμπων—ἔπεμψεν [six times]—πέμψει), 9:1 (τὸ ἀδύνατον—τῇ δυνάμει—δυνατοί), 9:5 (ἀνομία—δικαίῳ—ἀνόμους—δικαιώσῃ), 9:6 (τὸ ἀδύνατον—δυνατόν—τὰ ἀδύνατα). ὦ τῶν ἀπροσδοκήτων εὐεργεσιῶν (9:5) repeats the closing part of 8:2. Repetition frequently serves for emphasis. See the reiterated ταῦτα (2:5, 9; 7:9), ὡς (7:4), αὐτός (7:2; 9:2). The projection of words has the same effect (cf. τὴν αἰτίαν, 5:17).

Nevertheless, the author can effectively vary his expressions (cf. τοὺς ὑποδεεστέρους, 10:5; τοῖς ἐπιδεομένοις, 10:6; ἐπίγειος . . . θνητός . . . ἀνθρώπινος, 7:1). He plays skillfully with prepositional variations on the same root verb (συνέχω and κατέχω, 6:7; κατοικέω and παροικέω, 6:8; διατάσσω and ὑποτάσσω, 7:2; παρέχω and μετέχω, 8:11; καταγινώσκω and ἐπιγινώσκω, 10:7). We note the habit of repeating the same thought in different terms (e.g., διδόναι—γεραίρειν—παρέχειν, of man's offering to God, 3:4–6) or varying form ("the soul has been confined within the body," 6:7;

---

55. Puech, *Apologistes grecs*, 256, thinks that this is part of the technique which the author owed to the rhetorical schools, and points out that this form matches the author's view of the paradoxical character of the Christian faith (5:4): "antithesis is required here by thought." Similar Greek stylistic influence is apparent in Melito (see *Homily on the Passion*). But it is not improbable that we may detect also Semitic influence of the LXX (especially the Psalms and the Wisdom books) on both authors.

56. Cf. Rom 12:13ff (repeated διώκω, εὐλογέω, φρονέω), 2 Pet 2:1–3 (triple occurrence of ἀπώλεια). This stylistic artifice is patent in Melito's *Homily on the Passion* (ed. C. Bonner). See §59, 91 (δι' αὐτόν repeated five times), 93 (πικρός repeated twelve times).

"the soul, though immortal, dwells in a mortal tabernacle," 6:8). Note also the flesh hates the soul" (6:5), "the flesh which hates it (the soul)" (6:6). The same feature is observable in the rhetorical questions in ch. 2; cf. "another silver, which needs a man to guard it lest it be stolen" (2) with "those of silver and gold . . . lest they be stolen" (7). Note also σεσηπός (2:2) and σηπόμενα (2:4), φθαρτῆς ὕλης (2:3) and φθειρόμενα (2:4). Now and again the author anticipates possible objections—a rhetorical device. See "as one might suppose" (7:2, 3); "not at all . . . sins" (9:1), "He did not hate," etc. (9:2). He has one or two vivid metaphors (the Christian in the world is like the soul in the body, 6:1ff., deceptive custom must be "unloaded" like luggage, 2:1). He shows an ironical vein (cf. the epithet ἀξιόπιστος and the parenthesis in 8:2),[57] not to mention a refreshing candor.[58] He can also strike a moralizing note (6:10).

Among particular stylistic features we may name the careful use of tenses: note the discrimination between the present and aorist infinitive (τὸ λέγειν . . . εἰπεῖν, τὸ ἀκούειν . . . ἀκοῦσαι, 1:1), the perfect and aorist infinitive (μεμαθηκέναι . . . μαθεῖν, 4:6), the perfect and present tenses (6:2, 7; 7:2; 8:2, 6, 11), and the full force of the perfect indicative (ἐγκέκλεισται, 6:7, etc.). There is an abundance of adjectives in ἀ-privative (thirty-three instances in the epistle), which Aristotle[59] accounts a mark of elevated style. We observe the frequency of μέν . . . δέ (twenty-two times), of particles (see p. 64), and of resumptive οὗτος (6:1; 7:2; 10:6). Compound verbs abound (ninety-six in all, four being double compounds). Sometimes a compound verb is resumed by its simplex form with no appreciable difference of meaning (cf. κατοικέω . . . οἰκέω, 5:4, 5).[60] In 6:5 hiatus is avoided by the use of διότι (note causal ὅτι in the same section). Once (2:9) γάρ ends a sentence. Diminutives are entirely lacking.[61]

5. Authorship and Date

As so often in early literature, the authorship is veiled. External evidence is entirely lacking. The epistle itself is curiously impersonal. It is clear that

---

57. Speaking of "those specious philosophers" who say that God is fire, he adds: "they call that God whereunto they themselves are destined to go." See also 2:9, note (ταύτης τῆς κολάσεως).

58. See note on κράτιστε Διόγνητε (1:1).

59. *Rhet.* 3.6.7.

60. A classical idiom surviving in NT Greek (Moulton, *Grammar*, 1:115).

61. σιτίον (6:9), ὅριον (11:5), and χωρίον (12:2) are diminutives in form only. A frequent use of diminutives is a sign of colloquialism. Their absence from our epistle is in keeping with its literary quality.

the author is a man of furnished mind, who handles his theme with considerable skill but gives no clue to his identity. He never even allies himself explicitly with the Christians, though his personal faith is unmistakable.[62] The phrases: "a disciple of apostles"[63] and "a teacher of the gentiles" are vague in meaning and relate only to the writer of the appended chapters. One negative finding may be taken as assured. Few scholars would now accept the traditional ascription to Justin Martyr.[64] Language and style, apart from other features, are decisive on this point. The door of speculation thus stands open, and many have not hesitated to enter boldly in. Bunsen's view that the epistle (chs. 1–10) came from Marcion before his secession from the Church is very improbable.[65] Buonaiuti has revived this theory.[66] It is true that there are general features common to Marcion and Diognetus: the emphasis on the practical aspects of religion, the marked soteriological interest, the anti-Judaic temper, and the insistence on the uniqueness and newness of Christianity. But the differences are fundamental. The epistle shows no sign of Marcion's dualism, the hard, just Demiurge of the Old Testament, the loving Father-God of the New. Diognetus indeed credits the Jews with the worship of "the one God of the universe" (3:2). For Marcion the supreme God can have no contact with matter; the creator of the visible world is the Demiurge. Diognetus, on the other hand, speaks of "the all-creating God" (ὁ παντοκτίστης, 7:1), Creator of the universe (8:7), the world (10:2), the elements (8:2), and things (4:2). It uses similar language about the Son: "the very Artificer and Maker of the universe" (7:2). Man, according to Marcion, is the offspring of the creator of the world; he has no kinship with the God of love. Diognetus (10:2) affirms that God made man in his own image. Marcion takes the Pauline view of faith as trust in the unmerited grace of God revealed in Christ; in the epistle "faith" seems to have a more intellectual content.[67] The Docetism of Marcion is hardly consistent with Diognetus, 7:4: "He sent him as man to men." Finally, Diognetus, 5:6, regards marriage as the normal state, whereas the strict asceticism of Marcion leads him to condemn wedlock and parentage.[68]

Even less probable are the views which ascribe Diognetus to Clement of Rome (Baratier) and Apollos (Gallandi). Dorner would assign it to

---

62. "A believer is speaking" (Bardy, *Vie Spirituelle*, 90).
63. See note on 11:1.
64. See below, pp. 60–61.
65. Bunsen, *Christianity and Mankind*, 1:150ff.
66. See Molland, "Diognetbriefes," 301ff.
67. See below, p. 39.
68. See Tertullian, *Marc.* 1.29; 4.34.

I. Introduction

Quadratus,[69] the earliest apologist, a fragment of whose work is preserved in Eusebius.[70] Doulcet and Kihn[71] assign it to the author of the *Apology of Aristides*.[72] Other names suggested are Apelles (Dräseke),[73] Lucian the martyr (Chapman),[74] Ambrosius (Birks),[75] Hippolytus (Connolly).[76] Donaldson indeed was put to such straits in this matter that he was disposed to make its first editor (Stephanus, 1592) its author![77] But he states, "I am inclined to think it more likely that some of the Greeks who came over to Italy when threatened by the Turks may have written the treatise, not so much from the wish to counterfeit a work of Justin's as to write a good declamation in the old style." "But," he went on to add, "there is no sound basis for any theory with regard to this remarkable production." Similarly, Overbeck called into question the literary honesty of the writer of the epistle.[78] "There are no

---

69. Dorner, *Person of Christ*, 1.1:374f.

70. *Hist. eccl.* 4.3. See below, 176–79.

71. Kihn, "Diognet," 601–12.

72. See below, 58–60.

73. Dräseke, "Diognetus," 466.

74. Chapman, "Epistle of Diognetus," 8–9.

75. Birks, "Epistle to Diognetus," 162ff. See also his revised article in Wace and Piercy, *Dictionary of Christian Biography*, 257ff., holds that the heading "of the same" does not directly attribute Diognetus to Justin but relates it to the author of the treatise *To the Greeks* which immediately preceded it in the manuscript (see below, pp. 67–68). In support he points out features of style and diction common to both documents. Cureton, *Spicilegium Syriacum*, had given from a sixteenth or seventeenth century MS a Syriac version of a discourse almost identical with *To the Greeks*, ascribed to "Ambrosius, a chief man of Greece, who became a Christian, and all his fellow-councilors raised a clamor against him." Birks, therefore, thinks that both *To the Greeks* and *To Diognetus* came from the hand of Ambrosius. He suggests that probably an old copy exhibited three works of Ambrosius—an avowal of Christianity and answers *To the Greeks* and *To Diognetus*. The first document is lost; the second is a sample of numerous controversial works; the third, Diognetus, though fragmentary, is unique, apologetic but also catechetical in character, chs. 11–12 forming, as he is disposed to think, part of the same discourse as chs. 1–10 (see below, p. 63).

76. Connolly, "Date and Authorship," 347ff. Connolly argues that the similarity between Diogn. 7:1–5 and Hippolytus, *Philos.* 10.33 points to common authorship. These two passages are alike not only in theme and argument, but also in structure, and in two places they show such close resemblances in thought and language that "accidental coincidence seems out of the question."

77. Donaldson, *Critical History*, 2:141f.

78. Overbeck, *Brief; Studien*, vol. 1. Drummond, "Researches on the Epistle to Diognetus," 27–29, favorably reviews Overbeck's case for a late origin of the epistle. More recently Thomsen, "Review of *Der Brief an Diognetus* by J. Geffcken," *Philologische Wochenschrift*, 561–63, hazards a Byzantine authorship of the twelfth century.

adequate means of determining its authorship," says Westcott.[79] "But," he continues, "it is enough that we can regard it as the natural outpouring of a Greek heart holding converse with a Greek mind in the language of old philosophers."

The question of the date is only to a less degree indeterminate. The internal evidence is far from conclusive. The references to persecution are general in character and allow no sure deduction.[80] No chronological significance attaches to the description of Christianity as "this new race or practice" (1:1), since Tertullian and Eusebius can both speak of Christianity in their times in similar terms. Nor again does the fact that the author writes of Jewish sacrifices and ritual in the present tense necessarily imply that the Temple was still standing. For not only does it appear that sacrifices continued to be offered after 70 CE in various places,[81] but a Christian writer might naturally speak of the Jewish ritual as still obligatory, as indeed the pious Jew firmly held it to be.[82] On the other hand, it is precarious to infer a late date from the use of the term οἰκονομικῶς (9:1; Codex Argent.), which fourth- and fifth-century writers employ to denote the inner relations of the Godhead. This theological nicety is foreign to the thought of the epistle, and it is safer to adopt Lachmann's emendation οἰκονομηκώς ("planned").

The very universality of thought and tone makes it hard to fix the period of the epistle.[83] Westcott would place it as early as 117 CE. If that is too early, Overbeck's post-Constantinian date and Cotterill's fantastic theory[84] of an eighth- or ninth-century composition are patently far too late. Otto and Bunsen place it about 135 CE; Ewald between 120–30 CE. Keim and Cruttwell suggest the reign or Marcus Aurelius.[85] Wilamowitz-Moellendorff and Geffcken assign it to 250 CE, Zahn 250–310. Harnack prefers still wider

---

79. Westcott, *Canon*, 86f. Aubé, *Justin*, 94, impressed by the philosophic temper of the writer, offers no name; but "this unknown author undoubtedly spent his youth in Athens among the sophists."

80. Renan, *Marc-Aurèle*, 424, however, thinks that they fit the last years of Marcus Aurelius. See below, pp. 37–39.

81. See the evidence given in Donaldson, *Critical History*, 2:135f.

82. The use of the present tense is often a mere literary convention. Cf. Heb 7:8; Josephus, *Ant.* 3.6–12. See Harnack's note on 1 Clem. 41:2 in *Patrum Apostolicorum Opera*, vol. 1.1, and Lightfoot, *Apostolic Fathers*, vol. 1.2, on the same passage.

83. Dorner, *Person of Christ*, 1.1:377: "It breathes an air of eternity; it is marked by inner harmony and clearness; and precisely because it was so direct an expression of the eternal element in Christianity, does it bear so few traces of any particular period."

84. Cotterill, "Justin Martyr's Epistle to Diognetus and the Oration to the Gentiles"; Cotterill, *Peregrinus Proteus*. The theory is usefully summarized in Radford, *Diognetus*, 13–15.

85. See note on 7:4 (below).

limits (170–310). The prevailing view is that the epistle derives from the middle or latter half of the century. Puech puts it soon after Justin Martyr;[86] Connolly leans "to the close of the second century, and to the age of Hippolytus, at the earliest."[87] Lightfoot,[88] Bardenhewer,[89] and Krüger favor about 150 CE. Some general considerations point to this relatively early date: the condemnation in common of paganism and Judaism; freedom in handling the NT writings; the lack of the tendency to identify the ideal of Christian excellence with the ascetic life, and the absence of traces of sacerdotalism; the relatively simple Christology less elaborate than that of Origen; the dominance of the doctrine of the Logos with no doctrine of the Holy Spirit;[90] the problem why the Son had come late in time, which appears in Justin but finds little place in later apologists; the apparent unawareness of formulated heresies, apart from possible hints of the Gnostic emphasis; the traditional assignment of the epistle to Justin and its place in the Codex with other writings ascribed to him.

Nothing is known of the place of origin of the epistle. Bunsen, Dräseke, and others would assign it to Rome. Doulcet to Athens.

For the authorship and origin of the appended chapters (11–12) see below, pp. 65–67.

6. Teaching

i. Chapters 1–10

The theological content of Diognetus lies mainly in chs. 7–9. It indicates a simple form of belief. There is no elaboration, for example, in the author's doctrine of the Logos, nor does he seem aware of the philosophic difficulties involved in the idea of the incarnation of the Son of God.[91] Moreover, there are noticeable omissions. No explicit mention is made of the Old Testament.[92] This is the more strange in that some Christian apologists made

86. Puech, *Apologistes grecs*, 263.
87. Connolly, "Date and Authorship," 351. See note on 7:5 (below).
88. Lightfoot, *Apostolic Fathers*, 1.2:533; *Biblical Essays*, 94.
89. Bardenhewer, *Geschichte*, 1:322.
90. See below, p. 50.
91. Celsus (Origen, *C. Cels.* 4.2; 2.31), writing ca. 177 CE, argues that incarnation involves limitation and change, and that such is unthinkable in an immutable God. It would mean a "change from good to bad" (4.14).
92. The reference to the "fear of the law" and "the grace of the prophets" is found in the Appendix (11:6). Cf. also τὰ γεγραμμένα (12:3) of a passage in Genesis (2:8–9). For echoes of OT passages see below, pp. 52–53.

great play with Old Testament prophecies as supposed predictions of the coming of Christ,[93] and generally correlated the old revelation in the Law and the Prophets with the new revelation in Christ. The silence of the epistle in this regard is due not to Gnostic contempt for the Old Testament so much as to the author's polemic against Jewish tenets and customs as a foil to the Christian religion. Moreover, Diognetus was addressed to a heathen and intended primarily for gentiles to whom the Old Testament would make little or no appeal.[94] But, above all, the proof of the truth of Christian claims lies elsewhere, namely in the purity and nobility of Christian lives. More striking is the fact that the author has only a general reference to the historic life of the Son, and none to his miracles, suffering, death, and resurrection.[95] He comes nearest to this in the passage: "himself gave up his own Son as a ransom for us," etc. (9:2). Nor are forgiveness and the need of a new birth brought clearly into view. There is no indication of Church order or sacraments or indeed of any credal form such as is adumbrated in the *Apology of Aristides* (ca. 140 CE).[96] Too much must not be made of these omissions, since the discussion is limited by the supposed queries of Diognetus. But the simplicity of the theological contents is not without significance for the question of the date of the epistle. In temper the author of Diognetus is to be classed among the sub-apostolic writers, of whom Sanday says: "There is no conscious speculation or systematizing; and yet thought is at work; language and usage are in process of becoming more fixed; the foundations of more developed doctrine are really being laid, but laid, as it were, underground."[97] The Preaching of Peter, with which Diognetus shows kinship,[98] belongs also to this transitional type.

The teaching of Diognetus may be considered under the following heads:

---

93. Cf. Justin Martyr, *1 Apol.* 30 (cited below, p. 60). See also Athenagoras, *Suppl.* 9; Theophilus, *Autol.* 2.9 *al.*

94. This is not to deny that some cultured pagans had studied the Jewish Scriptures. Justin, Tatian, and Theophilus attribute their conversion to that source.

95. Suppression of the distinctive Christian elements is noticeable in other apologists, e.g., Tatian, Athenagoras, Minucius Felix. Justin is an exception. For reasons for this suppression, see below, p. 46.

96. See Harris, *Aristides*, 1.1:13ff., 24f.

97. Sanday, *Christologies*, 12.

98. See below, p. 57.

I. Introduction

a. God

Before the coming of the Son man was ignorant of the knowledge of God (8:1, see note). It is in the conception of God that both pagan idolatry and Jewish superstition stand condemned. The worship of stocks and stones is offered to senseless images and is therefore utterly foolish. The Jews, it is true, recognize the one God and Master of the universe. But they too are foolish and even impious; for by their sacrifice they suppose that God is in need of such offerings, and by their ridiculous ritual observances they misconceive his character and wisdom. The theories of the "plausible philosophers" who identified God with fire or water or some other created element are obviously absurd, since any one identification has equal claim with the rest. All such strivings after God are discredited. Our author makes no recognition of the revelation of God through nature[99] or through the OT witness[100] or through the soul "naturally Christian." Man's knowledge of the deity came from God himself. God "manifested himself through faith, by which alone it is given to see God" (8:6).

The God[101] thus self-revealed is primarily "the one God of the universe" and "Master" (3:2), "the all-sovereign, all-creating, and invisible God" (7:2), "Master and Maker of the universe, who created all things and disposed them in their *due* order" (8:7; cf. 3:4; 8:2). The Logos is the agent of creation,[102] but God its primal source (7:2). The providence of God ordains the seasons (4:5) and bestows on all men what they lack, while he himself is beyond all need (3:3ff.). As to his character God is "not only a lover of men" (φιλάνθρωπος) but also "long-suffering" (μακρόθυμος). And this he is unchangingly, "kind and good and free from anger and true, and he alone is good" (8:8). The author insists that "force [βία] is no attribute of God" (7:4, see note and p. 42, below). The power (δύναμις) that he wields is moral (9:1–2).

---

99. He affirms, of course, that God creates and controls all natural phenomena (3:4; 4:5 al.).

100. If this is implied in the bald statement that the Jews worship the one God of the universe (3:2), it is offset by their δεισιδαιμονία (see below, p. 98).

101. The author seems to use θεός with and without the article sometimes indifferently (sixteen times with and twenty without), both usages being found occasionally in the same context (8:2; 9:2; etc.). Cf. ὁ λόγος and λόγος (11:2, 3). The title πατήρ occurs rarely (10:1; 11:2; 12:9), perhaps because he is writing for gentile readers, for whom the concept of God as "Father" would have less meaning than that of "God" or "King" (cf. Wis 11:10). For the significance of the term "Father" in Greek thought, see Manson, *Teaching of Jesus*, 90f.

102. See below, p. 26.

But the dominant conception is the "goodness" and "love" of God. The author's mind moves within the circle of God's moral qualities denoted by χρηστότης (4:1 *al.*; cf. χρηστὸς καὶ ἀγαθός, 8:8), ἀγάπη, ἀγαπάω (4:4; 7:5), φιλάνθρωπος, φιλανθρωπία (8:7; 9:2). These qualities are reflected in all the divine dealings with men. His majesty (μεγαλειότης) is a majesty of beneficent love (10:5; see note). It was love of mankind that moved God to make the world (10:2), to subject all earthly things to man, to endow men with reason and mind,[103] to grant them the power to aspire to himself whose image they bear, to promise the kingdom in heaven to those who loved him. The gifts of God attest his love and care, and it is not possible to discriminate among these gifts; all are necessary and useful to men (4:2). It is, however, in the fact of redemption that the author sees most clearly the manifestation of the goodness of God. Chapters 7–9 set forth the divine plan of salvation. Here we have a clearer exposition of the atonement from one point of view than any before Irenaeus, who gives a careful analysis of the work of redemption. We shall indeed look in vain for any developed theory of atonement in Christian writings of the early period. The time for a formal statement of the doctrine had not yet come. But certain features of our author's view may be plainly discerned and are of interest as indicating in a personal utterance of faith one trend of Christian thought.[104]

The need for redemption lay in man's sin, which entailed the inevitable reward of spiritual incapacity and death. See below, pp. 28–29. Nothing, we note, is said of the view held generally by the apologists (cf. Justin Martyr, *Dial.* 30) that deliverance is from the power of the demons. Belief in demons, i.e., intermediary spirits who operate in all departments of human life as agents of the gods[105] was widely prevalent in ancient pagan thought.[106] Most of the apologists shared this belief in a modified form[107] and addressed themselves to the task of proving the reality and extent of the malign influence of the demons. The author of Diognetus gives no hint that he held the general view, though we may not, *e silentio*, conclude the contrary.

---

103. God "bestows on us *the power* both of speaking and of hearing" (1:1).

104. "By far the most complete statement at this period of the work of Christ is contained in that very attractive little work, the *Epistle to Diognetus*—a work which may be dated about the year A.D. 160" (Bishop of Gloucester, Article in *Church Quarterly Review*, 5).

105. Cf. Origen, *C. Cels.* 8:35.

106. Cf. Plato, *Symp.* 202E; Plutarch, *Def. orac.* 13.

107. Whereas the pagans made a distinction between the classes of demons, some being of a morally lower order, others good (cf. Origin, *C. Cels.* 8.60), for the Christians all demons were wholly bad.

I. Introduction

Redemption springs from God himself, but is effected in the Son. He indeed shares the counsel of the Father and is the appointed agent of salvation. But the initiative lies with God, who "first loved" men (10:3) and who in the beginning (cf. 8:11) purposed to save: "having conceived a great and unutterable design he communicated it to his child alone" (8:9) "He planned everything already in his own mind with his child" (9:1). It was God himself who "established among men and fixed firmly in their hearts the truth and the holy and incomprehensible word" (7:2). The primacy of God comes out clearly throughout the epistle. The role of the Father in the redemptive plan is differentiated from that of the Son as sender is from sent. The Son was "sent"[108] in gentleness and meekness to save and persuade and to call men in love, not to compel nor to judge (7:4). In this commission of the Son it was God himself moving towards men in redeeming love: "He did not hate us or repel us or remember our misdeeds, but was long-suffering, bore with us, himself in mercy took on him our sins, himself gave up his own Son as a ransom for us" (9:2; see note). That some phrases point also to the Son's activity in redemption only illustrates the author's view of the perfect accord of will between Father and Son.

Redemption is rooted in God's love and goodness. The execution of the plan determined in the heavenly counsels from the beginning (8:2; 9:1) was deferred until the appointed time. God waits till man, self-convicted by his own deeds, has learned his moral impotence. And this, not because God is neglectful of man (8:10) or takes pleasure in sins, but out of his long-suffering (8:7) and forbearance (9:2). Then he shows forth the Savior.[109] Here is the answer to Diognetus's third question, namely, why Christianity had not appeared at an earlier time.[110] God wanted to show that man could not save himself. The picture is not that of an offended or implacable deity, but of a patient God who yearns to save (is he not free from wrath and hatred? 9:2). "The entire conception and process of redemption is, from first to last, a revelation of unimaginable love; a love which can only elicit, from men who have eyes to see it, the profoundest motions of amazement and of adoration; and this love is, at least, not less emphatically the love of the Father, than the love of the Son who died" (Moberly).[111] Hence our author shares the Pauline wonder at the saving purpose of God as being wholly contrary to all human expectation. See 7:3; 8:11; 9:5.

---

108. This note is frequent in the Gospels (Mark 9:37; Luke 4:18; John 5:38 *al.*), especially the Fourth, where it is "a divine title" (Moulton and Howard, *Grammar*).

109. See note on 8:10–11, and cf. the purport of Wis 11:23; Acts 17:30; Rom 2:4; 3:25f.

110. On this theme see Origen, *C. Cels.* 6.78; Arnobius 2.75. See below, p. 146–47.

111. Moberly, *Atonement and Personality*, 331.

The immediate result of redemption is that man is enabled "to enter into the kingdom of God" (9:1), a new experience and status which lead to holy and joyous living. Redemption and sanctification are linked together. After describing the redemption through the Son and the faith and knowledge by which it is apprehended, the author continues, "with what joy do you think you will be filled? . . . loving him you will imitate his goodness" (10:3–4). Thus the redeemed man, "justified" (δικαιωθῆναι, see note on 9:4) by the Son, brings forth ethical fruits. Henceforth God is in him as "mind, light, honor, glory, strength, life." So also the writer finds evidence of God's "presence" (παραουσία) in the endurance and triumph of the Christian martyrs (7:9).

It is clear that in the main the author conceives the atonement from the point of view of "moral influence." Redemption is achieved by the love of God awakening its response of love in man. "How *greatly* will you love him who so first loved you?" (10:3).[112] But that is not all. There is a strain in the epistle which suggests that atonement is more than the expression of God's love. God "gave up his own Son as a ransom for us" (λύτρον ὑπὲρ ἡμῶν, 9:2). The term λύτρον in current Greek usage has the nuance of transaction, and the notion of equivalent price for deliverance[113] is dominant in both the Greek word and its common Hebrew correlative (*kopher*). Further, the words "for what else could cover our sins but his righteousness?" (9:3) seem to approach the idea of satisfaction, and possibly there is a hint of the substitution of the Son for sinners in the exclamation, "O the sweet exchange" (ἀνταλλαγή, 9:5).[114] Scott Lidgett, referring to crucial parts of Diogn. 7 and 9 says: "these passages will show that this epistle might stand with equal propriety at the head of the so-called moral doctrines of the atonement, and of those which look upon it as a satisfaction for sin."[115] It is clear that, while the moral theory of the atonement predominates in our author's thought, it is not exclusive of other elements which later developed into the substitutionary and penal theories.[116]

In this regard it is important to observe that it is in virtue of his righteousness (δικαιοσύνη) that the Son redeems. In an eloquent passage the

---

112. A Johannine thought (1 John 4:19).

113. The root idea of both verb and noun seems to be "deliverance." See Blake, "Contributions and Comments," 142. See Taylor, *Jesus and His Sacrifice*, 102ff.

114. The phrase, however, is ambiguous. The "exchange" is probably that of man's wickedness for righteousness, an internal change not an external transfer.

115. Lidgett, *Spiritual Principle of Atonement*, 424.

116. Rashdall, *Idea of Atonement*, 206n1, entirely minimizes the passage (9:2–5) as "after all only a rhetorical paraphrase of the ransom passage in the Gospel, read in the light of Isaiah 53 and of St. Paul."

epistle names the moral qualities of the Savior: he is holy, innocent, just, incorruptible, immortal. It then singles out δίκαιος as apparently the crucial term. By the *righteousness* of the Son man's sins are "covered" (see note on 9:3). "In that righteousness we are justified. The Pauline term is used, but the meaning has become much less forensic. The thought is not that of an externally imputed righteousness, but of a real change in the sinful heart of man, and the writer seems to feel that the righteousness of Christ becomes actually ours."[117] The death of Christ is obviously in mind, though not expressly named. But the necessity of the death is not considered, nor does the author show how it actually effects redemption, apart from the response of love evoked from men. His language trembles on the verge of the substitutionary principle. But the decisive step is not taken. It is sufficient for our author to declare that the source of redemption is in God and that it is as the righteous one that the Son saves, without particularizing the method by which atonement is made. The broad lines of the author's view are clear, but it is neither developed nor complete. He is, however, thoroughly evangelical in conviction; none can enter into the kingdom of God except through the Son, who is able to save even creatures devoid of *moral* power (9:2–6).[118] Lightfoot says of the central part of the epistle (5–7) that "it seems to embody the very spirit of the Gospel."[119] It is to be noted that the author gives small place to man's part in the atonement. Man must "believe on God's goodness" (9:6), a faith which he must first "desire" (10:1).[120] But redemption is solely the work of divine grace.

b. Son

Specific titles are "his child" (παῖς, 8:9; 9:1),[121] "his beloved child" (8:11), "the Son" (υἱός) of God" (9:4), "his own Son" (9:2), "his only-begotten (μονογενής) Son" (10:2), "the Savior" (9:6), "the Lord" (7:7; cf. 12:9), and in the Appendix "Son" (11:5), and "Word" (11:2, 3, 7; 12:9). To these we may add the terms descriptive of Christ's moral qualities named above (p. 25). One phrase describes the Son's cosmic function: "the very Artificer and Maker of the universe" (7:2).[122] In 7:4ff. he is viewed under the categories

---

117. Grensted, *Atonement*, 15.
118. Cf. Herm. Sim. 9.12.5–8.
119. Lightfoot, *Historical Essays*, 7.
120. This is not the Pauline conception of faith whereby man is "justified." See below, p. 39.
121. For παῖς and υἱός see on 8:9.
122. See below, p. 134.

of "King," "God," "Man," "Judge." Two expressions of uncertain reference remain: "the truth," and "the holy and incomprehensible word."[123]

We note the absence of the Jewish titles "Messiah" and "Son of Man," naturally of no interest to a gentile reader. The name "Jesus" is not found, and his earthly life is practically ignored,[124] although the explicit statement "He sent him as man to men" (7:4; cf. also 11:3) excludes any suggestion of Docetism (ἄνθρωπον, however, in 7:4 is Lachmann's insertion).

The Christology is simple and unscholastic.[125] It is plainly of the "pneumatic" type. The Son is a heavenly being who descended, being "sent" to appear to men. No precise definition of the relation of the Son to the Father is attempted. It is clear, however, from the use of the various titles, and from the whole idea of the "child" sharing God's heavenly counsel, being "sent" to men, given as "ransom" and shown as "Savior," that the author thinks of the Son as not only pre-existent, but subordinate to the Father. The frequency of the term "Son" bears this out.[126] The filial life as such implies subordination. But the passage describing the sending of the Son (7:2) emphasizes his majestic nature and office. The "sent" was no minister to men, or angel, or ruler, or one of those who direct earthly things, or of those entrusted with the dispensations in heaven. He was "the very Artificer and Maker of the universe himself" (substantially the same title is applied to God, 8:7), whom the author exalts in a lengthy description of his universal dominion over nature. So also the plan of salvation was disclosed "to his child alone" (8:9; 9:1), and revealed "through his beloved child" (8:11). Donaldson holds in reference to 8:1 that the author did not identify the Son with the Father but thought that he was possessed of a divine nature (θεός), "and therefore was capable of exhibiting to man the properties of a divine nature."[127] See "He sent him as God (θεός)" (7:4). But we may go further and say that the author shared the view held by the apologists that in essence the Son is one with the Father while distinct in person and subordinate in function. "He is God so truly that his coming can be described as the coming of God, his atonement as God's taking upon him our sins, his revelation as God's revelation of

---

123. Allen, *Continuity*, 26, thinks that the latter phrase denotes "Christ in his spiritual being." But see below on 7:2.

124. A "blanched Christology" (Moffatt, *Introduction*, 471).

125. See Little, *Christology*, 68–75.

126. "There is an intractable element of subordination in the functions which he (St. Paul) assigns to the Son" (cf. 1 Cor 15:27f) (Taylor, *Atonement*, 129). Cf. also 1 Cor 11:3; Gal 4:4; Phil 2:9. See Beyschlag, *New Testament Theology*, 2:74ff. A similar strain appears in Hebrews (1:2, 6; 5:5; 13:20) and the Fourth Gospel (5:19, 30; 6:38; 7:16; 10:36), and it is well marked in Justin Martyr (*1 Apol.* 12, 13; *2 Apol.* 13).

127. Donaldson, *Critical History*, 2:129.

I. Introduction

himself."[128] All this suggests a dignity inherent in the Son comparable with that of the Father himself.

The function of the pre-incarnate Son is conceived particularly in relation to the world. He was its creative principle, agent rather than author of creation.[129] But the writer's interest is more religious than philosophical.[130] He looks upon the Son as essentially Revealer and Redeemer. Diognetus, like Justin Martyr,[131] recognizes a didactic purpose in the incarnation. God by sending the Son "established among men the truth and the holy and incomprehensible word and fixed it firmly in their hearts" (7:2). But the revelation is not so much of the mind of the Father as of his will to save. This further redemptive function he effects in the Son, who is given as "ransom" for men. Justin Martyr excepted, the apologists generally tend to stress the work of Christ in creation rather than in redemption. But not so with our author. The soteriological aspect is set in the forefront. The Son not only reveals the true knowledge of the Father (8:1), but also fulfills the plan of salvation in his mission of love to men (see above, pp. 22–23).[132] When he returns it will be as judge (7:6). See p. 41.

---

128. Radford, *Diognetus*, 39. See also above, p. 22.

129. Here, as elsewhere, the author's mind is dominated by Johannine teaching. Later Jewish thought expressed the idea of the divine activity in creation and revelation by the personification of Wisdom. See Prov 8:22ff. In Wis 9:1–2, Wisdom is aligned with the Word of the OT (Gen 1:1; Ps 33:6 *al.*) and each credited with a share in the work of creation. To convey this idea of mediatorial agency in creation Philo adopted a term long current in Hellenic philosophical circles, namely, "Logos," which for him corresponded to both the creative Word of the OT and the immanent reason of Stoicism. Cf. *Leg. Alleg.* 3.96: σκιὰ δὲ ὁ λόγος αὐτοῦ ἐστιν, ᾧ καθάπερ ὀργάνῳ προσχρησάμενος ἐκοσμοποίει. So also *Migr. Abr.* 6; *Sacerdot.* 81. The thought is echoed in Paul (Col 1:16; 1 Cor 8:6) and the *auctor ad Hebraeos* (Heb 1:2), but the term itself is lacking (for possible reasons of this omission, see Howard, *John*, 42ff.). The word "Logos" comes into Christian use first in the Prologue of the Fourth Gospel (John 1:1ff., 14). There the Logos, the agent of creation (1:3, 10), is conceived as personal and incarnate, a marked advance upon Philonic thought. Moreover, in the Fourth Gospel the term "Logos" as a personal title is confined to the Prologue. In the body of that Gospel ὁ υἱὸς (τοῦ θεοῦ) becomes the characteristic title. It is to the NT, and especially to John, that the author of Diogn. 1–10 owes his general conception and particularly his preference for the terms "Son," "child." The title "Logos" occurs only in the appended chapters, with the doubtful exception of 7:2. See below, p. 160–61, and Additional Note C.

130. In both the Fourth Gospel (1:3) and our epistle (7:2) there is but a single clear reference to the cosmic creativeness of the Word or Son. In Diogenetus (8:7; 10:2) creation is attributed directly to God.

131. *1 Apol.* 23; *Dial.* 83.

132. It was reserved for Athanasius to develop this *religious* meaning of the incarnation. It is, however, noticeable how Diognetus makes the incarnation of the Word pivotal. It is in the coming of the Son, not in any moral precepts or philosophical doctrine of the faith as such, that our author finds the source of the new and vigorous life of Christians in the world.

c. Man and the Christian Community

Man is a moral being and the object of God's love. God made him in his own image and for his sake created the world.[133] To man he gave dominion over all things in the earth, endowed him with reason and mind,[134] and empowered him for heavenly aspirations.[135] God's love was shown in part in his forbearance with man's sins (8:7; 9:1), but still more by his implanting in man "the truth and the holy and incomprehensible word," by sending his Son as man to men, and by the promise of the kingdom in heaven "to those who loved him."

The author will have no truce with natural religion, not even with the Platonic view that man's reason can apprehend God, since God and man are kin.[136] It is the revelation through faith that enables man to see God (8:6) and to share in his blessings (8:11). He repeatedly insists that Christianity is supernatural in character. As it is beyond all human thought and devising (5:3; 7:1), so its "mystery" cannot be learned from man (4:6). Man too is not naturally immortal. His iniquity may bring "its reward of punishment and death" (9:2).[137] Free-will is implied in his capacity to become "a new man" (2:1), and in God's attitude of appeal rather than compulsion (7:4). It was by his own consent (ὡς ἐβουλόμεθα, 9:1) that man was in "the former time" "borne along by unruly impulse," the prey of "pleasures and lusts"; hence he was self-convicted as "unworthy of life" and unable of himself "to enter into the kingdom of God." The author's doctrine of sin is baldly stated, but the terms he uses suffice to show its heinousness in his eyes. He speaks of "inordinate impulses," "iniquity," "misdeeds," "wickedness and impiety," and finds sin's crowning effect in man's moral impotence to attain life (ζωή). He stresses the latter point. Man of himself and in "the former time" lack moral power. There is no hint of the idea that man has an innate bias towards evil,[138] though the σάρξ is in one passage (5:8; see note), after the Pauline usage, predominantly ethical, the seat of sin. Nor, unlike Justin Martyr, Athenagoras, and other apologists, does the author attribute sin to

---

133. A familiar thought in the apologists. See note on 10:2. Celsus (Origen, *Cels.* 4.24) controverts this idea. God cares for the whole, for irrational creatures no less than for man. See also Origen, *Cels.* 4.99.

134. Cf. Justin Martyr, *1 Apol.* 10: "the rational faculties (λογικῶν δυνάμενων) he has himself endowed us with."

135. See note on 10:2 (οἷς ... ἐπέτρεψεν).

136. See the discussion in Justin Martyr, *Dial.* 4.

137. See note on 6:8.

138. For the *yezer hara* cf. Sir 15:14 (Heb); 21:11 *al.*; Let. Aris. 108; 277; and for rabbinic citations, see Strack and Billerbeck, *Kommentar zum Neuen Testament*, 4:466–83.

I. Introduction

the malice of demons—a point in which our epistle is like the *Apology of Aristides*. In general, the ultimate source of evil lies in man's ignorance of God (see on 8:1; 10:3). Hence God's forbearance "during the former time and the implication that "complete knowledge of the Father" is given in the Christian faith (10:1). But the author's concern is less with the cause of sin than with its tragic results.

The remedy lies wholly in the redemption made in Christ. No place is given to Judaism as a *praeparatio evangelica*. The scheme of salvation was disclosed "to his child alone." Our author is to be classed with those apologists who recognize no progressive moral approach to the incarnation. The pre-Christian world, pagan and Jewish alike, stands under condemnation, an attitude first taken in Barnabas and discernible in Tatian and Irenaeus. Here there is no question of an embryonic goodness in mankind, maturing in the course of time. The redemption is that of an evil world, a wholly new and unforeseen manifestation of God's grace. "O the inscrutable working, O the unexpected blessings!" (9:5).

Of the Christians as a καινὸν γένος (ch. 1)[139] and the "soul" of the world (ch. 6) the author paints a glowing picture. See chs. 5–6; which culminate in the thought that Christians are divinely appointed to their high rank. Granted that this section[140] portrays an ideal of character and life,[141] yet the ideal cannot have been entirely remote from the actual.[142] The writer suggests rather than states how the moral transformation was effected. In the Son, God has manifested his love for men. This love begets in men a corresponding love towards God,[143] and this in turn leads to the *imitatio Dei*. Then love shown by man to man naturally follows. The wheel comes full circle in the striking affirmation that whoever imitates the goodness of God in helping others becomes a god to his fellows.[144] Stress is laid on love as the cardinal virtue of the Christian life, but it is love universalized. Diognetus had asked "what is the love which they (the Christians) have for

---

139. See note on p. 94. Jewish apologists had to rebut the imputation that their nation was of recent origin. Cf. Josephus, *C. Ap.* 1.1ff. Christian defenders laid great stress on the point. See Tatian, *Or. Graec.* 31; Theophilus, *Autol.* 3.20ff.

140. No summary can do justice to this famous passage in which both language and style accord with the theme. For a close paraphrase rather than a translation (in French), see Renan, *Marc-Aurèle*, 425–27. See below on ch. 5 (*ad init.*).

141. Harnack, *Expansion*, 1:252n1, takes an adverse view of its historical worth, dismissing Diogn. 5:6 as "a fine piece of rhetoric, but not much more than that." So also Workman, *Persecution in the Early Church*, 168n1. For a juster view see Gwatkin, *Early Church History*, 1:213.

142. See some balanced remarks in Dobschütz, *Christian Life*, xxxivf.

143. "How *greatly* will you love him who so first loved you?" (10:3).

144. See Additional Note B.

one another?"¹⁴⁵ Significantly, when the author takes up this point, he widens the reference. "Christians," he says, "love all men" (5:11; see note), even "those who hate them" (6:6). Here he sounds a prominent note in the apologies. Love to enemies was a principle which had marked apologetic value. Christians were accused of "hatred of the human race."¹⁴⁶ Their answer was to point to the centrality of love in Christianity as embodied in their own attitude towards their enemies.

Christians are conceived as forming a spiritual organism. Chapter 6 elaborates the thesis that "what the soul is in the body, that Christians are in the world." In the epistle proper (1–10) there is no hint of the Church,¹⁴⁷ ministry, or sacraments. Too much should not be made of this silence, but it suggests that the author did not regard Church order as of primary importance. Cruttwell says that the author of Diognetus is perhaps the only writer of the early period who presents, "pure and unadulterated,"¹⁴⁸ the idea of the Church as essentially a spiritual society.¹⁴⁹ It is difficult to see on what grounds Puech feels in the epistle "an ecclesiastical anointing."¹⁵⁰

d. Pagan Idolatry and Philosophy

The treatment of heathen idol-worship (ch. 2) follows the conventional lines.¹⁵¹ All images are of perishable material and mutable in form (do they not vary according to the skill or caprice of the artificer who carves or molds or forges them into their several shapes?). They are dumb and blind; they lack soul, feeling, and power of motion, and are subject to decay.¹⁵² To

---

145. Cf. the familiar heathen gibe: "Behold how these Christians love one another!" (Tertullian, *Apol.* 39).

146. "*Odium humani generis*" (Tacitus, *Annals* 15.44). The genitive is probably objective. A partial analogy is found in the familiar charge against the Jews of "misanthropy." For an exposition of the phrase in Tacitus, see Cuq, "De la nature." He concludes that "the *odium generis humani* was therefore the result of certain acts which, for the Romans, had the character of evil spells" (p. 128). See also Ramsay, *Church in the Roman Empire*, 236f.

147. τάξις (6:10) is used in a general sense rather than of the Church as the "*militia Dei*." See note *ad loc.*

148. Cruttwell, *Literary History*, 2:539ff.

149. But see Barn. 16:7ff., where the Pauline description of the Church as a spiritual temple is unfolded. Cf. also Ign. *Eph.* 15:3. The thought may derive from Mark 14:58.

150. Puech, *Apologistes grecs*, 252; *Histoire*, 2:219.

151. Cf. Isa 40:18–20; 44:9–20; Jer 10:1–16; Jub 1:9–11; Philo, *Decal.* 7ff.; Rom 1:18f.; Justin Martyr, *1 Apol.* 9.

152. Common characteristics. Cf. Ps 115:5ff; Wis 33:16; Let. Aris. 135; Sib. Or. 5:77ff.

discriminate among such "gods," leaving those of stone and earthenware unguarded while protecting with great care those of silver and gold, what is this but mockery of the god? The author stresses the senselessness of idolatry rather than its evil character and accompaniments (he does not touch on the shameless immoralities of pagan worship). Yet the latter are not lacking. Idolatry deceives (ἀπατῶσάν σε συνήθειαν, 2:1; see note),[153] and—the most fatal count in the indictment—the worshiper ultimately becomes like the idol that he worships (see notes on 2:5). In general, heathen idolatry was for our author merely blind worship of stocks and stones.

Edwyn Bevan, in a penetrating study of image-worship,[154] shows that with respect to pagan gods the general view of the OT is that the image has behind it no reality.[155] Hence pagan idolatry, since it treats mere inanimate matter as though it were a living being, is judged to be utterly absurd. He illustrates this view by citations of Ps 135:15f.; Isa 44; Wis 12:10–19; Epistle of Jeremiah (Bar 6:4–22). The *wickedness* of idolatry appears when it seeks to make in Israel a similitude of Jehovah, the one true God to whom alone worship should be offered. As for Christian writers, while they shared in some degree this view that an idol was a nonentity, generally they accepted the pagan claim that the images were animated by spirits, which, however, they deemed to be wholly evil. The images were tenanted by devils.[156] Bevan further affirms that educated pagans would not actually identify the image with the god which it represents. "It is hardly possible that anyone thought of the deity worshipped as simply the image he saw and nothing more . . . The deity was certainly conceived of as a person active in the world apart from the image."[157] In a recent review the same scholar adversely criticizes our epistle on the ground that it rests on the supposition that the heathen did identify the images with the gods they worshiped, a view which, he thinks, would appear contemptible in the eyes of Diognetus, presumably an enlightened pagan.[158]

153. Cf. Isa 44:20; Wis 12:24; T. Naph. 3:3: ἔθνη πλανηθέντα . . . ὑπήκουσαν ξύλοις καὶ λίθοις, πνεύμασι πλάνης.

154. Bevan, *Holy Images*, 17ff.

155. We may point out that some scholars hold that the terms used by the eighth-century prophets ("no gods," etc.) denote not the absolute non-existence of foreign deities but their "utter powerlessness and insufficiency" in comparison with the supreme might of Yahweh. See Whitehouse, "Demon, Devil," 1:591.

156. Cf. Minucius Felix, *Oct.* 27: "now these unclean spirits, the demons, as the magi and philosophers have shown, conceal themselves in statues and consecrated images."

157. Bevan, *Holy Images*, 20. See also on this point Geffcken, *Zwei griechische Apologeten*, 77–78; 241.

158. See Bevan, "Review of *The Epistle of Diognetus* by E.H. Blakeney," *Hibbert Journal* (1943), 378. Cf. also Donaldson, *Critical History*, 2:136–37.

Now it is clear that the writer of the epistle takes the general OT point of view in this regard. He is concerned with pagan idolatry, not with that apostasy in Israel which sought to make a likeness of Yahweh in some visible symbol. Hence he dwells on the irrationality of image-worship rather than its wickedness. To call lifeless images "gods" and to serve and worship them is a ridiculous delusion. Further, it is true that Diognetus makes no explicit distinction between the images and the beings they visibly represent,[159] such as some pagan writers imply.[160] This may betray a lack of clarity of thought and perhaps, in view of Diognetus's presumed reaction, bad tactics on the part of the author. Probably it can be explained, if not excused, by the author's earnestness and passion, qualities which do not always permit a fair statement of a case! In any event, his treatment is at least in line with the conventional Jewish and Christian protest, which did not commonly distinguish between the image and that which it symbolizes.[161]

Again, unlike the majority of the apologists, the writer of the epistle does not advance the view that the idol-gods were the abode of demons. He seems rather to share the concurrent opinion that images were, in Justin's phrase, ἄψυχα καὶ νεκρά.[162] That both views could be held in the mind without a sense of conflict may be seen in Paul, who assures his Corinthian readers that, while "we know that no idol is *anything* in the world, and that there is no God but one" (1 Cor 8:4),[163] to sacrifice to idols is to sacrifice to demons and thereby to have fellowship with demons.[164]

There is no reference to edible sacrifices such as are mentioned in the Preaching of Peter (Clem. Alex., *Strom.* 6.5.39ff.), unless these are implied in the phrase "by worshipping them with blood and steaming fat" (2:8).

---

159. Is there a hint of this distinction in the words "these you worship and in the end you become like them!" (2:5)? Obviously, the worshiper could not become like the god in its form. But probably what is meant is likeness in the qualities of the god (dumbness, blindness, etc.).

160. Bevan, *Holy Images*, 22, cites Plutarch, *Isis and Osiris* 71, and other sources. See also his article "Idolatry" in *Edinburgh Review*, 261.

161. But cf. 1 En. 99:7; Rev 9:20, where εἴδωλα and δαιμόνια are differentiated.

162. 1 *Apol.* 9.

163. Even if this part of a statement of belief sent by the Corinthians in a letter to Paul which he here quotes (see Lock, "1 Corinthians 8:1–8," 65ff.), it probably reflects the standpoint of his previous preaching to the Corinthians.

164. "What say I then? that a thing sacrificed to idols is anything, or that an idol is anything? But I say, that the things which the gentiles sacrifice, they sacrifice to devils, and not to God; and I do not wish for you to have communion with devils" (1 Cor 10:19–20). Cf. Deut 32:17; Bar 4:7. There is probably no fundamental inconsistency here. For Paul the gods *as such* are nonentities. Yet behind the material representations of the gods lurk demoniacal powers which can corrupt the worshipers.

I. Introduction

The treatment of idolatry is slight compared with that in the Book of Wisdom. Our author implies (2:2) but does not elaborate the argument of Wis (14:1–11) that the idol-maker is perverting created things from their divinely-intended use.[165] Perhaps this is one of the points which, as he naïvely remarks, he had in reserve (2:10)!

The contemptuous dismissal of the Greek philosophers is briefer still (8:2–4). It was but natural that some of the apologists who had come from the philosophic schools should seek to commend Christianity as a kind of philosophy.[166] Justin Martyr, who as a Christian teacher continued to wear the philosopher's cloak, has his condemnation of philosophy, but on the whole takes a just and sympathetic view. Indeed he explicitly recognizes some affinity of ideas between Christianity and Greek philosophic thought (see 1 Apol. 20). But while he reveres the great names he holds that Plato and the Stoics were only partially inspired by the spermatic Logos (2 Apol. 13). Christian teaching is "above all human philosophy" (2 Apol. 15).[167] Athenagoras too inclines to a charitable judgment. He affirms in Suppl. 7 that poets and philosophers are moved by "their affinity with the afflatus from God" (though their conclusions are uncertain and contradictory, being drawn "each one from himself"), and he makes free use of philosophic material and form. Platonic influence on Athenagoras is marked. It was generally argued that philosophy with its self-contradictions could not rival Christianity, which is a divine revelation: At the same time apologists recognize in the philosophic systems certain elements of universal truth, which they explain as either seed sown by the Logos in the heathen world or borrowings from the Scriptures.[168] The author of Diognetus, however, will have none of this. He is to be classed with Theophilus (2:4), Tertullian (Apol. 46–47), and Arnobius (2.9–10) in his adverse view of the Greek sages, though his tone is hardly as bitter as that of Tatian, who more than any other apologist repudiates Greek religion and culture (see Or. Graec. 2; 3). Our author roundly rejects "the vain and foolish statements of those specious philosophers" who identify God with one or other of the elements as "mere miracle-mongering

---

165. Cf. also the Preaching of Peter (Clement of Alexandria, Strom. 6.5.39: "[forgetting] their [i.e., wood, stones, etc.] material and *proper* use" [τῆς ὕλης αὐτῶν καὶ χρήσεως]).

166. See Friedländer, *Roman Life and Manners*, 3:227. Harnack, *History of Dogma*, 2:177, speaks of "the marvellous attempt to present Christianity to the world as the religion which is the true philosophy, and as the philosophy which is the true religion."

167. *Dial.* 8: "I found this philosophy (Christianity) alone to be safe and profitable."

168. "What poet," cries Tertullian (*Apol.* 47), "what sophist is there who has not drunk from the fountain of the prophets?" See Harnack, *Expansion*, 1:365n1.

and deceit of the magicians," and adds parenthetically a tart reminder of their final destination!¹⁶⁹

This censure of the philosophes, however, is less drastic than it seems. The author's own mind moves in Platonic grooves,¹⁷⁰ and his language and style alike attest the influence of the rhetorical schools.¹⁷¹ But even so, his preconceptions are always Christianized.¹⁷² He shares the idea (held by Plato and others¹⁷³) of the imitation of God by man, but deepens it by his insistence that such imitation is made possible only by divine grace (see note on 10:4). The overwhelming sense of the uniqueness of the Christian religion dominates his thought.¹⁷⁴ The Christian "mystery" is revealed by God, not discovered by man. It was left to Clement of Alexandria to see in idolatry and philosophy preparatory stages in the religious training of the nations.¹⁷⁵

e. Jewish Worship

The condemnation of Judaism is downright but superficial and warped. Most Christian apologists take the view that the Mosaic Law was merely a temporary dispensation, being superseded by the new Law written in the hearts of Christians; that the Old Testament itself foretells the coming of Christ; and that the Jews cannot rightly claim the exclusive favor of God, the gentiles being now incorporated in the new spiritual Israel, the Church. The author of the epistle does not avail himself of these contentions. He

---

169. Probably he has in mind Heraclitus, though he does not name him. See notes on 8:2. We remark a milder note in Aristides, *Apol.* 3: heathen philosophers have "erred" in deifying images made in honor of the elements. So also the author of *Cohort. ad Gent.* (3–4), though his tone hardens later (11).

170. Platonic parallels or reminiscences and affinities with Stoic thought are pointed out in the Notes (see especially ch. 6), though Geffcken, *Zwei griechische Apologeten*, 26, overrates them as "infinitely frequent." In particular, the figure of the dispersal of the soul in the body and the idea of the soul sustaining the body may be traced to Stoic sources. Platonic influence appears in the idea of the soul as imprisoned in the body (6:4, 7; see notes there).

171. See above, p. 14n55.

172. Molland, "Diognetbriefes," 306: "In fact, the letter is surprisingly little Platonizing and Stoicizing. The constituent thoughts of the author have a completely different character, and a closer analysis of the content shows that the Hellenistic-philosophical features are superficial and did not shape the Christian conception of the letter."

173. See Additional Note A.

174. "Everywhere and always, he is a conscious Christian, if ever there was one" (Puech, *Apologistes grecs*, 260).

175. See especially *Strom.* 1.2, 4–5, 13, 17, 19; 5.13; 6.8. Cf. 6.17: "there is no absurdity in philosophy having been given by divine providence as a preparatory discipline for the perfection which is by Christ."

I. Introduction

makes first a general indictment of Jewish δεισιδαιμονία.[176] The Jews offer God worship in the same fashion[177] as the Greeks; Jewish sacrifices are as foolish as pagan offerings, the latter because they are made to senseless and deaf images, the former because they rest on the view that God, the provider of all, is in need of these things. Then he fastens upon particular matters such as Jewish food taboos, the rite of circumcision, Sabbath punctiliousness, observance of feasts according to lunar periods. These he assails with great severity.[178]

It is important to see how radical is the author's attitude towards the Jewish Law. It was the ethical and spiritual meaning of the Law that was stressed by many Hellenistic-Jewish writers such as Aristeas and Philo, and is reflected in Barnabas.[179] The Mosaic requirements are symbols of moral demands upon God's people. All regulations of the Law "have been framed with a view to righteousness" (Let. Aris. 168; cf. 151, 161). Similarly, Barn. 10 brings out the spiritual or mystical significance of the Mosaic injunctions. They are symbolic of moral prohibitions. It is apparent that this allegorical interpretation of the Jewish Law prepared the way for the Christian position that the Law, while of divine origin and authority, was, as regards its external ordinances, abrogated in Christ. The obligation to observe them held no longer in the new Israel (so Paul);[180] what was merely symbolic and shadowy was done away in Christ (so the *auctor ad Hebraeos*). But it was recognized that the Jewish ceremonial Law, though now superseded, was valid for pre-Christian times.

Our author, however, sharply diverges here from the main Christian view. He neither admits the divine origin or ordering of the ceremonial observances, nor suggests that they were formulated to convey a moral lesson or serve as an aid to righteousness. It is not even conceded that they were "an educational necessity, to meet the stubbornness and idolatrous tendencies of the nation (being, in fact, a safeguard of monotheism)."[181] These rites

---

176. See note on the term (Diogn. 1).

177. ὁμοιοτρόπως (3:2). Cf. *Apology of Aristides* 14 (*sub fin.*): εἰσὶ παρόμοιοι τῶν ἐθνῶν.

178. It may be observed that Aristides (*Apol.* 14), while condemning these specific ceremonial observances, says nothing about Jewish sacrificial offerings.

179. Aristeas, while allegorizing the Law, makes no suggestion that its ceremonial observance need not be literally practiced. Philo, indeed, carefully insists that the allegorical elucidation does not destroy the literal force of the enactments of the Law nor dispense with the necessity of its external observance (*Migr.* 89ff.). See Drummond, *Philo Judaeus*, 1:20. Barnabas (9:4), however, is unequivocal: the literal observance of the Law is a seduction of the evil one.

180. Cf. Rom 10:4; Gal 3:23ff.

181. Harnack, *Expansion*, 1:68.

are absurd and even impious, an exhibition of Jewish "meddlesomeness and pride" (4:6). In denouncing Jewish sacrifices the author might well have enlisted the authority of the Hebrew prophets, who condemned them unsparingly (Amos 5:21f.; Isa 1:11, etc.). But, unlike Justin (*Dial.* 22) and Tertullian (*Adv. Jud.* 5), he disdains even this reinforcement of his plea. Judaism is anathema. The only relief in the picture is that he does not, after the manner of the Preaching of Peter,[182] charge the Jews with contaminating their monotheistic worship with homage to angels. He admits that "they worship the one God of the universe and think of him as Master" (3:2).

Edwyn Bevan sees in the wholesale condemnation of Jewish ritual practices an evidence of the author's intellectual inability to think out its implications.[183] It is inconsistent with the Scriptures, accepted as infallible and authoritative by the Church. In particular, it conflicts with the New Testament view that the Jewish ritual Law had been really given by God to Israel and had been of obligation before the death of the Messiah. Moreover, it is difficult to harmonize this severe treatment of material rites and observance of sacred days with the practices of the Church in regard to baptism, the Eucharist, and Easter, of which the author, though he makes no mention of them, must have been fully aware.

But does not the cogency of the former argument posit a relatively late date for the epistle? The fact that the author takes a view of the Jewish Law inconsistent with that of the NT does not necessarily point to his intellectual immaturity; rather it may indicate that he writes at a time when the NT books had not gained special sanctity or authority. We have already seen (pp. 18–19) that the epistle probably derives from about the middle of the second century CE, at which time the idea of a sacred canon of NT writings was not established (see below, p. 56). As to the latter point, it is true that in view of the denunciation of Jewish ceremonial as vain the mere observance of Christian baptism and the Eucharist could not logically claim to be efficacious. The author's inconsistency (if such it is) in this regard is shared by Justin and other apologists.

It may be that the author's strictures are made not so much of historical Judaism as of the Jewish practice of his own day in its conflict with Christianity. He has perhaps in mind the religion of the rabbis rather than that of the prophets. Be that as it may, he is in the succession of earlier writers;[184]

---

182. "They (the Jews) know him not, serving angels and archangels, the month and the moon" (Clem. Alex., *Strom.* 6.5.41). Cf. also *Apology of Aristides* 14 (Syr.).

183. Bevan, "Review of *The Epistle of Diognetus* by E.H. Blakeney," *Hibbert Journal*, 377ff. See also his *Hellenism and Christianity*, 39f.

184. For severe criticism of the Jews see the Fourth Gospel (*passim*); Jas 5:6 ("you murdered the just"); Rev 2:9 ("a synagogue of Satan"); Did. 8 ("hypocrites"); Gospel of

I. Introduction

the apologists as a whole take a more lenient view.[185] Our author's temper is Marcionite in its ignoring of the historical link between Judaism and Christianity.[186] His overwhelming sense of the incomparable worth of the new faith left little room for a just evaluation of pre-Christian as of non-Christian systems. Hence it cannot be said that on these two matters the author really answered Diognetus or the educated constituency that he represents. For in addressing cultured circles it was inept to treat both pagan idolatry and Jewish sacrifices so superficially. The one he seriously misrepresented as mere worship of stocks and stones, showing no appreciation of its higher aspects; upon the other he poured such unqualified contempt as would alienate or antagonize one who, like Diognetus, was especially concerned (μάλιστα ποθεῖν, 3:1) to know the difference between Jewish and Christian worship. The author's *apologia* suffers from defects of excessive zeal.

f. Persecution of the Christians

Almost up to the end of the first century the Christian religion appeared to gentile eyes as a special sect of Judaism; hence it shared the tolerance which Judaism enjoyed in the main as a recognized national cult. Persecutions under Nero and Domitian had been the outcome of personal rancor rather than of State policy. But by the time of Trajan (98–117 CE) Christianity was making itself felt as a power which might well prove subversive of the imperial order itself. Its treasonable character, deduced from the refusal of Christians to swear loyalty to the emperor as "Lord," became apparent. From this time on, the State joined with the Jews in systematic oppression of the Christians.[187] This continued through the reigns of Trajan, Hadrian, Antoninus Pius, and Marcus Aurelius. After the death of the last-named

---

Peter; Barnabas is still more drastic in denouncing historical Judaism and all its works. Aristides, *Apol.* 14 (Syr.) has a much milder tone. In their monotheism the Jews are "much nearer to the truth than all the peoples," as also in their imitation of God in works of compassion. Nevertheless, their observance of Sabbaths and new moons and the Passover and the great feasts, etc., is really service to angels, not to God. Moreover, Jesus "was pierced by the Jews" (2 [Syr.]). Justin Martyr, *1 Apol.* 63, adds that this was at the instigation of the devils. Cf. *Dial.* 16.

185. For example, Justin's tone, though occasionally severe (*1 Apol.* 37), is conciliatory on the whole. He even addresses the Jews as "my brothers" (*Dial.* 137).

186. See above, pp. 15–17.

187. Against Harnack's view (*Expansion*, 1:58f.; 2:104) that the Jews were as a rule the instigators of "bloody persecutions" of Christians in general. Abrahams, *Pharisaism*, 56ff., insists that the persecution related to *Jewish* Christians and not to *gentile* Christians as such.

(180 CE) there was a lull of more than fifty years. Then persecution broke out afresh. The State now stood alone in its hostility to Christians.

The references in the epistle to persecution are as follows. Christians "despise death" (ch. 1),[188] "suffer all things as strangers" (5:5), "are persecuted by all men," are "condemned," "put to death," "dishonored," "spoken evil of," "abused," "insulted," "buffeted," "warred upon by the Jews as foreigners and persecuted by the Greeks" (5:11ff.), "thrown to wild beasts" (7:7), "punished" (7:8; 10:7), "endure for the sake of righteousness the fire which is but for a season" (10:8).

These references are general in character[189] and allow but little inference about the place or date of the epistle.[190] The tone suggests that persecution was taken more or less for granted as the normal lot of Christians. But two points may be observed. First, the author suggests some of the grounds for the hatred towards Christians, namely, their refusal to acknowledge heathen gods (1:1; 2:5–6, 10), their distinctive manner of life (5:4), their opposition to the pleasures of the world (6:5), and probably their rejection of emperor-worship.[191] He rebuts by implication the charges of immorality (5:7–8) and aloofness from state service and loyalties (5:4–5, 10). Secondly, he insists that persecution leads to increase in the number of Christians (6:9; 7:8)—a feature not confined to any one period. Again we note that persecution is not attributed to the energies of demons as in Justin Martyr (*1 Apol.* 5; *2 Apol.* 1).

As to the attitude towards the civil power the author's tone indicates that he shares in the disparagement of government in general and of the Roman Empire in particular. It is not that he is hostile. There is no suggestion that Church and State must be in fundamental opposition, the note we hear in the book of the Revelation and in Ignatius.[192] On the contrary his tone is conciliatory. He affirms that Christians "share all things as citizens" (5:5) and "obey the appointed laws" (5:10).[193] But he views earthly government as belonging to the transient order. He says that God in sending his Son did

---

188. See below, pp. 97–98.

189. The persecutors are specified only in one passage (5:17). The Roman government is not named.

190. Bunsen, *Christianity and Mankind*, 1:170, and others find in 5:17 an allusion to the Jewish war of Bar-Kokhba, and hence assign the epistle to 134–35 CE. But the reference appears to be quite general.

191. "*Do you not see them* thrown to wild beasts, that they may deny the Lord?" (7:7). Cf. also 10:7.

192. Cf. Rev 14:8; 18:21.

193. Cf. Justin Martyr, *1 Apol* 17; Athenagoras, *Suppl.* 3. So the NT (Rom 13:1ff.; 1 Pet 2:13).

not send a "servant or an angel or ruler, or one of those who administer the affairs of earth" (7:2). And the Son came in gentleness and meekness, an implied contrast to earthly rulers who tyrannize by fear.[194] So also he rules out "dominion over one's neighbors" (10:5). This general attitude of inward aloofness to the temporal order is rooted in the conviction that the true life of the Christian is above. On earth he is a stranger and pilgrim, because his citizenship is in heaven.[195]

g. Moral and Religious Values

Repentance is not specifically named in the epistle, though implied. The stress lies on God's action rather than on man's moral response as the supreme factor in salvation. The divine delay in the plan of salvation was not, as was frequently explained,[196] to lead men to repent. Its purpose was to magnify the goodness and power of God in rescuing man impotent in his sins (9:1-2).[197] On the other hand, the author makes faith primary: "He manifested himself through faith (διὰ πίστεως),[198] by which alone it is given to see God" (8:6). This, however, is not the Pauline notion of faith. It does not signify that moral assent whereby man appropriates God's free gift of justifying grace. The author does not specify the object of faith, that is, God or Christ, or suggest its nature as an inward disposition of trust and surrender. The term here denotes belief in the divine revelation, this belief being the basis of true knowledge.[199] Cf. 10:1 where "this faith" is antecedent to "knowledge of the Father" (in 11:2 disciples, being πιστοί, gain "knowledge of the mysteries of the Father"). The divine intention in effecting the redemption of man is "that we should believe his goodness" (9:6), and grace "rejoices over the faithful" (or "believers"), 11:5. In the later writer's phrases, "the pledges of faith," "the faith of the gospels" (11:5, 6), the term πίστις becomes objective signifying almost "system of belief." See note *ad loc.*

---

194. Cf. Justin Martyr, 2 *Apol.* 1. Tatian says, "The construction of the world is excellent, but its πολίτευμα is bad" (19). So also Athenagoras, *Res.* 19, speaks of the "robber or prince or tyrant" who could not by one death make restitution for his evil deeds.

195. See below, pp. 40-41.

196. Cf. Wis 11:23; Acts 17:30; Rom 2:4; 2 Pet 3:9; Justin Martyr, 1 *Apol.* 28.

197. So Paul: man's former sins are passed over in the forbearance of God (Rom 3:25).

198. The term is used in its active sense "belief," "trust," as predominately in NT use.

199. The Fourth Gospel foreshadows this more intellectual content of "believing" (πιστεύειν). See Scott, *Fourth Gospel*, 267-70, and Tennant, *Nature of Belief*, 65f.

A few miscellaneous points may be mentioned. Almsgiving is prescribed (10:6).[200] Poverty seems to be commended (5:13), and, conversely, covetousness and love of wealth condemned or at least their perils pointed out (10:5).[201] There is no marked ascetic strain in the teaching of the epistle. The probable hint at fasting (6:9) merely indicates in general terms its moral value.[202] The author regards marriage and the procreation of children as normal.[203] He does not share the tendency of some early Christian writers to exalt celibacy.[204] On the contrary, he stresses the purity of the Christians in the married state (5:7–8), and that not merely as an answer to heathen charges of immorality (see above, p. 38). The wedded state, it would seem, is commended in and for itself. Prayer is mentioned only once ("I ask from God," etc., 1:1). Happiness (εὐδαιμονεῖν) defined in negative terms, with the positive implication that it consists in helping others (10:5–6).

For ideas prominent in chs. 11–12, see below, pp. 49–52.

h. Eschatology

Eschatological references are not numerous. The author tends to belittle earthly things as transient. His gaze is fixed on the higher and freer life hereafter. "The soul, though immortal, dwells in a mortal tabernacle; and Christians sojourn among corruptible things, awaiting the incorruptibility which is in heaven" (6:8). The kingdom is perhaps regarded in one passage as a future consummation. God promises men "the kingdom in heaven; and he will give it to them who loved him" (10:2).[205] But the hope of future reward is nowhere made the ground of morality (cf. Aristides[206]). As in New Testament teaching[207] the kingdom is also a present experience; the eschatology approaches the "realized" type. This is suggested by the phrase "to enter into the kingdom of God" (9:1), but is more apparent from the various features in the picture of the Christian's life in the world (chs. 5 and 6). It is of an other-worldly order, "the true life in heaven," though lived out here on

---

200. Cf. Aristides, *Apol.* 15; 2 Clem. 16:4; Justin Martyr, *1 Apol.* 15.
201. Cf. Tatian, *Graec.* 11; Justin Martyr, *1 Apol.* 15.
202. See note *ad loc.*
203. Cf. 1 Clem. 33:5f.; Justin Martyr, *1 Apol.* 29; Athenagoras, *Res.* 12.
204. Herm. Sim. 9.11; Acts of Paul and Thecla 5–16.
205. So also the Eucharistic prayer in the Didache (10:5) suggests a *future* kingdom.
206. Christians keep the commandments "in the hope and expectation of the world to come" (*Apol.* 15; cf. 16 Syr.). So Justin Martyr, *1 Apol.* 14: "that they may become partakers with us of the same joyful hope of a reward from God."
207. Cf. Matt 12:28; Col 1:13; Heb 6:5; 1 John 2:8.

earth (10:7). The body, while not despised (note, however, the depreciatory reference to the flesh in 6:5), is viewed as the temporary abode of the soul, as is also the world in relation to Christians. As the soul is "not of the body," so Christians are "not of the world." The θεοσέβεια of the Christians remains invisible. It is a mystery hidden from men (4:6). It is true that Christians live in their own fatherlands, but as πάροικοι; they share in the general life of men, but as ξένοι. Their citizenship is of a "remarkable and admittedly strange order" (5:4). It is "in heaven" (5:9).[208] The one brief reference to the parousia (in 7:9 the reference is probably to the "presence" of God; see note) makes no suggestion of its nearness (7:6). The return of Christ involves judgment. If he came first as "King," as "God," as "Man," he will come again as "Judge." Here the thought is thoroughly Pauline (2 Thess 1:7ff.; 1 Cor 4:4–5; 2 Cor 5:10) and indeed primitive (Acts 10:42). Our author describes judgment in general terms (condemnation, punishment, death, 9:2; 10:7). The one definite feature is "eternal fire," which shall punish "up to the end" (μέχρι τέλους, see on 10:7).[209] The main thought is, as in most Christian writers of the period, the certainty of judgment. See Aristides, *Apol.* 17 (*sub fin.*), Justin Martyr, *1 Apol.* 8, 12, 17, 45; *2 Apol.* 9.[210] It is noticeable that the epistle contains no allusion to the resurrection.[211] It is rather the resurrection life lived in this world that is in clear view.

208. Paul's conception of life in the Spirit is analogous (Gal 5:25–26; Rom 8:9ff.).

209. Bevan, "Review of The *Epistle of Diognetus* by E. H. Blakeney," *Hibbert Journal*, 378, points to the inconsistency of this view of God's judgment by fire with the previous statement that "force is no attribute of God" (7:4), and sees here a proof of the author's "feeble intellectual grasp." But the contrast is more apparent than real. The statement that "force is no attribute of God" is made expressly to illustrate the sending of the Son in gentleness and meekness; it stands, however, side by side in the same context with the idea of judgment to come. Judgment is less the forcible exertion of God's power over men than the just and inevitable "reward" of sin in "punishment and death" (9:2). The author's language suggests that these penalties work impersonally. He may have viewed them much in the manner of Paul, for whom the wrath of God means not some feeling or attitude on his part towards men, but the inescapable nemesis of sin seen in events "an inevitable process of cause and effect in a moral universe" (Dodd, *Romans*, 20ff.). This would tally entirely with the insistence in Diognetus that God is personally ἀόργητος (8:8). Be that as it may, that an author may not have thought out the implications of his view of God so that he holds positions seemingly at variance is by no means a rare occurrence!

210. Geffcken, *Apologeten*, 27, points out that these threats of future judgment appear at the *end* of Diognetus, as also in Aristides, *Apol.* 17; Justin Martyr, *1 Apol.* 68.

211. Note, however, the words "they (Christians) are put to death, yet they are endowed with life" (5:12), which may illustrate more generally the statement that the soul is immortal (6:8). Similarly, references to the resurrection are rare in the Apostolic Fathers. Cf. 1 Clem. 24:1; 42:3; Barn. 5:6; 15:9.

i. Relation to Current Thought

It may be of interest to note here the degree in which the author of the epistle accommodates himself to the presumed intellectual standpoint and convictions of his inquirer and the public that he represents. It is difficult to infer, except in general outline, what may have been Diognetus's religious tenets. As an educated man he would be fully aware of that complex intellectual and spiritual beliefs which marked second-century non-Christian thought. It is perhaps reasonable to assume that in the prevalent eclecticism[212] Roman Stoicism was for him a predominate element. How far then does the author adjust himself to the point of view of his questioner, and how much in the epistle can be taken as common ground between them?

Now the epistle seems to some extent an *argumentum ad hominem*.[213] This may be deduced in part from the conciliatory manner in which the author approaches Diognetus's inquiry. His tone is respectful and pleasing. He commends both Diognetus's zeal to learn about Christians, and the character of his questions. He prays that he himself may so speak that his addressee may be profited as much as possible and have the grace of hearing (1:1). The fact that these are conventional traits (see notes *ad loc.*) does not lessen the author's obvious sincerity. At the same time he is candid with his questioner. The latter must clear his mind of prejudice, use his intelligence, and indeed become, as it were, from the beginning a new man, as one too who is to hear a new story (2:1).

Similar frankness is shown concerning the recognition and worship of heathen gods. Here the tone is quite uncompromising. Idolatry is empty and foolish, a deceiving "custom" in which Diognetus must have no complicity (see note on 2:1). The author hints at the intellectual debasement to which it leads and charges his inquirer(s) with hating Christians because they reject such pagan worship.[214] How far Diognetus could justly be charged with belief in crude Greek polytheism is uncertain. He would, however, in company with the cultivated pagans of his time, doubtless tolerate and even reverence the popular religion of many gods.[215] In any event, the author's language

---

212. On the philosophic syncretism, see Bevan, *Stoics and Sceptics*, 91ff., and Bevan, Chapter in *Cambridge Ancient History*, 11:690–91.

213. See Telfer, "Review," 222ff., for a suggestive elaboration of this view.

214. In 5:17 Christians are hated without cause; elsewhere various causes are assigned. See pp. 38–39.

215. "From the time of Socrates an earnest belief in the gods of the Greek mythology became an impossibility to a philosophic mind" (Donaldson, *Critical History*, 2:19). "But the majority of philosophers did not deem it worth while to interfere with popular belief . . . they had no wish to indoctrinate men who were not philosophers with disparaging ideas of their national religions" (Donaldson, *Critical History*, 2:22). See also Zeller, *Outlines of the History of Greek Philosophy*, 254.

is pointed and personal (2:5ff.) and the tone openly contemptuous. In the invective against the Jewish δεισιδαιμονία the note is less directly personal. It is evident that Diognetus has some knowledge of Jewish worship (3:1) and observances (4:1). His attitude, however, is one of interest, not of allegiance. He desires to know why Christians do not worship in the same manner as Jews. The author commends the Jews' acknowledgment of "the one God of the universe," but perhaps covertly alludes thereby to the many heathen gods which Diognetus avows (cf. 2:5ff.). The God of the Jews is also the Creator of heaven and earth (by implication contrasted with the gentile gods which are manmade). The Jewish sacrificial worship, however, is in no respect better than pagan idolatry, and the ritual practices are utterly absurd.[216] Christians are right in rejecting the religion of both Jews and Greeks. Then comes the pertinent reminder that the "secret" of the Christians' religion does not yield to human inquiry. It is as though the author, while welcoming Diognetus's quest, would show him its necessary limits.[217] Christian truth ("no human doctrine") is not discovered so much as disclosed (4:6; 5:3; 7:1f.), and that to faith (8:6).

It is in ch. 6 that the author comes nearest to Diognetus's preconceptions. These are partly Platonic and partly Stoic.[218] The Stoic conceived of the world as a living Whole,[219] permeated and controlled by one energy. *Phusis*, the urge towards perfection, is everywhere at work, a life-force pervading all matter as the soul of a man permeates all his limbs.[220] It is the soul of the world.[221] Man by virtue of his rationality is a part of the Whole. Hence all men are akin and members of a world-state. Our author, it would seem, aligns his thought with this philosophic postulate of the world-soul. What the soul is in the body that Christians are in the world. In his conception of the cosmic role of Christians he moves in the intellectual orbit of his inquirer. The universalism of the function of Christians in the world corresponds to the Stoic emphasis on man's kinship with the whole of humanity. Similarly, the view of the Christians' loyalty to civil and political duties

216. For the superficiality of the author's account of pagan idolatry and Jewish sacrifices, see above, pp. 30–31.

217. See Minucius Felix, *Oct.* 5: "human insignificance is quite incapable of investigating things divine." Cf. Ps.-Justin, *Cohort. ad Gent.* 8 (cited below, p. 132).

218. Stoicism was familiar with the idea of the soul dispersed in the body and sustaining it. The notion of the soul as imprisoned in the body goes back to Orphic and Pythagorean doctrine (cf. Diogn. 6:2, 4, 7).

219. Cf. Marcus Aurelius 4.40; 5.8; 6.9 *al.*

220. Stoicism was familiar with the idea of the soul dispersed in the body and sustaining it. The notion of the soul as imprisoned in the body goes back to Orphic and Pythagorean doctrine (cf. Diogn. 6:2, 4, 7).

221. See Murray, *Stoic, Christian and Humanist*, 102ff.

as subordinate to their heavenly citizenship (5:9–10; 6; *passim*) is quite in line with Stoic cosmopolitanism.[222] But although the thought-forms are the same,[223] the content they carry for our author is different. New Testament teaching is his primary source.[224] Christians are the soul of the world in the sense that they are a spiritual influence which permeates the whole social order. The Gospel figures of light, leaven, and salt are not explicit but may be present to his mind. Johannine reflections in particular are traceable in this section. Note the meaning of the term κόσμος (6:1 et al.) and the thought of Christians as in the world but not of it (6:3; cf. 5:5).

In the conception of God our author, though holding views in common with current religious thought on some characteristics of the Deity,[225] is pronouncedly Christian. He openly challenges Diognetus with the query: "do you accept the vain and foolish statements of those specious philosophers" who "identify God with one of the created elements (8:2)? The stress laid on the creative power of God is marked (3:4; 4:2, 5; 7:2; 8:7). The material world is the divine handiwork wrought through the Logos as agent (7:2). God too is all-provident, ordaining the seasons and bestowing on men all that they need. The whole tenor of the epistle is that "the one God of the universe" is personal, and that man's knowledge of God derives solely from his self-manifestation through faith. This is far removed from the Stoic idea of an elemental Fire (as in the earlier theory of Heraclitus) in which the divine creative Reason is immanent and operative (at bottom a kind of materialistic pantheism), or even of a world-spirit permeating and governing the whole cosmic process in accordance with plan.[226]

Again the epistle implies belief in a divine purpose in history, "a great and unutterable design" (8:9). This was revealed and effected in the sending of the Son. His advent was timed to synchronize with man's acute awareness of sin and moral impotence. And that purpose was redemptive. The Son came to save, not to compel nor to condemn, the end being that man might believe his goodness, etc. (9:6). That the contemporary world of Diognetus felt increasingly the need for some sure revelation of God

---

222. See Zeller, *Outlines*, 252, and below, p. 46n242

223. As we have seen (pp. 34), the author, though nominally contemptuous of Greek philosophy, is necessarily influenced by it.

224. See pp. 53–56.

225. E.g., the idea that God needs nothing, a widespread notion in Greek thought. See note on 3:3, and Blakeney, *Diognetus*, 40ff.

226. Later, the religious element in Stoicism becomes more personal and intimate. The idea of a world-providence merges into that of a Guardian who cares for the individual. This note sounds in Seneca, Epictetus, and Marcus Aurelius.

and for its own redemption is clear.²²⁷ The Stoic indeed held that Providence and Plan were at work in the universe, but he hardly apprehended a personal purpose in history. The end conceived by Stoic thinkers—perfection, reached after many cyclic rounds, by reabsorption into the original fiery substance²²⁸—offered a vague and chilling prospect. It led only to "the infinite tedium of human history."²²⁹

At some points there are similarities between the author's view of man and that in current philosophic thought. But here again Christianization appears. For example, the author shares with pagan thought a high view of the dignity of man. The idea that God made the world for man's sake is frequent in Stoic teaching and became a commonplace in the Christian Fathers.²³⁰ Man was divinely endowed with reason (λόγος)²³¹ and was so made that he could look upwards to God. But our author derives the last conviction not from its Stoic analogue but from the Scriptures.²³² Similarly, the idea of man's imitation of God in love and beneficence (10:4–6), though reflected in philosophic and religious thought,²³³ is probably colored by and perhaps based on Pauline teaching. Again the deification of man by way of kindly offices to his fellows is familiar in the thought of the time.²³⁴ Goodness, so the Stoic held, consists in working along with God in the service of man. The good man co-operating with God in well-doing becomes a god.²³⁵ But the epistle reshapes the idea in the light of Johannine teaching.²³⁶ Further, the author believes that the soul is immortal by virtue of union with the divine Spirit.²³⁷ Christians, he says, though put to death are made alive (ζωοποιοῦνται, 5:12; cf. 5:16). See 6:8; 10:2. Seneca indeed sometimes approximates to the Christian hope;²³⁸ but for the most part Stoicism left only limited room for belief in a life after death. The soul is reabsorbed at the next

---

227. See Angus, *Religious Quests*, 16ff.
228. Cf. Marcus Aurelius 4.21; 10.7.
229. Bevan, *Later Greek Religion*, xxxvii. See also his *Stoics and Sceptics*, 47ff.
230. See Blakeney's full note in *Diognetus*, 74ff.
231. The earlier Stoic idea was that man's reason was itself a particle of the divine Being. So Epictetus later: σὺ ἀπόσπασμα εἶ τοῦ θεοῦ (*Diss.* 2.8, 11).
232. See note on 10:2.
233. See Additional Note A.
234. See Additional Note B.
235. See Murray, *Stoic, Christian and Humanist*, 107.
236. See below, p. 173.
237. Cf. Tatian, *Graec.* 13; 15.
238. Seneca, *Ep.* 102.

conflagration into the primary being.[239] In one further point the difference of view is acute. Roman Stoicism in particular emphasized man's own moral resources. He has all-sufficiency (αὐτάρκεια) in himself. Not only can he by stern self-restraint gain complete "apathy," but he can himself win his way to the higher life. A man's reason will suffice to attain salvation. There is no need of a Savior or of divine grace.[240] But the heart of the teaching of our epistle is man's moral and spiritual helplessness apart from the redeeming action of God manifested in the Son.[241]

In short, the author plainly tries, if not to come to terms with Diognetus, at least to win from him a hearing by a reasonable measure of intellectual accommodation.[242] Such ideas and beliefs as they held in common[243] are made the basis of his Christian *apologia*, and the terms in which this is framed are not alien from Diognetus's mode of thought.[244] Moreover, the silence of the epistle on some aspects of the Christian faith[245] is significant. It may be due in part to the author's desire not to irritate his pagan interrogator by protruding peculiarities of the Christian faith which might prove uncongenial or incredible.[246] He is accordingly economical in his statement of Christian belief. Such restrictions may be due also to the limited questions put by Diognetus. The author does not confine himself strictly to Diognetus's queries, but in the main moves within their bound. He naïvely states that he could say more (2:10)! In this regard the epistle is only in part an "apology"; it is more of a special plea. At any rate, it is clear that

239. See Sidgwick, *Outlines of the History of Ethics*, 102ff.; Lightfoot, *Philippians*, 320ff.; Arnold, *Roman Stoicism*, 125f., 262ff.

240. This tends to be modified in later Roman Stoicism. "Indeed no man can be good without the help of God. Can anyone rise superior to fortune unless God helps him to rise?" (Seneca, *Ep.* 41:2). But even this is the God who indwells every good man and whom he knows not.

241. See especially ch. 9.

242. The author is really more of a philosopher than he knows. He is among those apologists who, though keen opponents of philosophy, "to a man occupied philosophic ground, and indeed Platonic ground" (Harnack, *Expansion*, 1:295). The practical temper too of the epistle, which sets forth Christianity as a "way of life" (see below, p. 48), would at once evoke the sympathy of a Stoic.

243. For example, the idea that man's true abode is the city of God. Stoicism held that man was a member of a world-city, consisting of gods and men (Seneca, *Otio* 4.1; 12.36 et al.; Marcus Aurelius 2.16; 3.11; 12.36 *al.*). For the author's use of this conception mainly in its Pauline setting see notes on 5.5. See also Lightfoot, *Philippians*, 303ff.

244. See Westcott's verdict in *Canon of the New Testament*, 18. Cf. such terms as εἰκαιότης (4:6) and δόγμα (5:3). See notes *ad loc.*

245. See above, p. 20.

246. The absence of some specifically Christian beliefs in the *Octavius* of Minucius Felix springs from a similar consideration.

I. Introduction

the inquirer's need is kept constantly in view.[247] At the same time, the author never surrenders his convictions, never comprises with vital Christian truth. If no complete conspectus of Christian belief appears, its core stands plainly revealed.[248]

As stated above,[249] the presuppositions common to our author and his correspondent are always Christianized.[250] Where their tenets part company, the divergence is marked and deep.

j. Summary

The aid lent to the development of Christian theology by the apologists calls for fuller recognition. Their endowments were in the main slender, their writings had little distinction, and their theology is fairly described as "tentative, exploratory."[251] But their work was lasting, if judged less by any immediate effects[252] than by its preparatory and pioneer quality. In the writings of these men we find the beginnings of Patristic philosophy. But theirs was the philosophy of a revelation. Although they availed themselves of the best

---

247. Perhaps this partial *ad hominem* character of the epistle is not unconnected with the neglect which the document seems to have suffered in early Christian literary history. See p. 3.

248. There was a constant danger that the apologists in their desire to represent Christianity as the reasonable religion of mankind should rationalize unduly and impoverish the faith by dilution. See Bevan, *Later Greek Religion*, xxxvi. The author of Diognetus, however, is not open to this charge. He has a firm grasp of the essentials of the faith, and shows a no less firm insistence upon them.

249. See pp. 34–35.

250. Naturally this would not be realized by Diognetus himself at his present stage. Telfer, "Review," 222ff., points out that *ad hominem* apologies consist of a succession of *doubles entendre*. Statements which, though consonant with the Christian faith, are intelligible and acceptable to the uninitiated reader (because they are part of his thought-world) disclose their deeper and Christian meaning only after his conversion. Dr. Telfer cites the words τὸν ἴδιον υἱὸν ἀπέδοτο (9:2), which could mean for Diognetus nothing more than a supposed epiphany of the divine Logos (cf. τοῦτον πρὸς αὐτοὺς ἀπέστειλεν, 7:2) "as providing the manumission-price (λύτρον) delivering us from the bonds of habitual sinning against the divine law in Nature." The words would, however, assume for Diognetus their richer Christian significance if and when he became a Christian. We may compare 10:3, 7, 8, where "knowledge" (ἐπιγινώσκω) is one of the fruits of Christian conversion.

251. Burkitt, "Pagan Philosophy in the Christian Church," 463. See also Donaldson, *Critical History*, 2:15f.

252. Nock, *Conversion*, 192: "In the second century literary works were written in defense of the new Faith, but there is no indication that they were read by any save Christians or men on the way to be such or professed students of the movement such as Celsus."

elements in pagan thought, their convictions were basically Christian. The Christian "secret" had been disclosed to faith; it was their task to interpret it in the light of reason and align it with the best ethical and religious thought of the pagan world.[253] The apologists took the lofty moral truths preached in the philosophic schools and gave them the sanction of Christianity as a supernatural revelation. Here in an incipient form is that accommodation between Christianity and the highest philosophic thought which was to be made more complete by the great Alexandrian teachers of the third century. The apologists may claim at least the honor of the pathfinder.

In this dignity the little epistle to Diognetus has its share. But its real merit lies elsewhere. Most marked is its emphasis on the spiritual and mystical aspect of the faith. This appears in the wholesale condemnation of material and outward worship pagan and Jewish alike. It is perhaps not without significance that the author says nothing of Christian institutional religion or Church order. The Christian θεοσέβεια is invisible (6:4). It consists in the true knowledge of God and in the consequent change wrought in the heart by the atoning Son. The mystical element further appears in the comparison drawn between Christians in the world and the soul in the body (ch. 6). It is indeed integral to the author's temper and outlook.

The author's mind never moves very far from the practical implications of the faith. In glowing terms he set forth the Christian ethos. A new spirit of moral earnestness has come into the world. It is exercised within the earthly order, but its source and strength are from above. The note is one of joyous, almost rapturous, faith. Dialectic is not to our author's taste. His mind is of the pragmatic order. Conscious of Christianity as the revelation of the divine love, he sees its practical outworking negatively in deliverance from sin and positively in the imitation of God by love and beneficence towards men.[254] Hence he points to the purity and nobility of the lives of the Christians, their constancy under persecution, and their works of benevolence, as unmistakable evidence of the truth of their religion. These things, he seems to suggest, speak more loudly than any elaborate literary defense. It must of course be admitted that there is little that is new or creative in the epistle. But that is only to say that it is typical of second-century Christian

---

253. As stated above (pp. 1–5), they had a precedent in the apologetic aim of the Alexandrian Jews of the second and first century CE, who, having gained through constant contact with Hellenism a wider and more hospitable outlook than their Palestinian brethren, endeavored to make Greek philosophy subserve the interests of Israel's faith.

254. Aubé, *Justin*, 95: "Imitation of God is here, as in Platonic doctrine, the final word in morality." Cf. Theaetetus 176. Burnet, Article in *ERE* 10, 526, thinks that Plato adopted the doctrine from Pythagoreanism.

I. Introduction

writings as a whole. Moral and spiritual emancipation is the characteristic feature of apostolic Christianity. But of necessity there followed a period when that freedom was to be interpreted and secured. If the first task is to create, the second is to conserve. The epistle proper stands nearer in this regard to the apostolic age. We cannot fail to detect in its pages the "experimental" note. It has something of the glow of fresh discovery and creative experience. There is here no appeal to a body of Christian tradition. But this later note sounds in the appended chapters: "the faith of the gospels is established, and the tradition of the apostles is guarded" (11:6).

ii. Chapters 11–12

It may be convenient to summarize here the teaching contained in the two appended chapters. God, twice spoken of as "Father" (11:2; 12:9; cf. 10:1), plants in Paradise the tree of knowledge and the tree of life (12:3), sends the Word into the world (11:3; cf. 12:2ff.),[255] is the author of spiritual blessings (12:1, 8) and is glorified through the Word (12:9). The teaching regarding the Word or Son is fuller. The Word was "sent" to appear to the world, and "speaking plainly" revealed to disciples the secrets of God. He was indeed dishonored by the chosen people, but preached by the apostles, and believed by the heathen. The Word is eternal. He is from the beginning, yet is ever young in that he is born in the hearts of the saints (11:4). As Son[256] he enriches the Church by revealing and increasing grace among the saints. The once-incarnate Word can still speak to those whom he will (11:7); he is ever the teacher of the saints (12:9). Thus the historic incarnation and the abiding spiritual presence of the Word are linked together. We note here the lack of any explicit mention of the person and work of the Holy Spirit, as also in 1–10. It may be indeed, as Radford suggests,[257] that the quasi-personal use of χάρις (11:5–7) which "reveals" and "rejoices" and which is not to be "grieved"[258] hints at the Spirit. It is, however, plain that if the Spirit is here in view it is not as a separate personality but rather as an agency of the Word.[259] Other apologists also, for example Theophilus (*Autol.* 2.10),[260] are

---

255. In 10:2 the one "sent" is "the only-begotten Son."
256. See Additional Note C.
257. Radford, *Epistle to Diognetus*, 41.
258. Cf. Eph 4:30: "grieve not (μὴ λυπεῖτε) the Holy Spirit of God."
259. Harnack, *History of Dogma*, 2:209, thinks with regard to the apologists that "their conception of the Logos continually compelled them to identify the Logos and the Spirit." So Hermas earlier: "that Spirit is the Son of God" (Sim. 9:1).
260. "The Word, being God's Spirit, came down upon the prophets and spoke by

so concerned with the doctrine of the Logos or Son that they either fail to dwell on the Holy Spirit, or sometimes ascribe to the Son functions usually falling to the Spirit. Justin Martyr speaks now of the Son and now of the Spirit as the inspiration of men of old, though elsewhere he distinguishes between the two persons (1 *Apol.* 6, 13). Similarly, in Diognetus it is the Word by whom the Church is enriched (11:5) and the Word who speaks through those whom he chooses (11:7).[261] Radford finds in this doctrine of the Logos as being "still the dominant truth of Christian theology" an indication of a second-century period.

As we have seen, the epistle proper does not propound the idea of an organized Christian society. In the Appendix, however, we detect a conception of the Church[262] as an institution aligned with the Law, the Prophets, the Gospels, and the apostolic tradition (11:5–6). But even here the stress falls not on the ordered life of the Church but on its spiritual power meditated through the Son "through whom the Church is enriched and grace is unfolded and multiplied among the saints." Hence the exultant "grace" of the Church. If Diognetus does not "grieve this grace" he will understand what the Word wills to say through those whom he chooses. Divine revelation is thus continuous, and the authority of the faith is found in the written word and the living voice.[263] In ch. 12 the author avails himself of a current allegorical interpretation[264] which regards Paradise as representing the Church. The Church as the company of "those who love him rightly" is, as it were, a tree all-fruitful and flourishing.

Apparently two grades of Christians are specified by the author of these chapters. He sounds the catechetical note and describes himself as both "a disciple of apostles" and "a teacher of the heathen." What he has received from apostolic tradition he ministers to "those who are becoming disciples

---

them." But Theophilus (*Autol.* 2.15) is also careful to distinguish the two persons and was the first Christian writer to use the term τριάς of the Godhead.

261. Again we note the didactic office of the Logos. He is primarily revealer and teacher (11:2–3, 8). Nothing is said of his cosmic creativeness, dominion over nature, or redemptive function (as in chs. 7–9).

262. ἐκκλησία only in 11:5–6. For a full survey of the term, see Schmidt, "ἐκκλησία," 3:502ff. In Diognetus the term has the ecumenical sense, the whole body of Christians. Cf. Phil 3:6; Col 1:18, 24.

263. See Westcott, *Introduction to the Study of the Gospels*, 431ff. So also Cruttwell, *Literary History*, 1:280: "the canon of the truth in all the apologists is the same, namely, the teaching of Christ and His apostles preserved in the written evangelical records and in the general tradition of the Church."

264. See Routh, *Reliquiae Sacrae*, 1:16: certain early Christian writers and their followers "spiritualiter sunt contemplati de Christi ecclesia ea quae scripta sunt de paradiso."

of the truth," i.e., catechumens (11:1). He speaks of "disciples" who, being accounted πιστοί, receive divine revelation from the Word (11:2). He probably has in view two classes here, the catechumens and the full disciples. The latter are also named "saints" (ἅγιοι, 11:4, 5). Here he adds the mystical note. The saints are not only taught by the Word (11:7; 12:9), but are indwelt by him (11:4) and through him enriched by grace (11:5).

We observe the author's respect for the old dispensation and for tradition. Note the phrases "the fear of the law" and "the grace of the prophets" (11:6), the OT reminiscences (12:1–3), the references to apostolic tradition (11:1, 6) and the decrees of the Fathers (11:5).[265]

Three religious ideas are noticeable in this section.

Grace. The term χάρις (11:5–7) is used in the Pauline sense, denoting the free favor of God springing from his good pleasure and wholly apart from human merit (Rom 2:5 *al.*). Such grace is "multiplied" (πληθύνεται)—perhaps an echo of the Petrine epistolary greeting (1 Pet 1:2; 2 Pet 1:2), though Paul dwells much on the same thought; cf. 2 Cor 4:15 (πλεονάζω ... περισσεύω) and 9:8 (περισσεύω). That grace is "given" (δωρουμένη) is a note constantly struck by Paul (Rom 12:3, 6; 1 Cor. 1:4; Eph 3:8). The phrase "the grace of the prophets" may reflect 1 Pet 1:10, i.e., "the coming grace proclaimed by the prophets," or the meaning may be "grace which comes through the prophets." First Clement 8 speaks of the prophets as "ministers of the grace of God." For the "grace of the Church," see note on 11:6.

Faith. πίστις as used in the epistle proper denotes belief in the divine revelation and is the basis of true knowledge. So also in 11:2 "knowledge of the mysteries of the Father" comes to the disciples who are πιστοί. But in the phrases "the pledges of faith," "the faith of the gospels" (11:5, 6), the term πίστις becomes objective. See above, p. 39 and note *ad loc.*

Knowledge. In chs. 1–10 the concept of knowledge as such finds little place. It is sufficient for the author to insist that the knowledge of God cannot be reached by man. It is given by God himself through faith and begets fullness of joy (10:3). In chs. 11–12, however, knowledge looms large. Faith is intimately conjoined with gnosis. In the fertile world of Christian life both the tree of knowledge and the tree of life are found. "The tree of knowledge does not kill; but disobedience kills" (12:2). That is, gnosis has its due place in the religious life. On the other hand, its place is subordinate. God planted first in the garden of Eden the tree of life, the path to which was indicated by the tree of knowledge. "For there can be neither life without knowledge nor sound knowledge without true life. Wherefore each (tree) stands planted near the other" (12:4). Hence the apostle (Paul) blamed the

---

265. See below, pp. 163–64.

gnosis which is divorced from the truth that leads to life (1 Cor 8:1). Dorner finds "all through the twelfth chapter the pursuit of a middle path between Gnosticism and abstract piety."[266] The author of this Appendix (chs. 11–12) sets high value upon a true gnosis as an essential element in the Christian life. Christianity is the highest philosophy and is in accord with reason. Yet it is revealed to faith, apprehended only by men enlightened by God, and attested by life.

7. Literary Relationships

a. Old Testament (LXX)

3:4: ὁ γὰρ ποιήσας . . . ἐν αὐτοῖς. See note on that passage under (b) NT.

7:6: καὶ τίς αὐτοῦ τὴν παρουσίαν ὑποστήσεται; cf. Mal 3:2: ἢ (καὶ A) τίς ὑποστήσεται ἐν τῇ ὀπτασίᾳ αὐτοῦ;

10:2: οὓς ἐκ τῆς ἰδίας εἰκόνος ἔπλασε. Derived from Gen 1:26f., with the variations of ἐκ τῆς εἰκόνος (for κατ' εἰκόνα) and πλάσσω (for ποιέω). The idea is very frequent. See 1 Clem. 33:4: ἄνθρωπον . . . ἔπλασεν τῆς ἑαυτοῦ εἰκόνος χαρακτῆρα. See note on 10:2 (below).

11:5: ὁ σήμερον υἱὸς λογισθείς. See Ps 2:7, and see note on 11:5.

12:1: οἱ γενόμενοι παράδεισος τρυφῆς. See Gen 3:23f, ὁ παράδεισος τῆς τρυφῆς (the garden of Eden; cf. Joel 2:3). It is frequently mentioned as a type of a fertile well-watered place (Gen 13:10; Ezek 31:8f.). Our author allegorizes it to typify the "fruitfulness" of those who love God rightly. See note on 12:1.

12:2–3: Plainly reminiscent of Gen 2:9, as the underlined and numbered points in common will show:

Gen 2:8–9	Diogn. 12:2–8
καὶ ἐφύτευσεν[1] κύριος ὁ θεὸς παράδεισον ἐν Εδεμ κατὰ ἀνατολὰς καὶ ἔθετο ἐκεῖ τὸν ἄνθρωπον, ὃν ἔπλασεν. καὶ ἐξανέτειλεν ὁ θεὸς ἔτι ἐκ τῆς γῆς πᾶν ξύλον ὡραῖον εἰς ὅρασιν καὶ καλὸν εἰς βρῶσιν καὶ τὸ ξύλον τῆς ζωῆς[2] ἐν μέσῳ[3] τῷ παραδείσῳ καὶ τὸ ξύλον τοῦ εἰδέναι[4] γνωστὸν καλοῦ καὶ πονηροῦ.	ἐν γὰρ τούτῳ τῷ χωρίῳ ξύλον γνώσεως[4] καὶ ξύλον ζωῆς[2] πεφύτευται·[1] ἀλλ' οὐ τὸ τῆς γνώσεως[4] ἀναιρεῖ, ἀλλ' ἡ παρακοὴ ἀναιρεῖ. οὐδὲ γὰρ ἄσημα τὰ γεγραμμένα, ὡς θεὸς ἀπ' ἀρχῆς ξύλον γνώσεως[4] καὶ ξύλον ζωῆς[2] ἐν μέσῳ[3] παραδείσου ἐφύτευσε, διὰ γνώσεως ζωὴν ἐπιδεικνύς.

With ἐξανέτειλεν (Gen 2:9) see ἀνατείλαντες (Diogn. 12:1) and with παράδεισον ἐν Εδεμ (Gen 2:8) see παράδεισος τρυφῆς (Diogn. 12:1).

---

266. Dorner, *Person of Christ*, 1:260n1.

I. Introduction

There is no direct citation from the Greek OT and no introductory formulae. In two instances (3:4; 7:6) the verbal correspondence is close. In the latter passage the author has the common παρουσία instead of the late and in the sense of "appearance" less familiar ὀπτασία.[267] He simplifies and shortens the τὸ ξύλον τοῦ εἰδέναι γνωστὸν καλοῦ καὶ πονηροῦ of Gen 2:9 into ξύλον γνώσεως and inverts the order "tree of life"... "tree of knowledge." These scanty data suggest that the author is drawing loosely and paraphrastically upon OT passages, giving echoes of LXX language with a more or less free application of ideas. In particular the Genesis story of the garden is allegorically interpreted by the writer of the appended chapters and adapted to the purpose of his homily (ch. 12). No reminiscence of the Apocrypha appears, unless τοῦ δοκοῦντος ἐνθάδε θανάτου (10:7; see note) recalls Wis 3:2.

b. New Testament

2:1: καθάρας σεαυτὸν κτλ. A probable reminiscence of Eph 4:22-24. See note.

3:4: ὁ γὰρ ποιήσας ... ἐν αὐτοῖς. See Exod 20:11; Ps 145:6; Acts 14:15. But Diogn. 3:4 (see note *ad loc.*) differs from all three passages in omitting (καὶ) τὴν θάλασσαν (omitted also in the B text of Exod 20:11). Probably the immediate source of 3:4 is Acts 14:15, since in both contexts God's creative activity is associated with his beneficence, "which provides us all with what we need" (cf. Acts 14:17).

4:4: there is some correspondence here with Rom 11:28. See note on Diogn. 4:4.

5:8: ἐν σαρκὶ ... κατὰ σάρκα. See 2 Cor 10:3 and the τοῦ κατὰ σάρκα ζῆν of Rom 8:12f.

5:9: a reminiscence of Phil 3:20.

5:12f.: see 2 Cor 6:9-10 and see note on Diogn. 5:12-13 for similarities and differences.

5:15: see 1 Cor 4:12 λοιδορούμενοι εὐλογοῦμεν. For the contrasted terms see 1 Pet 3:9.

5:16: perhaps an echo of 2 Cor 6:10. But the notion of "rejoicing" in tribulation is common. See note on Diogn. 5:16.

---

267. The possibility lies open that this form of the prophetic text may be drawn from early Christian *testimonia*. The passage was familiar in messianic prophecy. The first part (Mal 3:1) is cited in Matt 11:10, Luke 7:27, and Mark 1:2, and applied to John the Baptist. See Harris and Burch, *Testimonies*, 2:64-65; Sanday and Headlam, *Romans*, 282.

Diogn. 6:3	John 17
καὶ Χριστιανοὶ ἐν κόσμῳ οἰκοῦσιν οὐκ εἰσὶ δὲ ἐκ τοῦ κόσμου.	καὶ αὐτοὶ ἐν τῷ κόσμῳ εἰσίν (17:11). οὐκ εἰσὶν ἐκ τοῦ κόσμου (14) (cf. v. 16 and John 15:19).

6:5: may reflect Gal 5:17. But again the notion is common in both Christian and pagan thought. See on 6:5. For the hatred of Christians by the world, see John 15:18-19; 17:14. Diognetus supplies a reason for the hatred of the soul by the flesh and of Christians by the world respectively, the latter reason being more pointed than the general statement of John 15:19; 17:14. In the latter passages Christians are hated because they "are not of the world"; in Diognetus because they resist the world's pleasures.

6:6: an echo of Matt 5:44 (Luke 6:27).

6:8: may possibly reflect 1 Cor 15:53f.

7:1: οἰκονομίαν μυστηρίων πεπίστευνται. See 1 Cor 9:17, οἰκονομίαν πεπίστευμαι.

7:4: ἐν ἐπιεικείᾳ καὶ πραΰτητι. A possible reminiscence of 2 Cor 10:1. But the combination is a familiar one. See note on Diogn. 7:4.

7:4-5: ὡς σώζων . . . οὐ κρίνων. This antithesis in relation to the purpose of the Son may be a Johannine echo (John 3:17; 12:47).

8:8: καὶ μόνος ἀγαθός ἐστιν. A reminiscence of Mark 10:18 (= Matt 19:17; Luke 18:19).

8:10-11: see note *ad loc*.

9:1: τῷ τότε τῆς ἀδικίας καιρῷ . . . τὸν νῦν τῆς δικαιοσύνης. See note *ad loc.* for NT references (Rom 3:21-26 *al.*)

9:1: ἀδύνατον . . . θεοῦ. See John 3:5: οὐ δύναται εἰσελθεῖν εἰς τὴν βασιλείαν τοῦ θεοῦ, and also Mark 10:27.

9:2: ἦλθε δὲ . . . θεοῦ. See Titus 3:4-5, and see note on Diogn. 9:2.

9:2: ἀπέδοτο λύτρον ὑπὲρ ἡμῶν. See note *ad loc.* for NT references.

9:2: τὸν δίκαιον ὑπὲρ τῶν ἀδίκων. A reminiscence of 1 Pet 3:18.

9:3: for the "covering" of sins see note *ad loc*.

9:6: περὶ . . . μεριμνᾶν. A probable gloss drawn from Matt 6:25, 28, 31.

10:2: ὁ γὰρ θεὸς . . . ἠγάπησε. A free recollection of John 3:16.

10:2: πρὸς οὓς . . . μονογενῆ. See the close parallel in 1 John 4:9.

10:2: οἷς . . . αὐτόν. A possible borrowing from Jas 2:5.

10:3: for the notion of being "filled with joy," see 1 John 1:4; 2 John 12.

10:3: ἢ πῶς . . . σε; from 1 John 4:19 (cf. vv. 10, 11). See p. 155.

10:6: ἀλλ' ὅστις . . . βάρος. A possible reflection of Gal 6:2. But see on Diogn. 10:6.

10:7: ὅτι . . . πολιτεύεται. See Eph 6:9. With μυστήρια θεοῦ λαλεῖν, see 1 Cor 14:2; 2:1-7.

I. Introduction

11:2: οἷς ἐφανέρωσεν ὁ λόγος φανείς. The language has a Johannine ring.
11:3: διὰ . . . ἐπιστεύθη. Perhaps reminiscent of 1 Tim 3:16. See note.
11:4: οὗτος ὁ ἀπ' ἀρχῆς. See 1 John 1:1: ὃ ἦν ἀπ' ἀρχῆς (cf. 2:13, 14).
12:5: ἡ γνῶσις . . . οἰκοδομεῖ. The only citation (from 1 Cor 8:1).
12:6: ἐπ' ἐλπίδι. A Pauline phrase (Rom 4:18; 5:2; 8:20; 1 Cor 9:10).
12:9: δι' οὗ . . . δοξάζεται. See John 13:31; 14:13.

The influence of the phraseology of the New Testament pervades the epistle. Some references are more explicit than others. Both earlier and later apologists made little *direct* use of Scripture.[268] In this the epistle to Diognetus is true to type. It gives but one precise citation (12:5), the passage (1 Cor 8:1) being ascribed to the "apostle."[269] But we hear abundant echoes, especially of the Pauline writings.[270] Words and phrases from the Corinthian letters in particular[271] are interwoven into the epistle. There is a not inconsiderable debt to the Fourth Gospel and 1 John.[272] The Synoptic Gospels are less directly in evidence. Further points of kinship with the Pastorals and with James and 1 Peter serve to show that the author is familiar with most of the NT books (1 and 2 Thessalonians, Philemon, Hebrews, 2 Peter, 3 John, Jude, and Revelation seem not to be represented). But he gives no indication

---

268. This is true in the main of the Apostolic Fathers also, though their language is throughout influenced by the apostolic diction. The early apologists had little need of recourse to Scripture, since their gentile readers would attach no authority to the sacred books.

269. Similarly, Polycarp, *Phil.*, while drawing freely on the apostolic books, only once, following a quotation, mentions the sacred writer by name ("*sicut Paulus docet*"; 11:2). Cf. Ps.-Clem., *Epistles concerning Virginity* (1.12), where the citation of 2 Cor 11:29 is introduced by the words "as the apostle has said." Clement of Alexandria has now the title and now the personal name. Cf. *Protr.* 5 p. 50, 10 (Stählin) where a citation of Gal 4:9 is introduced by ᾗ φησιν ὁ ἀπόστολος. In 9, p. 64, 19, he quotes 1 Tim 4:8: κατὰ τὸν Παῦλον.

270. Ewald, *History of Israel*, 174, says of the author of the epistle: "in him there seemed to be no other than Paul himself come back to life to speak to this age." For Pauline words in the Epistle see p. 10.

271. The Corinthian letters figure plentifully in the NT citations made in general by early Christian writers of the second century. See Oxford Society, *New Testament in the Apostolic Fathers*, 137.

272. The degree or actual literary dependence is not clear. Sanders, *Fourth Gospel in the Early Church*, 19, finds that chs. 1–10 point to a type of theology akin to that of the Fourth Gospel and 1 John. As regards chs. 11–12 he thinks that "the similarity in underlying doctrine and the use of the personal Logos" may suggest that these two chapters and the Fourth Gospel were both written in the same church. Neither in the epistle proper nor in the two appended chapters does he find any *certain* literary dependence on the Johannine writings. Be that as it may, the kinship with the Fourth Gospel is too marked to warrant the view of the author of *Supernatural Religion*, 2:357f., that the resemblance "is merely superficial and accidental."

that in his view any special sanctity or authority attached to these writings. Indeed his free handling of them along with the absence of the name of any sacred writer suggests that the idea of a New Testament canon was as yet dimly, if at all, conceived.[273] For the writer of the appended chapters (11–12), however, the Old Testament and the New form the authoritative Scriptures. Not only is the fear of the law sung and the grace of the prophets known, but the faith of the Gospels is established, and the tradition of the apostles "guarded" (11:6).[274] Here a fixed orthodoxy or canon of truth seems to be in view. At the same time the author recognizes the inspiration of the living Word along with that of the written Scriptures (11:7–8). He uses the phrase τὰ γεγραμμένα (12:3) to denote an OT passage (Gen 2:8–9),[275] but names no book of Scripture.

As the element of actual citation is negligible, it is not possible to draw any inference concerning the character of the NT text implied. We may, however, notice that 10:3 (ἢ πῶς ἀγαπήσεις τὸν οὕτως προαγαπήσαντά σε), which is apparently a free recollection of 1 John 4:19, perhaps reflects the influence of the reading preserved in 33 ℵ al. (ἡμεῖς ἀγαπῶμεν τὸν θεόν) or in some codices (αὐτόν), as against that which is read by AB al. (ἡμεῖς ἀγαπῶμεν).

c. The Apologists

Even a cursory reading of the early Christian apologies shows that they have much in common in both matter and form. The general likeness is so marked that it is easy to posit direct borrowing of one apologist from another. Close verbal correspondence is therefore needed as proof of such dependence.

---

273. This feature is, as far as it goes, consistent with the probable date of Diognetus (ca. 150 CE). "No witness of this period (the middle of the second century) knows any collection of New Testament writings, even a provisional and incomplete one" (Reuss, *History of the Sacred Scriptures*, 299). But Marcion's truncated canon (ca. 140 CE) and the growth of gnostic heresy were soon to accelerate, by way of reaction, a process of canonization.

274. See note *ad loc*. Jacquier, *Nouveau Testament*, 1:131, cites this passage as proof that at the time it was written "the gospels and apostolic writings were brought together in a collection. Here we have the same titles that we will find in subsequent writings: τὸ εὐαγγέλιον and ὁ ἀπόστολος, which designated the two collections of the New Testament writings."

275. So also Clement (1 Cor 13:1) writes ποιήσωμεν τὸ γεγραμμένον, followed by an OT passage introduced by λέγει γὰρ τὸ πνεῦμα τὸ ἅγιον.

I. Introduction

1. *The Preaching of Peter (ca. 100–130 CE)*[276]

This early writing is known from quotations made by Clement of Alexandria, *Stromateis* 1.29.182; 6.5.39ff., etc. It marks the transition from early Christian literature to the apologetic writings, and appears to have wielded much influence upon second-century Christian writings.[277] A comparison of Diognetus with the fragments of the Preaching reveals close similarity. Robinson marshals evidence to show that the Preaching lies behind both the *Apology of Aristides* and our epistle.[278] By inference from parallels between these two documents he records eleven points which presumably appeared in the Preaching. But it may be noticed that some of these points are held in common with other Christian writers of the period and apparently reflect conventional religious thought and terminology, e.g., παντοκράτωρ and ἀόρατος as epithets of the Deity, the ideas that the world was made for the sake of man and that God has no need of sacrifices, etc. Similarly, the notions of creation by the Word and of Christians as a new or third γένος have older and wider currency. Moreover, there are some minor differences between the Preaching of Peter and Diognetus. The Preaching is impressed by the ignorance (ἄγνοια)[279] of the idolaters, "not knowing God as we do, according to the perfect knowledge" (cf. Diogn. 10:1). The epistle dwells rather on their utter irrationality (ἀφροσύνη).[280] The offering of animal and edible sacrifices, pagan oblations which deny God's existence (Preaching), finds no mention in Diognetus. The description of Jewish worship differs in one material point, in that the Preaching ascribes to the Jews the worship of angels and archangels.

---

276. See Harris and Robinson, *Aristides*, 86ff.; Dobschütz, *Kerygma Petri*; Preuschen, *Antilegomena*, 88–91, 192–95; James, *Apocryphal New Testament*, 16ff.

277. See Reagan, *Preaching of Peter*.

278. Harris and Robinson, *Aristides*, 97f.

279. See also the *Apology of Aristides*, which stresses this aspect: the Greeks erred "as men who are destitute of knowledge," and former sins were wrought in ignorance (ch. 17 Syr.).

280. But cf. 8:1: "what man had any knowledge at all of what God is, before he came?"

2. The *Apology of Aristides* (ca. 140 CE)[281]

Doulcet[282] and Kihn[283] advocated the view that the *Apology of Aristides* and Diognetus came from the same hand. Robinson, while not affirming common authorship, has shown that the *Apology* has points in common with Diognetus.[284] To the specific similarities he gives we may add others of a more general kind. Both writings set forth the faith as eminently reasonable and as the source of moral power, and are marked by freshness and simplicity, especially in the pictures of the life of the Christians. In both, the polemic against heathen idolatry is conventional and superficial[285] and no element of revelation is credited to the Jewish religion. Both ignore the Old Testament as far as actual citation is concerned, and neither uses the argument from prophecy. Some ideas reflected in both documents are shared by early apologetics in general, e.g., that God is above all personal need (*Apol.* 1, 13 Syr.; Diogn. 3:4; *Clem. Recogn.* 5.15–16). But some verbal similarities with the Greek version suggest at least acquaintance of our author with the *Apology*:

Apol.	Diogn.
13: τὰ κωφὰ καὶ ἀναίσθητα εἴδωλα. Epithets of the Deity: ἀόρατος (4; 14) παντοκράτωρ (14) κτίστης καὶ δημιουργὸς τῶν ἁπάντων (15), and τεχνίτης (4).	2:4: οὐ κωφὰ πάντα . . . οὐκ ἀναίσθητα; 7:2: ὁ παντοκράτωρ . . . ἀόρατος θεός. 7:2: (cf. 8:7) ὁ τεχνίτης καὶ δημιουργὸς τῶν ὅλων.

We may notice also the occurrence of such terms as the following: μόρφωμα and ἐκτύπωμα (*Apol.* 3). See μεταμορφόω and ἐκτυπόω (Diogn. 2:3); προσδέομαι (*Apol.* 10; Diogn. 3:4); εἰς χρῆσιν (ἀνθρώπων) (*Apol.* 4; 5; 7; Diogn. 2:2; 4:2); οἰκονομία (*Apol.* 15, *bis*; Diogn. 4:5) of the divine "dispensation"; πραεῖς καὶ ἐπιεικεῖς (of Christians, *Apol.* 15); ἐν ἐπιεικείᾳ καὶ πραΰτητι (of the Son, Diogn. 7:4).

---

281. See Harris and Robinson, *Aristides*; Hennecke, *Aristides*; Raabe, *Apologie des Aristides*; Geffcken, *Zwei griechischen Apologeten*, 1–96.

282. Doulcet, "Apologie," 601–12.

283. Kihn, *Ursprung des Briefes an Diognet*, 95–154.

284. Harris and Robinson, *Aristides*, 95ff. Molland, "Diognetbriefes," 295ff., gives a recent and careful examination of the relationship between the two documents.

285. Aristides, however, deals with the matter more fully than Diognetus, which impatiently dismisses heathen worship with the remark: "I think it needless to say more" (2:10).

It is true that most of these terms are part of the stock-in-trade of Jewish and Christian writers in general. But when, as is the case in our two documents, they occur in similar contexts we may reasonably presume actual contact.

At the same time there are noticeable differences between the *Apology* and Diognetus. This may be seen in the respective attitudes towards the Jewish religion. Aristides's almost friendly tone (see ch. 14) is in sharp contrast to Diognetus's severity and contempt. Diognetus knows nothing of the adoration of angels, which Aristides (and the Preaching of Peter) attributes to the Jews. Conversely the idea of creation by the Word, found in our epistle and the Preaching, is lacking in Aristides. Aristides (15) sets forth the Christian way of life as issuing from Christian belief and finding its incentive in the hope of future reward: "they know and believe in God, the Maker of heaven and earth, in whom are all things and from whom are all things: He who has no other god as his fellow: from whom they have received those commandments which they have engraved on their minds, which they keep in the hope and expectation of the world to come; so that on this account they do not commit adultery . . ." (15 Syr.; Harris's translation). Diognetus inverts the order, picturing first the life of the Christians and then passing to their doctrinal belief. It does not suggest the hope of future bliss as a motive for morality, though Christians "await the incorruptibility which is in heaven" (6:8). More significant perhaps is the view of the quest of God presented by each writer. In the *Apology* (15; 16, Syr.) Christians "have found the truth" "by going about and seeking." Diognetus gives man little or no part in the discovery. It was God who "established among men and fixed firmly in their hearts the truth and the holy and incomprehensible word" (7:2). While commending Diognetus's zeal to understand the religion of the Christians (1:1), he insists that the knowledge of God lies beyond man's unaided power (5:3; 7:1).[286] God has manifested himself through faith, "by which alone it is given to see God" (8:6).

The data undoubtedly attest some contact of Diognetus with the *Apology*.[287] But the parallels are not sufficiently close to posit direct borrowing or a common authorship. Puech indeed thinks that, if Diognetus and the *Apology* have certain ideas in common, the former has made a quite different use of them,[288] and he credits the author of Diognetus with a far higher degree of literary skill.[289] We can hardly go further than

---

286. See note on 4:6 (*sub fin.*).

287. Molland discusses the various possibilities raised by this relationship.

288. Puech, *Apologistes grecs*, 251. See also his *Histoire*, 2:218.

289. See also Geffcken, *Zwei griechische Apologeten*, xli–xlii; Molland, "Diognetbriefes," 298.

Pfleiderer's verdict of "the acquaintance of the author of Diognetus with the earlier *Apology of Aristides*."[290]

3. Justin Martyr

It is convenient to summarize here the grounds on which the presumed authorship by Justin is inadmissible. As stated above,[291] Cod. Argent. ch. 9 contained Diognetus among a number of treatises ascribed to Justin Martyr. Tillemont (1691) was the first to suspect the Justinian authorship, which came to be rejected by many older scholars (Groshcim, Semisch, Hefele, and others) and practically all modern writers. Otto himself in the third edition of his *Corpus Apologetarum* gave up his former advocacy of Justin's authorship. Even a cursory review confirms that judgment. Justin shows himself more charitable towards both pagan and Jewish religion; Diognetus rejects both outright as ἀφροσύνη and μωρία. Justin names Socrates, Heraclitus, Abraham, and others as "Christians," being men who lived μετὰ λόγου.[292] "What man," says our author, "had any knowledge at all of what God is, before he (the Son) came?" (8:1; cf. 2–5). See above, pp. 20–21. Diognetus seems to deny reality to the Greek gods, whereas Justin invests them with demoniacal powers. Diognetus dubs Judaism as "superstition" but one removed from Greek idolatry, and pours ridicule on Jewish religious scruples. Justin, on the other hand, recognizes the divine origin of the Mosaic ordinances as a preparation for the gospel (*Dial.* 40–43). Diognetus makes little use of the OT;[293] Justin cites the LXX abundantly, and finds in the argument from prophecy strong proof of the truth of the faith.[294] There is a marked difference in the theology of redemption. Both writers offer a reason for the delay in carrying out the divine plan. It was in order to demonstrate man's moral helplessness and need of a Savior. So Diognetus. But Justin's view is that God, having given man the power of choice, had reinforced him by the partial indwelling of the Logos. So that God did not even seem to neglect man as Diogn. 8:10 hints. Justin shows but little Pauline influence; Diognetus is rich in Pauline echoes. Our author works out

---

290. Pfleiderer, *Primitive Christianity*, 4:482.

291. See p. 5.

292. *1 Apol.* 46. Man has a partial knowledge of God through "the seed of the Word" sown in all men (*2 Apol.* 13; cf. 10).

293. See pp. 52–53.

294. An argument, ἥπερ μεγίστη καὶ ἀληθεστάτη ἀπόδειξις (*1 Apol.* 30; cf. *1 Apol.* 53).

I. Introduction

his theme in orderly fashion; Justin's writing lacks logical arrangement, is often discursive and marked by frequent parentheses. The language of Justin is mainly on the level of the common dialect, and is sometimes careless and irregular. Diognetus, on the other hand, approaches classical standards in both vocabulary and style. There are naturally coincidences of thought between the two writers.[295] But these are shared for the most part with other apologists of the early and later periods.

4. Clement of Alexandria

Harnack suggests that there is a literary connection between Diognetus and the *Protrepticus* of Clement.[296] Geffcken[297] points out that both writers share the same Hellenistic-Christian mode of thought and show similar features in rhetorical style,[298] rhythmical ending of sentences, and metrical periods. The results of a comparison of the two documents are mostly given in the Notes, but may for convenience be assembled here. References in the second column are to chapters of the *Protrepticus* with the page and line of Stählin's edition.

Diogn.	Protr.
2:1: καθάρας σεαυτὸν ... συνήθειαν ἀποσκευασάμενος.	1.10.8ff.: σὺ δὲ ἐι ποθεῖς ἰδεῖν ὡς ἀληθῶς τὸν θεόν, καθαρσίων μεταλάμβανε θεοπρεπῶν.

συνήθεια, probably meaning "custom" of idolatry (see note), is frequent in that sense in the *Protr.* (4.35.13; 10.72.2 *al.*).

Diogn.	Protr.
2:4: οὐκ <u>ἀναίσθητα</u>; 2:8: <u>αἵματι καὶ κνίσαις</u>. 2:8: αἷς δὲ δοκεῖτε <u>τιμαῖς</u> προσφέρειν. 2:7: οὐ πολὺ μᾶλλον αὐτοὺς χλευάζετε καὶ <u>ὑβρίζετε</u>.	4.39.19ff.: ἀλλὰ γὰρ <u>ἀναισθήτῳ</u> λίθῳ καὶ ξύλῳ καὶ χρυσίῳ πλουσίῳ οὐδ' ὁτιοῦν μέλει, οὐ <u>κνίσης</u>, οὐχ <u>αἵματος</u>, οὐ καπνοῦ, ᾧ δὴ <u>τιμώμενοι</u> καὶ τυφόμενοι ἐκμελαίνονται. ἀλλ' οὐδὲ <u>τιμῆς</u> οὐχ <u>ὕβρεως</u>.

---

295. To take a minor point only: the apologists comment on the folly of appointing men as the guardians of the gods against theft. Cf. Justin Martyr, *1 Apol.* 9; Diogn. 2:2.

296. Harnack, *Geschichte*, 1:758; 2.1:514.

297. Geffcken, *Diognetos*, 5. Also Geffcken, "Diognetos," 348–50.

298. E.g., the exclamatory ὤ with genitive (Diogn. 9:2) frequently appears in Clement of Alexandria. To the reference given (p. 62) add *Protr.* 2.17.11f.; 9.63.2.

For the idea of the worshiper "mocking" the gods (χλευάζω, Diogn. 2:7) see *Protr.* 2.29.13 (παίζω).

Diogn.	Protr.
2:5: τούτοις προσκυνεῖτε, τέλεον δ' αὐτοῖς ἐξομοιοῦσθε.	4.48.3–4: ὅπως δὲ αὐτοὶ μὴ ὅμοιοι δι' ἀναισθησίαν τοῖς ἀνδριᾶσιν ἀποτελεσθῆτε, οὐ φροντίζετε.
8:4: ἀλλὰ ταῦτα μὲν τερατεία καὶ πλάνη τῶν γοήτων ἐστίν.	2.12.18f.: τὰ ὄργια ... ἀπάτης καὶ τερατείας ἔμπλεα.
8:6: διὰ πίστεως, ᾗ μόνῃ θεὸν ἰδεῖν συγκεχώρηται.	1.10.15: αἱ τοῦ λόγου πύλαι, πίστεως ἀνοιγνύμεναι κλειδί.
9:2 ὢ τῆς ὑπερβαλλούσης φιλανθρωπίας.	9.62.11: ὢ τῆς ὑπερβαλλούσης φιλανθρωπίας.

It must again be observed that some of the terms in the accounts of idolatry are common to most Greek writers on that theme. Similarly, some of the figures which Geffcken names to prove connection between the two documents are familiar literary devices, e.g., paronomasia,[299] the exclamatory ὢ with the genitive, and a series of rhetorical questions.[300] The idea of the worshiper becoming like the idol is also commonplace in polemics against idolatry (see note on 2:5). The evidence is not sufficient to warrant the view that Diognetus is dependent on the *Protrepticus*, or that its author "shines only as a satellite of the star of Clement."[301] We can hardly affirm more than a general resemblance between Diognetus and the *Protrepticus* due to the fact that both writings move in the same orbit of thought and deal in part with the same themes. The same observation may be made of the suggested parallels between Diognetus and Tertullian's *Apology*,[302] which are remarked in the Notes (pp. 95ff). For possible literary indebtedness to Irenaeus see note on 7:4 (ὡς πείθων ... τῷ θεῷ),[303] and for wider literary affinities see discussion at 6:7; 8:5–8. The possible relationship of Diogn. 9–12 to Hippolytus and Melito is discussed below (pp. 65–67).

---

299. κοινὴν ... κοίτην, 5:7. Cf. *Protr.* 10.68.9, ἀνονήτους καὶ ἀνοήτους τρυφάς and other examples. See above, p. 13n54.

300. Diogn. 2:2ff.; *Protr.* 2.13.13.

301. Geffcken, "Diognetos," 350. In our view (see pp. 18–19) Diognetus probably antedates the *Protrepticus* (ca. 190 CE) by some thirty years.

302. Set forth by Lipsius, "Review of *Über den pseudojustinischen Brief an Diognetus* by Franz Overbeck." See also Dräseke, "Diognetus."

303. Molland, "Diognetbriefes," 294, says: "The identical formulation, however, remains strange. Nevertheless, these words hardly suffice as a basis for a literary-critical hypothesis."

I. Introduction 63

8. Integrity

Two questions will be discussed: (1) the relation of chs. 1–10 to 11–12, and (2) the authorship and origin of chs. 11–12.

i. The Relation of Chs. 1–10 to 11–12

Codex Argent. 9 shows a lacuna at the close of ch. 10 (after ἐπιγνῷς) with a marginal note: "and here the copy had a break."[304] Stephanus first noted the incongruity of the last two chapters with the preceding ten, and nearly all later writers agree that 11–12 are a fragment of a work by a later author or editor.[305] Some editors indeed print only chs. 1–10.[306] The case for the separation of 11–12 from the epistle proper rests on:

a. General Considerations, Chiefly of Content and Teaching

The plan outlined in ch. 1 is completed in the main in the following nine chapters, and 11–12 appear to be extraneous to the original scheme. In ch. 1 the author states that he is moved to write his Epistle by Diognetus's zeal to learn; according to 11:8 he writes by command of the Word and under stress to share what has been revealed. In chs. 11–12 there is no suggestion of an earnest seeker whose inquiries are answered. On the contrary, these chapters deal with the blessings of true teaching and of friendship with the Word,[307] as embodied in the Church, and they have in view "those who are becoming disciples of the truth" (11:1), i.e., presumably catechumens in course of instruction. These differences, it is true, are not irreconcilable with the view that the same author is addressing Diognetus, who, convinced by the case set forth in 1–10, may now be regarded as typical of the class of nascent disciples. But there are more serious divergences. There is a marked difference in the attitude towards the Jewish dispensation. In the epistle proper the Mosaic ordinances (Sabbath, circumcision, fasts) are ridiculed

---

304. καὶ ὧδε ἐγκοπὴν εἶχε τὸ ἀντίγραφον.

305. Dorner, *Person of Christ*, 1.1:376, is a notable exception. These chapters (11–12), he says, "seem to me to exhibit the same compass of thought and Christian colouring as the rest, and first to bring the epistle to an appropriate conclusion." See also Kihn, *Ursprung*, 48; Birks, "Epistle of Diognetus," 258.

306. E.g., Wilamowitz-Moellendorff, Geffcken, Blakeney. Others detach and edit chs. 11–12. So Credner, *Geschichte*, 59–66.

307. For different aspects (in 11–12 compared with 7–10) of the Word or Son, see above, pp. 49–52.

and rejected (ch. 4), and prophecy is ignored, whereas in 11:6 the Law and the Prophets are equated with the Gospels and apostolic tradition as sources of enrichment for the Church. The primacy assigned to faith (8:6)[308] cedes to that of knowledge (12:3-7). Though 1-10 show abundant reminiscences of the New Testament,[309] there is no express citation; 12:5 has an exact quotation of 1 Cor 8:1 ascribed to "the apostle." The traces of allegorical interpretation (of the garden of Eden story) in ch. 12 are entirely lacking in 1-10. The two appended chapters give the impression that they are a portion of a homily[310] with vestiges of metrical form.[311]

b. Differences in Vocabulary and Style

In estimating vocabulary differences, it is necessary to bear in mind the relative extent of the two sections (1-10; 11-12), their different subject-matter, and the possible variation of mood in the author. But, with such allowances made, the following features are not without significance. Particles, plentiful and varied in 1-10, are rather limited in 11-12. οὐδέ, γάρ, ἀλλά, τε (only once, 12:5), δέ, and καί (*passim*) occur. But there are no instances of τε καί, γε, δή, ἄν. ὡς, especially frequent in 1-10, appears only once (12:3) and that in a different sense (= ὅτι). μὲν . . .δέ, abundant in 1-10, are entirely absent from 11-12. In prepositions, conjunctions, etc. 11-12 show ἄνευ, διό, εἶτα, μετά (all absent from 1-10); ἐξ ἀρχῆς (2:1; 8:11), but ἀπ' ἀρχῆς (11:4; 12:3 *bis*). Some words and phrases are alien from the general tenor of 1-10: ἁπλόω, γνῶσις, ἐξειπεῖν, συγχρωτίζω, συνετίζω, ἀποστόλων γενόμενος μαθητής, διδάσκαλος ἐθνῶν, ἀληθείας μαθηταί, λόγῳ προσφιλής,[312] οἱ ἅγιοι, οἱ πιστοί, ὅρκια[313*] πίστεως, ὅρια πατέρων, εὐαγγελίων πίστις, ἀποστόλων παράδοσις, ἐκκλησίας χάρις, ὁ ἀπόστολος (= St. Paul), τὸ κυρίου πάσχα, κηροί.

The argument from silence is precarious but the absence of some favorite words of the author of 1-10, e.g., ἴδιος, λοιπός, θεοσέβεια, may be noted. An estimate or style is largely subjective. But the total impression made by 11-12 is that these chapters derive from a writer other than the author of 1-10. The following features common in 1-10 are lacking in 11-12: ἄν with

---

308. See above, p. 39. Note the objective sense of πίστις in the usage of the later writer.

309. See pp. 53-56.

310. An Easter homily (Otto), an Epiphany homily (Lake).

311. For analogies in the New Testament and other early literature to the fusion of two distinct documents, see Harrison, *Polycarp's Two Epistles*, 20-24.

312. *Conjecture.

313. *Conjecture.

I. Introduction

potential optative, the rhetorical question, the use of synonyms, resumptive οὗτος, the habit of reiterating a keyword or construction. The high proportion of anarthrous nouns in 11–12 has no parallel in 1–10.

ii. The Authorship and Origin of Chs. 11–12

Bunsen was the first to assign the authorship of these chapters to Hippolytus, and in 1852[314] he claimed that they formed the concluding passage of Hippolytus's *Refutation of All Heresies* or the *Philosophumena*. Dräseke[315] and Di Pauli[316] supported this view. Bonwetsch agreed on the Hippolytean authorship, but did not assign the fragment to a particular treatise.[317] Ewald suggested that 11–12 form the end of a different book written some twenty or thirty years later than chs. 1–10, its object being to expound and commend the true gnosis.[318] Westcott was disposed to assign the fragment to a Jewish convert of Alexandria writing ca. 140–50 CE,[319] whereas Lightfoot,[320] equally impressed by its Alexandrian tone, suggested Pantaenus[321] (ca. 180–210) as its author.

Connolly had independently come to the conclusion (ca. 1916) that these chapters came from the hand of Hippolytus,[322] and later accepted the view that they formed the lost ending of the *Philosophumena*. He suggests that in the Codex (which contained various writings wrongly attributed to Justin Martyr) a portion (probably ch. 10) of the *Philosophumena* of Hippolytus stood immediately before chs. 11–12 of Diognetus. The parallels that Connolly draws differ in force and appositeness. The cumulative effect, however, is impressive, and a strong case has been built up by his careful study.

In his valuable study of Melito's *Homily* Campbell Bonner raises the interesting question whether Diogn. 11–12 "were once part of a homily by

---

314. Bunsen, *Hippolytus and His Age*, 1:414ff.
315. Dräseke, "'Refutatio Omnium Haeresium,'" 275ff.
316. Di Pauli, "Schlußkapitel," 28–36.
317. Bonwetsch, "Schlußkapitel," 621–34, and Article in *Göttingen Nachricht*, 27–28.
318. Ewald, *History of Israel*, 8:173n3.
319. Westcott, *Canon*, 88, 90, 93.
320. Lightfoot, *Apostolic Fathers*, 488–89, and *Biblical Essays*, 92. See also Batiffol, *Primitive Catholicism*, 179ff.
321. For Pantaenus see the references in Eusebius, *Hist. eccl.* 5.10.
322. Connolly, "Ad Diognetum xi–xii," 2ff. See Additional Note C below.

Melito."[323] A careful comparison of the text of all Melito's fragments[324] with the appended chapters of Diognetus yields interesting results but hardly conclusive. Bonner points out that the sound and rhythm of some sentences in these two chapters reveal stylistic affinities with writings of Melito:[325]

Diogn. 11:2: ὑπὸ ἀπίστων μὴ νοούμενος, μαθηταῖς δὲ διηγούμενος.

Diogn. 11:4: ὁ καινὸς φανεὶς καὶ παλαιὸς εὑρεθείς.

Diogn. 11:5: οἷς ὅρκια πίστεως οὐ θραύεται οὐδὲ ὅρια πατέρων παρορίζεται.

Diogn. 11:6: a sequence of four short clauses ending in -ται

Diogn. 12:9: a sequence of seven clauses ending in -ται. See Melito, *Homily* 16: ὁπότε τὸ πρόβατον σφάζεται καὶ τὸ πάσχα βιβρώσκεται καὶ τὸ μυστήριον τελεῖται καὶ ὁ λαὸς εὐφραίνεται καὶ ὁ Ἰσραὴλ σφραγίζεται. Note coordination in both writers.

The opening clauses of Diogn. 11:4, 5, in praise of the Word or Son (οὗτος ὁ ἀπ' ἀρχῆς ... οὗτος ὁ ἀεί) reminds us of the *Homily* 68–71, where a series of praises of Christ is expressed by eleven clauses introduced by οὗτός ἐστι with article and aorist participle. See also *Homily* 82–86, 104. The same locution is seen in Hippolytus, *Contra Noetum* 18.

Minor coincidences appear in:

Diogn.	*Homily*
11:3: ὑπὸ λαοῦ ἀτιμασθείς.	75: ἔδει αὐτὸν ἀτιμασθῆναι, ἀλλ' οὐχ ὑπὸ σοῦ (Israel).
11:2: τὰ διὰ λόγου δειχθέντα ("*by* the Word"; see note)	87: τὴν ἐκεῖ διατροφὴν διὰ τοῦ καλοῦ Ἰωσήφ ("*by* the good Joseph"). P.Oxy. 1600:[326] τον δι αδελ[φου φ]ονευομενον[327] ("*by* a brother").

The evidence gleaned is too meagre to establish the authorship of Diogn. 11–12 by Melito. But that the author belongs to the school of thought represented in Melito and Hippolytus seems certain. Bonner suggests that "it is conceivable that Hippolytus wrote the paragraphs now incorporated in the closing chapter of the Letter (i.e., Diognetus) in his younger days,

---

323. Bonner, *Homily on the Passion by Melito*.

324. Given in Routh, *Reliquiae Sacrae*, 1:113ff.; Otto, *Corpus Apologetarum*, 9:410ff.; Goodspeed, *Apologeten*; P.Oxy 13, 1600; Bonner, *Homily on the Passion by Melito*.

325. Bonner, *Homily on the Passion by Melito*, 60ff.

326. This papyrus of the fifth century CE was formerly ascribed to Hippolytus (so Bartlet and Bonwetsch). But it has since been identified as part of Melito's *Homily on the Passion* (Bonner and Martin).

327. The readings, however, are very uncertain.

I. Introduction

before he had developed his more elaborate style, and while he was still more patently under the influence of Melito than he was in his maturity."[328]

9. History of the Text

Of the original MS and its history, full accounts are given by various authorities.[329] It will be sufficient here to outline the story of the text. The original was a codex, probably of the thirteenth or fourteenth century,[330] which contained among other works[331] the following tractates: (1) *Concerning the Monarchy*, (2) *An Exhortation to the Greeks*, each entitled "of the holy Justin, philosopher and martyr," (3) *An Exposition of the faith concerning the right confession or concerning the Trinity*, by "Justin, philosopher and martyr," (4) *To the Greeks*, and (5) *To Diognetus*,[332] each ascribed "of the same" (τοῦ αὐτοῦ). The codex, apparently once in the possession of Reuchlin (d. 1522),[333] came to the monastery of Maurmünster in Alsace ca. 1560. Its subsequent history is obscure, but between 1793 and 1795 it arrived at Strassburg, where it was destroyed by fire on August 24, 1870, during the Franco-German war. The MS was known as Codex Argentoratensis Graec. 9, from the old Latin name of the city, Argentoratum.

Stephanus of Paris made a transcript of the MS in 1586 and published the *editio princeps* in 1592. About 1590 a copy of the codex had been made by Beurer of Freiburg. This copy seems to have perished, but some of Beurer's readings were incorporated by Stephanus in an appendix to his edition (1592) and by Sylburg (1593). Stephanus's transcript is extant at Leyden (Codex Graec. Voss., Q. 30). Until 1880, therefore, Diognetus was known only through Stephanus's manuscript. In that year, however, Dr. Neumann of Halle discovered an earlier transcript in the University Library at Tübingen. This copy (Codex Misc. Tübing., M.b. 17) had been made by B. Haus in 1580.

---

328. Bonner, *Homily on the Passion by Melito*, 62.

329. See Gebhardt, *Patrum Apostolicorum Opera*, 1.2:142–46; Otto, *Corpus Apologetarum*, 3:xiiiff.; Kihn, *Ursprung*, 35ff.; Harnack, *Geschichte*, 1:757–58; and idem, "Überlieferung," 1.2:79f., 79f., 85, 161ff.

330. Harnack, "Überlieferung," 85, suggests that the codex may be traced to an earlier text of the sixth to seventh century CE.

331. Notably two treatises of Athenagoras, *Petition on behalf of the Christians* and *Concerning the Resurrection*.

332. For full title see above, pp. 5–6.

333. The back of the codex bore a note in Rechlin's handwriting stating that the MS had been in his custody and that he had bought it from the Carthusian brotherhood in his native town.

Various editions of Diognetus appearing between 1742 and 1839[334] led up to the important work of Otto, *Corpus Apologetarum Christianorum saeculi secundi (Justini Philosophi et Martyris Opera)*, vol. 2, Jena (1843), 2nd ed. (1849), 3rd ed. (1879).[335] For Otto's first edition Cod. Argent. had been collated by Cunitz in 1842, and again for his third edition by Reuss in 1861. Among modern editors are Gildersleeve (1877), Lightfoot and Harmer (1891), Gebhardt, Harnack, and Zahn (6th ed. 1920), Geffcken (1928), and Lake (1913, reprinted in 1930).[336] The text of Funk, *Patres Apostolici I*, 2nd ed. (1901), which incorporates the results of an examination of the Tübingen transcript of 1580, is that followed in the present study,[337] though comparison has been made throughout with the texts of Otto, Lightfoot, Geffcken, and Lake. The original codex was defective in several places,[338] and the readings in not a few instances are highly doubtful. All subsequent editors are indebted to the emendations made by Lachmann and Bunsen which appear in the latter's *Analecta Ante-Nicaena*, 1:103–21 (1854).

The following abbreviations are used in the *apparatus criticus*: MS = Cod. Argentoratensis Graec. 9; h = the transcript by Haus; b = Beurer's readings; conj. = conjecture.

10. Select Bibliography

The following list includes books and articles bearing upon Diognetus (or upon general questions involved) which have been read or consulted in the preparation of this study. With few exceptions, only works published after 1879 (the date of Otto's text in the third edition of his *Corpus Apologetarum Christianorum saeculi secundi*, vol. 3) are specified here. For a list of prior editions, translations, and studies, see Otto, *Corpus Apologetarum*, 3:xxxiiiff., livff.; Gebhardt, Harnack, and Zahn, *Patrum Apostolicorum Opera*, 1.2, 2nd ed., 147f., 153f.; and Richardson, *Bibliographical Synopsis* (this gives editions up to 1881, translations to 1884). The Select Bibliography presented here may, it is hoped, afford an adequate guide to the modern interpretation of Diognetus. Additional works are named in the body of this book. Abbreviations used for works frequently cited appear in square brackets.

---

334. Prudentius of S. Maur (1742), Gallandi (1765), Oberthür (1777), Böhl (1826), Hefele (1839), all based on Stephanus's text.

335. Note also Otto, *Epistola ad Diognetum* (1st ed. 1845; 2nd 1852).

336. See Bibliography. That of Blakeney, *Diognetus*, is the most recent edition.

337. Some slight deviations from Funk's text are pointed out in the Notes.

338. Lacunae appear at 7:6; 10:1, 8.

I. Introduction

A. Editions and Translations

Blakeney, Edward Henry. *The Epistle to Diognetus.* London: Macmillan, 1943. [Blakeney]
Funk, Franz Xaver. *Patres Apostolici.* Vol. 1. 2nd ed. Tübingen: Laupp, 1901. [Funk]
Gebhardt, Oskar von, Adolf Harnack, and Theodor Zahn. *Patrum Apostolicorum Opera.* Leipzig: Hinrichs, 1878.
Geffcken, Johannes. "Der Brief an Diognetus." In *Neutestamentliche Apokryphen,* edited by Edgar Hennecke, 619–23. 2nd ed. Tübingen: Mohr Siebeck, 1942. [Geffcken]
———. *Der Brief an Diognetos.* Heidelberg: C. Winter, 1928.
Gildersleeve, B. L. *The Apologies of Justin Martyr. To Which Is Appended the Epistle to Diognetus.* New York: Harper & Brothers, 1877. [Gildersleeve]
Heinzelmann, Wilhelm. *Der Brief an Diognet, "die Perle des christlichen Altertums."* Erfurt: H. Neumann, 1896.
Lake, Krisopp. *The Apostolic Fathers.* Vol. 2. Loeb Classical Library. Cambridge: Harvard University Press, 1913. Repr. ed. 1930.
Lightfoot, John B., and J. R. Harmer. *Apostolic Fathers.* London: Macmillan, 1891.
Otto, Johann Carl Theodor von. *Epistola ad Diognetum Justini philosophi et martyris nomen prae se ferens.* 2nd ed. Leipzig: T. O. Weigel, 1852.
———. *Corpus Apologetarum Christianorum saeculi secundi.* Vol. 3. 3rd ed. Jena: Prostat apud F. Mauke, 1879. [Otto]
Radford, Lewis Bostock. *The Epistle to Diognetus.* London: SPCK, 1908. [Radford]
Rauschen, Gerhard. *Frühchristliche Apologeten und Märtyrerakten.* Vol. 1. München: Kösel, 1913.
Roberts, Alexander, James Donaldson, and W. S. Walford. *The Epistle to Diognetus.* Ante-Nicene Christian Library. Buffalo, NY: Christian Literature, 1867.
Walford, Walter Shirley. *Epistle to Diognetus: The Greek Text, with Introduction, Notes, and Translation.* London: James Nisbet, 1908.
Wilamowitz-Moellendorff, U. von. *Griechisches Lesebuch.* Vol. 1.2. 3rd ed. Berlin: Weidmann, 1906.
———. *Griechisches Lesebuch.* Vol. 2.2. 2nd ed. Berlin: Weidmann, 1906.

B. General

Altaner, Berthold. *Patrologie.* Freiburg: Herder, 1938.
Bardenhewer, Otto. *Geschichte der altkirchlichen Literatur.* Vol. 1. 2nd ed. Freiburg im Breisgau: Herder, 1913.
———. *Patrology: The Lives and Works of the Fathers of the Church.* Freiburg: Herder, 1908.
Batiffol, Pierre. *Anciennes Littératures chrétiennes. La Littérature grecque.* Paris: Lecoffre, 1897.
Bauer, Walter. *Griechisch-Deutsches Wörterbuch zu den Schriften des Neuen Testaments und der übrigen urchristlichen Literatur.* 3rd ed. Berlin: Alfred Töpelmann, 1937. [*Wörterbuch*]
Bethune-Baker, J. F. *An Introduction to the Early History of Christian Doctrine to the Time of the Council of Chalcedon.* London: Methuen, 1903.

———. *An Introduction to the Early History of Christian Doctrine to the Time of the Council of Chalcedon.* 5th ed. London: Methuen, 1933.
Birks, E. B. "Epistle to Diognetus." In *Dictionary of Christian Biography, Literature, Sects and Doctrines*, edited by William Smith and Henry Wace, 2:162–67. London: Murray, 1880.
———. "Epistle of Diognetus." In *Dictionary of Christian Biography*, edited by Henry Wace and William Piercy, 2:257ff. 2nd ed. London: Murray, 1911.
Blass, Friedrich, and Albrecht Debrunner. *Grammatik des neutestamentlichen Griechisch.* 5th ed. Göttingen: Vandenhoeck & Ruprecht, 1921. [Blass-Debrunner]
———. *Nachträge zur 5. Auflage.* 5th ed. Göttingen: Vandenhoeck & Ruprecht, 1931.
Bonner, Campbell, ed. *The Homily of the Passion by Melito, Bishop of Sardis, and Some Fragments of the Apocryphal Ezekiel.* Studies and Documents 12. London: Christophers, 1940.
Cadbury, Henry J., F. J. Foakes Jackson, and Krisopp Lake. *Christian Beginnings.* London: Macmillan, 1933.
Cadoux, C. J. *The Early Church and the World: A History of the Christian Attitude to Pagan Society and the State down to the Time of Constantinus.* Edinburgh: T. & T. Clark, 1925.
Carrington, Philip. *Christian Apologetics of the Second Century in Their Relation to Modern Thought.* London: SPCK, 1921.
Chapman, John. "Epistle of Diognetus." In *Catholic Encyclopedia*, edited by Charles G. Herbermann and Edward A. Pace, 5:8–9. Appleton: New York, 1909.
Connolly, Richard Hugh. "Ad Diognetum xi–xii." *Journal of Theological Studies* 37 (1936) 2–15.
———. "The Date and Authorship of the Epistle to Diognetus." *Journal of Theological Studies* 36 (1935) 347–53.
Cruttwell, Charles Thomas. *A Literary History of Early Christianity, Including the Fathers and the Chief Heretical Writers of the Ante-Nicene Period.* Vols. 1–2. London: Charles Griffin, 1893.
Deissmann, Adolf. *Bible Studies: Contributions from Papyri and Inscriptions to the History of the Language, the Literature, and the Religion of Hellenistic Judaism and Primitive Christianity.* Translated by Alexander Grieve. Edinburgh: T. & T. Clark, 1901. [*Bible Studies*]
———. *Light from the Ancient East: The New Testament Illustrated by Recently Discovered Texts of the Graeco-Roman World.* Translated by Lionel R. M. Strachan. London and New York: Hodder & Stoughton, 1890. [*Light from the Ancient East*]
Dittenberger, W. *Sylloge Inscriptionum Graecarum.* 3rd ed. Leipzig: Hirzel, 1915–24. [Ditt. Syll.]
Donaldson, James. *A Critical History of Christian Literature.* Vols. 1–3. London: Macmillan, 1864–66.
Doulcet, Henry. "L'Apologie d'Aristide et l'Épître à Diognète." *Revue des Questions Historiques* 28 (1880) 601–12.
Dräseke, Johannes. "Der Brief an Diognetus." *Jahrbücher für protestantische Theologie* 7 (1881) 213–83 and 414–84.
———. "Zur 'Refutatio Omnium Haeresium' des Hippolytos." *Zeitschrift für wissenschaftliche Theologie* 45 (1902) 263–88.
Ewald, Heinrich. *History of Israel.* Vols. 1–5. London: Longmans, 1869–74.

I. Introduction

Field, Frederick. *Notes on the Translation of the New Testament.* Cambridge: Cambridge University Press, 1899.

Funk, Franz Xaver. "Das Schlusskapitel des Diognetus Briefes." *Theologisches Quartalschrift* 85 (1903) 638–39

———. *Zwei griechische Apologeten.* Leipzig: Teubner, 1907.

Glover, Terrot Reaveley. *The Conflict of Religions in the Early Roman Empire.* 12th ed. London: Methuen, 1932.

Goodenough, Erwin Ramsdell. *The Theology of Justin Martyr.* Jena: Frommann, 1923.

Goodspeed, Edgar J. *Index Patristicus.* Leipzig: J. C. Hinrichs, 1907.

———. *Index Apologeticus.* Leipzig: J. C. Hinrichs, 1912.

Harnack, Adolf. *Geschichte der altchristlichen Literatur.* Vol. 1. Leipzig: Hinrichs, 1893.

———. *Geschichte der altchristlichen Literatur.* Vol. 2.1. Leipzig: Hinrichs, 1897.

———. *Geschichte der altchristlichen Literatur.* Vol. 2.2. Leipzig: Hinrichs, 1904.

———. *History of Dogma.* Vol. 1. Translated by Neil Buchanan. London: Williams & Norgate, 1894.

———. *History of Dogma.* Vol. 2. Translated by Neil Buchanan. London: Williams & Norgate, 1896.

———. *The Mission and Expansion of Christianity in the First Three Centuries.* Translated by James Moffatt. 2 vols. 2nd ed. London: Williams & Norgate, 1908. [*Expansion*]

———. "Die Überlieferung der griechischen Apologeten des 2. Jahrhunderts in der alten Kirche und im Mittelalter." In *Texte und Untersuchungen* 1, 1–300. Leipzig: Hinrichs, 1882.

Harris, James Rendel, and J. Armitage Robinson. *The Apology of Aristides on behalf of the Christians. From a Syriac Ms. Preserved on Mount Sinai.* Cambridge Text and Studies 1.1. Cambridge: Cambridge University Press, 1891.

Hatch, Edwin. *Essays in Biblical Greek.* Oxford: Clarendon, 1889. [*Essays*]

———. *The Influence of Greek Ideas and Usages upon the Christian Church.* 6th ed. London: Williams & Norgate, 1897.

Howard, W. F. *Christianity according to St. John.* London: Duckworth, 1947.

Jannaris, Antonius N. *An Historical Greek Grammar.* London: Macmillan, 1897.

Jülicher, A. "Diognetos." In *Real-encyclopädie der classischen Altertumswissenschaft*, edited by August Pauly and Georg Wissowa, 5:786. Stuttgart: Metzler, 1905.

Kennedy, Henry Angus Alexander. *Sources of New Testament Greek. Or, The Influence of the Septuagint on the New Testament.* Edinburgh: T. & T. Clark, 1895.

Kihn, Heinrich. *Der Ursprung des Briefes an Diognet.* Herder: Freiburg i.B., 1882.

———. "Zum Briefe an Diognet." *Theologisches Quartalschrift* 28 (1880) 601–12.

Kittel, Gerhard [and Otto Bauernfeind], ed. *Theologisches Wörterbuch zum Neuen Testament.* Stuttgart: Kohlhammer, 1933–[1979].

Krüger, Gustav. *History of Early Christian Literature.* London and New York: Macmillan, 1897.

Lechler, Gotthard Victor. *Das apostolische und das nachapostolische Zeitalter mit Rücksicht auf Unterschied und Einheit in Leben.* 3rd ed. Karlsruhe: Reuther, 1885.

Legge, F. *Philosophumena or the Refutation of All Heresies.* London and New York: SPCK, 1921.

Mansel, S. "The Apologists." In *Dictionary of Christian Biography, Literature, Sects and Doctrines*, edited by William Smith and Henry Wace, 1:140–47. London: Murray, 1877.

Mayser, Edwin. *Grammatik der griechischen Papyri aus der Ptolemäerzeit*. Vol. 1. Leipzig: Teubner, 1906. [Mayser]

———. *Grammatik der griechischen Papyri aus der Ptolemäerzeit*. Vol. 2. Leipzig: Teubner, 1938. [Mayser]

McGiffert, Arthur Cushman. *A History of Christian Thought*. New York: Scribner's and Sons, 1932–33.

Meecham, Henry G. *Letter of Aristeas*. Manchester: Manchester University Press, 1935.

Meyer, Ed. *Ursprung und Anfänge des Christentums*. 3 vols. Stuttgart: Cotta, 1921–23.

Molland, Einar. "Die literatur- und dogmengeschichtliche Stellung des Diognetbriefes." *ZNTW* 33 (1934) 289–312.

Moulton, James Hope. *A Grammar of New Testament Greek*. Vol. 1. 3rd ed. London: Hodder & Stoughton, 1908. [*Prolegomena*]

Moulton, James Hope, and George Milligan. *The Vocabulary of the Greek New Testament*. London: Hodder & Stoughton, 1914.

Moulton, James Hope, and Wilbert Francis Howard. *A Grammar of New Testament Greek: Prolegomena*. Edinburgh: T. & T. Clark, 1906.

Neumann, Karl Johannes. "Ueber eine den Brief an Diognet enthaltende Tübinger Handschrift." *Zeitschrift für Kirchengeschichte* 4 (1881) 284–87.

Norden, Eduard. *Die antike Kunstprosa*. Vol. 2. 2nd ed. Leipzig: Teubner, 1909.

Overbeck, Franz. Review of *Der Brief an Diognetus* by Dräseke. *Theologische Literaturzeitung* (1882) 28ff.

———. *Studien zur Geschichte der alten Kirche*. Vol. 1. Schloss-Chemitz: Schmeitzner, 1875.

Puech, Aimé. *Les apologistes grecs du IIe siècle de notre ère*. Paris: Librairie Hachette, 1912.

Radermacher, L. *Neutestamentliche Grammatik: Das Griechisch des Neuen Testaments im Zusammenhang mit der Volkssprache*. 2nd ed. Tübingen: Mohr, 1925.

Richardson, E. C. "Bibliographical Synopsis." In *Ante-Nicene Fathers*, 10:5–7. Buffalo, NY: 1887; repr. ed. 1917.

Rivière, Jean. *St. Justin et les apologistes du second siècle*. Paris: Bloud, 1907.

Scheibe, C. "Zur Kritik der Epistola ad Diognetum." *Theologische Studien und Kritiken* 35 (1862) 576–88.

Seeberg, R. "Die Apologie des Aristides." *Forschungen zur Geschichte des neutestamentlichen Kanons und der altkirchlichen Literatur* 5 (1893) 239–43.

Stählin, Otto. "Christliche Schriftsteller." In *Geschichte der griechischen Literatur*, edited by Wihelm von Christ, 2.2:907–1244. 5th ed. München: C. H. Beck, 1913.

Streeter, B. H., F. C. Burkitt, H. Lietzmann, and N. H. Baynes. *Cambridge Ancient History*. Vol. 11. Cambridge: Cambridge University Press, 1936.

———. *Cambridge Ancient History*. Vol. 12. Cambridge: Cambridge University Press, 1939.

Taylor, Vincent. *The Atonement in New Testament Teaching*. London: Epworth, 1941.

Thackeray, Henry. *A Grammar of the Old Testament in Greek according to the Septuagint*. Vol. 1. Cambridge: Cambridge University Press, 1909.

Tixeront, Joseph. *A Handbook of Patrology*. London: Herder, 1920.

Uhlhorn, Gerhard. "Der Brief an Diognet." In *Realenzyklopädie für protestantische Theologie und Kirche*, edited by Johann Jakob Herzog, Albert Hauck, and Hermann Caselmann, 4:675ff. Leipzig: Hinrichs, 1898.

I. Introduction

Weiss, Johann. *The History of Primitive Christianity.* 2 vols. New York: Wilson-Erickson, 1937.

Wendland, Paul. *Die hellenistisch-römische Kultur in ihren Beziehungen zum Judentum und Christentum: Die urchristlichen Literaturformen.* Handbuch zum Neuen Testament 1. Tübingen: Mohr, 1912.

———. *Hippolytus Werke.* Vol. 3, *Refutatio omnium Haeresium.* Die Grieschischen Schriftseteller der ersten drei Jahrhunderte. Leipzig: Hinrichs, 1916.

Note: Texts used in citations from early writers are:

Apostolic Fathers: Krisopp Lake. *The Apostolic Fathers.* Vol. 2. Loeb Classical Library. Cambridge: Harvard University Press, 1913. Repr. ed. 1930.

Aristeas: Henry Thackeray. *The Letter of Aristeas.* Appendix to Henry Barclay Swete, *An Introduction to the Old Testament in Greek.* 2nd ed. Cambridge: Cambridge University Press, 1902.

Athenagoras: Eduard Schwartz. *Griechische Apologeten.* Texte und Untersuchungen 4. Leipzig: Hinrichs, 1888–93.

Clement of Alexandria: Otto Stählin. *Clemens Alexandrinus.* 4 vols. Berlin: Akademie Verlag, 1905–36.

Josephus: B. Niese. *Flavii Josephi Opera.* 6 vols. Berlin: Weidmann, 1889–95.

Justin Martyr: Johann Carl Theodor von Otto. *Corpus Apologetarum.* Jena: Prostat apud F. Mauke, 1851–1888.

Philo: Leopold Cohn, Siegfried Reiter, and Paul Wendland. *Philonis Alexandrini Opera quae supersunt.* Berlin: Reimer, 1896–1930. References are to their sections.

Tatian: Eduard Schwartz. *Griechische Apologeten.* Texte und Untersuchungen 4. Leipzig: Hinrichs, 1888–93.

Testament of the Twelve Patriarchs: Robert Henry Charles. *The Greek Versions of the Testament of the Twelve Patriarchs.* Oxford: Clarendon, 1908.

Where I have not made my own English renderings from the original of the Apostolic Fathers and the Apologists, I have availed myself of the *Ante-Nicene Christian Library* translation series. References are to book and chapter.

For the Greek Bible, LXX citations are made from Rhalfs's *Septuaginta* (1935), with occasional recourse to the texts of Swete (3rd ed., 1901) and Brooke and McLean (1906–). New Testament citations are from Eberhard Nestle's text, revised by Erwin Nestle, 15th ed. (1932). The texts of Westcott and Hort and Souter have been consulted at times.

Passages underlined in the Greek text of Diognetus below denote close correspondences with the language of the Greek Bible.

NOTE: I regret that I have not been able to gain access to two studies of Diognetus, namely:

Buonaiuti, Ernesto. *Lettera a Diogneto, testo, traduzione e note.* Scrittori christiani antichi 1. Rome: Libreria di Cultura, 1921.

Fermi, M. "L'apologia di Aristide e la lettera a Diogneto." *Ricerche religiose* 1 (1925) 541–47.

An elaborate discussion of Diognetus has recently appeared:

Andriessen, Dom Paul. "L'apologie de Quadratus conservée sous le titre d'Épître à Diognète." *Recherches de Théologie ancienne et médiévale* 13 (1946) 5–39, 125–49, 237–60.

These articles are summarized by their author in *Vigiliae Christianae* 1.2 (1947). I have offered a brief account of Andriessen's thesis in Additional Note E (see below).

II. Text

ΕΠΙΣΤΟΛΗ ΠΡΟΣ ΔΙΟΓΝΗΤΟΝ

Title: τοῦ αὐτοῦ πρὸς Διόγνητον.

Chapter 1

1 Ἐπειδὴ ὁρῶ, κράτιστε Διόγνητε, ὑπερεσπουδακότα σε τὴν θεοσέβειαν τῶν Χριστιανῶν μαθεῖν καὶ πάνυ σαφῶς καὶ ἐπιμελῶς πυνθανόμενον περὶ αὐτῶν, τίνι τε θεῷ πεποιθότες καὶ πῶς θρησκεύοντες αὐτὸν[1] τε κόσμον ὑπερορῶσι πάντες καὶ θανάτου καταφρονοῦσι καὶ οὔτε τοὺς νομιζομένους ὑπὸ τῶν Ἑλλήνων θεοὺς λογίζονται οὔτε τὴν Ἰουδαίων δεισιδαιμονίαν φυλάσσουσι, καὶ τίνα τὴν φιλοστοργίαν ἔχουσι πρὸς ἀλλήλους, καὶ τί δή ποτε καινὸν τοῦτο γένος ἢ ἐπιτήδευμα εἰσῆλθεν εἰς τὸν βίον νῦν καὶ οὐ πρότερον· ἀποδέχομαί γε τῆς προθυμίας σε ταύτης καὶ παρὰ τοῦ θεοῦ, τοῦ καὶ τὸ λέγειν καὶ τὸ ἀκούειν ἡμῖν χορηγοῦντος, αἰτοῦμαι δοθῆναι ἐμοὶ μὲν εἰπεῖν οὕτως, ὡς μάλιστα ἂν ἀκούσαντά[2] σε βελτίω γενέσθαι, σοί τε οὕτως ἀκοῦσαι, ὡς μὴ λυπηθῆναι τὸν εἰπόντα.

Chapter 2

1 Ἄγε δή, καθάρας σεαυτὸν ἀπὸ πάντων τῶν προκατεχόντων σου τὴν διάνοιαν λογισμῶν καὶ τὴν ἀπατῶσάν σε συνήθειαν ἀποσκευασάμενος, καὶ γενόμενος ὥσπερ ἐξ ἀρχῆς καινὸς ἄνθρωπος, ὡς ἂν καὶ λόγου καινοῦ, καθάπερ καὶ αὐτὸς ὡμολόγησας, ἀκροατὴς ἐσόμενος· ἴδε μὴ μόνον τοῖς ὀφθαλμοῖς, ἀλλὰ καὶ τῇ φρονήσει, τίνος ὑποστάσεως ἢ τίνος εἴδους τυγχάνουσιν, οὓς ἐρεῖτε καὶ νομίζετε θεούς. **2** οὐχ ὁ μέν τις λίθος ἐστίν, ὅμοιος τῷ πατουμένῳ, ὁ δ' ἐστὶ χαλκὸς οὐ κρείσσων τῶν εἰς τὴν χρῆσιν ἡμῖν κεχαλκευμένων σκευῶν, ὁ δὲ ξύλον, ἤδη καὶ σεσηπός, ὁ δὲ ἄργυρος, χρῄζων ἀνθρώπου τοῦ φυλάξαντος, ἵνα μὴ κλαπῇ, ὁ δὲ σίδηρος, ὑπὸ ἰοῦ διεφθαρμένος, ὁ δὲ ὄστρακον, οὐδὲν τοῦ κατασκευασμένου

---

1. αὐτὸν τόν τε] conj. Lachmann; αὐτόν τε MS, h.
2. ἀκούσαντά] conj. Stephanus; ἀκοῦσαι MS.

II. Translation

The Epistle to Diognetus

Chapter 1

Since I perceive, most excellent Diognetus, that you are exceedingly zealous to learn the religion of the Christians and are making very clear and careful inquiry about them—both who is the God in whom they trust and how they worship him, so that all disdain the world and despise death, and neither account those to be gods who are esteemed such by the Greeks, nor observe the superstition of the Jews; and what is the affection which they have for one another; and why it is that this new race of men or mode of living has entered into our world now and not formerly—I welcome this eager desire in you, and I ask of God, who bestows on us *the power* both of speech and of hearing; that it may be given to me so to speak that you may be edified as much as possible by your hearing, and to you so to hear that I by my speaking may experience no regret.

Chapter 2

¹ Come then, clear yourself of all the bias that occupies your mind, and get rid of the habit that deceives you, and become as it were from the beginning a new man, as one too who is to hear a new story, even as you yourself also acknowledged. See not only with your eyes, but also with your understanding, what substance or form they happen *to have* whom you declare and esteem to be gods. ² Is not one a stone, like that which we tread on, another bronze, no better than the implements which have been forged for our use, another wood already decayed, another silver, which needs a man to guard[55] it lest it be stolen, another iron eaten through by rust, another earthenware,

---

55. Reading φυλάξοντος. See note *ad loc.*

πρὸς τὴν ἀτιμοτάτην ὑπηρεσίαν εὐπρεπέστερον; **3** οὐ φθαρτῆς ὕλης ταῦτα πάντα; οὐχ ὑπὸ σιδήρου καὶ πυρὸς κεχαλκευμένα; οὐχ ὃ μὲν αὐτῶν λιθοξόος, ὃ δὲ χαλκεύς, ὃ δὲ ἀργυροκόπος, ὃ δὲ κεραμεὺς ἔπλασεν; οὐ πρὶν ἢ ταῖς τέχναις τούτων εἰς τὴν μορφὴν τούτων³ ἐκτυπωθῆναι, ἣν ἕκαστον⁴ αὐτῶν ἑκάστῳ, ἔτι καὶ νῦν⁵ μεταμεμορφωμένον; οὐ τὰ νῦν ἐκ τῆς αὐτῆς ὕλης ὄντα σκεύη γένοιτ' ἄν, εἰ τύχοι τῶν αὐτῶν τεχνιτῶν, ὅμοια τοιούτοις; **4** οὐ ταῦτα πάλιν, τὰ νῦν ὑφ' ὑμῶν⁶ προσκυνούμενα, δύναιτ' ἂν ὑπὸ ἀνθρώπων σκεύη ὅμοια γενέσθαι τοῖς λοιποῖς; οὐ κωφὰ πάντα; οὐ τυφλά; οὐκ ἄψυχα; οὐκ ἀναίσθητα; οὐκ ἀκίνητα; οὐ πάντα σηπόμενα; οὐ πάντα φθειρόμενα; **5** ταῦτα θεοὺς καλεῖτε, τούτοις δουλεύετε, τούτοις προσκυνεῖτε, τέλεον δ' αὐτοῖς ἐξομοιοῦσθε. **6** διὰ τοῦτο μισεῖτε Χριστιανούς, ὅτι τούτους οὐχ ἡγοῦνται θεούς. **7** ὑμεῖς γὰρ αἰνεῖν⁷ νομίζοντες καὶ οἰόμενοι,⁸ οὐ πολὺ πλέον αὐτῶν καταφρονεῖτε; οὐ πολὺ μᾶλλον αὐτοὺς χλευάζετε καὶ ὑβρίζετε, τοὺς μὲν λιθίνους καὶ ὀστρακίνους σέβοντες ἀφυλάκτως, τοὺς δὲ ἀργυρέους καὶ χρυσοῦς ἐγκλείοντες ταῖς νυξὶ καὶ ταῖς ἡμέραις φύλακας παρακαθίσαντες,⁹ ἵνα μὴ κλαπῶσιν; **8** αἷς δὲ δοκεῖτε τιμαῖς προσφέρειν, εἰ μὲν αἰσθάνονται, κολάζετε μᾶλλον αὐτούς· εἰ δὲ ἀναισθητοῦσιν, ἐλέγχοντες αἵματι καὶ κνίσαις αὐτοὺς θρησκεύετε. **9** ταῦθ' ὑμῶν τις ὑπομεινάτω, ταῦτα ἀνασχέσθω τις ἑαυτῷ γενέσθαι. ἀλλὰ ἄνθρωπος μὲν οὐδὲ εἷς ταύτης τῆς κολάσεως ἑκὼν ἀνέξεται, αἴσθησιν γὰρ ἔχει καὶ λογισμόν· ὁ δὲ λίθος ἀνέχεται, ἀναισθητεῖ γάρ. οὐκ οὖν τὴν αἴσθησιν αὐτοῦ ἐλέγχετε. **10** περὶ μὲν οὖν τοῦ μὴ δεδουλῶσθαι Χριστιανοὺς τοιούτοις θεοῖς πολλὰ μὲν ἂν¹⁰ καὶ ἄλλα εἰπεῖν ἔχοιμι· εἰ δέ τινι μὴ δοκοίη κἂν ταῦτα ἱκανά, περισσὸν ἡγοῦμαι καὶ τὸ πλείω λέγειν.

Chapter 3

1 Ἑξῆς δὲ περὶ τοῦ μὴ κατὰ τὰ αὐτὰ Ἰουδαίοις θεοσεβεῖν αὐτοὺς οἶμαί σε μάλιστα ποθεῖν ἀκοῦσαι. **2** Ἰουδαῖοι τοίνυν, εἰ μὲν ἀπέχονται ταύτης τῆς προειρημένης λατρείας, καλῶς¹¹ θεὸν ἕνα τῶν πάντων σέβειν καὶ δεσπότην ἀξιοῦσι φρονεῖν· εἰ δὲ τοῖς προειρημένοις ὁμοιοτρόπως τὴν θρησκείαν προσάγουσιν αὐτῷ ταύτην, διαμαρτάνουσιν. **3** ἃ γὰρ τοῖς ἀναισθήτοις καὶ κωφοῖς προσφέροντες οἱ Ἕλληνες

---

3. (μορφὴν) τούτων] MS, h; ταύτην conj. Böhl.
4. ἕκαστον] conj. Prud. M.; ἕκαστος MS, h.
5. ἔτι καὶ νῦν] MS, h. εἰκάζειν conj. Lachmann.
6. ὑμῶν] ἡμῶν MS.
7. αἰνεῖν] conj. Lachmann. οἱ νῦν MS
8. οἰόμενοι] MS, h. σεβόμενοι conj. Lachmann.
9. παρακαθίσαντες] conj. Krenkel; παρακαθίσαντες MS, h.
10. μὲν ἂν] Lachmann. μὲν MS, h.
11. καλῶς] conj. Hilgenfeld. καί εἰς MS.

not a bit more pleasing than that made for the insignificant service? **3** Are not all these of perishable matter? Have they not been forged by iron and fire? Did not the sculptor fashion one of them, the brass-worker another, the silversmith another, the potter another? Before they were modelled by these men's art into the form of these *gods*, was not each of them subjected to transformation and still *is so* even now—at the hands of each artificer? Might not the vessels now formed out of the same material, if they met with the same workmen, be made similar to such *images* as these? **4** Again, could not these things which are now worshiped by you become at the hands of men vessels like the rest? Are they not all dumb? Are they not blind? Are they not without souls? Are they not destitute of feeling? Are they not without motion? Are they not all rotting away? Are they not all in course of decay? **5** These things you call gods! These are what you serve! These you worship and in the end you become like them! **6** For this reason you hate (the) Christians—because they do not think that these are gods. **7** For it is not you, who, although you consider and think that you are praising *the gods*, are much more despising them? Are you not rather mocking and insulting them, when you worship those of stone and earthenware, which you leave unguarded, and yet those of silver and gold you lock up at night and in the daytime set guards by them, lest they be stolen? **8** And by the honors that you think to offer them you are punishing them rather, if indeed they are endued with sense; but, if they lack sensibility, you are refuting[56] them by the very fact of worshiping them with blood and steaming fat. **9** Let anyone of you endure this treatment, let him bear with these things being done to him! Nay, there is not a single man who will, if he can help it, suffer this infliction, for he has sense and reason. But the stone suffers it, for it has no feeling. You do not then (by your offering) show up its sensibility![57] **10** Well, I could say many other things about the fact that Christians are not in bondage to such gods. But if to anyone even these arguments should not seem sufficient, I think it needless to say more.

Chapter 3

1 In the next place I suppose that you are especially anxious to hear why they (Christians) do not worship in the same manner as the Jews. **2** The Jews indeed, since they abstain from the religion described above, rightly deem that they worship the one God of the universe and think of him as Master; but in

---

56. Perhaps better "exposing," "showing them up." See note *ad loc.*, and cf. 2:9.
57. See note for this rendering.

ἀφροσύνης δεῖγμα παρέχουσι, ταῦθ' οὗτοι, καθάπερ προσδεομένῳ τῷ θεῷ λογιζόμενοι παρέχειν μωρίαν εἰκὸς[12] μᾶλλον ἡγοῖντ' ἄν, οὐ θεοσέβειαν. **4** <u>ὁ γὰρ ποιήσας τὸν οὐρανὸν καὶ τὴν γῆν καὶ πάντα τὰ ἐν αὐτοῖς</u> καὶ πᾶσιν ἡμῖν χορηγῶν, ὧν προσδεόμεθα, οὐδενὸς ἂν αὐτὸς προσδέοιτο τούτων ὧν τοῖς οἰομένοις διδόναι παρέχει αὐτός. **5** οἱ δέ γε θυσίας αὐτῷ δι' αἵματος καὶ κνίσης καὶ ὁλοκαυτωμάτων ἐπιτελεῖν οἰόμενοι καὶ ταύταις ταῖς τιμαῖς αὐτὸν γεραίρειν, οὐδέν μοι δοκοῦσι διαφέρειν τῶν εἰς τὰ κωφὰ τὴν αὐτὴν ἐνδεικνυμένων[13] φιλοτιμίαν· τῶν μὲν μὴ δυναμένοις[14] τῆς τιμῆς μεταλαμβάνειν, τῶν δὲ δοκούντων[15] παρέχειν τῷ μηδενὸς προσδεομένῳ.

Chapter 4

1 Ἀλλὰ μὴν τό γε περὶ τὰς βρώσεις αὐτῶν ψοφοδεὲς καὶ τὴν περὶ τὰ σάββατα δεισιδαιμονίαν καὶ τὴν τῆς περιτομῆς ἀλαζονείαν, καὶ τὴν τῆς νηστείας καὶ νουμηνίας εἰρωνείαν, καταγέλαστα καὶ οὐδενὸς ἄξια λόγου οὐ[16] νομίζω σε χρῄζειν παρ' ἐμοῦ μαθεῖν. **2** τό τε γὰρ τῶν ὑπὸ τοῦ θεοῦ κτισθέντων εἰς χρῆσιν ἀνθρώπων ἃ μὲν ὡς καλῶς κτισθέντα παραδέχεσθαι, ἃ δ' ὡς ἄχρηστα καὶ περισσὰ παραιτεῖσθαι, πῶς οὐκ ἀθέμιστον;[17] **3** τὸ δὲ καταψεύδεσθαι θεοῦ ὡς κωλύοντος ἐν τῇ τῶν σαββάτων ἡμέρᾳ καλόν τι ποιεῖν, πῶς οὐκ ἀσεβές; **4** τὸ δὲ καὶ τὴν μείωσιν τῆς σαρκὸς μαρτύριον ἐκλογῆς ἀλαζονεύεσθαι ὡς διὰ τοῦτο ἐξαιρέτως ἠγαπημένους ὑπὸ θεοῦ, πῶς οὐ χλεύης ἄξιον; **5** τὸ δὲ παρεδρεύοντας αὐτοὺς ἄστροις καὶ σελήνῃ τὴν παρατήρησιν τῶν μηνῶν καὶ τῶν ἡμερῶν ποιεῖσθαι, καὶ τὰς οἰκονομίας θεοῦ καὶ τὰς τῶν καιρῶν ἀλλαγὰς καταδιαιρεῖν[18] πρὸς τὰς αὐτῶν ὁρμάς, ἃς μὲν εἰς ἑορτάς, ἃς δὲ εἰς πένθη· τίς ἂν θεοσεβείας καὶ οὐκ ἀφροσύνης πολὺ πλέον ἡγήσαιτο[19] δεῖγμα; **6** τῆς μὲν οὖν κοινῆς εἰκαιότητος καὶ ἀπάτης καὶ τῆς Ἰουδαίων πολυπραγμοσύνης καὶ ἀλαζονείας ὡς[20] ὀρθῶς ἀπέχονται Χριστιανοί, ἀρκούντως σε νομίζω μεμαθηκέναι· τὸ δὲ τῆς ἰδίας αὐτῶν θεοσεβείας μυστήριον μὴ προσδοκήσῃς δύνασθαι παρὰ ἀνθρώπου μαθεῖν.

12. εἰκὸς] MS, h. εἰκότως Stephanus.
13. ἐνδεικνυμένων] conj. Beurer, Stephanus. ἐνδεικνύμενοι MS, h.
14. τῶν μὲν μὴ δυναμένοις] Gebhardt. τῶν μὴ δυναμένων MS, h.
15. τῶν δὲ δοκούντων] Lachmann. τὸ δὲ δοκεῖν τινα MS, h.
16. οὐ] Stephanus inserts.
17. οὐκ ἀθέμιστον] Gebhardt. οὐ θέμις ἐστί MS, h.
18. καταδιαιρεῖν] καταδ... εῖν MS, h.
19. ἡγήσαιτο] Lachmann. ἡγήσεται.
20. ὡς] Bunsen inserts.

offering this service to him in like fashion to those already mentioned they go utterly astray. **3** For whereas the Greeks furnish an example of foolishness by making offerings to *images* void of sense and hearing, these Jews ought rather to consider it folly maybe, not piety, in thinking that they are offering these things to God as though he were in need of them.[58] **4** For "He who made the heaven and the earth and all things that are in them" and provides us all with what we need would not himself need any of these things which he himself supplies to those who imagine that they give to *him*. **5** But those who think that they are rendering due sacrifices to him by blood and fat and whole burnt offerings, and that they are showing him reverence by these tributes, seem to me in no way better than those who show the same lavish honor to deaf images. For the one class seem to offer *sacrifices* to things unable to partake of the honor, the other to him who is in need of nothing.

Chapter 4

1 But, in truth, I do not think that you need to learn from me that, after all, their qualms concerning food and their superstition about the Sabbath, and the vaunting of circumcision and the sanctimoniousness of fasting and new moon, are utterly absurd and unworthy of any argument. **2** For how can it be other than unlawful to receive some of the things created by God for man's use as created "good" and to refuse others as useless and superfluous? **3** And is it not impious to slander God as though he forbids the doing of a good deed on the Sabbath day? **4** And to glory in the mutilation of the flesh as evidence of their election, as if they were on this account especially beloved by God—does this not call for derision? **5** And their star-gazing and watching of the moon, so as to observe months and days and to distribute at their own inclinations the orderings of God and the changes of the seasons, making some into feasts and others into times of mourning—who would consider this an example of piety and not much more of folly? **6** Well then, I think that you have learned sufficiently that Christians are right in keeping aloof from the general fatuity and deceit and from the meddlesomeness and pride of the Jews; but as for the mystery of the Christians' own religion, do not expect to be able to learn this from man.

---

58. For the rendering of this passage see note *ad loc.*

Chapter 5

1 Χριστιανοὶ γὰρ οὔτε γῇ οὔτε φωνῇ οὔτε ἔσθεσι διακεκριμένοι τῶν λοιπῶν εἰσὶν ἀνθρώπων. **2** οὔτε γάρ που πόλεις ἰδίας κατοικοῦσιν οὔτε διαλέκτῳ τινὶ παρηλλαγμένῃ χρῶνται οὔτε βίον παράσημον ἀσκοῦσιν. **3** οὐ μὴν ἐπινοίᾳ τινὶ καὶ φροντίδι πολυπραγμόνων ἀνθρώπων μάθημα τοῦτ'[21] αὐτοῖς ἐστιν εὑρημένον, οὐδὲ δόγματος ἀνθρωπίνου προεστᾶσιν, ὥσπερ ἔνιοι. **4** κατοικοῦντες δὲ πόλεις ἑλληνίδας τε καὶ βαρβάρους, ὡς ἕκαστος ἐκληρώθη, καὶ τοῖς ἐγχωρίοις ἔθεσιν ἀκολουθοῦντες ἔν τε ἐσθῆτι καὶ διαίτῃ καὶ τῷ λοιπῷ βίῳ θαυμαστὴν καὶ ὁμολογουμένως παράδοξον ἐνδείκνυνται τὴν κατάστασιν τῆς ἑαυτῶν πολιτείας. **5** πατρίδας οἰκοῦσιν ἰδίας, ἀλλ' ὡς πάροικοι· μετέχουσι πάντων ὡς πολῖται, καὶ πάνθ' ὑπομένουσιν ὡς ξένοι· πᾶσα ξένη πατρίς ἐστιν αὐτῶν, καὶ πᾶσα πατρὶς ξένη. **6** γαμοῦσιν ὡς πάντες, τεκνογονοῦσιν· ἀλλ' οὐ ῥίπτουσι τὰ γεννώμενα. **7** τράπεζαν κοινὴν παρατίθενται, ἀλλ' οὐ κοίτην.[22] **8** <u>ἐν σαρκὶ</u> τυγχάνουσιν, ἀλλ' <u>οὐ κατὰ σάρκα</u> ζῶσιν. **9** ἐπὶ γῆς διατρίβουσιν, ἀλλ' ἐν οὐρανῷ πολιτεύονται. **10** πείθονται τοῖς ὡρισμένοις νόμοις, καὶ τοῖς ἰδίοις βίοις νικῶσι τοὺς νόμους. **11** ἀγαπῶσι πάντας, καὶ ὑπὸ πάντων διώκονται. **12** ἀγνοοῦνται, καὶ κατακρίνονται· θανατοῦνται, καὶ ζωοποιοῦνται. **13** <u>πτωχεύουσι, καὶ πλουτίζουσι πολλούς</u>· πάντων ὑστεροῦνται, καὶ ἐν πᾶσι περισσεύουσιν. **14** ἀτιμοῦνται, καὶ ἐν ταῖς ἀτιμίαις δοξάζονται· βλασφημοῦνται, καὶ δικαιοῦνται. **15** <u>λοιδοροῦνται, καὶ εὐλογοῦσιν</u>· ὑβρίζονται, καὶ τιμῶσιν. **16** ἀγαθοποιοῦντες ὡς κακοὶ κολάζονται· κολαζόμενοι χαίρουσιν ὡς ζωοποιούμενοι. **17** ὑπὸ Ἰουδαίων ὡς ἀλλόφυλοι πολεμοῦνται, καὶ ὑπὸ Ἑλλήνων διώκονται· καὶ τὴν αἰτίαν τῆς ἔχθρας εἰπεῖν οἱ μισοῦντες οὐκ ἔχουσιν.

Chapter 6

1 Ἁπλῶς δ' εἰπεῖν, ὅπερ ἐστὶν ἐν σώματι ψυχή, τοῦτ' εἰσὶν ἐν κόσμῳ Χριστιανοί. **2** ἔσπαρται κατὰ πάντων τῶν τοῦ σώματος μελῶν ἡ ψυχή, καὶ Χριστιανοὶ κατὰ τὰς τοῦ κόσμου πόλεις. **3** οἰκεῖ μὲν ἐν τῷ σώματι ψυχή, οὐκ ἔστι δὲ ἐκ τοῦ σώματος· καὶ Χριστιανοὶ ἐν κόσμῳ οἰκοῦσιν, <u>οὐκ εἰσὶ δὲ ἐκ τοῦ κόσμου</u>. **4** ἀόρατος ἡ ψυχὴ ἐν ὁρατῷ φρουρεῖται τῷ σώματι· καὶ Χριστιανοὶ γινώσκονται μὲν ὄντες[23] ἐν τῷ κοσμῷ, ἀόρατος δὲ αὐτῶν ἡ θεοσέβεια μένει. **5** μισεῖ τὴν ψυχὴν ἡ σὰρξ καὶ πολεμεῖ μηδὲν ἀδικουμένη, διότι ταῖς ἡδοναῖς κωλύεται χρῆσθαι· μισεῖ καὶ Χριστιανοὺς ὁ κόσμος μηδὲν ἀδικούμενος, ὅτι ταῖς ἡδοναῖς ἀντιτάσσονται. **6** ἡ ψυχὴ τὴν μισοῦσαν ἀγαπᾷ σάρκα καὶ τὰ μέλη· καὶ Χριστιανοὶ τοὺς μισοῦντας ἀγαπῶσιν. **7** ἐγκέκλεισται μὲν ἡ ψυχὴ τῷ σώματι,

---

21. μάθημα τοῦτ'] α. ε. εὑρημένον] Prud. M. μαθήματι τοῦτ' α. ε. εἰρημένον MS.

22. κοίτην] conj. Prud. M. κοινήν MS, h.

23. μὲν ὄντες] conj. Stephanus. μένοντες MS, h.

Chapter 5

1 For Christians are distinguished from the rest of men neither by country nor by language nor by customs. **2** For nowhere do they dwell in cities of their own; they do not use any strange form of speech or practice a singular mode of life. **3** This lore of theirs has not been discovered by any design and thought of prying men, nor do they champion a mere human doctrine, as some men do. **4** But while they dwell in both Greek and barbarian cities, each as his lot was cast, and follow the customs of the land in dress and food and other matters of living, they show forth the remarkable and admittedly strange order of their own citizenship. **5** They live in fatherlands of their own, but as aliens. They share all things as citizens, and suffer all things as strangers. Every foreign land is their fatherland, and every fatherland a foreign land. **6** They marry, like all others; they breed children, but they do not cast out their offspring. **7** Free board they provide, but not carnal bed. **8** They are "in the flesh," but they do not live "after the flesh." **9** They pass their days on earth, but they have their citizenship in heaven. **10** They obey the appointed laws, yet in their own lives they excel the laws. **11** They love all men, and are persecuted by all. **12** They are unknown, yet they are condemned; they are put to death, yet they are made alive. **13** "They are poor, yet they make many rich." They suffer the lack of all things, yet they abound in all things. **14** They are dishonored, and yet are glorified in their dishonor. They are slandered, yet are vindicated. **15** "They are reviled, and they bless"; insulted, they repay with honor. **16** When doing good they are punished as evil-doers; suffering punishment, they rejoice as if brought to life. **17** By the Jews they are warred against as foreigners, and are hunted down by the Greeks. Yet those who hate them cannot state the cause of their hostility.

Chapter 6

1 Broadly speaking, what the soul is in the body, that Christians are in the world. **2** The soul is dispersed through all the members of the body, and Christians throughout the cities of the world. **3** The soul dwells in the body, but is not of the body; and Christians dwell in the world, but "are not of the world." **4** The soul, itself invisible, is guarded in the body which is visible; so Christians are known as being in the world, but their religion remains unseen. **5** The flesh hates the soul, and, though it suffers no wrong, wars *against it*, because the flesh is hindered from indulging its pleasures; so too the world, though in no way wronged, hates Christians, because they set themselves against its pleasures. **6** The soul loves the flesh that hates it, and

συνέχει δὲ αὐτὴ τὸ σῶμα· καὶ Χριστιανοὶ κατέχονται μὲν ὡς ἐν φρουρᾷ τῷ κόσμῳ, αὐτοὶ δὲ συνέχουσι τὸν κόσμον. **8** ἀθάνατος ἡ ψυχὴ ἐν θνητῷ σκηνώματι κατοικεῖ· καὶ Χριστιανοὶ παροικοῦσιν ἐν φθαρτοῖς, τὴν ἐν οὐρανοῖς ἀφθαρσίαν προσδεχόμενοι. **9** κακουργουμένη σιτίοις καὶ ποτοῖς ἡ ψυχὴ βελτιοῦται· καὶ Χριστιανοὶ κολαζόμενοι καθ᾽ ἡμέραν πλεονάζουσι μᾶλλον. **10** εἰς τοσαύτην αὐτοὺς τάξιν ἔθετο ὁ θεός, ἣν οὐ θεμιτὸν αὐτοῖς παραιτήσασθαι.

Chapter 7

1 Οὐ γὰρ ἐπίγειον, ὡς ἔφην, εὕρημα τοῦτ᾽ αὐτοῖς παρεδόθη, οὐδὲ θνητὴν ἐπίνοιαν φυλάσσειν οὕτως ἀξιοῦσιν ἐπιμελῶς, οὐδὲ ἀνθρωπίνων οἰκονομίαν μυστηρίων πεπίστευνται. **2** ἀλλ᾽ αὐτὸς ἀληθῶς ὁ παντοκράτωρ καὶ παντοκτίστης καὶ ἀόρατος θεός, αὐτὸς ἀπ᾽ οὐρανῶν τὴν ἀλήθειαν καὶ τὸν λόγον τὸν ἅγιον καὶ ἀπερινόητον ἀνθρώποις ἐνίδρυσε καὶ ἐγκατεστήριξε ταῖς καρδίαις αὐτῶν· οὐ, καθάπερ ἄν τις εἰκάσειεν, ἀνθρώποις ὑπηρέτην²⁴ τινὰ πέμψας ἢ ἄγγελον ἢ ἄρχοντα ἤ τινα τῶν διεπόντων τὰ ἐπίγεια ἤ τινα τῶν πεπιστευμένων τὰς ἐν οὐρανοῖς διοικήσεις, ἀλλ᾽ αὐτὸν τὸν τεχνίτην καὶ δημιουργὸν τῶν ὅλων, ᾧ τοὺς οὐρανοὺς ἔκτισεν, ᾧ τὴν θάλασσαν ἰδίοις ὅροις ἐνέκλεισεν, οὗ τὰ μυστήρια πιστῶς πάντα φυλάσσει τὰ στοιχεῖα, παρ᾽ οὗ τὰ μέτρα τῶν τῆς ἡμέρας δρόμων ὁ ἥλιος εἴληφε φυλάσσειν, ᾧ πειθαρχεῖ σελήνη νυκτὶ φαίνειν κελεύοντι, ᾧ πειθαρχεῖ τὰ ἄστρα τῷ τῆς σελήνης ἀκολουθοῦντα δρόμῳ· ᾧ πάντα διατέτακται καὶ διώρισται καὶ ὑποτέτακται, οὐρανοὶ καὶ τὰ ἐν οὐρανοῖς, γῆ καὶ τὰ ἐν τῇ γῇ, θάλασσα καὶ τὰ ἐν τῇ θαλάσσῃ, πῦρ, ἀήρ, ἄβυσσος, τὰ ἐν ὕψεσι, τὰ ἐν βάθεσι, τὰ ἐν τῷ μεταξύ· τοῦτον πρὸς αὐτοὺς ἀπέστειλεν. **3** Ἆρά γε, ὡς ἀνθρώπων ἄν τις λογίσαιτο, ἐπὶ τυραννίδι καὶ φόβῳ καὶ καταπλήξει; **4** οὐ μὲν οὖν· ἀλλ᾽ ἐν ἐπιεικείᾳ καὶ πρᾳΰτητι ὡς βασιλεὺς πέμπων υἱὸν βασιλέα ἔπεμψεν, ὡς θεὸν ἔπεμψεν, ὡς ἄνθρωπον²⁵ πρὸς ἀνθρώπους ἔπεμψεν, ὡς σῴζων ἔπεμψεν, ὡς πείθων, οὐ βιαζόμενος· βία γὰρ οὐ πρόσεστι τῷ θεῷ. **5** ἔπεμψεν ὡς καλῶν, οὐ διώκων· ἔπεμψεν ὡς ἀγαπῶν, οὐ κρίνων. **6** πέμψει γὰρ αὐτὸν κρίνοντα, καὶ τίς αὐτοῦ τὴν παρουσίαν ὑποστήσεται;²⁶ ... **7** [οὐχ ὁρᾷ]²⁷ παραβαλλομένους θηρίοις, ἵνα ἀρνήσωνται τὸν κύριον, καὶ μὴ νικωμένους; **8** οὐχ ὁρᾷς, ὅσῳ πλείονες κολάζονται, τοσούτῳ πλεονάζοντας ἄλλους; **9** ταῦτα ἀνθρώπου οὐ δοκεῖ τὰ ἔργα· ταῦτα δύναμίς ἐστι θεοῦ· ταῦτα τῆς παρουσίας αὐτοῦ δείγματα.²⁸

---

24. ἀνθρώποις ὑπηρέτην] MS, h. conj. Bunsen ἄνθρωπος, ὑπηρέτην.
25. ἄνθρωπον] Lachmann and Bunsen insert.
26. ὑποστήσεται] Here MS, h. show a lacuna and a marginal note. See on 7:6 [below].
27. οὐχ ὁρᾷς] Stephanus inserts.
28. δείγματα] Stephanus. δόγματα MS, h.

the limbs; so Christians love them that hate them. ⁷ The soul is enclosed within the body, but itself curbs[59] the body; and Christians are detained in the world as in a prison, but themselves restrain the world. ⁸ The soul, though immortal, dwells in a mortal tabernacle; and Christians sojourn among corruptible things, awaiting the incorruptibility which is in heaven. ⁹ When faring ill in food and drink the soul becomes better; so Christians when buffeted day by day flourish the more. ¹⁰ To so high a rank has God appointed them, and it is not right for them to refuse it.

Chapter 7

¹ For this is not, as I said, an earthly discovery which was committed to them, and no mortal idea which they think it their duty to guard with such care, nor have they been entrusted with the stewardship of mere human mysteries. ² But in truth God himself, the all-sovereign and all-creating and invisible God, himself from heaven established among men the truth and the holy and incomprehensible word and fixed it firmly in their hearts, not, as one might surmise, by sending to men some servant, or an angel, or ruler, or one of those who administer the affairs of earth, or one of those entrusted with the ordering of things in heaven, but the very Artificer and Maker of the universe himself, by whom he created the heavens, by whom he confined the sea in its own bounds; whose mysteries all the elements faithfully guard, from whom the sun has received the measure of its daily rounds to keep, whom the moon obeys as he bids her shine by night, whom the stars obey as they follow the course of the moon, by whom all things have been ordered and determined and placed in subjection, the heavens and the things in the heavens, the earth and the things therein, the sea and what is in the sea, fire, air, abyss, the things in the heights, the things in the depths, the things in the realm between—him he sent to them. ³ Did he send him, as a man might conclude, to rule in tyranny and terror and awe? ⁴ Not so, but in gentleness and meekness he sent him, as a king sending a son who is a king, he sent him as God, he sent him as man unto men. He was as it were saving when he sent him, (as) persuading, not compelling (for force is no attribute of God). ⁵ When he sent him God was calling, not pursuing; he sent him as in love, not in judgment. ⁶ For he will send him to be our judge, and who shall stand at his coming? ⁷ *Do you not see*[60] *them* thrown to wild beasts that they may deny the Lord, and yet unconquered? ⁸ Do you not see

---

59. For this rendering see note *ad loc.*
60. There is a lacuna in the MS at this point. See note *ad loc.*

Chapter 8

1 Τίς γὰρ ὅλως ἀνθρώπων ἠπίστατο, τί ποτ' ἐστὶ θεός, πρὶν αὐτὸν ἐλθεῖν; **2** ἢ τοὺς κενοὺς καὶ ληρώδεις ἐκείνων λόγους ἀποδέχῃ τῶν ἀξιοπίστων φιλοσόφων, ὧν οἱ μέν τινες πῦρ ἔφασαν εἶναι τὸν θεόν (οὗ μέλλουσι χωρήσειν αὐτοί, τοῦτο καλοῦσι θεόν), οἱ δὲ ὕδωρ, οἱ δ' ἄλλο τι τῶν στοιχείων τῶν ἐκτισμένων ὑπὸ θεοῦ. **3** καίτοι γε, εἴ τις τούτων τῶν λόγων ἀπόδεκτός ἐστι, δύναιτ' ἂν καὶ τῶν λοιπῶν κτισμάτων ἓν ἕκαστον ὁμοίως ἀποφαίνεσθαι θεόν. **4** ἀλλὰ ταῦτα μὲν τερατεία καὶ πλάνη τῶν γοήτων ἐστίν· **5** ἀνθρώπων δὲ οὐδεὶς οὔτε εἶδεν[29] οὔτε ἐγνώρισεν, αὐτὸς δὲ ἑαυτὸν ἐπέδειξεν. **6** ἐπέδειξε δὲ διὰ πίστεως, ᾗ μόνῃ[30] θεὸν ἰδεῖν συγκεχώρηται. **7** ὁ γὰρ δεσπότης καὶ δημιουργὸς τῶν ὅλων θεός, ὁ ποιήσας τὰ πάντα καὶ κατὰ τάξιν διακρίνας, οὐ μόνον φιλάνθρωπος ἐγένετο, ἀλλὰ καὶ μακρόθυμος. **8** ἀλλ' οὗτος ἦν μὲν ἀεὶ τοιοῦτος καὶ ἔστι καὶ ἔσται, χρηστὸς καὶ ἀγαθὸς καὶ ἀόργητος καὶ ἀληθής, καὶ μόνος ἀγαθός ἐστιν· **9** ἐννοήσας δὲ μεγάλην καὶ ἄφραστον ἔννοιαν ἀνεκοινώσατο[31] μόνῳ τῷ παιδί. **10** ἐν ὅσῳ μὲν οὖν κατεῖχεν ἐν μυστηρίῳ καὶ διετήρει τὴν σοφὴν αὐτοῦ βουλήν, ἀμελεῖν ἡμῶν καὶ ἀφροντιστεῖν ἐδόκει· **11** ἐπεὶ δὲ ἀπεκάλυψε διὰ τοῦ ἀγαπητοῦ παιδὸς καὶ ἐφανέρωσε τὰ ἐξ ἀρχῆς ἡτοιμασμένα, πάνθ' ἅμα παρέσχεν ἡμῖν, καὶ μετασχεῖν τῶν εὐεργεσιῶν αὐτοῦ καὶ ἰδεῖν καὶ νοῆσαι, ἃ τίς[32] ἂν πώποτε προσεδόκησεν ἡμῶν;

Chapter 9

1 Πάντ' οὖν ἤδη παρ' ἑαυτῷ σὺν τῷ παιδὶ οἰκονομηκὼς μέχρι μὲν[33] τοῦ πρόσθεν χρόνου εἴασεν ἡμᾶς, ὡς ἐβουλόμεθα, ἀτάκτοις φοραῖς φέρεσθαι, ἡδοναῖς καὶ ἐπιθυμίαις ἀπαγομένους· οὐ πάντως ἐφηδόμενος τοῖς ἁμαρτήμασιν ἡμῶν, ἀλλ' ἀνεχόμενος, οὐδὲ τῷ τότε τῆς ἀδικίας καιρῷ συνευδοκῶν, ἀλλὰ τὸν νῦν[34] τῆς δικαιοσύνης δημιουργῶν, ἵνα ἐν τῷ τότε χρόνῳ ἐλεγχθέντες ἐκ τῶν ἰδίων ἔργων ἀνάξιοι ζωῆς νῦν ὑπὸ τῆς τοῦ θεοῦ χρηστότητος ἀξιωθῶμεν, καὶ τὸ καθ' ἑαυτοὺς φανερώσαντες ἀδύνατον <u>εἰσελθεῖν εἰς τὴν βασιλείαν τοῦ θεοῦ</u> τῇ δυνάμει τοῦ θεοῦ δυνατοὶ γενηθῶμεν. **2** ἐπεὶ δὲ πεπλήρωτο μὲν ἡ ἡμετέρα ἀδικία καὶ τελείως πεφανέρωτο, ὅτι ὁ μισθὸς αὐτῆς κόλασις καὶ θάνατος προσεδοκᾶτο, ἦλθε δὲ ὁ καιρός, ὃν θεὸς προέθετο λοιπὸν φανερῶσαι τὴν ἑαυτοῦ χρηστότητα

---

29. εἶδεν] conj. Stephanus. εἶπεν MS, h.
30. μόνῃ] h. μόνον MS.
31. ἀνεκοινώσατο] ἣν ἐκοινώσατο MS, h.
32. νοῆσαι, ἃ τίς] conj. Lachmann. ποιῆσαι τίς MS, h.
33. ἤδη . . . οἰκονομηκὼς μέχρι μὲν τοῦ] conj. Lachmann. ᾔδει . . . οἰκονομικῶς, μέχρι μὲν οὖν τοῦ MS, h.
34. τὸν νῦν] conj. Hefele. τὸν νοῦν MS.

that as more of them are punished, so much do others abound? These things do not seem to be the works of man; they are a mighty deed of God; they are proofs of his presence.

Chapter 8

1 For what man had any knowledge at all of what God is, before he came? **2** Or do you accept the vain and foolish statements of those specious philosophers of whom some said that God was fire (what they themselves are destined to go to, that they call God!), and others water, and others some other of the elements created by God? **3** And yet, if any of these arguments is admissible, each one of the other created things could in like manner be declared God. **4** But these things are mere miracle-mongering and deceit of the magicians. **5** No man has either seen or known *him*, but God manifested himself. **6** And he manifested himself through faith, by which alone it is given to see God. **7** For God, Master and Maker of the universe, who made all things and disposed *them* in their *due* order, proved himself not only a lover of man but also long-suffering. **8** Nay, such he ever was and is and will be, kind and good and free from anger and true, and he alone is good. **9** And having conceived a great and unutterable design he communicated it to his child alone. **10** And so long as he held it in a mystery and guarded his wise counsel he seemed to have no concern or care for us. **11** But when he revealed it through his beloved child, and manifested the things prepared from the beginning, he bestowed upon us all things at once, both to share in his blessings and to see and understand. Who of us would ever have expected these things?

Chapter 9

1 Having therefore planned everything already in his own mind with his child, he allowed us up to the former time to be borne along by unruly impulses, as we willed, in the clutches of pleasures and lusts. Not at all because he took pleasure in our sins, but out of his forbearance; not in approval of the season of iniquity which was then, but creating the season of righteousness which is now, so that we who in past time were from our own deeds convicted as unworthy of life might now by the goodness of God be deemed worthy, and when we had shown clearly that of ourselves it was impossible "to enter into the kingdom of God," might be made able by the power of God. **2** But when our iniquity was fulfilled and it has been fully manifest that its reward of punishment and death was awaited, and the season came

καὶ δύναμιν (ὦ³⁵ τῆς ὑπερβαλλούσης φιλανθρωπίας καὶ ἀγάπης³⁶ τοῦ θεοῦ), οὐκ ἐμίσησεν ἡμᾶς οὐδὲ ἀπώσατο οὐδὲ ἐμνησικάκησεν, ἀλλὰ ἐμακροθύμησεν, ἠνέσχετο, ἐλεῶν³⁷ αὐτὸς τὰς ἡμετέρας ἁμαρτίας ἀνεδέξατο, αὐτὸς τὸν ἴδιον υἱὸν ἀπέδοτο λύτρον ὑπὲρ ἡμῶν, τὸν ἅγιον ὑπὲρ τῶν ἀνόμων, τὸν ἄκακον ὑπὲρ τῶν κακῶν, <u>τὸν δίκαιον ὑπὲρ τῶν ἀδίκων</u>, τὸν ἄφθαρτον ὑπὲρ τῶν φθαρτῶν, τὸν ἀθάνατον ὑπὲρ τῶν θνητῶν. **3** τί γὰρ ἄλλο τὰς ἁμαρτίας ἡμῶν ἠδυνήθη καλύψαι ἢ ἐκείνου δικαιοσύνη; **4** ἐν τίνι δικαιωθῆναι δυνατὸν τοὺς ἀνόμους ἡμᾶς καὶ ἀσεβεῖς ἢ ἐν μόνῳ τῷ υἱῷ τοῦ θεοῦ; **5** ὦ τῆς γλυκείας ἀνταλλαγῆς, ὦ τῆς ἀνεξιχνιάστου δημιουργίας, ὦ τῶν ἀπροσδοκήτων εὐεργεσιῶν· ἵνα ἀνομία μὲν πολλῶν ἐν δικαίῳ ἑνὶ κρυβῇ, δικαιοσύνη δὲ ἑνὸς πολλοὺς ἀνόμους δικαιώσῃ. **6** ἐλέγξας οὖν ἐν μὲν τῷ πρόσθεν χρόνῳ τὸ ἀδύνατον τῆς ἡμετέρας φύσεως εἰς τὸ τυχεῖν ζωῆς, νῦν δὲ τὸν σωτῆρα δείξας δυνατὸν σῴζειν καὶ τὰ ἀδύνατα, ἐξ ἀμφοτέρων ἐβουλήθη πιστεύειν ἡμᾶς τῇ χρηστότητι αὐτοῦ, αὐτὸν ἡγεῖσθαι τροφέα, πατέρα, διδάσκαλον, σύμβουλον, ἰατρόν, νοῦν, φῶς, τιμήν, δόξαν, ἰσχύν, ζωήν, περὶ ἐνδύσεως καὶ τροφῆς μὴ μεριμνᾶν.

Chapter 10

1 Ταύτην καὶ σὺ τὴν πίστιν ἐὰν ποθήσῃς, καὶ λάβῃς³⁸ πρῶτον μὲν ἐπίγνωσιν πατρός. **2** ὁ γὰρ θεὸς τοὺς ἀνθρώπους ἠγάπησε, δι' οὓς ἐποίησε τὸν κόσμον, οἷς ὑπέταξε πάντα τὰ ἐν τῇ γῇ, οἷς λόγον ἔδωκεν, οἷς νοῦν, οἷς μόνοις ἄνω³⁹ πρὸς αὐτὸν⁴⁰ ὁρᾶν ἐπέτρεψεν, οὓς ἐκ τῆς ἰδίας εἰκόνος ἔπλασε, πρὸς οὓς <u>ἀπέστειλε τὸν υἱὸν αὐτοῦ τὸν μονογενῆ</u>, οἷς τὴν ἐν οὐρανῷ βασιλείαν ἐπηγγείλατο καὶ δώσει τοῖς ἀγαπήσασιν αὐτόν. **3** ἐπιγνοὺς δέ τίνος οἴει πληρωθήσεσθαι χαρᾶς; ἢ πῶς ἀγαπήσεις τὸν οὕτως προαγαπήσαντά σε; **4** ἀγαπήσας δὲ μιμητὴς ἔσῃ αὐτοῦ τῆς χρηστότητος. καὶ μὴ θαυμάσῃς, εἰ δύναται μιμητὴς ἄνθρωπος γενέσθαι θεοῦ. δύναται θέλοντος αὐτοῦ. **5** οὐ γὰρ τὸ καταδυναστεύειν τῶν πλησίον οὐδὲ τὸ πλέον ἔχειν βούλεσθαι τῶν ἀσθενεστέρων οὐδὲ τὸ πλουτεῖν καὶ βιάζεσθαι τοὺς ὑποδεεστέρους εὐδαιμονεῖν ἐστιν, οὐδὲ ἐν τούτοις δύναταί τις μιμήσασθαι θεόν, ἀλλὰ ταῦτα ἐκτὸς τῆς ἐκείνου μεγαλειότητος. **6** ἀλλ' ὅστις τὸ τοῦ πλησίον ἀναδέχεται βάρος, ὃς ἐν ᾧ κρείσσων ἐστὶν ἕτερον τὸν ἐλαττούμενον εὐεργετεῖν ἐθέλει, ὃς ἅ⁴¹ παρὰ τοῦ θεοῦ λαβὼν ἔχει, ταῦτα τοῖς ἐπιδεομένοις χορηγῶν θεὸς γίνεται τῶν λαμβανόντων, οὗτος μιμητής ἐστι θεοῦ. **7** τότε θεάσῃ τυγχάνων ἐπὶ

---

35. ὦ] Prud. M. ὡς MS, b. h. shows a gap.
36. καὶ ἀγάπης] conj. Lange. μία ἀγάπη MS.
37. ἐλεῶν] conj. Lachmann. λέγων MS, h.
38. καὶ λάβῃς] MS. κατάλαβε conj. Gebhardt. See note *ad loc*.
39. ἄνω] b. ἄ... MS. ἀεὶ h.
40. αὐτὸν] MS. οὐρανὸν conj. Lachmann.
41. ὃς ἅ] conj. van Hengel. ὅσα MS, h.

which God had appointed to manifest henceforth[61] his own goodness and power (O the exceeding kindness and love of God!), he did not hate us or repel us or remember our misdeeds, but was long-suffering, bore with us, himself in mercy took on him our sins, himself gave up his own Son as a ransom for us, the holy One for the wicked, the innocent for the guilty, "the just for the unjust," the incorruptible for the corruptible, the immortal for mortals. **3** For what else could cover our sins but his righteousness? **4** In whom was it possible for us, wicked and impious as we were, to be justified, except in the Son of God alone? **5** O the sweet exchange, O work of God beyond all searching out, O blessings past our expectation, that the wickedness of many should be hidden in one righteous man and the righteousness of the One should justify many wicked! **6** Having then convinced us in the former time of the powerlessness of our nature to gain life, and having now shown the Savior in his power to save even powerless creatures, in both these ways his will was that we should believe his goodness, and regard him as guardian, father, teacher, counsellor, healer, mind, light, honor, glory, strength, life, and have no anxiety about clothing and food.[62]

Chapter 10

1 If you also long for this faith and first obtain knowledge of the Father . . .[63] **2** For God loved men for whose sake he made the world, to whom he subjected all things which are in the earth, to whom he gave reason, to whom he gave mind, whom alone he permitted to look upward to him, whom he formed after his own image, to whom "He sent his only-begotten Son," to whom he promised the kingdom which is in heaven—and he will give it to them that have loved him. **3** And when you have this knowledge, with what joy do you think you will be filled? Or how will you love him who first loved you so? **4** Loving him you will imitate his goodness. And do not wonder that a man can become an imitator of God. By the will of God he can. **5** For happiness lies not in lordship over one's neighbors, nor in the desire to have more than one's weaker *brethren*, nor in being rich and coercing the more needy. Not in these things can any man imitate God. No, these things are outside his majesty. **6** But whosoever takes upon himself his neighbor's burden, whosoever wishes to benefit another who is poorer in that in which he himself is better off, whosoever by supplying to those in want the things which he has received and holds from God become a god to those who receive them—this

---

61. Or "at last."
62. For the last clause see notes *ad loc*.
63. For the apparent lacuna see note *ad loc*.

γῆς ὅτι θεὸς ἐν οὐρανοῖς πολιτεύεται, τότε μυστήρια θεοῦ λαλεῖν ἄρξῃ, τότε τοὺς κολαζομένους ἐπὶ τῷ μὴ θέλειν ἀρνήσασθαι θεὸν καὶ ἀγαπήσεις καὶ θαυμάσεις· τότε τῆς ἀπάτης τοῦ κόσμου καὶ τῆς πλάνης καταγνώσῃ, ὅταν τὸ ἀληθῶς ἐν οὐρανῷ ζῆν ἐπιγνῷς,[42] ὅταν τοῦ δοκοῦντος ἐνθάδε θανάτου καταφρονήσῃς, ὅταν τὸν ὄντως θάνατον φοβηθῇς, ὃς φυλάσσεται τοῖς κατακριθησομένοις εἰς τὸ πῦρ τὸ αἰώνιον, ὃ τοὺς παραδοθέντας αὐτῷ μέχρι τέλους κολάσει. **8** τότε τοὺς ὑπομένοντας ὑπὲρ δικαιοσύνης θαυμάσεις τὸ πῦρ τὸ πρόσκαιρον[43] καὶ μακαρίσεις, ὅταν ἐκεῖνο τὸ πῦρ ἐπιγνῷς.[44]

Chapter 11

1 Οὐ ξένα ὁμιλῶ οὐδὲ παραλόγως ζητῶ, ἀλλὰ ἀποστόλων γενόμενος μαθητὴς γίνομαι διδάσκαλος ἐθνῶν· τὰ παραδοθέντα ἀξίως[45] ὑπηρετῶ γινομένοις ἀληθείας μαθηταῖς. **2** τίς γὰρ ὀρθῶς διδαχθεὶς καὶ λόγῳ προσφιλὴς γενηθεὶς[46] οὐκ ἐπιζητεῖ σαφῶς μαθεῖν τὰ διὰ λόγου δειχθέντα φανερῶς μαθηταῖς; οἷς ἐφανέρωσεν ὁ λόγος φανείς, παρρησίᾳ λαλῶν, ὑπὸ ἀπίστων μὴ νοούμενος, μαθηταῖς δὲ διηγούμενος,[47] οἳ πιστοὶ λογισθέντες ὑπ' αὐτοῦ ἔγνωσαν πατρὸς μυστήρια; **3** οὗ χάριν ἀπέστειλε λόγον, ἵνα κόσμῳ φανῇ· ὃς ὑπὸ λαοῦ ἀτιμασθείς, διὰ ἀποστόλων κηρυχθείς, ὑπὸ ἐθνῶν ἐπιστεύθη. **4** οὗτος ὁ ἀπ' ἀρχῆς, ὁ καινὸς φανεὶς καὶ παλαιὸς εὑρεθεὶς καὶ πάντοτε νέος ἐν ἁγίων καρδίαις γεννώμενος. **5** οὗτος ὁ ἀεί, ὁ σήμερον υἱὸς λογισθείς, δι' οὗ πλουτίζεται ἡ ἐκκλησία καὶ χάρις ἁπλουμένη ἐν ἁγίοις πληθύνεται, παρέχουσα νοῦν, φανεροῦσα μυστήρια, διαγγέλλουσα καιρούς, χαίρουσα ἐπὶ πιστοῖς, ἐπιζητοῦσι δωρουμένη, οἷς ὅρκια[48] πίστεως οὐ θραύεται οὐδὲ ὅρια πατέρων παρορίζεται. **6** εἶτα φόβος νόμου ᾄδεται, καὶ προφητῶν χάρις γινώσκεται, καὶ εὐαγγελίων πίστις ἵδρυται, καὶ ἀποστόλων παράδοσις φυλάσσεται καὶ ἐκκλησίας χαρᾷ[49] σκιρτᾷ. **7** ἣν χάριν μὴ λυπῶν ἐπιγνώσῃ, ἃ λόγος ὁμιλεῖ δι' ὧν βούλεται, ὅτε θέλει. **8** ὅσα γὰρ θελήματι τοῦ κελεύοντος λόγου ἐκινήθημεν ἐξειπεῖν μετὰ πόνου, ἐξ ἀγάπης τῶν ἀποκαλυφθέντων ἡμῖν γινόμεθα ὑμῖν κοινωνοί.

---

42. ἐπιγνῷς] Lachmann, Bunsen. ἐπιγνώσῃ
43. πρόσκαιρον] conj. Syllburg. προσ... MS.
44. ἐπιγνῷς] the MS shows a lacuna and a comment. See note *ad loc*.
45. ἀξίως] conj. Hollenberg. ἀξίοις MS, h.
46. προσφιλὴς γενηθεὶς] Prud. M., Bunsen. προσφιλεῖ γεννηθεὶς MS.
47. διηγούμενος] MS. conj. Lachmann διηχούμενος.
48. ὅρκια] conj. Lachmann. ὅρια MS.
49. ἐκκλησίας χαρᾷ] MS. Conj. Lachmann χαρά.

man is an imitator of God. **7** Then though your lot is on earth you will see that God lives[64] in heaven, then you will begin to speak the mysteries of God, then you will both love and admire those who are being punished for their refusal to deny God, then you will condemn the deceit and error of the world, when you know what is the true life in heaven, when you despise the apparent death here below, when you fear the real death, which is kept for those that shall be condemned to the eternal fire, which shall punish up to the end those that were delivered to it. **8** Then you will admire those that endure for righteousness' sake the fire which is but for a season, and you will count them blessed when you know that other fire. . . .[65]

Chapter 11

1 My discourse is not of strange matter, nor is my quest perverse; but having been a disciple of apostles I have become a teacher of the heathen. What has been handed down I minister worthily to those who are becoming disciples worthy of the truth. **2** For who that has been rightly instructed and has become a lover of the Word does not seek to learn clearly the things that were openly shown by the Word to disciples, to whom the Word on his appearance manifested them, speaking plainly, not being perceived by unbelievers, but expounding them to disciples, who, deemed by him to be faithful, gained knowledge of the mysteries of the Father? **3** For which cause he sent the Word that he might appear to the world, who was dishonored by the chosen people, proclaimed by the apostles, believed on by the heathen. **4** This is he who was from the beginning, who appeared as new and was proved to be old, and being born in the hearts of the saints is ever young. **5** This is he who is the eternal one, who today was accounted a Son, through whom the Church is enriched and grace is unfolded and multiplied among the saints, grace which confers understanding, makes mysteries plain, announces seasons, rejoices over the faithful, is given to them that seek, that is, those by whom the pledges of faith are not broken nor the decrees of the fathers transgressed. **6** Then is the fear of the law sung, and the grace of the prophets is known, and the faith of the gospels is established, and the tradition of the apostles is guarded, and buoyant is the grace of the Church. **7** And if you do not grieve this grace you will understand what the Word speaks through those whom he chooses, when he will. **8** For in all things

---

64. Or "rules." See note *ad loc.*
65. See note *ad loc.*

Chapter 12

1 Οἷς ἐντυχόντες καὶ ἀκούσαντες μετὰ σπουδῆς εἴσεσθε, ὅσα παρέχει ὁ θεὸς τοῖς ἀγαπῶσιν ὀρθῶς, οἱ γενόμενοι παράδεισος τρυφῆς, πάγκαρπον ξύλον εὐθαλοῦν ἀνατείλαντες ἐν ἑαυτοῖς, ποικίλοις καρποῖς κεκοσμημένοι. **2** ἐν γὰρ τούτῳ τῷ χωρίῳ ξύλον γνώσεως καὶ ξύλον ζωῆς πεφύτευται· ἀλλ' οὐ τὸ τῆς γνώσεως ἀναιρεῖ, ἀλλ' ἡ παρακοὴ ἀναιρεῖ. **3** οὐδὲ γὰρ ἄσημα τὰ γεγραμμένα, ὡς θεὸς ἀπ' ἀρχῆς ξύλον γνώσεως καὶ[50] ξύλον ζωῆς ἐν μέσῳ παραδείσου ἐφύτευσε, διὰ γνώσεως ζωὴν ἐπιδεικνύς· ᾗ μὴ καθαρῶς χρησάμενοι οἱ ἀπ' ἀρχῆς πλάνῃ τοῦ ὄφεως γεγύμνωνται. **4** οὐδὲ γὰρ ζωὴ ἄνευ γνώσεως οὐδὲ γνῶσις ἀσφαλὴς ἄνευ ζωῆς ἀληθοῦς· διὸ πλησίον ἑκάτερον πεφύτευται. **5** ἣν δύναμιν ἐνιδὼν ὁ ἀπόστολος τήν τε ἄνευ ἀληθείας προστάγματος εἰς ζωὴν ἀσκουμένην γνῶσιν μεμφόμενος λέγει· Ἡ γνῶσις φυσιοῖ, ἡ δὲ ἀγάπη οἰκοδομεῖ. **6** ὁ γὰρ νομίζων εἰδέναι τι ἄνευ γνώσεως ἀληθοῦς καὶ μαρτυρουμένης ὑπὸ τῆς ζωῆς οὐκ ἔγνω, ὑπὸ τοῦ ὄφεως πλανᾶται, μὴ ἀγαπήσας τὸ ζῆν. ὁ δὲ μετὰ φόβου ἐπιγνοὺς καὶ ζωὴν ἐπιζητῶν ἐπ' ἐλπίδι φυτεύει, καρπὸν προσδοκῶν. **7** ἤτω σοι καρδία γνῶσις, ζωὴ δὲ λόγος ἀληθής, χωρούμενος. **8** οὗ ξύλον φέρων καὶ καρπὸν αἴρων[51] τρυγήσεις ἀεὶ τὰ παρὰ θεῷ ποθούμενα,[52] ὧν ὄφις οὐχ ἅπτεται οὐδὲ πλάνη συγχρωτίζεται· οὐδὲ Εὔα φθείρεται, ἀλλὰ παρθένος πιστεύεται· **9** καὶ σωτήριον δείκνυται, καὶ ἀπόστολοι συνετίζονται, καὶ τὸ κυρίου πάσχα προέρχεται, καὶ καιροὶ[53] συνάγονται καὶ πάντα μετὰ κόσμου ἁρμόζονται,[54] καὶ διδάσκων ἁγίους ὁ λόγος εὐφραίνεται, δι' οὗ πατὴρ δοξάζεται· ᾧ ἡ δόξα εἰς τοὺς αἰῶνας. ἀμήν.

---

50. ξύλον γνώσεως καὶ] Bunsen inserts.
51. αἴρων] conj. Otto (2nd ed.). . . . ρῶν MS. καρποῦ ἐρῶν b.
52. ποθούμενα] MS πορούμενα b. εὐπορούμενα conj. Bunsen.
53. καιροὶ] conj. Sylburg. κληροὶ MS. See note *ad loc.*
54. ἁρμόζονται] b. ἁρμόζεται MS.

which we were moved to declare under stress,[66] by the will of the Word who commands us, we become sharers with you, out of love for what has been revealed unto us.

Chapter 12

1 If you happen upon[67] these truths and listen earnestly to them you will know what things God provides for those who love him rightly, who have become "a paradise of delight," raising up in themselves a tree all-fruitful and flourishing, and are adorned with diverse fruits. **2** For in this garden has been planted "the tree of knowledge and the tree of life." But the tree of knowledge does not kill; disobedience kills. **3** For that which stands written is not without significance, how that God from the beginning planted "the tree [of knowledge and the tree] of life in the midst of paradise," showing that life is through knowledge. Because our first parents did not make pure use of this knowledge they were left naked[68] by the deceit of the serpent. **4** For there can be neither life without knowledge nor sound knowledge without true life. Therefore each (tree) stands planted near the other. **5** And when the apostle saw the force of this, he blamed the knowledge which is exercised apart from the truth of the commandment which tends unto life, and said, "Knowledge puffs up, but love edifies." **6** For he who thinks that he knows anything without knowledge that is true and attested by life has learned nothing, but he is deceived by the serpent, not having loved life. But he who has gained knowledge with fear and seeks after life plants in hope, expecting fruit. **7** Let your heart be knowledge, your life the true teaching received (into the heart). **8** If you bear the tree of this and pluck its fruit, you will ever gather in the things desired with[69] God, which the serpent does not touch and deceit does not taint; and Eve is not corrupted, but is believed on as a virgin. **9** And salvation is set forth, and apostles are given understanding,[70] and the Passover of the Lord advances, and the seasons[71] are gathered together and are arranged in order, and the Word rejoices in teaching the saints, the Word through whom the Father is glorified; to whom be glory forever. Amen.

---

66. Literally "with labor."
67. Or "read." See note *ad loc.*
68. Or "were deprived of it."
69. I.e., in the sight of God. See note *ad loc.*
70. See note *ad loc.*
71. See note *ad loc.*

Notes

(A brief explanatory section is prefixed to each chapter as a guide to the thought of the epistle.)

On the title of the epistle, see above, pp. 5–6.

Chapter 1

Diognetus, eager to be informed about the religion of the Christians, makes three pointed inquiries. The first of these, however, involves three dependent questions, which, though stated affirmatively, are virtually interrogative. The series, which we repeat here (see above, pp. 5–6) for convenience, is as follows:

1. Who is the God the Christians trust in, and what is the nature of the worship they offer him, that they are all led to (*a*) disregard the world and despise death, (*b*) deny those to be gods whom the Greeks consider as such, (*c*) refrain from the superstition of the Jews?

2. What kind of affection is this that the Christians have for one another?

3. Why has this new race or practice entered the world now and not formerly?

The author approves Diognetus's zeal and asks God's favor for both speaker and hearer.

How far these questions represent precise queries made by an inquirer is uncertain. As Geffcken remarks,[1] a demand to set forth the nature of the Christian God was general among the heathen. See Theophilus, *Autol.* 1.2; Origen, *C. Cels.* 6.66. We may suppose that the questions reflect some of the main issues raised in the mind of cultured pagans. The author's apologetic

---

1. Geffcken, *Diognetus*, 12.

aim may account for their particular form; it certainly determines the order of their treatment. He discusses first both pagan and Jewish worship, so as to bring out in sharp relief the religion of the Christians which he desires to commend. The major part of Question 1 is dealt with by implication in the discussion of 1(b) and 1(c) in chs. 2–4, and more directly in chs. 7ff. See also the note on 10:7. Question 2 is answered generally in the exposition of the Christian manner of life (5–6); it is significantly amended in the statements that "they love all men" (5:11), even their enemies (6:6). Question 3 falls into ch. 8 and particularly within 8:7–9.

Ἐπειδὴ ὁρῶ κτλ. The writer begins in the conventional manner by complimenting his addressee. Cf. the Letter of Aristeas addressed to Philocrates: "I know that you have a mind in love with learning" (1; cf. 5; 322). Similarly, Josephus, *Ant.* 1.8, acknowledges the literary stimulus that he received from Epaphroditus, "a man who is a lover of every kind of learning." Melito writing to "his brother Onesimus" speaks in the same vein (Eusebius, *Hist. eccl.* 4.26).

The causal clause (ἐπειδὴ ... αὐτῶν), amplified by the intervening words τίνι ... πρότερον, leads up to the main sentence (ἀποδέχομαί κτλ.). Note the similar structural opening of Melito's letter (Eusebius, *Hist. eccl.* 4.26), and cf. Theophilus, *Autol.* 2.1, ἐπειδὴ ... ἐγένετο λόγος ἡμῖν ... περὶ τῆς θεοσεβείας μου ἐξεθέμην σοι.

κράτιστε Διόγνητε. The semi-technical term κράτιστος, denoting status rather than moral character, is commonly used in the inscriptions and papyri in addressing men of high official position. Cf. Acts 23:26; 24:3; 26:25. As a polite form of address it was employed sometimes without special regard to the rank of the addressee. For this more personal and even intimate nuance, cf. Dion. Hal. *Ant. or.*, proem.: ὦ κράτιστε Ἀμμαῖε. Nothing is known of Diognetus's rank or identity (assuming that a real person and not a literary fiction is intended). The name was not uncommon. See the evidence assembled by Otto.[2] The view of Stelkens and Kihn that it is a mere appellative (= "born of Zeus") and that it referred to the emperor Hadrian is very improbable. Nor is the suggestion (Ceillier, Otto, Dräseke, Molland) that Diognetus may be identical with one of the tutors of Marcus Aurelius (cf. 1:6) more than conjecture. Renan thinks that the tutor was not sufficiently famous to be the addressee, whom he holds to be "undoubtedly a fictional character."[3] The epistle itself does not lend us the aid of any personal touches (as, e.g., Josephus, *C. Ap.* 2.1: τιμιώτατέ μοι Ἐπαφρόδιτε), since the name does not recur. We may surmise that Diognetus was a pagan of high but not necessarily official status, who was interested in the Christian religion and

---

2. Otto, *Epistola ad Diognetum*, 2nd ed., 21–22.
3. Renan, *Marc-Aurèle*, 424.

evidently had some knowledge of Jewish worship. The κράτιστε Θεόφιλε of Luke 1:3 is a parallel to this personal sense of the title.[4]

The author while respectful is no less candid; Diognetus must shed all prejudice and use his intelligence (2:1)!

On the custom of dedicating books to individuals, see p. 8.

ὑπερεσπουδακότα. Idiomatic participle (cf. πυνθανόμενον) after a verb of perception (ὁρῶ). Cf. 7:8 (πλεονάζοντας). For the infinitive (μαθεῖν) cf. Menander, Sam. 4 ὑπερεσπουδακὼς τὰ τοῦ γάμου πράττειν, Josephus, Ant. 15.69 ὑπερεσπουδακὼς . . . ἐπιδεῖξαι. Beurer's copy read ὡς ὑπερεσπουδακότα.[5]

τὴν θεοσέβειαν. This classical word and the late cognate verb are favorite terms of the author (3:1 al.). Cf. Sir 1:25; 1 Tim 2:10 (here only in the NT). It is common in the apologists to denote the distinctive "religion" of the Christians, which, according to Diogn. 6:4, is invisible, being a μυστήριον not learned from man (4:6; 5:3). On the name Χριστιανοί, see Cadbury.[6]

πάνυ. Goes with both adverbs, as in 2 Macc 12:43. Note the effective change from the perfect participle (ὑπερεσπουδακότα) to the present (πυνθανόμενον) "are exceedingly zealous" (existing state) . . . "are making inquiry" (action in progress). Cf. πεποιθότες . . . θρησκεύοντες (below). For πυνθάνομαι περί, cf. Esth 6:4; Acts 23:20; P.Oxy. VI, 930 (2–3 CE) πυθέσθαι περὶ τῆς ὑγίας σου.

τίνι . . . πεποιθότες. The usual constructions in the Greek Bible are πέποιθα ἐπὶ τὸν θεόν (or τῷ θεῷ) or ἐν κυρίῳ. For the simple dative (of person), cf. Sir 32:24; 2 Cor 10:7.

Θρησκεύοντες αὐτὸν τον τε κόσμον. So Lachmann, Bunsen, and others. αὐτὸν κόσμον τε (Krenkel), αὐτόν τε κόσμον (others). Stephanus conjectures αὐτόν τε τὸν κόσμον. In the Greek Bible θρησκεύω is confined to Wisdom (11:15; 14:17), both passages in a derogatory setting. Similarly, θρησκεία (cf. Wis 14:18, 27, of the worship of idols) is not commonly used of Christians. Note, however, Jas 1:26f. (see Mayor's note) and Clem. Hom. 7.8: ἡ ὑπὸ θεοῦ ὁρισθεῖσα θρησκεία. The terms usually denote the ritual and external aspect of worship.[7] For κόσμος, see the note on 6:1.

ὑπερορῶσι. "They disregard," "make light of." Cf. 2 Macc 7:11, 23. In the NT only in Acts 17:30 in the extended sense ("overlook"). The meaning is that in virtue of their faith (πεποιθότες) and cultus (θρησκεύοντες) they are led to condemn the world and despise death, etc. The Christians' disregard of death would contrast the more strikingly with the wide and deep-seated

---

4. See Meyer, Ursprung und Anfänge, 1:6; Cadbury in Beginnings, 2:505ff.
5. See Otto, Epistola ad Diognetum, 2nd ed., 158–59.
6. Cadbury, Beginnings, 2:383ff.
7. Cf. 2:8; 3:2; and see Hatch, Essays, 55ff.; Trench, Synonyms, §xlviii.

fear of death which pervaded the ancient world.[8] Early Christian writers base the Christian contempt of death on various grounds. "Those with Peter" are led to defiance of death by their contact with the revivified flesh of Jesus (Ignatius, *Smyrn.* 3). For Justin Martyr it lies in the expectation of a divine future kingdom and in the fact that death is inevitable (*1 Apol.* 11–12, 39, 59; *2 Apol.* 11–12). Cf. also *Acts of Apollonius* §25–28. Marcus Aurelius (11.3) attributes the Christians' scorn of death to their irrational obstinacy, while Lucian of Samosata (*The Passing of Peregrinus* 13) bases it on their conviction that they are immortal for all time. For our author it is explained by the divine presence (παρουσία) that sustains the martyr (7:7–9), and the transcendence of the "apparent" death of this world by knowledge of "the true life of heaven" (10:7). So also the Christians' slighting of the world (cf. 1 John 2:15ff.; 5:19) is familiar in the literature of the period. Cf. the parallel in Justin Martyr, *Dial.* 119: μέχρι τοῦ ἀποθνήσκειν πᾶσι τοῖς ἐν τῷ κόσμῳ ἀπεταξάμεθα.[9]

οὔτε ... φυλάσσουσι. Cf. Eusebius, *Dem. Ev.* 1.6.62–63, who speaks of a third division (i.e., Christians) which "as it has escaped Greek godlessness ... so it has left behind Jewish unprofitable observances," etc. For the Christian refusal to acknowledge heathen gods see below (2:6, 10). The heathen turned the tables on the Christians by charging them with "atheism," an inference drawn from the fact that the Christians neither set up images nor offered sacrifice. For Christian replies to the charge, see Justin Martyr, *1 Apol.* 6 and 13; Athenagoras, *Suppl.* 4; Tertullian, *Apol.* 24.

τοὺς νομιζομένους ... θεούς. For the common classical νομίζειν θεούς (Xen., *Mem.* 1.1 *al.*), cf. 2:1; Wis 13:2. τῶν Ἑλλήνων, i.e., the gentiles. So also 5:17. For this sense of the term, cf. Acts 14:1; Gal 3:28. See notes by Lightfoot on Col 3:11 and Swete on Mark 7:26. The article occurs here and in 3:3, but not in 5:17. Ἰουδαίων generally without the article as a collective term. Cf. 3:1, 2; 4:6; Acts 25:10; 26:2, and frequently in the Pauline Epistles. So with Χριστιανοί (2:6, 10; 4:6 *al.*).

δεισιδαιμονίαν. *Per se* the term is morally neutral. Cf. Acts 25:19 (of the Jews). Most modern translators incline to the good sense (cf. Josephus, *Ant.* 10.42) in Acts 17:22 (adj.), as against the Revised Version, Field,[10] Hatch.[11] Here the sense is derogatory as appears from 4:1 ("superstition about the Sabbath").[12]

---

8. See Bevan, *Hellenism and Christianity*, 81–82.
9. Cited in Otto, *Epistola ad Diognetum*, 2nd ed., 159.
10. Field, *Notes*, 125ff.
11. Hatch, *Essays*, 43ff.
12. See notes in Gildersleeve, *Apologies*, 238–39; Lake and Cadbury, *Beginnings*,

φυλάσσουσι. "They keep," "observe." For the active in this sense, see John 12:47. In the LXX and NT we find both in the middle (Mark 10:20) and active (Gen 26:5) voice with this meaning. See Blass-Debrunner § 316.1.

φιλοστοργίαν. Practically a κοινή word, being first found in Xen., *Cyr.* 1.4.3. It is appropriately used of strong *family* love (4 Macc 15:6, 9) and so here of Christians as a family. Cf. Rom 12:10 (adj.). Diodorus Siculus 4.44.1 defines it as ἡ φυσικὴ τῶν γονέων εἰς τέκνα φιλοστορφία. Minucius Felix includes among charges made against Christians that "they love one another after the briefest acquaintance" (*Oct.* 9.2). It is interesting to see how our author turns this particular query of Diognetus by asserting the love of Christians for *all* men, even enemies (5:11; 6:6).

καινὸν ... ἐπιτήδευμα. γένος either "kind" (Wis 19:21; Matt 13:47; and often in the papyri), or, more probably, "race" (1 Pet 2:9). ἐπιτήδευμα "practice," "mode of life," frequent in the LXX (Ezek 20:44 *al.*).

For Christians as a new γένος (cf. καινὸς ἄνθρωπος, 2:1) see chs. 5 and 9, where its character is set forth. See also Origen, *C. Cels.* 1.26 and the references in Otto's note.[13] Add Aristides, *Apol.* 16.4 (Syr.), "truly this people (i.e., Christians) is a new people," Arnobius, *Adv. Gent.* 2.69, "but our name is new (we are told), and the religion which we follow arose but a few days ago." The heathen found it difficult to place the Christians and their novel faith. Harnack has pointed out that Diognetus's classification into three peoples (Jews, Greeks, Christians) goes back to the threefold division of *worshipers* in John 4:21–22.[14] This classification is taken up in the Preaching of Peter (in Clement of Alexandria, *Strom.* 6.5.39 and 41), which asserts that Christians are a new or third γένος "a new covenant he has made with us, for that of the Greeks and Jews is old, but you worship him anew in the third manner are Christians," i.e., of the three classes Christianity is the new or third genus of worship. Diognetus takes the further step and separates into three *peoples*. The threefold classification lends some support to the Greek text of Aristides, *Apol.* 2, which Geffcken[15] and F. C. Burkitt[16] accept as original. The Syriac and Armenian versions of Aristides have a fourfold division (Barbarians, Greeks, Jews, Christians). The idea may derive ultimately from 1 Pet 2:9f. Cf. also 1 Cor 10:32 (Jews, Greeks, the Church of God).

4:214f., 311; Blakeney, *Diognetus*, 32; Moulton and Howard, *Grammar*, 291.

13. Otto, *Epistola ad Diognetum*, 2nd ed., 160.
14. Harnack, *Expansion*, 1:247ff.
15. Geffcken, *Apologeten*, 46.
16. Burkitt, "Pagan Philosophy in the Christian Church," 464n1.

τὸν βίον. Used apparently in the late sense "world" (of men). Cf. Philo, *Post.* 2, and (probably) Wis 10:8; 14:21. Cf. 4 Macc 17:14: ὁ τῶν ἀνθρώπων βίος ἐθεώρει. In Diogn. 5:2 ("manner of life"); 5:4 ("livelihood").

νῦν καὶ οὐ πρότερον. For the question why Christianity had not appeared earlier, see Origen, *C. Cels.* 4.7: "after so long a period of time, then, did God now think himself of making men live righteous lives, but neglect to do so before? To which we answer that there never was a time when God did not wish to make men live righteous lives." Cf. also 6.78. Arnobius, *Adv. Gent.* 2.75, dealing with the question "why was the Savior sent forth so late?" argues that there are fitting seasons for the relief of particular moral conditions and that God judged the period when he sent forth Christ to be proper to man's need at that time.

ἀποδέχομαι with accusative of person and genitive of source, after the pattern of θαυμάζω τινά τινος (*Thuc.* 6.36). Cf. P. Oxy IV, 705[59] ἀποδεχόμεθα σε ταύτης τῆς ἐπιδόσεως. Gildersleeve calls attention to the respectful tone of the word here and in Acts 24:3. The commendation of the "hearer" is conventional. Cf. Cyprian, *Don.* 1: "a listener, too, with an eagerness proportioned to your affection." For the MS reading γε Bunsen, Scheibe, and others conjecture τε. The two particles are often interchanged by the scribes. See Otto on Justin Martyr, *1 Apol.* 4n1.

παρὰ τοῦ θεοῦ ... αἰτοῦμαι. Puech thinks that this is a recollection, probably conscious, of the traditional formula by which ancient Attic writers won the goodwill of their hearers.[17] Otto points out the similar prayer at the beginning of the *Cohort. Ad Gent.*, where, he thinks, the author imitates the exordium of Demosthenes, *De Corona*.[18] Prayer at the beginning of an oration was not unusual among the ancients. Cf. the opening of Lycurgus's speech against Leocrates. The formula may well have been adapted to their own use by Christian writers. See the note on p. 33. The middle (αἰτοῦμαι) perhaps emphasizes the earnestness of the action.[19]

χορηγοῦντος. Frequent of divine "supply," as in 3:4. Cf. Sir 1:26; 2 Cor 9:10.[20]

ἂν ἀκούσαντά σε. So Bunsen, Gildersleeve, Lake, and others, against the MS. ἂν ἀκοῦσαί σε. The participle is clearly to be preferred, to correspond to εἰπόντα, just as εἰπεῖν and ἀκοῦσαι answer to each other. We then have εἰπεῖν and τὸν εἰπόντα (of the writer) in antithesis to ἀκούσαντα and ἀκοῦσαι (of Diognetus). Otto and other editions prefer to read τὸν ἀκούσαντα, substituting

---

17. Puech, *Histoire*, 253.
18. Otto, *Epistola ad Diognetum*, 2nd ed., 160.
19. See Mayor on Jas 4:3–4, Moulton, *Grammar*, 1:160–61.
20. See note in Blakeney, *Diognetus*, 34.

the article for ἄν and the participle for ἀκοῦσαί σε, thus securing a complete correspondence (τὸν ἀκούσαντα ... τὸν εἰπόντα). Scheibe follows Otto but would retain ἄν, connecting it with γένεσθαι to denote the future.

βελτίω = βελτίονα (acc. masc. sing.). Cf. βελτίω γεγονότα (Plato, *Gorgias* 514E).

σοί τε. Against Stephanus's conjecture δέ (balancing ἐμοὶ μέν) Otto cites passages where a τε (or καί) balances a μέν. On the other hand, our author regularly employs the familiar antithesis μὲν ... δέ (2:2; 3:5 *al.*).

The implication of the prayer ("I ask of God," etc.) is that man, apart from divine aid, is unable to speak about God (cf. 4:6 *sub fin.*). We may compare the probable interpretation of the Greek text of the *Apology of Aristides* (2 *init.*) τούτων οὕτως εἰρημένων περὶ θεοῦ, καθὼς ἐμὲ ἐχώρησε περὶ αὐτοῦ λέγειν.

For the twofold division into speaker and hearer and prayer offered on behalf of both, cf. Hippolytus, *Anti*. 2 (*sub fin.*) "since, then, in this there is a work assigned to both parties together, namely to him who speaks, that he speak forth faithfully without regard to risk, and to him who hears, that he hear and receive in faith that which is spoken, I beseech you to strive together with me in prayer to God" (S. D. F. Salmond's trans.).

Chapter 2

Pagan idolatry and Jewish superstition must alike be dismissed before the faith and practice of the Christians is expounded. See above, pp. 30–31. Polemics against idol-worship are abundant in both Jewish and Christian literature (see references on pp. 30–31). Our author follows the conventional mode of attack. He has little or nothing fresh to say, but says it with some warmth and severity in a series of rhetorical questions. What impresses his mind is not so much the wickedness of idolatry as its absurdity (cf. 3:3).

1. ἄγε δή. Interjectional, as often in Homer. Cf. Judg 19:6 B (ἀρξάμενος A) and ἄγε νῦν (Jas 4:13; 5:1).

καθάρας κτλ. The language is perhaps reminiscent of Eph 4:22–24 (note καινὸς ἄνθρωπος, the influence of ἀπάτη, and ἐξ ἀρχῆς which may be a terse way of expressing the idea of man's original endowment κατὰ θεόν stated in Eph 4:24. Cf. Paul's καινὴ κτίσις [2 Cor 5:17; Gal 6:15]). Geffcken cites Clement of Alexandria, *Protr*. p. 10, 8ff (Stählin) σὺ δὲ εἰ ποθεῖς ἰδεῖν ὡς ἀληθῶς τὸν θεόν, καθαρσίων μεταλάμβανε θεοπρεπῶν. ... Note Attic καθαίρω, not Hellenistic καθαρίζω. καθαίρω in the LXX (3) and NT (1 simplex and 3 in compound form).

λογισμῶν. In classical usage the word has a morally neutral sense, "reasoning." So 2:9 (sing.). The present context favors the bad sense frequently found in Hellenistic Greek (cf. Wis 1:3, 5; 11:15; 2 Cor 10:4).

ἀπατῶσάν. The simple verb is infrequent in later Greek. But see Gen 3:13 *al.*, Eph 5:6.[21]

συνήθειαν. The term may refer to pagan "custom" in general. But in view of the following polemic it probably relates to the "habit" of idol-worship. συνήθεια is frequent in Clement of Alexandria, *Protr.* in this sense (see pp. 61–62). Cf. 1 Cor 8:7 for a similar connection. In the LXX the term is confined to 4 Maccabees (*four times*). Diognetus must free himself alike from general preconceptions (λογισμῶν) and a particular habit (συνήθειαν).

ἀποσκευασάμενος. A vivid figurative use, "having packed off" (of baggage). It is perhaps the author's equivalent of Paul's ἀποθέσθαι, if he has the Ephesian passage (4:22) in mind. Cf. Polyb. 2.26.2, ταῦτα δ' ἀποσκευασαμένους, "having got rid of these encumbrances," Athenagoras, *Suppl.* 9, ὅπως μετὰ τοῦ προσήκοντος λογισμοῦ τὴν καθ' ἡμᾶς ἐπήρειαν ἀποσκευάσησθε. A late word used literally in the Greek Bible (only in Lev 14:36 *act.*, and Acts 21:15 *variant*). See Ditt., *Syll.* 3rd ed., 588.50; 633.65.

ἐξ ἀρχῆς. Cf. 8:11 (in 11:4 ἀπ' ἀρχῆς). For the Greek Bible cf. Sir 15:14; John 6:64, ἀπ' ἀρχῆς being much more frequent.

ὡς ἂν ... ἐσόμενος. A rare construction. See Gildersleeve's note,[22] and add P. Par. 26 (163–62 BCE): ὑπέδειξαν ὡς ἂν εὐτακτηθησομένων ἡμῖν τῶν καθηκόντων.[23] For ὡς ἄν, with present participle, cf. 2 Macc 1:11; 12:4.

λόγου καινοῦ. For the significance of the epithet "new" ("a new race," "a new man," "a new story"), see p. 99. Cf. Clement of Alexandria, *Paed.* 1.5.20: χρὴ γὰρ εἶναι καινοὺς λόγου καινοῦ μετειληφότας. The author's use of the term λόγος reflects its elasticity of meaning. (1) "story," "narrative" (2:1); (2) "statement," "argument" (4:1; 8:2, 3); (3) "word," "teaching" (7:2; 12:7); (4) "reason" (10:2); (5) "the Word" (11:2, 3, 7; 12:9).

καθάπερ. Cf. 3:3; 7:2. "Thoroughly Attic and a slight literary touch."[24] Cf. Gen 12:4. In NT 17 times, all in Paul (Rom 4:6 *al.*) except Heb 4:2. The καί strengthens the correspondence indicated by καθάπερ (cf. 2 Cor 1:14).

ὡμολόγησας, i.e., implicitly in Diognetus's third question about the "new race or practice" (1:1).

ἴδε. The zeugma (ἴδε relating to both ὀφθαλμοῖς and φρονήσει) is natural. Cf. "the mind's eye." ἴδε has its imperatival force here (cf. Isa 69:18; Rom

---

21. See Moulton and Milligan, *Vocabulary*, 54.
22. Gildersleeve, *Apologies*, 240–41.
23. Cited in Milligan, *Selections*, 14–15.
24. See Robertson, *Grammar*, 967.

11:22), though frequently it is stereotyped into an interjection (cf. Mark 15:35). Cf. ἄγε (2:1). For the accent on ἴδε see p. 12.

ὑποστάσεως, "substance" or "real nature" (cf. Heb 1:3 RV), as opposed to "form" (εἴδους). It is practically synonymous here with ὕλη (2:3), which in Aristotle is often contrasted with εἶδος. Note μορφή (2:3). For the εἶδος of divine beings cf. Isa 53:2–3; John 5:37.

τυγχάνουσιν. Absolute use, practically equivalent to εἰσίν. Cf. 5:8; Xen., *Anab.* 3.1, 3; Tob 5:14; P.Oxy. VII, 1070[18] (3rd c. CE) σὺ αὐτὴ μήτηρ τυγχάνουσα τοῦ τέκνου.

ἐρεῖτε. The use of the future here rather than the present (cf. the correlative νομίζετε) has led to various conjectures: αἱρεῖτε (Sylburg), αἰνεῖτε (Lachmann). But ἐρῶ sometimes bears in later usage (possibly earlier; cf. Aesch. *Eumen.* 45) a present sense. Cf. Athenaeus, *Deipn.* 400a. Note the transition to the plural ἐρεῖτε, νομίζετε. For the most part in addressing Diognetus the singular is used (1:1; 2:1; 3:1; etc.); but the plural occurs here and in 2:5–6, perhaps suggestive of Diognetus as a representative of the pagan world. This alternation of singular and plural occurs also in 11–12. Cf. 11:7 with 11:8 ὑμῖν, 12:1 with 12:7–8.

Otto points out that the "substance" (ὑπόστασις) is illustrated in the following section, "is not one stone . . . iron and fire" (2–3), and the "form" (εἶδος) in the words "have they not been forged . . . in process of decay" (3–4); then the words "whom you declare and esteem to be gods" are taken up in the phrases "these things . . . you worship" (5).

2. Now follows a series of rhetorical questions which imply an affirmative answer, the initial οὐκ controlling the correlative clauses which follow. For this stylistic feature, see p. 13.

ὁ μέν τις . . . ὁ δέ. The pleonastic τις in this locution is frequent in Xen. (*Cyrop.* 3.1.41 *al.*). See below, 8:2, οἱ μέν τινες . . . οἱ δ'. . . οἱ δ', with which cf. Justin Martyr, *Dial.* 35; οἱ μέν τινες καλούμενοι Μαρκιανοί, οἱ δὲ Οὐαλεντινιανοί κτλ.

κρείσσων. On the spelling, see p. 11.

τῶν . . . κεχαλκευμένων σκευῶν. Genitive of comparison. Cf. τοῦ κατεσκευασμένου (below). The phrase is amplified in 3 (ὑπὸ σιδήρου . . . κεχαλκευμένα). Note in this and the following section the perfect participles of existing state. For εἰς τὴν χρῆσιν ἡμῖν cf. 4:2.

σεσηπός. In the passive sense, "rotted." Cf. Job 16:7, and for the metaphorical usage Jas 5:2 (of wealth). Note σηπόμενα (2:4), and for the habit of style, see p. 14.

ὁ δὲ ἄργυρος . . . κλαπῇ. Again the thought is repeated in §7 (*sub fin.*). The idea of gods being stolen is frequent. Cf. the Epistle of Jeremiah 57ff.; Aristides, *Apol.* 3.2; *Clement Recognitions* 5.15 (cited under 2:7 below).

For τοῦ φυλάξαντος (so the MS and some editions) Stephanus prefers to read τοῦ φυλάξοντος, the future participle expressing purpose (cf. Acts 8:27 al.). So also Otto and Geffcken. The aorist participle may indeed be used in Hellenistic Greek in a futuristic or purposive sense.[25] The present occurrence, however, is not parallel to the usage illustrated there, since the aorist participle here is not conjoined with a main finite verb (of motion or appointment). If the *aorist* participle is to be read here, it may reflect its timeless use. Cf. Gen 4:15; John 16:2 (πᾶς ὁ ἀποκτείνας). But the change to the *future* participle is very slight.

The article marks the attributive character of the participial clause. Cf. 1 Pet 1:7 (χρυσίου τοῦ ἀπολλυμένου).

ὑπὸ ἰοῦ, the "rust" being viewed as an inanimate agent. Cf. ὑπὸ σιδήρου καὶ πυρός (2:3). Cf. Xen., *Anab.* 1.5.5; Matt 11:7. For ἰός = "rust," cf. Jas 5:3.

οὐδὲν ... εὐπρεπέστερον. The passage shows some verbal similarity to Wis 13:11b. πρός is a stylistic variation of εἰς (εἰς τὴν χρῆσιν) above. Cf. Paul's "a vessel unto honor, and another unto dishonor" (ἀτιμία, Rom 9:21), and 2 Tim 2:20.

3-4. These "gods" of perishable material were molded by men, to whom they owe their particular shapes. The implication is that to worship such gods is to honor the created thing rather than its creator (cf. Rom 1:25). Aristides, *Apol.* 3, makes the point openly: "he who creates is greater than that which is created." So also Athenagoras, *Suppl.* 16: "how can I call those objects gods of which I know the makers to be men?"

οὐ φθαρτῆς ... τάντα; cf. 2:4: οὐ πάντα φθειρόμενα; see note on style, p. 13.

ὃ μὲν ... ὃ δέ. There is no need to write ὁ μὲν ... ὁ δέ, as Funk. The use in these correlative clauses of the relative with demonstrative force is common in prose after Demosthenes. See 4:2, 5; Polyb. 1.7.3; Matt 21:35, etc.

λιθοξόος, "sculptor." Late word. Cf. Plut., *Mor.* 74E, and inscriptions. For ἀργυροκόπος "silversmith," cf. Plut., *Mor.* 830E: χρυσοχόους καὶ ἀργυροκόπους, Jer 6:29; Acts 19:24.

The list of the four artificers answers to four of the six materials specified in §2, ξύλον and σίδηρος being left without their corresponding craftsmen. But, as Otto acutely observes, they are covered by the phrase ὑπὸ σιδήρου καὶ πυρός, "since wood needs the service of iron implements (e.g., the axe) and iron needs that of fire."

ἔπλασεν. The verb goes with all four subjects though more appropriately with κεραμεύς (cf. Wis 15:7). It is used of God, below (10:2).

---

25. See articles by Chambers, "Aorist," and Howard, "Futuristic Use."

οὐ πρὶν ἤ κτλ. For the thought see Epistle of Jeremiah 45. πρὶν ἤ (cf. πρίν, 8:1) is only occasional in Attic prose, though frequent in Herodotus and common in late Greek. Cf. Exod 1:19; Matt 1:18; Justin Martyr, *1 Apol.* 23, 30. The infinitive here with πρίν (after the negative principal sentence) may be explained by the facts that (1) the initial οὐ postulates an *affirmative* answer to the question, making the sentence virtually positive, (2) the πρὶν ἤ clause precedes the main sentence, suggesting that the temporal ideal ("before") is dominant in the writer's mind (cf. Mark 14:30).

τούτων (the artificers) ... τούτων (the gods). Lightfoot and Geffcken (after Böhl) emend the latter pronoun to ταύτην.

ἦν ἕκαστον ... μεταμεμορφωμένον; the text is corrupt and difficult. See translation above. ἕκαστον is read by most editions for the MS. ἕκαστος. For ἔτι καὶ νῦν Lachmann substitutes εἰκάζειν, which Bunsen accepts. So also Lightfoot, getting the general sense "made to resemble these several utensils." Geffcken suggests ὅ, τι, καὶ νῦν. Gildersleeve with some reserve inserts ὡς before ἔτι καὶ νῦν, "as still happens." The drift of the passage is clear, namely, that these "gods" owe their form to the caprice of the craftsman. He first roughly shaped his material and then formed it into an idol, although he was free (and is so now) to mold it into any form that he desired. Accordingly, the same material which now serves to make vessels of ordinary use could be shaped by the craftsman into a "god." Cf. Horace, *Satires* 1:8 (*ad init.*).

ἑκάστῳ, dative of agent ("by each artificer") after the perfect participle passive (μεταμεμορφωμένον). For μεταμορφόω, cf. Rom 12:2.

τὰ νῦν. The following sentence τὰ νῦν ... προσκυνούμενα suggests that νῦν here goes with ὄντα rather than with γένοιτ' ἄν.

For γένοιτ' ἄν (potential optative), cf. δύναιτ' ἄν (4). See p. 12.

τοιούτοις, i.e., the objects fashioned into the shape of gods. Cf. 2:10.

4. Conversely it would surely be possible for these "gods" now worshiped by you to be converted by the craftsmen into such vessels.

ὑμῶν. So Stephanus for the MS. ἡμῶν.

κωφά. The word means both "dumb" and "deaf." Cf. 3:3, 5. The "dumbness" of idols is frequently remarked. Cf. Hab 2:18; 1 Cor 12:2; Sib. Or. 5.84, etc. So also their ἀναισθησία (cf. 3:3). Cf. Let. Aris. 135: "obviously the images lack feeling" (τὴν ἀναισθησίαν). For ἄψυχα, cf. Wis 13:17; 14:29.

Note the three adjectives in ἀ-privative. See p. 15.

5. It is difficult to decide whether the sentences of §§5–6 are affirmative or interrogative. Most editions and translators take the former view, Lake the latter. It is perhaps a point in favor of the affirmative rendering that all the rhetorical questions (§§2–4, 7) are put in the negative form. To think that you call such inanimate things gods and then serve and worship them!

It is the irrationality of idol-worship that impresses the author, but he goes on to point out its psychological effect, namely, that the worshiper becomes like the idol, void of feeling and liable to decay. Thus in a double sense he provides an ἀφροσύνης δεῖγμα (3:3), because he regards mere things without life and motion as gods, and thereby shares their nature.

Otto suggests that the thought of the worshiper's conformity to the idol goes back to Ps 115:8 (118:16 LXX; cf. 134:18). Funk compares *Clem. Recogn.* 5.15: "but I should like if those who worship idols would tell me if they wish to become like those whom they worship," etc. For our author as for the psalmist the "likeness" consists in mental rather than moral degradation. Idolatry leads to aesthetic failure, incapacity to perceive that the idol is nothing but a mere molded form. Cf. Clem. Alex., *Protr.* 4.48.3–4: "you exercise no care to guard against your becoming like images for stupidity" (δι' ἀναισθησίαν).

ταῦτα ... τούτοις ... τούτοις. The emphasis and reiteration are impressive. Cf. 2:9; 7:9. In Hellenistic Greek προσκυνέω takes either accusative or dative (Gen 24:26; John 4:23). τέλεον. An adverbial use found in late prose (Lucian, Clement of Alexandria, 3 Macc 1:22; papyri). Either "in the end" (so Lightfoot, Lake) or "completely" (= τελέως, thus Otto). Cf. Justin Martyr, *1 Apol.* 29 and 62. ἐξομοιοῦσθε (Herodotus, Plato). Cf. 2 Macc 4:16; Epictetus 1.2.18; Justin Martyr, *1 Apol.* 6.

6. διὰ τοῦτο ... ὅτι κτλ. The demonstrative is expanded by the ὅτι clause: "for this reason, namely," etc. Cf. Isa 24:6; John 5:16. For the hared of Christians see note on οὔτε ... φυλάσσουσι (1:1), and cf. 5:17; 6:5. For the omission of the article with Χριστιανούς see note (1:1).

7–8. You are deluding yourself. Your worship means not praise but contempt for the gods. For, to discriminate between your idol-gods, setting close guard over some but not others—this is not to worship but to ridicule and to insult them. And the gods themselves, if they have powers of perception, will not be deceived by your homage, but will feel aggrieved (κολάζετε) by such discrimination. If, on the other hand, they lack perception, by worshiping them with blood and steaming fat you are really showing them up (ἐλέγχοντες) for what they are, mere insensible idols. For a kindred view see Tertullian, *Apol.* 12.

ὑμεῖς ... οἰόμενοι. The text is uncertain. The MS reads οἱ νῦν νομίζοντες καὶ οἰόμενοι. Otto substitutes σεβόμενοι for οἰόμενοι. So also Lightfoot and Geffcken. Bunsen, following Lachmann, reads ὑμεῖς γὰρ αἰνεῖν (for οἱ νῦν) νομίζοντες καὶ σεβόμενοι. Gebhardt, Funk, and Lake similarly, with οἰόμενοι for σεβόμενοι.

πολὺ πλέον. Cf. 4:5. The comparison is implied, αὐτῶν (= the gods) being genitive after καταφρονεῖτε. Cf. 4 Macc 1:8. So πολὺ μᾶλλον (below).

Cf. Heb 12:9. The alternative, to take αὐτῶν as genitive after πλέον and refer it to the Christians (so Radford and Blakeney), would leave both αἰνεῖν and καταφρονεῖτε without an object expressed, and is less likely. For πλέον see p. 10.

σέβοντες. The active form (cf. 3:2) is rarer in prose than the middle. But cf. Xen., *Mem.* 4.4.19 and 4 Macc 5:24; P.Oxy. XII, 1464⁵ (250 CE) σέβειν θεοῖς.

Stephanus emends ἀφυλάκτως (so MS and Haus's copy) to ἀφυλάκτους.

ἀργυρέους. Otto and other editions prefer the contracted form ἀργυροῦς (cf. the following χρυσοῦς). Note the addition of gold, not mentioned among the "gods" in §2. ἐγκλείοντες. Cf. 6:7 (of the soul "locked up" in the body), 7:2 (of the "enclosing" of the sea).

παρακαθιστάντες. The foregoing present participle (ἐγκλείοντες) favors this emendation (Krenkel) of the MS reading παρακαθίσαντες. For φύλακας καθιστάναι cf. Justin Martyr, *1 Apol.* 9.

Clementine Recognitions 5.15 remarks in similar fashion that men guard gods of silver and gold "and even of brass," but leave those of stone and earthenware unguarded since none would steal such.

8. αἷς . . . αὐτούς. Geffcken thinks that this is the only thought in the author's diatribe against idolatry which, "so far as I know," is not otherwise known from literature.[26] τιμαῖς, i.e., sacrificial offerings (3:5). προσφέρειν is frequent in the LXX and Epistle to Hebrews (20 times) for the "offering" of sacrifices. εἰ μὲν αἰσθάνονται. The author has already denied the sensibility of these gods (2:4). But here he grants the hypothesis for the sake of his argument.

κολάζετε. The verb may have the weaker meaning, "harm," "wrong." Cf. κόλασις (9). The passive has this sense in Aelian, *N.A.* 3.24: ἀπαλά τε ὄντα τὰ νεόττια . . . οἶδε καλῶς . . . ὅτι κολασθήσεται ἀλγοῦντα. It occurs later in Diognetus in the stronger sense of the "punishment" of Christians in persecutions (5:16; 6:9; 7:8; 10:7). Cf. Mart. Poly. 2.4.

ἀναισθητοῦσιν. For the "insensibility" of idols see Epistle of Jeremiah 19 and 23. ἐλέγχοντες . . . θρησκεύετε. The participle takes the main emphasis: "you are refuting them by the very fact of worshiping them" (= ἐλέγχετε . . . θρησκεύοντες), as in 2 Pet 1:16. ἐλέγχω may here have the sense "expose" "show them up" (for what they are). Cf. 2:9 (note), Xen., *Mem.* 1.7.2; Eph 5:11,[27] and papyri. For the slightly stronger nuance "convince," "convict," cf. 9:6. For θρησκεύετε see note (1:1).

---

26. Geffcken, *Diognetos*, 13, 14.
27. See the note by Abbott, *Ephesians*, on this verse.

αἵματι καὶ κνίσαις. Cf. 3:5. κνῖσα a Homeric word (κνίση). Cf. Sib. Or. 8.391: οὐ χρήζω . . . οὐ κνίσσης μιαρῆς, οὐχ αἵματος ἐχθίστοιο.

9. ταῦθ' . . . ταῦτα. Emphasis and repetition. "These things" are the sacrifices of blood and steaming fat, ironically referred to below as "this punishment." ὑμῶν τις, i.e., Diognetus and those who think with him.

ταύτης τῆς κολάσεως. See note above (ταῦτα). The accusative is more usual with ἀνέχομαι. For the genitive, cf. Plato, *Prot.* 323A; 2 Macc 9:12; 2 Tim 4:3. For λογισμόν, see note on 2:1.

ὁ δὲ λίθος. The "stone" is singled out as a familiar type of "those whom you declare and esteem to be gods." It stands first in the list (2:2).

ἀναισθητεῖ γάρ. The laconic sentence ending with γάρ recalls Mark 16:8 ἐφοβοῦντο γάρ). Brief sentences ending in γάρ are not without precedent in Greek literature. See the articles cited by R. H. Lightfoot who reports other instances from classical Greek prose, the papyri, Justin Martyr, and the Hermetic writings.[28] The present passage (Diogn. 2:9) may be added as typical of this locution: the γάρ ends a brief statement which gives the reason for what precedes. Note the *two* γάρ clauses here (the second of which shows the final γάρ), as in Mark 16:8, and also in Plato, *Prot.* 328C: τῶνδε δὲ οὔπω ἄξιον τοῦτο κατηγορεῖν. ἔτι γὰρ ἐν αὐτοῖς εἰσιν ἐλπίδες. νέοι γάρ.[29]

οὐκ οὖν . . . ἐλέγχετε. A cryptic sentence, the meaning depending on (*a*) the reading (οὐκ οὖν or οὐκοῦν), (*b*) the meaning of ἐλέγχω ("prove," or with negative sense "refute"), (*c*) the interpretation of the sentence as a statement or a question. The general sense of the passage is: no one would willingly endure such offerings (i.e., blood and fat) made to himself, because he has perception and reason. The fact that the stone endures such shows that it lacks sensibility. (1) You do not then (οὐκ οὖν) *by offering such sacrifices* show up its sensibility! No. Quite the contrary—an ironical comment. (2) Do you not then (οὐκ οὖν) refute its sensibility, i.e., prove that it has none (ἀναισθητεῖ)? (3) So then (οὐκοῦν) you refute its sensibility.

Of these renderings (1) is perhaps to be preferred since (*a*) it lends to ἐλέγχω the same sense as above (2:8), (*b*) a statement seems more natural in the context than a question, (*c*) the ironical touch is quite in the author's vein (see above, p. 15).

For various emendations of the sentence see Otto[30] and Gildersleeve.[31] αὐτοῦ *sc.* τοῦ λίθου.

---

28. R. H. Lightfoot, *Locality*, 1ff.
29. Cited by R. H. Lightfoot, *Locality*, 11.
30. Otto, *Epistola ad Diognetum*, 2nd ed., 167.
31. Gildersleeve, *Apologies*, 243.

10. For the thought, cf. Melito (in Routh, *Reliquiae Sacrae* 1:118) "we are not servants [θεραπευταί] of stones that have no feeling, but of God alone."

δεδουλῶσθαι, with the full force of the perfect, "to be in a state of bondage." For περὶ τοῦ, with the infinitive, cf. 3:1 and see p. 12. ἄν. So several editions, following Lachmann. The MS omits ἄν, Krenkel places it after ἔχοιμι. For the familiar ἔχω, with infinitive (= δύναμαι), cf. Heb 6:13, and 5:17 (below).

κἄν. This crasis is sometimes used in later Greek as an equivalent of intensive καί = "even." Cf. Mark 5:28; Acts 5:15.

περισσὸν ἡγοῦμαι. Cf. Wilcken: περισσὸν ἡγοῦμαι διεξοδέστερον ὑμῖν γράφειν (ca. 117 CE).[32] Cf. 2 Cor 9:1.

Chapter 3

The author turns now to the subject of Jewish worship raised in Diognetus's first question (1c). The Jews may rightly claim that they reverence the one true God. But in their ritual service they match the foolishness of the Greeks, who offer to "senseless and deaf images." For the Jews make their oblations on the assumption that God is in need of such offerings. But the Creator and Provider of all cannot himself stand in need of anything. Indeed, these very offerings are his gift to men. For both Greek and Jew it is absurd to consecrate such sacrifices, "for one seems to offer to those unable to partake of the honor, the other to him who is in need of nothing."

1. Ἑξῆς, "next" in order or sequence. In the NT always of time (Luke 9:37 *al.*) περὶ τοῦ ... θεοσεβεῖν. Cf. Preaching of Peter in Clem. Alex., *Strom.* 6.39ff: μηδὲ κατὰ Ἰουδαίους σέβεσθε. For κατὰ τὰ αὐτά, "after the same manner," cf. Let. Aris. 236; Luke 6:23, 26. For the omission of the article with Ἰουδαίοις, see p. 98, and for θεοσεβεῖν, see on θεοσέβεια (1:1).

αὐτούς, i.e., the Christians. The shortened form οἶμαι is common in Attic prose. For the accusative and infinitive construction cf. Gen 37:7; John 21:25; and papyri. In Jas 1:7 ὅτι ... For ποθεῖν with infinitive (aorist), cf. Barn. 16:10. The verb occurs below with the accusative (11:1) and in the passive (12:8).

2. λατρείας, (divine) "service." Cf. Plato, *Apol.* 23B; Exod 12:25; Rom 9:4. For its reference to the "service" of idol-gods as here, see Did. 6:3.

καλῶς ... φρονεῖ. The text is obscure. The various editorial reconstructions are fully set out in Otto's note.[33] We follow the reading suggested by

32. Wilcken, *Chrestomathie der Papyruskunde*, 238.II.4.

33. Otto, *Epistola ad Diognetum*, 2nd ed., 168–69. See also Gildersleeve, *Apologies*, 244.

Gebhardt and Hilgenfeld and adopted by Funk, Lightfoot, and Lake as least open to objection. Geffcken prints καὶ εἰ θεὸν ἕνα τῶν πάντων σέβειν καὶ δεσπότην ἀξιοῦσιν, ὀρθῶς δοκοῦσι φρονεῖν.

θεὸν ἕνα. Cf. 1 Cor 8:5–6. μόνος is very frequent in this connection (2 Macc 7:37; John 5:44, etc.).

τῶν πάντων. The universal sovereignty of God is a familiar idea in Jewish and Christian literature. Cf. ὁ πάντων δεσπότης, Job 5:8; Wis 6:7. Cf. 8:7 (below). Otto suggests that the author has also in mind the thought that God is God of all (Greek) gods, and cites Justin Martyr, *Dial.* 55; Deut 10:17; Ps 49:1. For σέβειν see note on 2:7, and for δεσπότης (of God) on 8:7.

ἀξιοῦσι with infinitive "think fit," "claim." Cf. 7:1; Acts 15:38; 28:22. In 9:1 (passive) "to deem worthy."

θησκείαν. See p. 98.

προσάγουσιν. The verb commonly connotes *sacrificial* "offering" in the LXX (Lev 3:12 *al*), but *moral* offering in Tob 12:12.

διαμαρτάνουσιν. Bunsen would read αὐτῷ, ταύτης διαμαρτάνουσιν "in this they go utterly astray." But for the absolute use of the verb, cf. Plato, *Theat.* 178A; Num 15:22; Herm. Mand. 4:1, 2; 1 Clem. 40:4.

The author does not charge the Jews with angel worship. See p. 36.

3. οἱ Ἕλληνες. See the note on p. 98.

ἀφροσύνης δεῖγμα. The phrase recurs in 4:5. παρέχουσι, a favorite word.

ταῦθ᾽ οὗτοι κτλ. Two renderings are possible according as παρέχειν is taken as epexegetic of λογιζόμενοι with ταῦθ᾽ as its object, or as infinitive with ἡγοῖντ᾽ ἂν having μωρίαν as object. (*a*) "These (the Jews) ought rather to consider it folly maybe, not piety, thinking that they are offering these things to God as though He were in need of them." (*b*) "These (the Jews) ought rather to consider that they are showing folly maybe not piety by crediting these things to God as though he were in need of them." It is better to adopt (*a*) since the infinitive seems more natural with the participle (cf. τοῖς οἰομένοις διδόναι, 3:4), and ἡγέομαι takes the direct object in 9:6.

For καθάπερ, see on 2:1.

προσδεομένῳ. Here of God (as in Plato, Aristotle, etc.[34]). In 3:4 it is used of God and man. The thought that God has need of nothing (ἀπροσδεής) is very frequent. Cf. 2 Macc 14:35; 3 Macc 9:2; Let. Aris. 211: "God is in need of nothing and is gentle"; Philo, *Deus* 57: "in addition to the fact of (God's) wanting nothing, he actually has everything." Cf. also Theophilus, *Autol.* 2.10; Tatian, *Or. Graec.* 4.[35]

---

34. See Bauer, *Wörterbuch*, 1188.

35. See Blakeney, *Diognetus*, 40–41.

μωρίαν. Possibly a stylistic variation of ἀφροσύνης (above). See 4:5, where ἀφροσύνη (like μωρία here) is predicated of the Jews and contrasted with θεοσέβεια. Herm. Sim. 9.22.2 has ἀφροσύνη μωρά. Both terms suggest moral as well as intellectual fault.

εἰκός. Some editions, following Stephanus, emend to εἰκότως or to εἶναι. Otto retains εἰκός and thinks that the word (= "perhaps") is so placed (*cum quadam urbanitate*) to moderate the notion of μωρία. In line with this suggestion we render "folly maybe." For θεοσέβειαν see p. 95.

4. ὁ γὰρ ... αὐτός. Note the omission here of the sea (cf. Exod 20:11; Ps 145:6; Acts 14:15; see below, pp. 52–53) among created objects. But cf. 7:2 (below). The thought may be reminiscent of Acts 14:15. The idea of God, however, as Creator and universal Provider and consequently as above all personal need is familiar. Cf. Justin Martyr, *1 Apol.* 10: "we have received by tradition that God does not need the material offerings which men can give, seeing that he himself is the Provider of all things." For χορηγῶν see p. 95.

ὧν. Antecedent omitted. In the next line the antecedent (τούτων) is supplied and the relative ὧν (= ἅ) is assimilated to it.

τοῖς οἰομένοις διδόναι. Perhaps an ironical touch. See above, p. 15. For the infinitive after οἴομαι, cf. 3:5; 1 Macc 5:61; Phil 1:17.

διδόναι, i.e., τῷ θεῷ.

αὐτός. Emphatic by position and repetition.

θυσίας ... ἐπιτελεῖν. Cf. Herodotus, *Hist.* 2.63. The verb is common in a ritual sense and setting. Cf. Lev 6:22 (15); 1 Esdr. 8:16; Heb 9:6; P. Tebt. 1.6.48 (140 BCE), ἐπιτελεῖν τὰ νομιζόμενα τοῖς θεοῖς.

Since the author is dealing now with Jewish sacrifices he adds "whole burnt offerings" (ὁλοκαυτωμάτων) to "blood and steaming fat" (2:8).

τιμαῖς, i.e., sacrificial offerings. Cf. 2:8 and 3:5 (τιμή).

γεραίρειν. Poetical word (Homer, Pindar), but found in Herodotus, Plato, and Xenophon. Cf. 3 Macc 5:17; Philo, *Sacr.* 117: ἀπαρχαῖς καὶ τιμαῖς γεραίρωμεν τὸ θεῖον.

ἐνδεικνυμένων (so Stephanus for the MS ἐνδεικνύμενοι), i.e., the Greeks.

φιλοτιμίαν. The noun along with its cognate adjective and verb originally connoted "emulation," "ambition." Cf. Wis 14:18. In later Greek generally the meaning develops into "zeal," as often in Polybius. Here we have the rarer sense "lavish honor," for which cf. Let. Aris. 227: πῶς τινα δεῖ φιλότιμον εἶναι ... φιλοτιμίαν δεῖν χαριστικὴν ἔχειν. Cf. also P.Oxy. VIII, 1153[16] (1st c. CE) ἐκ φιλοτιμίας αὐτοῦ κατηρτισμένα. Josephus, *Ant.* 10.25 has φιλοτιμία περὶ τὸν θεόν.

τῶν μὲν μὴ δυναμένοις κτλ. The text is corrupt. See Otto's full note. Stephanus reads τὰ μὴ δυνάμενα. So Gildersleeve. Geffcken follows Wilamowitz's reading τῶν μὲν τοῖς μὴ δυναμένοις. For further emendations, see Blakeney.[36] We adopt the text printed by Funk, Lightfoot, and Lake, following Gebhardt. For the grammatical construction of the sentence see p. 13.

Chapter 4

The author now particularizes his indictment of the Jews, and shows briefly the folly and impiety of their scruples concerning meats, the Sabbath, circumcision, fasting, and the new moon. These ritual observances are arbitrary and impugn the character of God. From all such error the Christians hold aloof. The secret of their religion is not learned from man.

1. We may compare Paul's list (Col 2:16), which varies the order, adds "drinking," but omits circumcision. Diognetus leaves out "drinks," perhaps because the Mosaic law was almost entirely concerned with meats. Only in a few special cases, e.g., of priestly ministration in the tabernacle (Lev 10:9) and of Nazarite vows (Num 6:3), were prohibitions laid down respecting drinks.

Ἀλλὰ μὴν τό γε κτλ. The particles mark the transition to another point (cf. Xen., *Mem.* 1.1.10).

τὰς βρώσεις. Literally "eatings," but here in the concrete sense "food." There was a tendency to identify the meaning of words ending in -μα and -σις. Cf. Let. Aris. 224, 229, where δόμα and δόσις are apparently used interchangeably. For βρῶσις = "food," cf. Thucydides 2.70; Gen 25:38; John 4:32; and the papyri.

ψοφοδεές, "qualms." "Skittishness," "shyness" (Gildersleeve). Cf. Plato, *Phaed.* 257D: εἰ αὐτὸν οὕτως ἡγεῖ τινα ψοφοδεᾶ, Plutarch, *Nic.* 2: τὸ δ' ἐν τῇ πολιτείᾳ ψοφοδεές.

τὰ σάββατα. Plural used of the single day. In the Greek Bible both plural and singular forms are found in the sense "the Sabbath." Cf. Josephus, *Ant.* 3.237: κατὰ δὲ ἑβδόμην ἡμέραν, ἥτις σάββατα καλεῖται.[37] Note ἡ τῶν σαββάτων ἡμέρα (4:3 below), for which cf. Exod 20:8; Acts 13:14 *al.* On δεισιδαιμονίαν see p. 98.

τῆς περιτομῆς, the rite (Gen 17:13; John 7:22 *al.*), or possibly here the state (Rom 3:1 *al.*) of circumcision.

ἀλαζονείαν . . . εἰρωνείαν. Cf. Aristotle, *Eth. nic.* 2.7.12, for the juxtaposition and see Cope's notes (*Aristotle's Rhetoric* 1.2 §7; 2.2 §24; 5 §11). ἀλαζονεία, "excessive self-assertion," implies both presumption and imposture. εἰρωνεία stands primarily for dissimulation and cunning. Cf. the Socratic εἰρωνεία, "mock" in conversation. Diognetus uses the terms of the

---

36. Blakeney, *Diognetus*, 42.
37. See Thackeray, *Grammar* 35; Swete, *Mark*, 17.

Jews to denote their empty vaunting (ἀλαζονεία) of circumcision and their "sham" or "sanctimoniousness" (εἰρωνεία) in respect of fasting and the new moon, with perhaps the implication, common to both terms, that such Jewish practices are "quackery" and "humbug." The notion of ἀλαζονεία is repeated in 4:6 (below) and in 4:4 (ἀλαζονεύομαι). For εἰρωνεία cf. 2 Macc 13:3. The Didache (8:1) has a stronger word: the Jews fast (and pray) as ὑποκριταί. Note the paronomasia ἀλαζονείαν, εἰρωνείαν . . . νηστείας, νουμηνίας.

νουμηνίας. Attic contracted spelling for νεομηίας. See p. 11. It refers to the Jewish monthly celebrations, as in Num 10:10; Col 2:16. See the similar condemnation of Jewish lunar observations in the Preaching of Peter (Clement of Alexandria, *Strom.* 6.5.39ff.), Aristides, *Apol.* 14 (Syr.).

οὐ νομίζω. The sense "need" for χρῄζειν (cf. 2:2) favors the insertion of οὐ made by Stephanus. The negative may easily have fallen out after λόγου. Otto, however, takes χρῄζειν = "desire," and follows the MS in omitting οὐ: "I think that you desire to learn," etc. But the brevity of treatment in the following sections (2–5), which relate, as Otto points out, to these four matters of food, Sabbath, circumcision, and lunar festivals respectively, rather supports the insertion of the negative: "I do not think that you need," etc. Jewish superstition may be summarily dismissed (ἀρκούντως σε νομίζω μεμαθηκέναι), since Diognetus's chief interest lies in the faith and worship of the Christians.

2. Now follows a series of rhetorical questions (πῶς οὐ κτλ) after the author's manner.

κτισθέντων. Of creation by God, as frequently (cf. 7:2; 8:2). Cf. Let. Aris. 185; Prov 8:22; Mark 13:19. We have ποιέω in 8:7; 10:2 (below), as in 3:4 (a citation); πλάσσω in 10:2.

εἰς χρῆσιν. Cf. 2:2.

ἃ μὲν . . . ἃ δ', "some" . . . "others." See note on 2:3 and cf. 4:5.

ὡς καλῶς κτισθέντα. Is this a possible reminiscence of the refrain (καὶ εἶδεν ὁ θεὸς ὅτι καλόν) in Gen 1:10, 12, 18 *al.*? Cf. 1 Tim 4:4: πᾶν κτίσμα θεοῦ καλόν.

παραιτεῖσθα (opp. παραδέχεσθαι). Cf. 6:10; 2 Macc 2:31; 1 Tim 4:7; 5:11; and papyri.[38] It bears here the strong sense "decline," "refuse."

πῶς οὐκ ἀθέμιστον. So Gebhardt for the MS reading πῶς οὐ θέμις ἐστί. For editorial emendations see Otto.[39] The Greek Bible, as the Koine generally, has the more correct prose form ἀθέμιτος (2 Macc 6:5; 1 Pet 4:3). The term is used here with reference to the Jewish code: "contrary to the Law" (which you Jews exalt). Cf. Acts 10:28.

---

38. Moulton and Milligan, *Vocabulary*, 484.
39. Otto, *Epistola ad Diognetum*, 2nd ed., 172.

3. τὸ δὲ καταψεύδεσθαι. Good classical word found once in the Greek Bible (Wis 1:11: στόμα καταψευδόμενον). Cf. Ignatius, *Trall.* 10: καταψεύδομαι τοῦ Κυρίου.

ὡς κωλύοντος. Of divine "restraint," as in 1 Kgs 25:26. For κωλύω with infinitive without article, cf. 1 Tim 4:3; P. Magd: 2 (221 BCE) Πόωρις κεκώλυκεν οἰκοδομεῖν. For the passive cf. 6:5 (below). ὡς with participle suggests the presumed reason.

For the thought see Mark 3:4 and the Synoptic parallels (Matt 12:12; Luke 6:9). With καλόν τι ποιεῖν, cf. the καλῶς ποιεῖν of Matt 12:12. See the discussion of the Sabbath in Barn. 15; Justin Martyr, *Dial.* 27; Tertullian, *Adv. Jud.* 4.

4. Circumcision, a ground of Jewish ἀλαζονεία, was regarded as a proof of special divine favor. Cf. Jub. 15:26f.: "and every one that is born, the flesh of whose foreskin is not circumcised on the eighth day, belongs not to the children of the covenant which the Lord made with Abraham, but to the children of destruction" (Charles's translation). Cf. Gen 17:13–14.

τὴν μείωσιν. Literally "the lessening," "contraction," the reference being to circumcision (4:1). In Polybius 9.43.5 of the "decrease" as opposed to the αὔξησις of the Euphrates. σάρξ here denotes the material part of a living being. See on 5:8; 6:5.

ἐκλογῆς. A common Attic word (Plato, Aristotle) found also in Polybius and papyri. It does not occur in the LXX (cf., however, Aquila Isa 22:7; Symmachus and Theodotion Isa 37:24), but is found seven times in the NT as a quasi-technical term, always of divine "choice" (Acts 9:15 *al.*). Cf. 1 Clem. 29:1, where Christians are styled ἐκλογῆς μέρος.

ἀλαζονεύεσθαι. Cf. ἀλαζονεία (4:1, 6). For the verb cf. Xen., *Mem.* 1.7.5; Wis 2:16. διὰ τοῦτο, i.e., because of their ἐκλογή.

ἐξαιρέτως. A late adverb (Plutarch, inscr.; papyri). Cf. Aquila Deut 32:12; Ign., *Smyrn.* 7:2.

ἠγαπημένους ὑπὸ θεοῦ. For the verb and noun (used of God) cf. 7:5; 9:2; 10:2, 3. Paul (Rom 11:28) finds the ground upon which the chosen people were "beloved" in the fact of their election (κατὰ δὲ τὴν ἐκλογήν). Earlier (1 Thess 1:4) he had applied the same thought (and language) to Christian brethren: εἰδότες, ἀδελφοὶ ἠγαπημένοι ὑπὸ (τοῦ) θεοῦ, τὴν ἐκλογὴν ὑμῶν.

For χλεύης ἄξιον cf. Philo, *Contempl.* 6: τοῦτό γε καὶ χλεύης ἄξιον. Cf. Philo, *Legat.* 71.

5. παρεδρεύοντας. Cf. Prov 1:21; 8:3; 1 Cor 9:13; Let. Aris. 81: τοῖς δὲ τεχνίταις παρήδρευεν ἐπιμελῶς, "he would attentively supervise the craftsmen."

Otto notes the chiasmus (for the figure cf. Gal 4:4–5):

ἄστροις καὶ σελήνῃ
μηνῶν καὶ ἡμερῶν

For the anarthrous ἄστροις καὶ σελήνῃ cf. 7:2. Terms denoting familiar natural phenomena may lack the article, being sufficiently definite in themselves. Cf. 4 Macc 17:5; 1 Cor 15:41; 1 Clem. 20:2ff.

τὴν παρατήρησιν . . . ποιεῖσθαι. The familiar periphrasis with ποιεῖσθαι. Cf. Let. Aris. 18; Plutarch, Mor. 363B. παρατήρησις, a late word (since Polybius). Cf. Luke 17:20. Note Paul's use of the cognate verb in connection with months and days in Gal 4:10: "you observe (παρατηρεῖσθε) days and months, and times and years." Cf. Josephus, Ant. 14.264: μηδένα κωλύεσθαι παρατηρεῖν τὴν τῶν σαββάτων ἡμέραν. The Jews dated the beginning of the Sabbath and other holy days from the rising of the stars. For example, none might work after three stars (= night) had appeared on Friday evening, the beginning of the Sabbath, without being guilty of sin. See the quotation from Böhl in Otto[40] and Funk.[41] The moon had similar significance. Cf. The Preaching of Peter (Clement of Alexandria, Strom. 6.5.39) "and if no moon be seen, they do not celebrate what is called the first sabbath, nor keep the new moon, nor the days of unleavened bread, nor the feast (of tabernacles?), nor the great day (of atonement)" (James's translation in Apocryphal New Testament).[42] μηνῶν, ἡμερῶν, objective genitives.

τὰς οἰκονομίας. The word οἰκονομία extends its meaning from "management of a household" to management or provision in general (cf. 7:1). It came to be used of the various operations of the divine will, particularly of God's "dispensation" effected in Christ for the salvation of men. So Eph 1:10; 3:2. Cf. Clement of Alexandria, Strom. 2.5.20 where Isaac is spoken of as τύπον ἐσόμενον ἡμῖν οἰκονομίας σωτηρίου. Cf. the use of the cognate verb in 9:1 (below), and see Robinson's note on Eph 1:10,[43] and Lightfoot.[44] Here the term relates to the divine "ordering" of the seasons, which may be specifically named as καιρῶν ἀλλαγάς. So Lake: "the changing seasons ordained by God." But it is better to take καί as the simple copula, "the orderings of God and the changes of the seasons." In Wis 7:18 man's knowledge of τροπῶν ἀλλαγὰς καὶ μεταβολὰς καιρῶν is a gift of God.[45] With ἀλλαγή cf. παραλλαγή (Jas 1:17).[46]

40. Otto, Epistola ad Diognetum, 2nd ed., 173.
41. Funk, Patres Apostolici, 396–97.
42. See note in Lietzmann, Galater, 24, 26.
43. Robinson, Ephesians, at comment on Eph 1:10.
44. Lightfoot, Apostolic Fathers, 2.2:75.
45. See Gass, "Das patristiche Wort οἰκονομία."
46. See notes by Mayor, James, and Knowling, James.

καταδιαιρεῖν. Otto thus fills the MS lacuna, καταδ . . . ειν. See his note for other editorial reconstructions.[47] καταδιαιρεῖν is a late word occurring four times in the LXX (Ps 47:13 al.), and in the papyri. Cf. Dion. Hal., Ant. 4.19; καταδιαιρῶν τὸ πλῆθος κτλ.

θεοσεβείας . . . ἀφροσύνης . . . δεῖγμα. A repetition of the language of 3:3.

ἃς μὲν . . . ἃς δέ. See note on p. 13. The "feasts" and "mourning" refer to the great Jewish festivals and the Day of Atonement respectively (Lev 23:27ff.).

ἂν . . . ἡγήσαιτο . . . δεῖγμα; so Lachmann, Scheibe, and others, for the MS reading ἡγήσεται τὸ δεῖγμα. Stephanus has ἡγήσηται τὸ δεῖγμα. See Gildersleeve's note.[48] For δεῖγμα, cf. 7:9.

6. τῆς . . . ἀπάτης, "the general fatuity and deceit," i.e., of the Greeks; τῆς . . . ἀλαζονείας, "the meddlesomeness and pride of the Jews." This interpretation is preferable to the view that all four faults relate to the Jews (Lightfoot-Harmer, Lake), for (a) the position of the word Ἰουδαίων confines it to the second clause, (b) the defects paired here (note the one article [τῆς] in each member) correspond to the author's general view of the Greek and Jewish cults respectively, the one "silly" (εἰκαιότης) and in some instances a deliberate "imposture" (ἀπάτη), the other "fussy" in its minute regulations (πολυπραγμοσύνη) and "proud" (ἀλαζονεία) of its privileges. On this view κοινῆς means "general" and refers to the Greek or pagan world as a whole in contrast to Jews, not, as Funk takes it, "common" to both alike. (c) 4:6 closes the *whole* discussion up to this point. The worship offered by both Greeks and Jews is now dismissed in a comprehensive, not to say caustic, phrase.

εἰκαιότητος. A late word found in Aquila Prov 30:8. Cf. Philo, *Deus* 10: ἐξ οὗ μοι δοκεῖς εἰκαιότητα καὶ εὐχέρειαν ἀπελέγχειν σεαυτοῦ . . . μνηύειν, Diog. Laert. 7.48: εἰς ἀκοσμίαν καὶ εἰκαιότητα. For ἀπάτη, cf. 10:7, τῆς ἀπάτης τοῦ κόσμου, and see note on 2:1.

πολυπραγμοσύνης. This good classical word seems to carry the double sense of "fussy or punctilious activity" and "prying." Cf. πολυπράγμων (5:3). See Blakeney's note.[49]

ἀλαζονείας, "pride" in keeping all the Jewish laws and customs, i.e., general. In 4:1 it is specified in regard to circumcision, as also the verb in 4:4.

ὡς. So Bunsen inserts. Gebhardt and most modern editions accept. Stephanus and others prefer ὅτι. For μανθάνω ὡς, cf. Thuc. 1.34; Prov 6:8a.

ἀρκούντως. Attic contraction for ἀρκεόντως. Cf. Thuc. 1.22. μεμαθηκέναι has the full force of the perfect, stressing the abiding result. Contrast μαθεῖν

---

47. Otto, *Epistola ad Diognetum*, 2nd ed., 174.
48. Gildersleeve, *Apologies*, 246.
49. Blakeney, *Diognetus*, 47.

(4:6), "to ascertain." This brief exposition of Jewish observances is quite "sufficient" for the purpose! See on 4:1 (οὐ νομίζω).

αὐτῶν, i.e., the Christians. ἴδιος here, as in 5:2, 5, 10 has its original force (one's own), not the weakened sense (= ἑαυτοῦ) as sometimes in late Greek.[50] For the conjunction of ἴδιος and the personal pronoun, cf. Wis 19:13; Acts 1:19; 2 Pet 3:3, 16.

μυστήριον. A favorite word of the author. He uses it in reference to the Christian religion (4:6), to the Father or God, whose "mysteries" the Christian can both apprehend (11:2) and utter (10:7). The term is used of God's secret ways in nature (7:2) and of the hidden plan of salvation (8:10). Only once does it refer to man (ἀνθρώπινα μυστήρια, 7:1).

The whole passage (6) serves as a transition to the picture of the Christian life (chs. 5 and 6). The concluding comment (τὸ δὲ κτλ) is to be interpreted in the light of the passages 5:3; 7:1ff. Diognetus had asked for information about the Christian θεοσέβεια. So far the author's references to the Christians have been more or less of a negative character (2:10; 3:1). In coming now to the positive exposition of the religion of the Christians, he is aware that it is a μυστήριον (cf. 1 Tim 3:16). It cannot be learned from man (παρὰ ἀνθρώπου) any more than its teaching ("no human doctrine") has been discovered by man. The "secret" is disclosed by God, who himself from heaven established among men and fixed firmly in their hearts "the truth and the holy and incomprehensible word." It is as though our author acknowledges that no argumentative skill or subtlety can avail to win Diognetus to the faith (there are signs of impatience in the previous discussion, as though he was eager to proceed to the heart of his theme; see 2:10; 4:1). Hence he points him now to the *life* of the Christians—the unanswerable proof.

Similarly Paul insists that his gospel, being οὐ κατὰ ἄνθρωπον, did not come to him παρὰ ἀνθρώπου but δι' ἀποκαλύψεως (Gal 1:12). Cf. Rom 16:25–26; Col 1:26.

Note that the direct personal address to Diognetus ceases after 4:6. The personal note is renewed in 7:8 (see note).

Chapter 5

The true distinction of the Christians lies not in their habitat, language, or customs—a statement briefly expanded in §2. It resides in the supernatural quality of their individual and corporate life. Just as their teaching is not of human origin or discovery, so their citizenship, whilst conforming to the ordinary life of men, is not of this world (ἐν οὐρανῷ πολιτεύονται, 5:9). The

---

50. See Deissmann, *Bible Studies*, 123–24, Moulton, *Prolegomena.*, 87ff.

rest of chapters 5 and 6 develops this latter principle. By terse contrast and paradox, which defy analysis, these sections bring out the positive features of the Christian ethos which attest its divine origin and nature.

This emphasis on the moral life of the Christians is significant for the apologetic. Nothing is said up to this point of the belief in God which is its *fons et origo*. The author comes to this later (see 8:6; 9:6; 10:1). He is in no doubt that the quality of the Christian life springs from the divine revelation in the incarnate and atoning Son. But his mind reverts to the practical aspects of faith (10:4-7). He is concerned to show that "by their fruits you will know them." See above, p. 48. Aristides, *Apol.* 15 inverts the order: "they know and believe in God . . . from whom they have received those commandments . . . so that on this account they do not commit adultery," etc. (Syr.).

This description of the Christian way of life may be compared with the accounts given in Aristides, *Apol.* 15 and Justin Martyr, *1 Apol.* 14-15. It is instructive to follow Renan's hint[51] and work out the contrast with the picture of the secular ideal state in Lucian's *Hermotimus* 22-24. Lucian depicts a blissful life for men in the enjoyment of legality, equality, and all good things. But in at least three features it is widely different from the picture of the Christian πολιτεία in Diognetus: (*a*) Lucian's city-state is set in the future. One day men will reach it, be naturalized, and gain their franchise; for Diognetus the Christian lives here and now in the heavenly city. (*b*) For Lucian earthly duties and domestic ties must alike be sacrifices to gain the ideal state; the Christians, says Diognetus, "share all things as citizens," conform in matters of clothing, food, and customs, and obey the appointed laws. Moreover, they enjoy and honor the privileges of family life. (*c*) Lucian's city is secular; for Diognetus the Christian's ideal is, though not expressly so named, the city of God. It is "in heaven."

1. ἔθεσι. For MS ἔσθεσι ("clothing"). But the threefold correspondence with 5:2 (cities, speech, life) favors the term "customs." Cf. τοῖς ἐγχωρίοις . . . βίῳ (5:4), where ἔθεσιν is the generic term inclusive of ἐσθής, etc. Trypho (Justin Martyr, *Dial.* 10) wonders why Christians, supposing themselves to be pious and better than other men, exhibit no mode of living distinct from that of the nations. Cf. Tertullian, *Apol.* 42: "people (Christians) who live among you, eating the same food, wearing the same attire, having the same habits, under the same necessities of existence."[52]

διακεκριμένοι . . . εἰσιν. Periphrastic perfect. Cf. ἐστιν εὑρημένον (5:3).

2. A particularization of 5:1. The Christians do not dwell in cities of their own (οὔτε γῇ); they do not use a strange form of speech (οὔτε φωνῇ);

---

51. Renan, *Marc-Aurèle*, 424ff.
52. Cited in Otto, *Epistola ad Diognetum*, 2nd ed., 175.

they practice no notable way of life (οὔτε ἔθεσι). Although the phrase τῶν λοιπῶν ἀνθρώπων suggests their distinctiveness from men in general, the author seems to point to a particular contrast with the Jews, who have their own city quarters (cf. the medieval ghetto), a stranger language, and practices of marked singularity (Sabbath, food taboos, circumcision). The first point ("country") and the third ("customs") are developed in the rest of ch. 5. The point of language is not further referred to.

ἰδίας. See note on 4:6. κατοικοῦσιν. Transitive here and in 5:4; intransitive in 6:8.

διαλέκτῳ. If any contrast with φωνή (5:1) is intended, διάλεκτος indicates variety of speech (*patois*). Cf. Strabo, *Georg.* 8.1.2 (of the ancient Greek "dialects").

παρηλλαγμένῃ, "strange." Cf. Polybius 2.29.1; 3.55.1; 2 Macc 3:16.

παράσημον, "notable," "singular," with a suggestion of reprehension. Cf. Plutach, *Mor.* 823B: οὐδὲ τοῖς εἰς τρυφὴν καὶ πολυτελείαν ἐπιφθόνοις παράσημος. Note the substantive in 3 Macc 2:29 ("emblem"). Acts 28:11 ("figure-head"). Their manner of life is not "singular," though their citizenship, being "in heaven," is of "a remarkable and admittedly strange order" (5:4).

3. πολυπραγμόνων. Used in its common disparaging sense ("meddlesome"). See note on 4:6. The meaning tends to be refined in later Greek, being used, for example, of the "research" of the historian. Cf. Diod. Sic. 1.37.4: Ἡρόδοτος ὁ πολυπράγμων, and the cognate verb in 2 Macc 2:30.

μάθημα ... εὑρημένον. For the MS and editorial readings see Otto.[53] The thought of man's inability to grasp the "mystery" of the religion of the Christians seems to interrupt the connection of §§2 and 4. But it is in the author's mind (cf. 4:6) and is developed in 7:1.

For μάθημα of Christian teaching, cf. Justin Martyr, *1 Apol.* 3: καὶ βίου καὶ μαθημάτων τὴν ἐπίσκεψιν, 2:2: τῶν Χριστιανῶν μαθημάτων. It became a quasi-technical term to connote Christian tradition. See note on τὰ παραδοθέντα (11:1). αὐτοῖς, dative of possession. For the periphrastic perfect, see p. 12.

προεστᾶσιν, with genitive. Cf. 4 Macc 11:27; Titus 3:8, 14. The thought that the Christians "champion" no human doctrine is taken up in 7:1: "it is no mortal idea which they think fit to guard with such care." It is probable that there is here, as Radford hazards,[54] a specific reference to rabbinical subtleties (πολυπραγμόνων ἀνθρώπων) and Greek philosophy (δόγματος ἀνθρωπίνου), since (*a*) πολυπράγμων is used of the Jews in 4:6, and (*b*) the

---

53. Otto, *Epistola ad Diognetum*, 2nd ed., 176.
54. Radford, *Diognetus*, 62.

author throughout seems to have the two main types, gentiles and Jews, in mind. Cf. especially 3:5; 4:6; 5:17.

The term δόγμα is employed in a sense akin to that of the Stoic use to denote "principles" of their teaching. Cf. Marcus Aurelius 2.3: ταῦτά σοι ἀρκείτω, ἀεὶ δόγματα ἔστω. The term is not infrequent in the fathers (Ign., *Magn.* 13; Did. 11:3; Barn. 1:6; 9:7). ἔνιοι, i.e., the philosophers.

The MS has a marginal note to the phrase οὐδὲ ... προεστᾶσιν, namely "because the Christians do not hold to the teaching of a man. For the apostle Paul says, 'I received it not from man' (Gal 1:12)." See note on μυστήριον (4:6).

4. So far (§§1–3) the distinctiveness of the Christians has been couched in negative terms. Now it is set forth mainly in a positive way (except §§6, 8).

πόλεις ... βαρβάρους. Otto understands "gentile" (ἑλληνίδας) and Jewish (βαρβάρους) cities," and compares the use of the two terms in Justin Martyr, *1 Apol.* 5, 7, 46.[55] But the more comprehensive range of βάρβαρος (cf. Thuc. 2.97) is not excluded. Cf. 6:2: "Christians *are dispersed* throughout the cities of the world" (see note). See Lightfoot on Col 3:11.[56]

τοῖς ... βίῳ. The author insists on the participation of the Christians in the common life of men as against the frequent charge of aloofness. Cf. 5:5.

ἀκολουθοῦντες (not ἕπομαι), as in the papyri, NT, and LXX (except 3 Macc 2:26).

ὁμολογουμένως. To be taken with παράδοξον, as perhaps also in 1 Tim 3:16 ("confessedly great"). Cf. Thuc. 6.90; P. Par. 15[66] (120 BCE) *al.*

παράδοξον, "beyond expectation," i.e., "strange." Cf. Let. Aris. 175: οὗ πᾶσι παραδόξου φανέντος, Luke 5:26; 1 Clem. 25:1.

τὴν κατάστασιν ... πολιτείας "the order of their own citizenship." Cf. Plato, *Leg.* 832D; Aristotle, *Ath. pol.* 42.1. πολιτεία, πολιτεύεσθαι (cf. 5:9), originally denoting *civic* condition or behavior, also came to have the general meaning "manner of life," "conduct." Cf. Let. Aris. 31; 2 Macc 11:25; Acts 23:1; Phil 1:27; Justin Martyr, *Dial.* 105, 119. Geffcken takes the word in this wider sense here, "Leben" (life), "Wesen" (being). But the context suggests that the idea of citizenship is here predominant. Cf. πολῖται ... ξένοι, 5:6.

5. The descriptive features in §§5–17 are reminiscent of Paul's epistles with perhaps an occasional echo of Heb 11:13–14 and 1 Peter (see following notes). Note the effective sequence of antithetical sentences extending from 5:5 to 6:9.

οἰκοῦσιν. The simplex resumes the compound (κατοικέω, 5:2, 4) with no appreciable diminution of meaning, a classical usage. Cf. John 1:11–12

---

55. Otto, *Epistola ad Diognetum*, 2nd ed., 176–77.
56. Lightfoot, *Colossians*.

(παρέλαβον ... ἔλαβον), Rev 10:10 (κατέφαγον ... ἔφαγον).[57] The verb, transitive here, is intransitive in 6:3. ἰδίας. See 4:6.

πάροικοι. The word is familiar as a metaphorical description of the Christians' status in the world. Cf. 1 Pet 2:11; Heb 11:13-14.[58] Note Χριστιανοὶ παροικοῦσιν ἐν φθαρτοῖς (6:8). For the thought see Herm. Sim. 1.1ff. Philo (Conf. 77f.) allegorizes all the wise men mentioned in the books of Moses as "sojourners" (παροικοῦντες), "for their souls are sent down from heaven upon earth as to a colony, ... looking upon the heavenly country in which they have the rights of citizens (πολιτεύονται) as their native land (πατρίδα) and the earthly abode in which they dwell for a while (παρῴκησαν) as a foreign land" (ξένην). So Clement of Alexandria, Paed. 3.8.1: πατρίδα ἐπὶ γῆς οὐκ ἔχομεν (of Christians).

On the use of πάροικος in the Greek Bible, see Kennedy, Sources, 102.

μετέχουσι ... πολῖται. On the general attitude of the Christians towards secular ordinances, see above, pp. 37-39. Tertullian, Apol. 42 insists that Christians take an active part in the observances and institutions of public life and engage in its ordinary callings.

ξένοι, "foreigners" in general, contrasted with πολῖται. Cf. Eph 2:19 for the combination of ξένοι καὶ πάροικοι contrasted with συμπολῖται.

ξένη, sc. γῆ. Lietzmann prefers to render "every strange city is their home town and every home town is strange" on the ground that the conception of "native land" in the patriotic sense was lacking in the ancient world.[59] But, while πατρίς properly means "native town" (Luke 4:23-24 and the papyri), it is better to give it here the wider connotation into which the term shades off (2 Macc 8:21), in view of the occurrence of πόλεις (4). Cf. 2 Macc 13:14.

For the sentiment see Blakeney's full note.[60]

6. γαμοῦσιν ... τεκνογονοῦσιν. For the absence of the ascetic note in the teaching of the epistle, see pp. 39-40. Cf. Justin Martyr, 1 Apol. 29: τὴν ἀρχὴν οὐκ ἐγαμοῦμεν, εἰ μὴ ἐπὶ παίδων ἀνατροφῇ. See Athenagoras, Suppl. 33; Resurr. 21. For the absolute use of γαμέω cf. 2 Macc 14:25; 1 Cor 7:28; P.Oxy. IX, 1213[4] (2nd c. CE) [εἰ] δέδοταί μοι γαμῆσαι;

(καὶ) τεκνογονοῦσιν. Otto, followed by Bunsen and Gildersleeve, inserts καί. But the asyndeton is characteristic. Cf. 2:9; 9:2. τεκνογονέω is a rare and later word. Cf. Anthol. Gr. 9.4: πέμφθη δ' εἰς ἀγέλην τεκνογονεῖν ἄφετος (of a heifer). The two verbs are here used of the Christians of both sexes. The

---

57. See Moulton, Prolegomena, 115.
58. See especially Moffatt, Hebrews, 174-75.
59. Lietzmann, Beginnings, 2:247.
60. Blakeney, Diognetus, 49-50.

fluidity in the use of γαμέω (in the active properly of the man; in later Greek of the woman also) probably attaches to τεκνογονέω (both verbs are used of the woman in 1 Tim 5:14).

ῥίπτουσι. "They throw out," "expose" (of children). Cf. Sophocles, *Oed. tyr.* 719; Gen 21:15. A *"verbum magis odiosum"* (Otto) than the more usual word ἐκτιθέναι (Herodotus, *Hist.* 1.112; Wis 28:5; Acts 7:21 [cf. 19]). See the famous passage in P.Oxy. IV, 744 (1 BCE) in which a certain Hilarion, writing to his sister (wife) Alis, says: "if—good luck to you—you bear offspring, if it is a male, let it live: if it is a female, expose it."[61] Too much must not be made of this somewhat rare allusion in the papyri. But exposure of (female) infants was common enough in the Graeco-Roman world to elicit protests from both Hellenistic Jews (cf. Ps.-Phocylides 185) and Christian writers (Justin Martyr, *1 Apol.* 27; Athenagoras, *Suppl.* 35; Tertullian, *Apol.* 9; Minucius Felix, *Oct.* 30; Did. 2:2).[62]

7. τράπεζαν . . . κοίτην. "Free board they provide—but no carnal bed," an interesting specimen of the author's terse and epigrammatic style. For τράπεζα κοινή cf. Justin Martyr, *1 Apol.* 14: ἑστίας κοινὰς μὴ ποιούμενοι. For παρατίθενται τράπεζαν, an old expression, cf. Homer, *Od.* 5.92; Acts 16:34.

κοίτην. The reading is uncertain. (1) κοινήν. So the MS, followed by Otto[63] and other editions. This makes an effective play upon the word, "a common board, but no polluted one." If κοινήν be read, the author may have in mind the question of Christians partaking of meats offered to idols, which vexed the Corinthian Church (1 Cor 8; 10). Cf. Justin Martyr, *Dial.* 34 (*sub fin.*). For this sense of κοινός cf. 1 Macc 1:62; Acts 10:14 *al.* Or possibly the allusion is to the calumnies circulated about the Christian love-feasts, namely, that promiscuous lewdness was commonly practiced at services after dark. See Athenagoras, *Suppl.* 3; Tertullian, *Apol.* 7. Radford inclines to think that the hospitality is not "profane," in the sense that it is "consecrated by the word of God and thanksgiving," 1 Tim 4:5.[64] Puech's suggestion that there is here a veiled allusion to the Eucharist is improbable.[65] (2) κοίτην. So Prudentius of Maur (1742) conjectures. This reading is adopted by Bunsen and many modern editions. See Justin Martyr, *2 Apol.* 2 of a Christian wife, ὁμοδίαιτος καὶ ὁμόκοιτος γινομένη, seeking divorce from a dissolute husband, and the much-quoted passage from Tertullian, *Apol.* 39: *omnia indiscreta sunt apud nos, praeter uxores.* The writer of Heb 13:2-4

---

61. See Deissmann, *Light*, 167ff.
62. See Blakeney, *Diognetus*, 50–51, for fuller references.
63. See his full note in Otto, *Epistola ad Diognetum*, 2nd ed., 178–79.
64. Radford, *Diognetus*, 64.
65. Puech, *Apologistes grecs*, 255n2, 262; see also Blakeney, *Diognetus*, 52.

enjoins hospitality (φιλοξενία), but insists that the marriage-bed be undefiled (ἡ κοίτη ἀμίαντος).

For the paronomasia κοινὴν ... κοίτην, see p. 13. It is gratuitous to suggest, as Geffcken does, that Clement of Alexandria is the model here. Paronomasia is a literary feature of general occurrence. See above, p. 62.

8. ἐν σαρκὶ ... κατὰ σάρκα. These Pauline borrowings (2 Cor 10:3; Rom 8:4) illustrate the twofold sense in which the apostle uses the term σάρξ. "In the flesh," i.e., physically, "after the flesh," i.e., ethically, the σάρξ being viewed as the material medium through which the lower senses are gratified, and hence the seat of sin. Cf. Rom 7:18; Gal 5:19ff.

For τυγχάνουσιν see note on 2:1.

9. The thought that the Christians' "native land" is in heaven frequently recurs in the writings of the period. But the other-worldliness of our epistle is healthy. There is no escapist strain such as we find in Tertullian, who, placing the true Christian abode in heaven (*scit se peregrinam in terris agere ... dignitatem in caelis habere*, Tertullian, *Apol.* 1), would hasten the Christians' progress thereto (*nihil nostra refert in hoc aevo, nisi de eo quam celeriter excedere*, Tertullian, *Apol.* 41). Plato, *Rep.* 592B, had already envisaged the pattern of an ideal city in heaven, the practices of which the wise man will adopt.

διατρίβουσιν. Absolute as in 2 Macc 14:23; John 3:22. Frequent in papyri. ἐν οὐρανῷ πολιτεύονται, "they live (as citizens) in heaven," where God "lives" (πολιτεύεται, 10:7). For ἐν οὐρανῷ, cf. ἐν οὐρανοῖς (6:8; 10:7). The thought is plainly reminiscent of Phil 3:20. It recurs often in 1 Clement. See 1 Clem. 2:8 and especially 54:4: ταῦτα οἱ πολιτευόμενοι τὴν ἀμεταμέλητον πολιτείαν τοῦ θεοῦ ἐποίησαν καὶ ποιήσουσιν. See on πολιτεία (5:4).

10. The meaning is that Christians excel the laws in that they exhibit a higher type of life than mere legal requirements demand (cf. Athenagoras, *Suppl.* 32 and 34 *ad fin.*). This kind of life is exemplified in general terms in the statements that follow (11–16). Love as being "the fulfillment of the law" holds the first place (Rom 13:10). The "laws" here are the ordinances laid down by the secular authority, obedience to which Paul had enjoined (Rom 13:1ff.), and which Christians, in the thought of our author, "overcome" in the sense that they fulfill (πληροῦν) them. It is more probable that the author is here indebted, as so often, to Paul than to classical precedents (Aristotle, Varro, Horace) which Geffcken cites.[66] For the insistence on the Christians' loyalty to lawful state demands, see pp. 37–39. Cf. Lactantius, *Div. Inst.* 6.23: *nec tantum legibus publicis pareat: sed sit supra omnes leges, qui legem dei sequitur.* We have an analogy in the transcendence of the Jewish law by

---

66. Geffcken, *Diognetos*, 18.

Christians, which is implicit in both the teaching of Jesus (see especially Matt 5:17–18) and Paul's view of "the fruit of the Spirit" as above the law (Gal 5:23). Cf. 1 Tim 1:9: "the law is not made for a righteous man."

καί, here and similarly in 11–16, introduces a mild antithesis, almost "yet." Cf. John 1:10; 3:11; P. Tebt. 2.278³⁰: ζητῶι καὶ οὐχ εὑρίσκωι.

11. ἀγαπῶσι πάντας. The verb is used here (as in 6:6; 10:7) of man's love to man; to God (10:3). Note how the scope of Diognetus's original question, "what is the love which they have for one another?" is here enlarged ("all men") and later particularized (6:6) into love of enemies. Cf. the universal note struck in 10:6: Christian love ministers to one's "neighbor" and to "those in need." Cf. Aristides, *Apol*. 15. Nock shows that "love of the brethren" has analogies in popular philosophy and pagan faiths. But it "was altogether more lively and more far-reaching in Christianity."[67] Our author gives but a slight treatment of Diognetus's question. Overbeck suggests that a fuller exposition of this point stood originally in the lacuna at 7:6–7.[68]

12–13. The language is clearly reminiscent of 2 Cor 6:9–10:

ἀγνοοῦνται.	ὡς ἀγνοούμενοι.
θανατοῦνται, καὶ ζωοποιοῦνται.	ὡς ἀποθνήσκοντες καὶ ἰδοὺ ζῶμεν, ὡς παιδευόμενοι καὶ μὴ θανατούμενοι.
πτωχεύουσι . . . πολλούς.	ὡς πτωχοὶ . . . πλουτίζοντες
πάντων . . . περισσεύουσιν.	ὡς μηδὲν . . . κατέχοντες.

But there is a marked difference. Our author applies to the Christian life in general what Paul sketches of his own ministry in particular. This difference appears in various details. (1) While Paul was misunderstood (ἀγνοούμενοι) by some, yet he was understood (ἐπιγινωσκόμενοι) by others (cf. 2 Cor 11:16). The Christians had no such recompense: it was their lot both to suffer wide ignorance or misunderstanding and to be condemned, (2) the apostle, while dying "daily," was inwardly sustained (cf. 2 Cor 4:10); Christians suffer death, but the life of the Christian society is renewed. For this latter idea, see 5:16; 6:9; 7:8.

ἀγνοοῦνται κτλ. For the passive cf. Gal 1:22. The connection appears to be that Christians are "not understood" and yet (or in consequence) are condemned. For this nuance of ἀγνοέω cf. Mark 9:32. It was commonly maintained by the apologists that the persecution of Christianity rested on the fact that the emperors were not rightly informed about its nature and objects, such ignorance or distortion being due (so Justin Martyr, *1 Apol*. 14) to the activity of the demons. Justin indeed appeals to the authorities

---

67. Nock, *Conversion*, 219.
68. Overbeck, *Studien*, 1:7.

to pass judgment on Christians only κατὰ τὸν ἀκριβῆ καὶ ἐξεταστικὸν λόγον (*1 Apol.* 2), for ἀκρίτως κολάξετε μὴ φροντίζοντες (*1 Apol.* 5). Cf. also *2 Apol.* 14. Similarly Tertullian, *Apol.* 1, *unum gestit interdum, ne ignoratur damnetur*, and again *Apol.* 1, *quid enim iniquius, quam ut oderint homines, quod ignorant*.

θανατοῦνται, καὶ ζωοποιοῦνται, "they are put to death, yet they are endowed with life" (cf. ζωοποιούμενοι, 5:16). For the collocation of the two verbs see 4 Kgs 5:7; 1 Pet 3:18.

πλουτίζουσι. Cf. Gen 14:23; 2 Cor 6:10.[69] πάντων ὑστεροῦνται. Christians are like OT worthies ὑστερούμενοι (Heb 11:37).

ἐν πᾶσι περισσεύουσιν: "they abound in all things" (opp. to ὑστερέω, cf. 1 Cor 8:8; Phil 4:12), a sense of the verb common in Paul. For περισσεύω ἐν, cf. 1 Cor 15:58; Phil 1:9.

14. ἀτιμοῦνται ... δοξάζονται may possibly reflect Paul's διὰ δόξης καὶ ἀτιμίας (2 Cor 6:8). Cf. 1 Cor 4:10 and for the collocation Sir 3:10. ἀτιμίαις, the plural indicating "the individual concrete manifestations of the abstract quality."[70] Cf. Dem. 18.205.

δοξάζονται. Here used of honor by men. Cf. Esth 3:1; 1 Macc 2:64. The verb receives enriched meaning in the NT (John 12:28 *al*).

βλασφημοῦνται, "are defamed." For this sense, calumny against *men*, cf. Rom 3:8; 1 Cor 10:30; Titus 3:2.

δικαιοῦνται, "justified" (in the sight of men), i.e., vindicated as to the calumnies they suffer (βλασφημοῦνται). Cf. Matt 11:19. In 9:4 (below) in the Pauline sense, "justified" (before God). See note.

15. λοιδοροῦνται καὶ εὐλογοῦσιν. A reminiscence of 1 Cor 4:12. Cf. also 1 Pet 3:9; Rom 12:14. So Aristides, *Apol.* 15. "those who grieve them they comfort and make them their friends." In classical Greek εὐλογέω = "to praise." Hellenistic adds the associated sense "to bless," as in Gen 14:19; Acts 3:26.

ὑβρίζονται, καὶ τιμῶσιν. Geffcken thinks that the "honor" is that paid by the Christians to the emperor, in that they regard him as ordained of God (cf. Rom 13) to his high office and pray for him and for the stability of the empire.[71] See Tertullian, *Apol.* 31ff.

16. ἀγαθοποιοῦντες, absolute as in Luke 6:9. The context (εὐλογοῦσιν, τιμῶσιν) favors the sense "to do good (to)," as in Let. Aris. 242; Num 10:32; Luke 6:33, 35. The verb sometimes carries the sense "to do what is morally

---

69. See Anz, *Subsidia*, 297.
70. Blass, *Grammatik*, 84.
71. Geffcken, *Diognetos*, 19.

right" (1 Pet 2:15, 20; 3 John 11).[72] For the suffering of the ἀγαθοποιοῦντες, cf. 1 Pet 3:17; for rejoicing in punishment, 2 Cor 6:10; 1 Pet 4:13; Col 1:24, etc. Note the epanastrophe κολάζονται. κολαζόμενοι, and cf. ἐπέδειξεν. ἐπέδειξε (8:5-6). κολάζω is a favorite word of the author (2:8, see note; 6:9; 7:8; 10:7).

17. For the hatred shown to Christians see 2:6 and 6:5. It is probable that the reference to Jewish bitterness is quite general (cf. John 15:18-19) and not to any specific persecution such as the Bar-Kokhba uprising (see above p. 38). Radford, following Otto, cites Justin Martyr, *1 Apol.* 31: "the Jews regard us with personal enmity (ἐχθρούς) and active hostility (πολεμίους), slaying and injuring us just as you gentiles do." Cf. also *Dial.* 16, 19, 133. At the final preparations for Polycarp's death the Jews were especially zealous "as is their custom" (ὡς ἔθος αὐτοῖς), Mart. Poly. 13:1. Cf. 1 Thess 2:14-16. ὑπὸ Ἑλλήνων, i.e., gentiles, as in ch. 1 (above).

καὶ τὴν αἰτίαν κτλ. Otto cites John 15:25 (= Pss 34:19; 68:5); but the parallel is closer in thought than in language. The statement relates to the general hatred of the Christians, for which their enemies can assign no cause—a confirmation of the fact that Christians ἀγνοοῦνται (5:12). Both Jews and Greeks could of course supply specific reasons for their hostile attitude, the one the Christians' acceptance of Jesus as the Messiah (cf. Justin Martyr, *1 Apol.* 36), the other their "atheism" and repudiation of heathen gods (2:6). The writer himself supplies some reasons. See above, p. 35.

For Jewish persecution of Christians see Harnack.[73] εἰπεῖν ... οὐκ ἔχουσιν. For the construction see 2:10 (above).

Chapter 6

An analogy between the function of the soul in the body and that of Christians in the world is elaborated in a series of antithetical statements. The section concludes with a moralizing touch: Christians must not refuse their divinely appointed rank.

1. ἁπλῶς δ' εἰπεῖν may mean "to speak simply" (or "shortly"; cf. Isoc. 4.154), or "to speak in general terms" (cf. Aristotle, *Pol.* 3.9.5; *Eth. nic.* 3.6.2). The latter rendering is perhaps to be preferred, since the specific features of the Christians' manner of life (ch. 5) are followed (ch. 6) by a broad statement of their relation to the world.

ὅπερ ... τοῦτ' ... For the form of the comparison Geffcken (p. 19) cites Philo, *Opif.* 53 (12M): ὅπερ γὰρ νοῦς ἐν ψυχῇ, τοῦτ' ὀφθαλμὸς ἐν σώματι.

---

72. See Hatch, *Essays*, 7.
73. Harnack, *Expansion*, 1:57ff.

ἐν κόσμῳ. The term κόσμος appears fourteen times in Diognetus, eight times in this chapter. The prevailing sense is ethical: the world of human affairs viewed as apart from and hostile to God. Cf. especially 10.7: "the deceit and error of the world." This sense is found in Paul (1 Cor 1:21), Jas (1:27), and is especially Johannine (John 14:17; 1 John 4:4, etc.). In 10:2 (below) and perhaps 12:9 the word appears in its classical sense: the world as an ordered system. Cf. Acts 17:24, etc.[74]

2. A vivid figure of the soul dispersed as seed (ἔσπαρται) through all the members of the body. For Christians as seed sown in the world, cf. Irenaeus, *Haer*. 3.11.8: κατέσπαρται ἡ ἐκκλησία ἐπὶ πάσης τῆς γῆς. Our author's statement (cf. 5:4) is more or less rhetorical and can hardly be cited as evidence for the spread of Christianity in the first two centuries.[75] Nevertheless numerous passages elsewhere have the same tenor. See the references on this point cited in Otto's note on Justin Martyr, *1 Apol*. 1. In 112 CE Pliny writes of the Christians: *multi enim omnis aetatis, omnis ordinis, utriusque sexus etiam vocantur in periculum et vocabuntur. Neque enim civitates tantum, sed vicos etiam atque agros superstitionis istius contagio pervagata est* (*Trajan* 10.96). Cf. Tacitus, *Ann*. 15.44; Eusebius, *Hist. eccl*. 2.3; 4.7, etc.

κατὰ πάντων τῶν μελῶν . . . κατὰ τὰς πόλεις. The genitive and accusative cases with κατά in a local sense here approximate in meaning, the accusative having perhaps a more distributive force, "throughout the several cities of the world." Cf. Luke 4:14 (genitive); Acts 8:1 (accusative). κατά with genitive "throughout," is Hellenistic (cf. Polybius 3.19.7, κατὰ τῆς νήσου διεσπάρησαν, Josephus, *Ant*. 8.297, τὸ ἔθνος κατὰ πάσης σπαρήσεται γῆς), though it is seen in classical Greek in the phrases καθ' ὅλου and κατὰ πάντος. In the NT it is Lukan (Gospel and Acts) and found always with ὅλος (Acts 9:31, etc.).[76]

3. Note here and in §§4, 7, 8 that each half of the analogy contains a contrast within itself.

καὶ Χριστιανοὶ κτλ. Cf. John 15:19; 17:11, 14, 16. The thought is akin to that of 5:5. It finds some correspondence in Pauline teaching (1 Cor 2:12; Gal 6:14).

ἀόρατος . . . ὁρατῷ. For the collocation cf. Col 1:16; Ignatius, *Trall*. 5:2. ἀόρατος is used of their "religion" (below) and of God (7:2). Cf. Ignatius, *Poly*. 3:2.

φρουρεῖται, "is guarded." The verb is commonly used in the (military) sense "to garrison," "to keep watch." So 1 Esdr. 4:56; 2 Cor 11:32; Phil 4:7. Here the sense is rather "to enclose," "to keep in ward," for which cf. Wis

---

74. See Burton, *Galatians*, 514.
75. See Harnack, *Expansion*, 2:25.
76. See Blass-Debrunner, *Grammatik*, §225.

17:15; Gal 3:23. The notion is virtually repeated below (6:7), where note the force of ἐγκέκλεισται and ἐν φρουρᾷ.⁷⁷ Cf. Plutarch, *Def. orac.* 29: οὐδὲ φρουρεῖν συγκλείσαντας ἐν ὕλῃ "nor keep them (gods) imprisoned by enclosing them with matter."

For the idea of the soul as the prisoner of the body see note on 6:7. Otto appositely cites (Ps.)-Plato, *Ax.* 365E, ed. Stephanus, ἡμεῖς μὲν γάρ ἐσμεν ψυχή, ζῷον ἀθάνατον, ἐν θνητῷ καθειργμένον φρουρίῳ.

καὶ Χριστιανοὶ κτλ. Throughout the chapter the parallelism between the soul on the one hand and Christians on the other is closely drawn. At this point it is somewhat extended. It is the *religion* of the Christians that is like the soul in being secret or invisible.

μὲν ὄντες. Later editions follow this conjecture for the MS. μένοντες. Note the correlative δέ. To join disparate words is a common scribal error. Cf. Justin Martyr, *Res.* 6: μὲν οὐσῶν (μενουσῶν, B and editions), Xenophon, *Oec.* 8.4: ἄτακτος μὲν οὖσα. For ἡ θεοσέβεια see on p. 97. Funk sees here a contrast between the externalism of pagan and Jewish religion and the spirituality of Christian worship. So also Otto. This is in line with the general connotation of θεοσέβεια as "*profession* of religion." But the nuance here may be the inner character of Christian piety, the life that is "his with Christ in God." Lightfoot's remark here is, by way of contrast, very pertinent: "it is next to impossible for us to realize the *ubiquity*, the *obtrusiveness*, the *intrusiveness* of polytheism."⁷⁸ But Christianity as "a spiritual religion from its very nature does not force itself on observation in the same way."

5–6. The ethical (Pauline) sense of σάρξ would fit the context here (see on 5:8). But, since the chapter deals with the body as opposed to the soul (cf. 1ff., 7ff.), the σάρξ is here virtually equivalent to the σῶμα. Cf. the μέλη of v. 6. At the same time, the gradations from the physical to the ethical nuance of the term σάρξ cannot always be clearly marked. For the opposition of flesh to soul see Plutarch, *Mor.* 101B; Gal 5:17; 1 Pet 2:11.

πολεμεῖ. Absolute as in 1 Macc 11:46; Jas 4:2. Cf. the passive use above (5:17). μηδέν. Adverbial accusative διότι, causal, as apparently always in the NT (Luke 1:13 *al.*), and three hundred times in the LXX.⁷⁹ It is used here instead of ὅτι probably to avoid hiatus after ἀδικουμένη as frequently in Polybius and the LXX. Cf. below ἀδικούμενος, ὅτι (casual).⁸⁰

---

77. See note by Hicks, "Political Terms," 7–8.
78. Lightfoot, *Historical Essays*, 15.
79. Thackeray, *Grammar*, 1:139.
80. See Meecham, *Letter of Aristeas*, 162–63.

ταῖς ἡδοναῖς. A depreciatory sense is implied. The word is found five times in NT in a bad sense (Luke 8:14 al.). For the plural cf. Let. Aris. 277; 4 Macc 5:23; Titus 3:3; and 9:1 (below).

κωλύεται χρῆσθαι. For the passive of κωλύω with the infinitive (without the article), cf. Acts 16:6; Heb 7:23, and see note on 4:3 above. For χρῆσθαι see p. 11.

ἀντιτάσσονται. Middle "they rage themselves against," "resist." Cf. Prov 3:34; Rom 13:2, etc. For the aloofness of the Christians from worldly pleasures, see Minucius Felix, Oct. 12: "you abstain from legitimate amusements, you never visit the shows, never join the processions, never attend the public banquets." Cf. also Tertullian, Apol. 38.

For the world's hatred of Christians, see 5:17 (note) and cf. 1 John 3:13.

6. ἡ ψυχὴ ... σάρκα. The thought is repeated from 6:5 (see p. 15). The soul loves also the limbs (τὰ μέλη), through which it is dispersed (6:2).

καὶ Χριστιανοὶ κτλ. Cf. the teaching of Jesus (Matt 5:44; Luke 6:27–28). See pp. 29–30.

7. The import of this section depends upon the meaning of συνέχω. (1) "hold together" (Gildersleeve cites Max. Tyr. 15.5: τὸ μὲν σῶμα συνέχεται, ἡ δὲ ψυχὴ συνέχει). The thought appears to be that the soul, though confined (ἐγκέκλεισται) within the body (cf. note on 6:4), avails to hold the body together, since they are spread abroad through its cities. Lake renders "sustain the world," and cites Aristides, Apol. 16, "I have no doubt but that the world stands through the intercession of Christians." The idea that Christians are the preservation of the world is common in early writers, a natural development of the figures used by Jesus of Christians as "salt," "light" (Matt 5:13ff.). Justin says that it is on account of the good and virtuous (i.e., Christians) that God has delayed the consummation (1 Apol. 45). See also 2 Apol. 7 (init.). In similar vein Tertullian (Apol. 32 and 39) states that Christians pray for emperors and for the stability of the Roman Empire, since it is the existence of the latter that delays the final dissolution of all things (see also ad Scap. 2). Cf. Clement of Alexandria, Quis dives salv. 36: "this is the seed (i.e., the elect) sent here as on a kind of foreign ... and all things are held together so long as the seed remains here." Origen (Cels. 8.70) has the Gospel figure of the salt: "men of God are assuredly the salt of the earth; they preserve the order of the world; and society is held together (συνέστηκε) as long as the salt is uncorrupted." Most commentators take the passage here in this sense. But (2) if συνέχω may be rendered "hold in charge," "keep under arrest," the parallelism becomes more exact. Just as the soul, though shut up in the prison of the body, yet keeps the body under control, so Christians, apparently imprisoned in the world, really hold mastery over it. For this sense of

συνέχω cf. Luke 22:63; 1 Clem. 20:5; and the papyri.[81] Cf. the force of συνέχει in 2 Cor 5:14, "keeps within bounds."

Otto thinks that the phrase ὡς ἐν φρουρᾷ τῷ κόσμῳ is reminiscent of Plato, *Phaedo* 62B, ὡς ἔν τινι φρουρᾷ ἐσμεν οἱ ἄνθρωποι, and that its following words, καὶ οὐ δεῖ δὴ ἑαυτὸν ἐκ ταύτης λύειν οὐδ' ἀποδιδράσκειν are echoed in 6:10. The notion of the soul as incarcerated in the body is of course widespread in both pagan and Christian literature. We may add Plato, *Phaedo* 82E, where the soul is described as διαδεδεμένην ἐν τῷ σώματι καὶ προσκεκολλημένην, *Tim.* 44B, ὅταν (ψυχὴ) εἰς σῶμα ἐνδεθῇ θνητόν, Cicero, *Somn. Scip.* 3, *hi vivunt qui e corporum vinculis tamquam e carcere evolaverunt*. For Philo (*Migr.* 9) the body is a δεσμωτήριον. Cf. Rom 7:22–23; 2 Cor 5:1–4.[82]

ἐγκέκλεισται, "is enclosed" (perfect). For the verb cf. 2:7; 7:2 (active). For κατέχω "detain," "imprison," cf. Gen 39:20. Often in the papyri "to arrest." φρουρά shows the ambiguity of its cognate verb and may mean "watch" and "prison." The whole context of this chapter supports the latter rendering. See note on φρουρεῖται (6:4).

8. The meaning is not that the soul is necessarily immortal. See above, p. 28. Several of the apologists reject the idea of natural immortality. See Justin Martyr, *Dial.* 5; Theophilus, *Autol.* 2.27. But the soul is capable of immortality by union with the divine Spirit. Cf. "they are put to death, yet they are endowed with life" (5:12). Cf. 5:16; 10:2 (the promise of the kingdom in heaven).

ἀθάνατος. A frequent epithet of the soul. Cf. Pausanias 4.32.4; 4 Macc 14:6. σκηνώματι, i.e., the bodily "frame," the temporary home of the soul. Cf. Wis 9:15, and 2 Cor 5:1 (σκῆνος), on which see Field[83] and 2 Pet 1:13–14. Eusebius, *Hist. eccl.* 2.25, speaks of the place where τὰ ἱερὰ σκηνώματα of Peter and Paul are laid. κατοικεῖ, intransitive. See above, p. 119.

παροικοῦσιν. See on πάροικοι (p. 121). There is no implied contrast between the two verbs here (as there is in Gen 37:1). As we have seen, κατοικέω is used quite generally by the author and παροικέω especially of the Christians' "sojourn."

φθαρτοῖς ... ἀφθαρσίαν. The collocation is familiar (cf. 1 Cor 15:53). φθαρτός is not specifically of the body (cf. Wis 9:15). It related to earthly things in general. Cf. 2 Clem. 6:6: τὰ ἐνθάδε ... φθαρτά (cf. Barn. 19:8) In 9:2 (below) φθαρτός is used of men. ἀφθαρσία is commonly employed by the apologists to denote God's manner of life as free from decay. Applied to

---

81. Moulton and Milligan, *Vocabulary*, 606b.
82. See Blakeney, *Diognetus*, 56, for references.
83. Field, *Notes*, 183.

Christians it suggests that their destiny was a divine existence of a similar quality. For ἀφθαρσία and ἀθανασία see 1 Cor 15:53.

ἐν οὐρανοῖς. See 5:9, and Hort's note on 1 Pet 1:5.

9. The author is content to remark the spiritual benefit of literal fasting, i.e., abstinence from food and drink. He says nothing about other forms of fasting or about the various motives which prompt it.[84] There is no suggestion that fasting is imposed upon Christians. In the early Christian period fasting is *commended* as a useful spiritual exercise; it must not, however, be a merely external observance. See Barn. 3; Justin Martyr, *Dial.* 15 (both cite Isa 58); Polycarp, *Phil.* 7; Herm. Sim. 5.1ff. Did. 8:1 enjoins a change of days for the Christians' two weekly fast. Later, great emphasis was laid on fasting (Tertullian, Cyprian, Jerome).

The author curtly dismisses *Jewish* fasts as a "shame" (εἰρωνεία, 4:1).

κακουργουμένη. The cognate noun is used in respect of the soul in Ps 34 (35):17. σιτίοις, "food" (Prov 24:57 [30:22]; Acts 7:12 [א AB]), ποτοῖς, "drink" (Ignatius, *Trall.* 2:3) are datives of respect. For the combination, cf. Xen. *Anab.* 7.1.33. For the association of the soul with food and drink, cf. Luke 12:19. See Otto's note for other references.

βελτιοῦται (passive). A late verb. Cf. Philo, *Sacr.* 42; Plutarch, *Mor.* 85C; inscriptions. Cf. Clement of Alexandria, *Paed.* 1.1.1: τὸ τέλος αὐτοῦ βελτιῶσαι τὴν ψυχήν ἐστιν.

καὶ Χριστιανοί . . . μᾶλλον. The thought (see below, πλεονάζουσι) is anticipated in 5:12, 16 and repeated in 7:8 (note κολάζω and πλεονάζω).

κολαζόμενοι. See note on 2:8. καθ᾽ ἡμέραν may be taken with either κολαζόμενοι or πλεονάζουσι. If the latter, the statement, though not the language, is parallel to Acts 2:47.

πλεονάζουσι. "Increase" in either (*a*) numbers (quantitative), or (*b*) strength (qualitative). The strict parallelism with βελτιοῦται would support (*b*). The soul improves the less the corporeal needs are tended. So Christians grow (inwardly) the more they are punished. Stephanus, Otto, and others take this view. But the NT usage of the verb (2 Pet 1:8 *al.*) generally seems to carry with it the notion of external or visible increase ("to flourish")—1 Thess 3:12 of *spiritual* increase is an exception—and this appears to be the sense in 7:8 (below). Moreover, the idea that the Christians increase in numbers in proportion as they are oppressed is very familiar in the apologetic writings. Cf. Justin Martyr, *Dial.* 110: "the more such things (tortures) happen, the more do others and in larger numbers become faithful and worshipers of God through the name of Jesus." So also Tertullian, *Apol.* 50: "the oftener we are mown down by you, the more in number we grow; the blood

---

84. See Ottley in *Lux Mundi*, 511ff.

of Christians is seed." See also *Scap.* 5: "this community will be undying; for be assured that just in the time of its seeming overthrow it is built up into greater power." See Lactantius, *Inst.* 5.19; Origen, *Cels.* 7.26.

εἰς τοσαύτην ... παραιτήσασθαι. Otto sees here a reflection of Plato, *Phaedo* 62B. See note on 6:7 (above). Plato, *Apol.* 29A is perhaps a closer parallel: Socrates will not desert the post (τάξιν) to which the god has ordained him. For the thought cf. Cicero, *Sen.* 73; *Tusc.* 1.74.

For παραιτέομαι see on 4:2. Lachmann prefers to read τοιαύτην here.

The τάξις is the place or rank of the Christians as the soul of the world, ch. 6 ending on the same note as that on which it begins. For this sense of the term, cf. Isocrates 6.2: τὴν ἰδίαν τοῦ βίου τάξιν διαφυλάττων, "by keeping the place appropriate to my years," Josephus, *Ant.* 20.183: παιδαγωγὸς ... τάξιν τὴν ἐπὶ τῶν Ἑλληνικῶν ἐπιστολῶν πεπιστευμένος. Lake thinks that the notion is that of the Church as the *militia dei* (Tertullian). But the context does not suggest the military flavor which τάξις often carries ("post"; cf. Plato, *Apol.* 29A, referred to above).

Chapter 7

The religion of the Christians is no human discovery, but a divine revelation. It was God who implanted in men the truth and the holy and incomprehensible word by sending to them "the very Artificer and Creator of the universe." He sent him in gentleness, meekness, and love to save and persuade, not to compel nor to judge ... Christian martyrs suffer and die but are not overcome. No, they multiply all the more. These things attest God's presence and power.

ὡς ἔφην, i.e., in v. 3 (see note, and cf. 4:6). The thought touched upon there is now resumed and developed (hence γάρ) and the language to some extent repeated. Cf. ἐπινοίᾳ (5:3) with θνητὴν ἐπίνοιαν, and εὑρημένον (5:3) with εὕρημα. Note ἀνθρωπίνων μυστηρίων as perhaps an echo of δόγματος ἀνθρωπίνου (5:3). Pseudo-Justin, *Cohort. ad Gent.* 8, insists that "our progenitors ... received from God the knowledge which also they taught to us. For neither by nature nor by human conception (ἀνθρωπίνῃ ἐννοίᾳ) is it possible for men to know things so great and divine," etc. Cf. Justin Martyr, 2 *Apol.* 10: "our doctrines, then, appear to be greater than all human teaching."

ἐπίγειον. Cf. 7:2. Note Paul's phrase οἱ τὰ ἐπίγεια φρονοῦντες (Phil 3:19) and the σοφία ἐπίγειος of Jas 3:15. For εὕρημα note the classical -ημα form, not the Koine preference for -εμα (cf. Sir 20:9; Strabo, *Georg.* 16.2.24).[85]

ἀξιοῦσιν. See note on 3:2.

οἰκονομίαν μυστηρίων πεπίστευνται. Cf. 1 Cor 9:17. Gildersleeve cites Theophilus., *Autol.* 1.11: [ὁ βασιλεὺς] τρόπῳ τινὶ οἰκονομίαν πεπίστευται. Verbs, which in the active take an accusative of the thing and a dative of the person (cf. John 2:24), have (in the passive) the latter (dative) as subject, while the former (accusative) is retained. Cf. 7:2 (below); Rom 3:2; Gal 2:7. For οἰκονομία, see on 4:5, and for μυστήριον, on 4:6. The perfect πεπίστευνται has its full force of completed past action with existing result (contrast the aorist παρεδόθη).

2. αὐτὸς ... αὐτός. The repeated pronoun adds emphasis. Cf. 9:2 and Rev 19:15. ὁ παντοκράτωρ (θεός). Cf. Let. Aris. 185; 2 Macc 8:18. In the NT the appellative παντοκράτωρ in reference to God ("All-Sovereign") is confined (except in 2 Cor 6:18, a quotation) to nine instances in Rev (1:8–9) but is very frequent in early Christian literature (1 Clem 2:3 *al.*).

παντοκτίστης. The word is not given in Liddell and Scott. It may be a coinage of the author, though an obvious formation from ὁ πάντων κτίστης (of God, 2 Macc 1:24; Sir 24:8; cf. 1 Pet 4:19).

ἀόρατος. Of God, as frequently in Greek, Jewish, and Christian thought. Cf. Aristotle, [*Mundo*] 399a; Col 1:15; Heb 11:27; 1 Tim 1:17; 2 Clem 20:5. See Josephus, *J. W.* 7.346: ἀόρατος ... ὥσπερ αὐτὸς ὁ θεός. For the thought, cf. John 1:18.

ἀπ' οὐρανῶν. The phrase should probably be taken not with αὐτός but with ἐνίδρυσε, "established from heaven," indicating the source of the divine action and the origin of the truth so established.

τὴν ἀλήθειαν ... ἀπερινόητον. A difficult passage due largely to the elasticity of the term λόγος. (*a*) "reason." This, though supported by 10:2: "to whom he gave reason" (λόγον, cf. 2:9, λογισμός) is, in view of the epithets, improbable. (*b*) "teaching." i.e., truth revealed in Christ, here spoken of as "established" and "fixed firmly" among men. So Lightfoot-Harmer. (*c*) the Word, i.e., the incarnate Son. Otto, who takes this view cites John 14:6 (for τὴν ἀλήθειαν) and Theophilus, *Autol.* 2.10 (ὁ λόγος ὁ ἅγιος). His further references to Justin Martyr, *1 Apol.* 32; *Dial.* 54, do not seem conclusive for the present passage. The terms ἅγιος and ἀπερινόητος fit either (*b*) or (*c*), and indeed, as Radford points out,[86] the two views (*b*) and (*c*) are not mutually exclusive. It may be that the author intends "the truth" and "the word" as personifications of Christ, as in the Preaching of Peter (Clement

---

85. See Thackeray, *Grammar*, 1:80; Moulton, *Prolegomena*, 46; Moulton-Howard, *Grammar*, 57, 354.

86. Radford, *Diognetus*, 68–69.

of Alexandria, *Strom.* 1.29.182), where the Lord is called "Law and Word." On the other hand, some support for (*b*) is found in the terms ἐνίδρυσε and ἐγκατεστήριξε and in the fact that the title Logos is used of Christ only in the Appendix (11:2, 3, 7; 12:9). The balance of probability lies on the side of (*b*). In contrast with the "earthly discovery" and the "mortal idea" and "mere human mysteries" (7:1) God has established among men the truth and the holy incomprehensible *teaching* by sending "the very Artificer" etc. On this view there would seem again to be kinship with Johannine thought. Note especially the connection of ἀλήθεια and λόγος. Cf. 1 John 1:8: ἡ ἀλήθεια (ὁ λόγος, 1:10) οὐκ ἔστιν ἐν ἡμῖν, 2:14: ὁ λόγος τοῦ θεοῦ ἐν ὑμῖν μένει, John 17:17: ὁ λόγος ὁ σὸς ἀλήθειά ἐστιν.

For ἀπερινόητον, cf. Theophilus, *Autol.* 1.3: μεγέθει ἀκατάληπτος, ὕψει ἀπερινόητος (of God). The word is used (in an active sense) of ἡ ψυχή in Athenagoras, *Suppl.* 27: ἀπερινόητος δὲ τοῦ πατρὸς καὶ ποιητοῦ τῶν ὅλων.

ἐνίδρυσε. Cf. Plutarch, *Mor.* 1008A: ἡ φύσις, ὥσπερ κυβερνήτην ἐνιδρύσασα τῇ κεφαλῇ τὸν λογισμόν.

ἐγκατεστήριξε. Rare word. Cf. Cornutus, *Nat. d.* 6: ὁ λίθος οὗτος ὃν καλοῦμεν γῆν, οἰονεὶ καταποθεὶς, ἐγκατεστηρίχθη.

καθάπερ. See note on 2:1.

εἰκάσειεν, ἀνθρώποις ὑπηρέτην κτλ. (MS). ἀνθρώποις may be due to dittography (cf. one line above). Otto emends to εἰκάσειεν ἀνθρώπων, ὑπηρέτην, and points to ὡς ἀνθρώπων ἄν τις λογίσαιτο (7:3). Bunsen and other editions read εἰκάσειεν ἄνθρωπος, ὑπηρέτην. For the stylistic trait see p. 15.

ὑπηρέτην τινὰ … διοικήσεις. The passage is difficult. (1) Are two classes in view, or more? (2) What is the connection of the clauses ("one of those who administer the affairs of earth" and "one of those entrusted with the ordering of things in heaven") with ἄγγελον and ἄρχοντα? (3) What precise meaning can be attached to ἄγγελος and ἄρχων here?

Otto takes ὑπηρέτην as a general term. "God has not sent to men just any of his ministering spirits," i.e., from the class of "angels" or "rulers"; the former are further specified as "those who administer the affairs of earth," the latter as "those entrusted with the ordering of things of heaven." On this view both "angel" and "ruler" denote heavenly officiants with different spheres of service. The one class ("angel") administers on earth; the other ("ruler") governs in heaven. This is perhaps to credit our author with too much precision. It may be that the terms and clauses are loosely strung together without careful differentiation. The order of the added clauses supports Otto's connection. On the other hand, the ἄρχοντα and the two explanatory clauses may be merely variations on the term ἄγγελον. God sent no minister to men whether we call him angel or ruler, an earthly governor or a heavenly ruler. But the general sense of the passage is clear. The one sent did not belong to any subordinate order of celestial beings; he was "the very Artificer and Maker of the universe." On the grades of the spiritual hierarchy see Lightfoot on Col 1:16.

The term ἄγγελος was apparently current in early Christian usage as a designation both of the nature and of the office of Christ. Justin Martyr, 1 Apol. 63 uses the term as a title of the Logos: "the Word of God is his Son . . . and he is called ἄγγελος καὶ ἀπόστολος." Harnack[87] cites a protest against this view in Apoc. Sophoniae, iv, frag., p. 10: "He appointed no Angel to come to us, nor Archangel, nor any power, but he transformed himself into a man that he might come to us for our deliverance."[88] Geffcken thinks that the passage in Diognetus is directly opposed (im deutlichen Gegensatze) to Justin's view.[89] But the context suggests that ἄγγελος is here used not as a title, but is descriptive of the role of the Son, in line with the terms ὑπηρέτης and ἄρχων.

The idea of angels exercising authority in heaven and earth is frequent in apologetic literature. See Athenagoras, Suppl. 10: "we recognize also a multitude of angels and ministers (ἀγγέλων καὶ λειτουργῶν) whom God the Maker and Framer of the world distributed and appointed to their several posts by his Logos, to occupy themselves about the elements, and the heavens and the world, and the things in it, and the goodly ordering of them all" (Pratten's translation). See also ch. 24.

ἄρχων is used generically, "ruler," whether in heaven or on earth. For the latter, cf. Bar. 3:16; Matt 20:25; Acts 4:26–28; 1 Clem. 60:2. Geffcken thinks that ἄρχοντα denotes "a demon who directs the στοιχεῖα, as in the Pauline sense: cf. 1 Cor 2:6–8."[90] But this is less probable here. Our author is apparently silent about the demons.[91]

τῶν διεπόντων, "those who administer." Cf. Wis 9:3 (of man); 12:15 (of God). The word is appropriately used here of God's "deputies." Cf. 1 Clem. 61:1–2.

διοικήσεις, "dispensations." Once in the Greek Bible (Tob 1:21, "state of affairs"). In 1 Clem. 20:1 the word is used of the divine "appointment" which controls the heavens. Cf. Epictetus 1.14.7: ἡ θεία διοίκησις.

For the accusative case, see on οἰκονομίαν μυστηρίων πεπίστευνται (7:1).

τὸν τεχνίτην καὶ δημιουργόν. Both terms relate to the Son. τεχνίτης is used of God in Wis 13:1, and both terms in juxtaposition (of God) in Heb 11:10[92]

---

87. Harnack, History of Dogma, 1:185n3.
88. See also Harnack, Geschichte, 1:758; 2.1:514n1, and Kirchenordnung, 69.
89. Geffcken, Diognetos, 20–21.
90. Geffcken, Diognetos, 21.
91. Geffcken, Diognetos, 22.
92. See Moffatt, Hebrews, ad loc.

and Philo, *Mut.* 29-31. In 8:7 (below) δημιουργὸς τῶν ὅλων is descriptive of God, with which cf. 1 Clem. 26:1; 59:2: ὁ δημιουργὸς τῶν ἁπάντων.

ᾧ... ἔκτισεν, ᾧ... ἐνέκλεισεν. A "remarkable" use of the instrumental dative.[93] Aall notes this passage and points out that the instrumental dative may be used rather than the usual διά with genitive, whenever the means is regarded as personal.[94] Cf. Xen., *Anab.* 6.4.27: ἐν δὲ τοῖς ὅπλοις ἐνυκτέρευον, φυλαττόμενοι ἱκανοῖς φύλαξι. Cf. also Soph., *Antig.* 164 (πομποῖσιν, "by means of messengers"). The function of the Logos in the creation of the world is commonly expressed by διά with genitive. Cf. John 1:3, 10; Heb 1:2. Philo speaks of God as the cause (αἴτιον) of the world by whom it was made (ὑφ' οὗ γέγονεν), but the Word as the medium through whom it was prepared (ὄργανον δὲ λόγον θεοῦ δι' οὗ κατεσκευάσθη, *de Cherub* 127). Cf. also *de Sacerd.* 81: λόγος δ' ἐστὶν εἰκὼν θεοῦ, δι' οὗ σύμπας ὁ κόσμος ἐδημιουργεῖτο. But Philo also uses the simple dative in this connection. Cf. *Deus* 57: δίδωσι δὲ λόγῳ χρώμενος ὑπηρέτῃ δωρεῶν, ᾧ καὶ τὸν κόσμον εἰργάζετο. The use dative in both Philo and our epistle may attest the feeling that the Logos is directly concerned in the act, being less the medium than the personal instrument of creation. We note that Diognetus has διά with genitive to indicate the office of the Word in revelation (8:11; 11:2), enrichment of the Church (11:5) and glorification of God (12:9).

For ἔκτισεν see on 4:2. ἐνέκλεισεν. Cf. 2:7; 6:7, and for the thought 1 Clem. 20:6-7; 33:3. See the glowing description of Wisdom in Prov 8:27ff.: "when he gave to the sea its bound" (5:29 RV. The LXX has no equivalent of this sentence. But not the reading of ℵAC A in Swete's text, footnote). Cf. Job 26:10; 38:8; Ps 104:9; Jer 5:22.

τὰ μυστήρια, i.e., the laws of nature as being divine "secrets" lying beyond man's knowledge. See on 4:6. πιστῶς, only once in the Greek Bible (4 Kgs 16:2). Cf. 1 Clem. 35:5; P.Oxy. IX, 1187[18] (254 CE) ὑγιῶς καὶ πιστῶς. In 8:2, τὰ στοιχεῖα = "the elements." See note. Here the term denotes the heavenly bodies ("luminaries") immediately named (sun, moon, stars), as in Justin Martyr, 2 *Apol.* 5: τὰ οὐράνια στοιχεῖα. Cf. 2 Pet 3:10, 12 (RV); Theophilus, *Autol.* 1.4.[95]

δρόμων. Used frequently of the "courses" of the sun and moon (cf. below). So 1 Esdr. 4:34; Josephus, *Ant.* 1.31. ὁ ἥλιος is lacking in the MS. Most editions insert (with or without the article), but some before εἴληφε (Bunsen, Otto), others before (Hefele) or after (Krenkel, Gildersleeve) φυλάσσειν.

---

93. Moulton, *Prolegomena*, 76n.

94. Aall, *Logos*, 2:370n1.

95. See the full notes in Moulton and Milligan, *Vocabulary*, 591; Burton, *Galatians*, 510ff.; Lietzmann, *Galater*, 23ff.

ᾧ πειθαρχεῖ. The phrase is immediately repeated. See p. 14 (ἡ) σελήνη. Otto inserts the article (lacking in the MS), pointing to τὰ στοιχεῖα (preceding) and τὰ ἄστρα (following). He thinks that H may easily have fused with the last two letters (E I) of the preceding word. Lightfoot and Lake omit the article. Note the anarthrous οὐρανοί, etc., in the following passage, and see note on 4:5. For νυκτί Gildersleeve reads ἐν νυκτί, but cf. 2:7 (ταῖς νυξί). For ἀκολουθοῦντα see on 5:4.

διώρισται. In Isa 45:18 of the divine action in creation, as here. The word is found in Herodotus, inscriptions, and the papyri.

καὶ ὑποτέτακται. Some interpret, "to whom (all things) have been subjected." Cf. 1 Cor 15:27. But it would be harsh in a writer as neat as the author to take ᾧ with the third verb in a different sense (dative of advantage) from that of the other two (dative of agent after the perfect passive = "by whom"). Otto renders, *a quo omnia disposita et suis limitibus circumscripta et (hominibus) subjecta sunt*. He thinks that the phrase, "the earth and the things in the earth," relates to ὑποτέτακται, and he completes the sense by adding "to men" on the analogy of 10:2: οἷς (i.e., to men) ὑπέταξε πάντα τὰ ἐν τῇ γῇ. For subjection to man cf. Gen 1:26; 9:2; Heb 2:8 (= Ps 8:6); Justin Martyr, *2 Apol.* 5: ὁ θεὸς . . . τὰ ἐπίγεια ἀνθρώποις ὑποτάξας.

ἐν οὐρανοῖς. It is unnecessary to insert the article τοῖς (as Otto), for, while it would match τῇ γῇ and τῇ θαλάσσῃ, the author's invariable practice is to omit the article in this prepositional phrase (5:9; 6:8; 10:2, 7). See note on σελήνη (above). Cf. ἐν ὕψεσι and ἐν βαθέσι (below).

τοῦτον. Emphatic and resumptive. Cf. 10:6 (*sub fin.*). ἀπέστειλεν (so 10:2), but πέμπω in 7:4–5. Both verbs are used in the NT of the Father "sending" the Son. Cf. 1 John 4:9, 14 (ἀποστέλλω); Rom 8:3 (πέμπω). It is hardly possible to refine between the two verbs in this connection.[96]

3. For ἆρά γε cf. Gen 37:10; Acts 8:30. ἄνθρωπος is used pleonastically as in 8:1, 5. ὡς . . . λογίσαιτο. For the stylistic feature see p. 15.

ἐπὶ τυραννίδι. The ἐπί is either (1) of accompaniment ("with," "in"), virtually equivalent to ἐν (cf. ἐν ἐπιεικείᾳ, 7:4). Cf. Rom 4:18; 2 Cor 9:6. Or more probably (2) of object or purpose ("to rule in tyranny," etc.). Cf. Wis 2:23; Gal 5:13; Eph 2:10. ἐν ἐπιεικείᾳ would then be differentiated, "in gentleness." See 1 Thess 4:7 for a similar variation of the prepositions. καταπλήξει. Classical word. Cf. 2 Esdr. 3:3; *B.G.U.*: 1209[16] (1st c. BCE) πρὸς κατάπληξιν τῶν τολμησάντων.

4. Here only, and that in a quite general way, does the author show any interest in the earthly life of the Son. Cf. also 11:3.

---

96. Contra Westcott, *John*, Additional Note, 298. On the incidence of the two verbs in the Johannine writings, see Howard, *John*, 25.

ἐν ἐπιεικείᾳ καὶ πραΰτητι. For the collocation cf. Philo, *Opif.* 103 and, with reference to Christ, as here, 2 Cor 10:1. Otto punctuates with a full stop after πραΰτητι, supplying in thoughts the words "He sent him." But the sense does not demand a stop after πραΰτητι. The passage has a rhythmical force, which suggests an excerpt from a Christian hymn (see on 9:2).[97] πραΰτης (a later form of πραότης) is a characteristic of the messianic king (Zech 9:9).

ὡς βασιλεὺς ... ἔπεμψεν. The accusative (three times) before the main verb ἔπεμψεν rather favors the rendering. "He sent him as king. He sent him as God" (Lake). But it is preferable to translate "He sent him, as a king sending a son who is a king," etc., since (*a*) the ὡς qualifies βασιλεύς not βασιλέα. (*b*) the apposition "the son who was a king" gives added point to ἐν ἐπιεικείᾳ καὶ πραΰτητι. Though he was a king, he did not come in tyranny and terror and awe, but in gentleness and meekness. (*c*) the antithesis "God"... "man" is more natural than the series "king," "God," "man."

Here Keim sees an allusion to Commodus being taken into the co-regentship by his father,[98] and hence dates the epistle in the time of Marcus Aurelius (ca. 177 CE).[99]

ὡς θεόν. See above, p. 26. ἄνθρωπον. So Lachmann conjectures. Lightfoot brackets the word.

ὡς πείθων ... τῷ θεῷ. Note the parallel in P.S.I., II, 120 (? 4th c. CE) εὐμετάβολος γὰρ ὁ θεός. πεῖσαι ζητεῖ μὴ βιάσασθαι. ὁ μὲν γὰρ βιασάμενος ἐχθρός, ὁ δὲ πείσας σοφός.[100] Connolly cites several passage from Irenaeus, *Haer.* on the point of God's not using "force," which in his view show that "Irenaeus is under contribution both by Hippolytus and in the Epistle to Diognetus."[101] In particular the words ὡς πείθων, οὐ βιαζόμενος (Diogn. 7:4) closely agree with Irenaeus, *Haer.* 5.1.1, *suadentem et non vim inferentem*, and the οὐ βιαζόμενος has "at least four other parallels in Irenaeus." Moreover, βία γὰρ οὐ πρόσεστι τῷ θεῷ (Diogn. 7:5) is precisely paralleled in the first half of Irenaeus's statement (4.59) *vis enim a Deo non fit, sed bona sententia adest illi semper* (βία [γὰρ] θεῷ οὐ πρόσεστιν. ἀγαθὴ δὲ γνώμη πάντοτε συμπάρεστιν αὐτῷ). Connolly argues that this close relationship posits literary indebtedness and that Diognetus has borrowed from Irenaeus and not vice versa.[102]

---

97. See the note in Otto, *Epistola ad Diognetum*, 2nd ed., 186.
98. Keim, "Die Zeit der Apologie Justin's," n13 and 14.
99. See Lightfoot and Harmer, *Apostolic Fathers*, 488.
100. Cited in Moulton and Milligan, *Vocabulary*, 110.
101. Connolly, "Date and Authorship," 349ff.
102. For the bearing of this point on the question of the date of the epistle, see pp. 18–19. See also Harnack, *Geschichte*, 1:758; 2.1:514; Grensted, *Atonement*, 36.

βία γάρ ... θεῷ. Otto brackets these words and suspects a gloss. οὐ βιαζόμενος. Middle "using no violence" (cf. Luke 16:16). Cf. 10:5 (translation); Thuc. 7:70, 72 (βιάζεσθαι τὸν ἔκπλουν); 4 Macc 2:8. It is probably passive in Matt 11:12, as in classical Greek.[103]

5. καλῶν. Used absolutely, a point which Connolly[104] notes in favor of the Hippolytean authorship of the epistle. See Hippolytus, *Philo.* 10.33.

6. The οὐ κρίνων (5) reminds the author of the second coming of Christ as judge. Hence κρίνοντα, the present participle expressing attendant circumstances ("in judgment") which easily shades off into purpose ("to judge"). It is unnecessary to emend (with Stephanus and Bunsen) to κρινοῦντα. For the occasional use of the *present* participle to imply purpose Blass-Debrunner cite Thuc. 7.25.9, ἔπεμψαν ... ἀγγέλλοντας (note the normal *future* participles which follow, δηλώσοντας, ἀξιώσοντας).[105] Cf. also Acts 3:26 where εὐλογοῦντα may be rendered purposively "to bless" (so RV, Moffatt, Goodspeed, Weymouth) and 15:27 (ἀπαγγελοῦντας D).

καὶ ... ὑποστήσεται; cf. Mal 3:2. See above, pp. 52–53. The wicked especially have cause to fear the judgment by Christ at his second coming. See Justin Martyr, *Dial.* 121. For ὑφίστημι, with accusative, cf. Jdt 6:3; Prov 13:8.

τὴν παρουσίαν. In classical Greek the word bears the general sense "presence," "arrival," as also in LXX (2 Esdr. 12, 6A; 2 Macc 8:12 *al.*) and the NT (2 Cor 10:10; Phil 2:12). In the papyri and inscriptions παρουσία has added a quasi-technical meaning denoting the "visit" of a royal or official personage. This particularized usage is reflected in the NT where the term is frequently and appropriately employed "to emphasize the nearness and the certainty" of the second advent of Christ (1 Thess 2:19 *al.*).[106] It is not certain whether our author uses the term here in the general sense "presence" or with the particularized meaning "coming." The meaning "presence" (of God) in 7:9 (see note *ad loc.*) favors the former view; the latter is supported by the context ("He will send him as judge").

7. The MS has a lacuna at this point with a marginal note: οὕτως καὶ ἐν τῷ ἀντιγράφῳ εὗρον ἐγκοπήν, παλαιοτάτου ὄντος. A considerable section may have been omitted (see on 5:11). Stephanus fills in the gap with the words οὐχ ὁρᾷς (cf. 7:8 *init.*). Otto has a full note on the suggestions made by various editions.[107] For παραβαλλομένους θηρίοις cf. Justin Martyr, *Dial.* 110.

---

103. See, however, Deissmann, *Bible Studies*, 258; Otto, *Kingdom*, 108–12; Moulton and Milligan, 109–10.

104. Connolly, "Date and Authorship," 349ff.

105. Blass-Debrunner, *Grammatik*, §339, 2.

106. See Milligan's elaborate study of the word in Milligan, *Thessalonians*, 145ff.

107. See also Geffcken, *Diognetos*, 22.

ἵνα ἀρνήσωνται τὸν κύριον. This was the head and front of the Christians' offence, that they would not offer sacrifice to the emperor and renounce Christ (cf. 10:7). For ἀρνέομαι, with personal accusative ("unclassical and seems to be confined to Christian literature"[108]), cf. Matt 10:33; 2 Clem. 17:7. For the title κύριος, cf. 12:9; in both instances it refers to the exalted Christ (Rom 14:8; Eph 4:5).

8. The direct address to Diognetus is here inserted in the exposition which began with ch. 5. It is repeated in 7:2; 10:1, 3, 4, 7, 8.

κολάζονται. The verb here and perhaps in 6:9 suggests the "punishment" of death. See 10:7: "you will love and admire those who are being punished (τοὺς κολαζομένους) because they will not deny God"... "the everlasting fire which shall punish (κολάσει) up to the end." Note κόλασις καὶ θάνατος (9:2). κολάζω is used probably in this sense in Wis 3:4. Cf. also Matt 25:46 (εἰς κόλασιν αἰώνιον).

πλεονάζοντας. See on 6:9. Funk queries whether Exod 1:12 is here in mind.[109]

9. ταῦτα ... ἔργα. Stephanus omits οὐ (dittography from the preceding ἀνθρώπου?) and takes the sentence as a question to which the words that immediately follow are the answer. "These things" are the endurance and triumph of the Christian martyrs (cf. 10:8). δύναμις, "mighty act," God's moral power (cf. 9:1, 2) at work, enabling impotent man.

τῆς παρουσίας αὐτοῦ δείγματα. The precise reference indicated by παρουσία is uncertain. (a) Christ's *first* coming. So Otto (*eum advenisse*), who points to the opening words of ch. 8 (πρὶν αὐτόν ἐλθεῖν). The connection, however, of the last-named clause with the end of ch. 7 is hardly conclusive, since 8:1 may introduce a new theme. Moreover, the notion of the *second* coming has already intervened (7:6), if παρουσία there is so interpreted. But is in favor of Otto's view that the bulk of the chapter (vv. 1–5) relates to the first coming. παρουσία commonly has this meaning (Ign. *Phil* 9:2). Justin Martyr (*1 Apol.* 52; *Dial.* 14; 32) uses the term of *either* advent. (b) Christ's *second* coming, as probably in 7:6. The thought in the present passage is consonant with this rendering: endurance by the Christians of persecution is a presage that Christ is soon to come again. Cf. Matt 24:9f.; Did. 16:3–8; Justin Martyr, *Dial.* 39; 110. (c) God's "presence." This is the most probable interpretation. The pronoun goes most naturally with the antecedent θεοῦ, and the twofold contrast of "man" and "God" is not marred by the introduction of a third factor (the coming of Christ). For παρουσία in reference to *God*, see T. 12 Patr., T. Jud. 22:2: ἕως τῆς παρουσίας θεοῦ τῆς

---

108. Mayor, *Jude*, 72.
109. Funk, *Patres Apostolici*, 401.

δικαιοσύνης. Cf. also Athanasius, *Inc.* 19:3: τὴν τοῦ δεσπότου παρουσίαν (in 31:2 of the "presence" of Christ).

δείγματα. So Stephanus for the MS reading δόγματα. See 4:5.

Chapter 8

The author now approaches Diognetus's third query. The answer is given more explicitly in ch. 9, to which he leads up by denying that any true knowledge of God existed before the coming of his Son. The theories held by "those specious philosophers" about the nature of God are palpably absurd. They savor too of deceit and magic. The true knowledge of God (that he is kind, good, and long-suffering) and of his purpose comes through faith, "by which alone it is given to see God." God manifested himself. So long as God's design remained secret man could charge God with indifference. But by the revelation through "His beloved child" that which had been prepared from the beginning was made known and all its benefits conferred. What unexpected gifts!

1. πρὶν αὐτὸν ἐλθεῖν. Not πρὶν ἤ as in 2:3 (see note). The general rule is observed that πρίν (= "before") commonly takes the infinitive after affirmative principal sentences. The αὐτόν relates to the Son, the meaning being that as θεός (cf. 7:4) he was able to reveal the nature of the divine. See above, p. 26. For the thought cf. John 1:18; Acts 17:23.

2. On the attitude to pagan philosophers, see pp. 33–34. In Heraclitus's view reality regarded in its material aspect is fire; the Logos, fire, and God are fundamentally the same conception.[110] Thales held that the origin of all things is water. Our author curtly dismisses such speculations. If God is to be identified with the elements, then one element is as good as another. The *Apology of Aristides* 4ff. (Syr.), discusses these theories more seriously and fully.

ληρώδεις, "foolish," a classical word (Plato, Aristotle). Cf. 2 Macc 12:44: περισσὸν καὶ ληρῶδες ὑπὲρ νεκρῶν εὔχεσθαι, B. G. U. 1011.2.15 (2nd c. BCE) πολλὰ ... ληρώιδη καὶ ψευδῆ. For ἀποδέχῃ, cf. Acts 2:41.

ἀξιοπίστων, "trustworthy" (Prov 28:20), perhaps used here ironically (Otto). It may, however, bear a later derogatory sense, "specious," "plausible," for which cf. Ign. *Phil.* 2, where heretical teachers are described as λύκοι ἀξιόπιστοι (see Lightfoot's note for further references). Lucian (*Alex.* 4) uses it in this ironical way. He characterizes Alexander's type of soul as πιθανὴν καὶ ἀξιόπιστον, "plausible and convincing."

---

110. See Adam, *Religious Teachers*, 212ff.

οἱ μέν τινες. So most editions. Otto brackets τινες (see his note). For ὁ μέν τις ... ὁ δέ, cf. 2:2 (note).

(οὗ μέλλουσι ... θεόν). A parenthesis in ironical vein ("this Christian unmannerliness," Gildersleeve). They are destined to go to τὸ πῦρ τὸ αἰώνιον (10:7, 8). To think they should give the name of God to that! οὗ = οἷ. In late Greek the notions of "where" and "to where" often coalesce. The distinction had not always been preserved even in the classical language.[111] For the Greek Bible (where οἷ does not occur) cf. Gen 11:3; Luke 10:1. μέλλουσι χωρήσειν. As often in classical Greek μέλλω takes the *future* infinitive, which is almost obsolete in the LXX, NT (*three times*), and the papyri.[112] For χωρεῖν, "to go," cf. Matt 15:17; Ign. *Eph.* 16:2 (εἰς τὸ πῦρ τὸ ἄσβεστον χωρήσει). For the passive in another sense see 12:7 (below).

τῶν στοιχείων, "the elements," often enumerated as four (fire, water, air, earth). Cf. Plato, *Timaeus* 32C; Wis 7:17. For ἐκτισμένων see on 4:2.

3. καίτοι γε introduces an objection or qualification. Cf. Xen., *Mem.* 1.2.3; John 4:2. καίτοι is rare in the Greek Bible (4 Macc 2:6; Acts 14:17), and is not found in the Apostolic Fathers.

ἀπόδεκτός ἐστι. Bunsen and other editions accent as a verbal form; Otto as an adjective (ἀπόδεκτος, cf. 1 Tim 2:3; 5:4). Cf. the cognate verb above (8:2).

δύναιτ' ἄν. Either the personal construction with ἓν ἕκαστον as subject (cf. 2:4), or "it would be possible," impersonal use followed by accusative and infinitive. Stephanus prefers δύναιν' ἄν, "they (the philosophers) would be able," etc. So also Geffecken.

4. ταῦτα, i.e., the content of the λόγοι of the philosophers (8:2, 3). τερατεία, "big talk," cf. Aristophanes, *Nub.* 318 ("humbug"); Polybius 2.17.6: περὶ ὧν οἱ τραγῳδιογράφοι ... πολλὴν διατέθεινται τερατείαν. Blakeney appositely cites two passages from Eusebius, *Praep. ev.* 63 and 132, for the conjunction of τερατεία with "deceit" (ἀπάτη).[113] τῶν γοήτων, "of the magicians," as often in classical Greek. Later the word frequently bears the sense "impostor." For their πλάνη see 2 Tim 3:13, where they are stigmatized as πλανῶντες καὶ πλανώμενοι. The term is used here in the active sense, "deceit." The passive sense, "error," probably holds in all NT occurrences of the word, "though the active meaning, 'deceit,' would sometimes be equally

---

111. Blass-Debrunner, *Grammatik*, §103.
112. See Moulton, *Prolegomena*, 114n.
113. Blakeney, *Diognetus*, 65.

appropriate."[114] Philo, *Sacr.* 315, speaks of the γόης as ψευδόμενος λόγια καὶ χρησμοὺς ἐπλάσσατο.[115]

5–8. It is not unlikely that the thought that God himself revealed himself (5) as eternally the same (8) echoes a passage in Sib. Orac. 3.15: ἀλλ' αὐτὸς ἀνέδειξεν αἰώνιος αὐτὸς ἑαυτόν ὄντα τε καὶ πρὶν ἐόντα, ἀτὰρ πάλι καὶ μετέπειτα. The Christian apologists, e.g., Justin Martyr, *1 Apol.* 44; Athenagoras, *Suppl.* 30; and especially Theophilus, *Autol.* 2.3.36, drew upon the Sibylline Oracles, as did Tertullian and Lactantius in the West. Blakeney gives further pagan parallels to the thought of §8.[116]

θεόν (§ *sub fin.*) must be understood as the object of εἶδεν and ἐγνώρισεν. The thought repeats that of 8:1. One might have expected the author to quote here John 1:18. ἐγνώρισεν, either (*a*) "has known," "recognized" (Lightfoot-Harmer), or (*b*) "has made known," "declared," a meaning rare in classical Greek, but predominant in Hellenistic (1 Sam 6:2; Eph 1:9; Phil 4:6). So Otto (*notum fecit*). The same uncertainty attaches to Phil 1:22 ("to know"; RV, "to make known," RV m). The context in Diogn. 8:5 leaves either rendering open, though εἶδεν (Stephanus's emendation of the MS εἶπεν) favors "has known," since "seeing" and "knowing" God are frequently associated (Irenaeus, *Haer* 4.20.6 and 11).

αὐτός, i.e., God. Emphatic, as in Matt 1:21; Acts 20:35.

6. ἐπέδειξε δέ sc. ἑαυτόν. Cf. John 21:1 (ἐφανέρωσεν δὲ οὕτως). The verb ἐπιδείκνυμι is used of God twice only in the Greek Bible (Isa 37:26; Heb 6:17). Cf. 12:3 below. διὰ πίστεως. Cf. Rom 3:25; Eph 3:17. For the meaning of "faith" in the author's thought, see p. 39, and the note on 9:4 (below). ᾗ μόνῃ "by which alone" (instrumental dative), rather than "to which alone." Faith enables men to see God who is ἀόρατος (7:2; cf. 8:5). Do we have here a reminiscence of Heb 11:27? συγκεχώρηται, "it is given," "conceded," perfect with the force of existing state. συγχωρέω, a classical word found in the LXX, inscriptions, and papyri.

7. From this point to the end of ch. 9 the author addresses himself particularly to Diognetus's third question. See p. 95.

ὁ γὰρ δεσπότης ... θεός. For the combined terms cf. 1 Clem. 20:11; 33:2. δεσπότης (cf. 3:2) is a title of God in the LXX (Wis 6:7 *al.*) and in the NT of both God and Christ (Luke 2:29; 2 Pet 2:1). For δημιουργός (of God) see on 7:2. It is frequent in later philosophy of God as Creator (Philo).

---

114. Robinson, *Ephesians*, 185.
115. See Blakeney's note in *Diognetus*, 65–66.
116. Blakeney, *Diognetus*, 66–67.

τῶν ὅλων is to be taken with both appellatives. Cf. Justin Martyr, 1 Apol. 36: ἀπὸ προσώπου τοῦ δεσπότου πάντων καὶ πατρὸς θεοῦ. For ὁ τῶν ὅλων δεσπότης see Justin Martyr, Dial. 140. With κατὰ τάξιν, cf. 1 Cor 14:40.

φιλάνθρωπος. The adjective and its cognates commonly denote the "humaneness" of a king towards his subjects. Cf. Let. Aris. 36; 208; 2 Macc 4:11; inscriptions and papyri. Here it is used of God (cf. φιλανθρωπία, 9:2), who while being ὁ δεσπότης καὶ δημιουργὸς τῶν ὅλων is also "a lover of men." Moulton and Milligan cite P.Oxy. VI, 925², ὁ θεὸς . . . φιλάνθρωπος καὶ δημιουρός (in a Christian prayer of the 5th/6th c. CE).[117]

μακρόθυμος, of God, as in 9:2 (the verb); Exod 34:6; Herm. Sim. 8.11.1. The cognate substantive is frequent (of God) in the Pauline Epistles (Rom 2:4 al.).

8. χρηστός. For the χρηστότης of God (Ps 144 [145]:7) cf. 9:1, 2, 6; 10:4. As so used in the NT it expresses God's (a) gracious long-suffering (Luke 6:25; Rom 2:4; cf. the substantive in Rom 11:22). (b) loving-kindness (Titus 3:4; 1 Pet 2:3). It is frequent in the Apostolic Fathers (1 Clem. 9:1 al.).

καὶ ἀγαθὸς . . . καὶ μόνος ἀγαθός ἐστιν. Not mere repetition. The second statement amplifies the first: "God is good . . . yes, he alone is good" (the sole source of goodness). For the thought, cf. Mark 10:18 (= Matt 19:17; Luke 18:19).

ἀόργητος. The only negative quality in the list. The word is not used of God in the Greek Bible, perhaps because of the frequent references to the ὀργή and θυμός of God. But Hellenistic-Jewish writers had already sounded this note (cf. Let. Aris. 254: "one must know that God directs the whole world with kindliness, all anger apart"), taken up by Christian writers. Cf. 1 Clem. 19:3: "let us consider how free from wrath (ἀόργητος) is he toward all his creatures"; Aristides, Apol. 1 (Syr.) "he does not possess anger and wrath." Athenagoras, Suppl. 21, marks the same feature in heathen gods. Per contra see Theophilus, Autol. 1.3: "is God angry? Yes, he is angry with those who act wickedly," etc.[118]

For an impressive passage on the moral qualities of God in "forbearing" with men see 2 Esdr. 7:62–68 [132–38].

9. The idea of God's counsel with the pre-existent Logos has been traced to Gen 1:26, ποιήσωμεν ἄνθρωπον κτλ. It is reflected in Herm. Sim. 9.12.2: "the Son of God is older than all his creation, so that he was the Counsellor [σύμβουλον] of his creation to the Father." Cf. also Barn. 5:5. Theophilus, Autol. 2.18, commenting on Gen 1:26, writes: "to no one else than his own Word and Wisdom did he say, 'Let us make,'" and again (2.22)

---

117. Moulton and Milligan, Vocabulary, 669.
118. See Bevan, Later Greek Religion, 215n2.

"for before anything came into being he had him (the Word) as his Counsellor [σύμβουλον], being his own mind and thought."

The above references relate to the counsel of the Son in *creation*. The thought in Diognetus is rather that the Son shares in the plan of *redemption*, which he was to effect by his being sent to men (8:11; 9:1). It may be that the author has in mind Isa 9:6 (אCA AV), where the ideal messianic king is described as θαυμαστὸς σύμβουλος, which Clement of Alexandria (*Paed.* 1.24) reproduces in his quotation. Cf. the *admirabilis, consiliarius, Deus fortis* of Irenaeus, *Haer.* 4.33.11. For the idea that the Logos not only shared in the divine counsel but also revealed it to men (Diogn. 8:11), perhaps suggested by the μεγάλης βουλῆς ἄγγελος of Isa 9:5, cf. Hippolytus, *Dan.* 3.9: ὁ δὲ λόγος ἀκούσας τὴν βουλὴν τοῦ πατρὸς καταβὰς ἀπὸ οὐρανῶν τὸ θέλημα τοῦ πατρὸς τοῖς ἀγγέλοις ἀνήγγειλεν. See also Justin Martyr, *Dial.* 56; 76; 127; 128, and the note above (on Diogn. 7:2, ἄγγελος).

ἄφραστον. Poetical word (Homer, Aeschylus), emerging again in later prose. Cf. T. Levi 8.15 (*variant*) of the παρουσία.

ἔννοιαν, "design," "intent" (Heb 4:12), i.e., the incarnation. Cognate accusative ἀνεκοινώσατο. So Bunsen, Gildersleeve, and others for the MS reading ἣν ἐκοινώσατο. For ἀνακοινόω (Plato, Xen.), cf. 2 Macc 14:20. For the thought, see 9:1.

μόνῳ τῷ παιδί. Stephanus and Krenkel think that some words have fallen out after τῷ παιδί. It would seem that παῖς and υἱός are used in the epistle as practical equivalents expressing the filial relationship of Christ to God. Note that the epithets ἀγαπητός and μονογενής (which may be virtually synonymous; see on 8:11) are used of παῖς (8:11) and υἱός (10:2) respectively. If we can at all refine here, Christ as παῖς shares and reveals the Father's plan of salvation (8:9, 11; 9:1); as υἱός he is "sent" and effects it (9:2, 4; 10:2). Note the interchange of the two terms in Wis 2:13, 18 (cf. 2:16), 12:19, 20–21, in John 4:46, 47, 50, 53 (nobleman's υἱός), 51 (παῖς, *variant* υἱός), and (of the Word) in Hippolytus (see the passages cited in Additional Note C, below).[119] παῖς, "in later Christianity easily fused with υἱός when applied to Jesus."[120] Cf. Origen, *Cels.* 7.9 (θεοῦ παῖς), 10 (θεοῦ υἱός).

The usage of παῖς in Acts (3:13, 26; 4:27, 30) probably arises from the LXX occurrence of the term in Second Isaiah to denote the "Servant" (52:13 *al.*), though it is also used in the OT of the great men of Israel (Moses, etc.). Matthew 12:18 specifically applies the παῖς of Isa 42:1 to Jesus. Cf. Did. 9:2f; Barn. 6:1; 9:2. In these passages παῖς is rightly rendered "servant."[121]

119. See Dalman, *Words of Jesus*, 277ff.

120. Cadbury, *Beginnings*, 5:369.

121. See the discussion in Cadbury, *Beginnings*, 1:391; 4:46f.; 5:29; Rawlinson, *New Testament Doctrine*, Additional Note II, 238ff.; Taylor, *Atonement*, 26n1.

It is the filial relationship of Christ to God that dominates our author's mind. Hence we render παῖς as "child," not "servant." Cf. especially Mart. Poly. 14:1: ὁ τοῦ ἀγαπητοῦ καὶ εὐλογητοῦ παιδός σου Ἰησοῦ Χριστοῦ πατήρ. See also 14:3. Lightfoot detects the higher sense of υἱός in the ambiguous word παῖς in 1 Clem. 59:2 (see his note *ad loc.*) and cites Apost. Const. 8.5, 14, 39, 40, 41.

10–11. The essential points in these sections (the divine design for long kept secret—the possible charge against God of neglect of man—the revelation through the Son of the plan prepared from the beginning—the consequent blessings contrary to all man's expectations) are drawn from Paul's teaching, and there is some similarity in language also. See especially Rom 16:25f.; 1 Cor 2:7–10; Eph 3:4f.; Col 1:26f. Note the prevalence of the terms μυστήριον, ἀποκάλυψις (ἀποκαλύπτω), φανερόω, and the idea of the prolonged "hiddenness" of the divine plan (cf. the phrases χρόνοις αἰωνίοις, πρὸ τῶν αἰώνων, ἑτέραις γενεαῖς, ἀποκεκρυμμένον ἀπὸ τῶν αἰώνων καὶ ἀπὸ τῶν γενεῶν). The ὅσα ἡτοίμασεν ὁ θεὸς τοῖς ἀγαπῶσιν αὐτόν of 1 Cor 2:9 (a citation) suggests τὰ ἐξ ἀρχῆς ἡτοιμασμένα of Diogn. 8:11, and Paul's question in Rom 8:32 the words πάνθ᾽ ἅμα παρέσχεν ἡμῖν (Diogn. 8:11; cf. also 1 Tim 6:17).

ἐν μυστηρίῳ is better taken with κατεῖχεν ("He held *it* in a mystery and guarded his wise counsel") rather than with the whole phrase κατεῖχεν . . . βουλήν. The second clause then virtually repeats the notion of the first.

αὑτοῦ. It is unnecessary to read αὐτοῦ with Bunsen and others. See 1 Pet 2:9 and cf. 1 Clem. 19:3: εἰς τὸ μακρόθυμον αὐτοῦ βούλημα.

ἐδόκει, "he seemed," personal use as in Acts 17:18.

For the marginal comment in the MS at the end of §10 see Radford[122]

11. τοῦ ἀγαπητοῦ παιδός, (*a*) "beloved child" (= ἠγαπημένος, cf. Ps 44 [45] title; 1 Clem. 59:2), or (*b*) "only child" (= μονογενής, cf. 10:2 below; Mart. Poly 20), a sense found in classical Greek (*Dem.* 21.165) and the LXX (Gen 22:2; Jer 6:26). ἀγαπητός is frequent in the Ascension of Isaiah (1.4 *al.*) as a title of the Messiah.[123] For φανερόω (of God) cf. 9:2, and (of the Word) 11:2.

τὰ . . . ἡτοιμασμένα. The idea of divine "preparation" from the beginning in the interest of God's people is familiar in the NT (Matt 20:23; 25:34; 1 Cor 2:9).

νοῆσαι, ἃ τίς. So Lachmann conjectures for the MS ποιῆσαι τίς.[124]

προσεδόκησεν. Cf. 9:5: "O the unexpected [ἀπροσδοκήτων] blessings!"

---

122. Radford, *Diognetus*, 73–74.

123. Cf. Mark 1:11; 9:7; and see Robinson, *Ephesians*, 229ff.; Turner, "ho huios," 113ff.

124. See Otto, *Epistola ad Diognetum*, 2nd ed., 192.

Chapter 9

To the third question as to why Christianity was late in appearing the author replies as follows. God permitted men during the pre-Christian period to be under the dominion of sin, until both their own inability to attain life and the inevitable reward of sin were fully manifest. This he did in his forbearance and by wise design. Then at the appointed time God in his patience and love gave his own Son as ransom for men. In none other than him, the righteous one, is there salvation.

1. πάντ' οὖν ἥδυ ... οἰκονομηκώς. So Lachmann's reconstruction, which most editions accept. Others follow the MS reading πάντ' οὖν ᾔδει ... οἰκονομικῶς, on the interpretation of which see Radford's note.[125] οἰκονομηκώς, "late for ᾠκονομηκώς" (Gildersleeve). For οἰκονομέω in the general sense "plan," "arrange," cf. 3 Macc 3:2; Polyb. 4.67.9. See note on οἰκονομία (4:5).

σὺν τῷ παιδί. σύν, "in association with," here only in the epistle though frequent in compounds. σύν is little used in Attic prose, apart from Xenophon. So also in the NT it is comparatively rare, being mainly Lukan (Luke 2:13; Acts 10:23 al.). In both the classical and Hellenistic language μετά with the genitive prevails, of which Diognetus shows only four instances, all in the Appendix (11:8; 12:1, 6, 9). For τῷ παιδί see note on 8:9.

τοῦ πρόσθεν χρόνου. Cf. 9:6: ἐν τῷ πρόσθεν χρόνῳ. The good classical word πρόσθεν seems to decline from the beginning of the Christian era. It is absent from both the LXX and the NT and is rare in the papyri of the period.

For the notion of the contrasted seasons (below), τῷ τότε τῆς ἀδικίας καιρῷ and τὸν νῦν τῆς δικαιοσύνης, Otto cites Pauline teaching (Rom 3:21–26; 5:20; Gal 4:4; Eph 2:1–9; Acts 17:30; add Titus 3:3–7). For our author this "former time" was not so much one of men's ignorance (cf. Acts 17:30, ἄγνοια) as of their "iniquity" (ἀδικία).

ἀτάκτοις φοραῖς, "inordinate impulses." The phrase has a philosophic ring. Milligan cites references to ἄτακτοι ἡδοναί from Plato, Leg. 2.660B; Plut. [Lib. ed.] §7 p. 5A.[126] For ἄτακτος, cf. 3 Macc 1:19. φοραῖς, cognate instrumental dative. Classical word found in inscriptions, papyri, and Polybius, but here in a late sense. Used of the "surge" of the passions in Longinus, [Subl.] 32.

ἡδοναῖς. See note on 6:5. For the collocation with ἐπιθυμίαις cf. 4 Macc 5:23; Titus 3:3.

---

125. Radford, Diognetus, 74–75.
126. Milligan, Thessalonians, 152.

ἀπαγομένους. So Otto conjectures for varying readings.[127] The figure is vivid, "in the clutches of pleasures and lusts," ἀπάγω having commonly the sense "to arrest," sometimes with the added nuance, "to lead away to death" (Gen 39:22; Acts 12:19; 1 Cor 12:2).

οὐ πάντως . . . ἀνεχόμενος, and οὐδὲ τῷ . . . δημιουργῶν, anticipating possible objections. See p. 15. ἐφηδόμενος, "gloating over," as in Xen, *Hell.* 4.5.18, ἐφηδομένους τῷ δυστυχήματι. ἀνεχόμενος. Cf. Isa 64:11 (of God); Matt 17:17 (of Christ). For the absolute use cf. Job 6:11; 1 Cor 4:12. Note the Pauline insistence on the "forbearance" of God (Rom 2:4; 3:25f).

καιρῷ, "season," "period" (9:2). Cf. χρόνος ("course of time"), below, and see Milligan's note.[128] If the change of word here is deliberate, then καιρός is used as the qualitative word (as properly in classical Greek and generally in the NT), being defined by ἀδικίας and δικαιοσύνης, whereas χρόνος is general, lacking a defining genitive. But it is not always possible to press the distinction (cf. Acts 1:7).

συνευδοκῶν, a late and common verb (Polybius, inscriptions, papyri), here with dative of thing (1 Macc 1:57; Luke 11:48).

τὸν νῦν (so Hefele, for the MS τὸν νοῦν). Sc. καιρόν (Rom 3:26; 8:18). τῆς δικαιοσύνης, i.e., the time of "the one righteous" (9:5). So also Christians endure martyrdom "for the sake of righteousness" (10:8). δημιουργέω is appropriately used of divine "fashioning" (cf. the substantive in 9:5). See Philo, *Opif.* 16; 1 Clem. 20:10; 38:3. For ἐλεγχθέντες see on 2:8.

ἐκ . . . ἔργων, "from," "out of" (source). But the sense approximates to that of instrument, "by our own works." Cf. 2 Cor 2:2; Rev 2:11.

ἀνάξιοι ζωῆς. Stated positively in §2, κόλασις καὶ θάνατος.

ὑπὸ . . . ἀξιωθῶμεν, "we may be deemed worthy by the agency (ὑπό) of God's goodness" (for χρηστότης see on 8:8). In verbs in—όω derived from adjective of *moral* meaning the factitive sense is modified = "to regard as," rather than "to make."[129] Note δικαιόω (9:4, below).

τὸ . . . ἀδύνατον. Otto refers to John 3:5. There may be also an echo of Mark 10:27 (= Matt 19:26; Luke 18:27). Note ἀδύνατον . . . τῇ δυνάμει . . . δυνατοί. See p. 14.

καθ᾽ ἑαυτούς, "of ourselves," a common periphrasis for the personal genitive. Cf. Let. Aris. 147: ἰσχύι τῇ καθ᾽ ἑαυτούς, 2 Macc 4:21: τῆς καθ᾽ αὐτὸν ἀσφαλείας, Eph 1:15: τὴν καθ᾽ ὑμᾶς πίστιν. Since man was long under the sway of "inordinate impulses" he came ultimately to complete moral

---

127. See his note in Otto, *Epistola ad Diognetum*, 2nd ed., 193.

128. Milligan, *Thessalonians*, 63.

129. See Moulton and Howard, *Grammar*, 397, and cf. Gen 31:28; 2 Thess 1:11; Heb 3:3.

impotence. "Unworthiness of life" (ἀνάξιοι ζωῆς) and "inability to enter the kingdom of God" (τὸ ... ἀδύνατον κτλ.) are regarded as virtually equivalent (cf. 9:6, τὸ ἀδύνατον τῆς ἡμέτερας φύσεως εἰς τὸ τυχεῖν ζωῆς). The two notions sometimes correspond in the NT (Mark 9:43–47; 10:17, 24, 25).

2. The thought and language show kinship with Titus 3:4–5 (note χρηστότης and φιλανθρωπία).[130]

πεπλήρωτο. The syllabic augment is omitted from the pluperfect passive, as also in πεφανέρωτο.[131]

πληρόω is used of ethical "fulfillment," whether good (John 16:24) or bad (Dan 8:23; Matt 23:32).

κόλασις καὶ θάνατος. In apposition to μισθός, "its reward, namely," etc. See note on 7:8.

προέθετο. Of the divine purpose, "set before himself," as in Eph 1:9. Cf. the technical Pauline πρόθεσις (Rom 8:28 al.).

λοιπόν. Probably "henceforth" (Heb 10:13 al.), though the sense "at last" (Acts 27:20) would fit the context. In either case the word should be taken with φανερῶσαι, not with προέθετο.

ὦ τῆς ὑπερβαλλούσης ... τοῦ θεοῦ. The text is uncertain. If the MS reading ὡς τῆς ... μία ἀγάπη be followed the sense would be "how" (ὡς) the one love of God in its surpassing kindness," etc. But Lange, followed by most editions, reads καὶ ἀγάπης.[132] For the exclamatory ὦ with the genitive, cf. 9:5 (*three times*).

For ἀγάπη see Meecham and the references given there[133] as well as especially Stauffer's treatment of ἀγαπάω.[134]

οὐκ ἐμίσησεν ... θνητῶν. Probst thinks that this is a fragment of a Christian hymn. See Otto, and notes on 7:4 (above), 11:3 (below).

ἀπώσατο, of God's "rejecting" his people, as in Rom 11:1–2 (Ps 93:14). The classical verb μνησικακέω occurs five times in the LXX (Gen 1:15 al.), but not of God. The thought, however, of the divine "forgetfulness" of man's sins is familiar (Isa 43:25; Jer 31:34). Cf. especially Herm. Sim. 9.23.4: εἰ ὁ θεὸς ... οὐ μνησικακεῖ τοῖς ἐξομολογουμένοις κτλ.

ἠνέσχετο ... ἀνεδέξατο. The MS has ἠνέσχετο λέγων κτλ. Lachmann reads ἐλεῶν for λέγων. Hefele omits λέγων (so Gildersleeve). Otto (text) omits the whole passage, ἠνέσχετο ... ἀνεδέξατο. He thinks that ἠνέσχετο

---

130. See Field, *Notes*, 147–48, 222–23.

131. For the usage in the Greek Bible see Thackeray, *Grammar*, 196–97; Moulton and Howard, *Grammar*, 190–91; Blass-Debrunner, *Grammatik*, §66.1.

132. See Otto's note in *Epistola ad Diognetum*, 2nd ed., 194–95.

133. Meecham, *Letter of Aristeas*, 63.

134. Stauffer, Entry in *Theologisches Wörterbuch*.

merely unfolds ἐμακροθύμησεν, that the words λέγων ... ἀνεδέξατο are a textual gloss from Isa 53:4, 11, and instances other possible glosses in 9:6 (*sub fin.*), 7:4 (βίᾳ ... θεῷ). The phrase "took upon himself our sins" means that God in his concern for man acted as though man's sin was his own and hence planned to do away with it by giving his own Son as ransom. Later Patripassianism is not here in view. For ἀνεδέξατο cf. Epictetus 3.24.64: ὃς οὕτως ἥμερος ἦν καὶ φιλάνθρωπος ὥστε ... τοσούτους πόνους ... ἄσμενος ἀναδέχεσθαι (of Diogenes). The verb is used in the papyri with a legal nuance ("become surety for"). Cf. 2 Macc 8:36, and see below (10:6). αὐτὸς ... αὐτός. Emphatic repetition (7:2).

ἀπέδοτο λύτρον ὑπὲρ ἡμῶν. The middle is appropriate, "to give up of one's own will," "part with" (so Moffatt on Heb 12:16). The thought is clearly based on Mark 10:45 (= Matt 20:28) δοῦναι τὴν ψυχὴν αὐτοῦ λύτρον ἀντὶ πολλῶν. Diognetus enlarges it in the following clauses: τὸν ἅγιον κτλ. The λύτρον was necessary,[135] since men were "in the clutches of pleasures and lusts" (9:1). Cf. Eph 1:7 (ἀπολύτρωσις); 1 Tim 2:6 (ἀντίλυτρον); Titus 2:14 (ὃς ἔδωκεν ἑαυτὸν ὑπὲρ ἡμῶν ἵνα λυτρώσηται κτλ).

No exegetical importance can be attached to the change from Mark's ἀντί to ὑπέρ. The two prepositions are not infrequently interchanged. In the probable reminiscence of the Markan saying in 1 Tim 2:6 we have ὑπὲρ πάντων (cf. Mark 14:24). ὑπέρ seems occasionally to approximate to the idea of substitution. Cf. Plato, *Gorgias* 515C: ἐγὼ ὑπὲρ σοῦ ἀποκρινοῦμαι, Xen, *Anab.* 7.4.9: ἐθέλοις ἄν, ὦ Ἐπίσθενες, ὑπὲρ τούτου ἀποθανεῖν; Phlm 13 ("as your deputy," Moffatt), P.Oxy. II 275 (66 CE) ἔγραψα ὑπὲρ αὐτοῦ μὴ ἰδότος γράμματα.

ἀνόμων. Otto prefers to read τῶν ἀνόμων to balance τῶν κακῶν, etc. For Christ's association with the "lawless" see Luke 22:37 (= Isa 53:12).

τὸν ἄκακον, "innocent" (Job 8:20; Jer 11:19). Used of Christ as high priest in Heb 7:26.

τὸν δίκαιον ... ἀδίκων, a reminiscence of 1 Pet 3:18. The alignment of the term δίκαιος with other adjectives shows that it is descriptive, not a title of the Son (as in Acts 3:14; 7:52; 22:14). This is made clear in 9:5 by the absence of the article ("in one who is righteous"). We may compare 1 John 2:1, "Jesus Christ, being, as he is, righteous."

τὸν ἀθάνατον. For the apparent redundancy after τὸν ἄφθαρτον Otto cites Justin Martyr, *Dial.* 117: ἀφθάρτους καὶ ἀθανάτους.

3. The "covering" of sins is a scriptural idea. See Ps 31 (32):1; 84 (85):3; Jas 5:20;[136] 1 Pet 4:8. The author's meaning is that the righteousness of Christ

---

135. See Westcott, *Hebrews*, 295ff.; Abbott, *Ephesians*, 11ff.
136. See Mayor, *Jude*, full note here.

"covers" men's sins in the sense of "making atonement" for them (cf. the force of the Hebrew כָּפֶּר in the Ps [65:4 *al.*]). Note that it is the δικαιοσύνη of the Son (cf. §5) that thus "covers" sins. See above, pp. 24–25. καλύπτω is a word of Ionic origin.[137] The simplex, common in Homer and the poets, is rare in Attic prose. For Hellenistic cf. Let. Aris. 87; Exod 24:15; Matt 10:26. For the form ἠδυνήθη, see p. 11.

4. δικαιωθῆναι, "to be justified." This rendering best preserves the ambiguity of δικαιόω (cf. §5), which means strictly "to declare or deem righteous" (see note on ἀξιόω, 9:1). But the notion "to make righteous" is not excluded when the verb is used of the divine dealings with men.[138] Our author's thought is deeply Pauline (cf. Rom 3:26, 30; 4:5; 8:30, 33; Gal 3:8). The place of "faith" in the work of justification is doubtless present to his mind, though not explicitly named. For the use of the term "faith" see p. 39.

ἀνόμους ... ἀσεβεῖς. For the conjunction cf. 1 Macc 7:5; Ps 50:15. The former term has here a positive ring, "those who violate law" (1 John 3:4).

5. ὢ τῆς γλυκείας ἀνταλλαγῆς. For exclamatory ὢ with the genitive, see 9:2, and for a rhetorical series of exclamations as here, Clement of Alexandria, *Quis div.* 35. The context suggests that the "exchange" is one of *state* rather than of *person*, of wickedness for justification, not the substitution of Christ for men. ἀνταλλαγή is a very rare word.

ὢ τῆς ἀνεξιχνιάστου δημιουργίας, "O heavenly workmanship past finding out!"[139] ἀνεξιχνίαστος is perhaps a "biblical" word, though formed on classical precedents (see LS on ἐξιχνεύω, Aesch. *Agam.* 368). It is found in Job 5:9 and 9:10, as here, in reference to God's creativeness, and perhaps borrowed by Paul (Rom 11:33; Eph 3:8). Cf. 1 Clem. 20:5. For δημιουργίας cf. 1 Clem 20:6, and see note on 9:1.

ὢ τῶν ἀπροσδοκήτων εὐεργεσιῶν, referring to 8:11 (ἃ τίς ... ἡμῶν), i.e., to share in his blessings (εὐεργεσιῶν).

ἵνα ἀνομία κτλ. The ἵνα clause is explanatory of the three preceding exclamations, the ἵνα, following late usage, denoting *content* not purpose (cf. John 15:13; 17:3 *al.*).

The contrast of the "one" righteous with the "many" wicked is drawn from Rom 5:12ff. (see especially vv. 15, 18). δικαίῳ ... δικαιοσύνη ... δικαιώσῃ. For the stylistic feature see p. 14. κρυβῇ: the second aorist passive form ἐκρύβην is late (Gen 3:10; John 8:59).[140]

---

137. Nägeli, *Wortschatz*, 27.

138. So Moberly, *Atonement*, 335n1; see Sanday and Headlam, *Romans*, 28; Dodd, *Romans*, 42ff.

139. Newman, *Grammar of Assent*, 474.

140. See Blass-Debrunner, *Grammatik*, §76.1.

6. ἐλέγξας. Sc. ὁ θεός, to which also the pronouns αὐτοῦ and αὐτόν (below) relate. For ἐλέγχω see on 2:8.

ἐν τῷ πρόσθεν χρόνῳ, i.e., before the Son came. Cf. 9:1, μέχρι τοῦ πρόσθεν χρόνου.

τὸ ἀδύνατον . . . φύσεως. This pregnant phrase resumes the thought of the second half of 9:1 (ἐν τῷ τότε . . . γενηθῶμεν). From the classical down to the Byzantine period the neuter singular of common adjectives is used with the article as a substantive expressing an abstract idea, often followed by a genitive as here. It is a frequent usage in the higher κοινή.[141] Cf. Let. Aris. 122; Rom 8:3; 1 Cor 1:25; 2 Cor 8:8.

εἰς τὸ τυχεῖν ζωῆς. The construction is used in place of the so-called object infinitive after τὸ ἀδύνατον (expressing *inability*).[142] It is a virtual equivalent of the construction ἀδύνατον εἰσελθεῖν (9:1; cf. δυνατὸν σῴζειν, 9:6). Cf. Hab 1:8: πρόθυμος εἰς τὸ φαγεῖν.

νῦν δὲ τὸν κτλ. The νῦν is emphatic and in contrast with ἐν τῷ πρόσθεν χρόνῳ. The term ὁ Σωτήρ is found here only in the epistle. It is infrequent also in Paul (Eph 5:23; Phil 3:20), the Gospels (*three times*), and the Apostolic Fathers (2 Clem. 20:5 al.).

τὰ ἀδύνατα. A cryptic phrase. Either (*a*) "even powerless creatures" or (*b*) "even in the sphere of the impossible," taking τὰ ἀδύνατα as accusative of respect. If so, σῴζω is used absolutely (Matt 8:25).

For the thought cf. Luke 28:27: τὰ ἀδύνατα παρὰ ἀνθρώποις δυνατὰ παρὰ τῷ θεῷ ἐστιν.

ἐξ ἀμφοτέρων. The position of the phrase suggests that it goes with ἐβουλήθη, "in both ways his will was," etc. The thought runs as follows. God has proved man's inability to attain life in time past and has now shown the Savior's ability to save. In both these ways his will was that men should believe his goodness and regard him as guardian, etc. Otto thinks that the passage shows the influence of Isa 11:2–3, 12:2 on our author. But the connection is not obvious. For a similar list of appellatives (of God) see Theophilus, *Autol.* 1.3.

τροφέα. This and the following terms are not titles of God, but descriptive of his role towards men. For τροφεύς cf. *Hermetica* 1:390, 392 (ed. Scott) τῷ δημιουργῷ ὡς πατρὶ ἀγαθῷ καὶ τροφεῖ χρηστῷ. The cognate verb is used of God in Bar 4:8. Cf. the variant τροφοφορεῖν in Deut 1:31; Acts 13:18. For σύμβουλος (of the Son) see note on 8:9 (above). For φῶς (of God) cf. 1 John 1:5, 7. τιμή and δόξα are frequently combined, usually in the reverse order, and used in reference to God in Ps 8:6; Rom 2:7, 10.

---

141. See Blass-Debrunner, *Grammatik*, 263.2.
142. See Goodwin, *Moods and Tenses*, §§747–49.

περὶ ... μεριμνᾶν. So the MS and most editions, including Lake. Otto and Lightfoot omit the words as a gloss (on τροφέα) drawn from Matt 6:25, 28, 31, "*in textum inepte importatum*" (Otto). This view is probably correct, for the notion of "care for clothing and food" is not only alien from the context, but almost from the entire epistle. God's provision of temporal necessities is stated in 3:4, but nowhere does the idea of man's anxiety in this regard occur. Moreover, the clause savors of an anticlimax, following the glowing description of *God's* moral qualities. On the other hand, some sequence is apparent: men believing on God's goodness will think of him as guardian, etc., and so be free from care for material needs. Atonement for man's sin and provision of his daily needs alike attest the χρηστότης of God, who "bestowed upon us all things at once" (8:1). Cf. Rom 8:32.

Chapter 10

The author now draws some practical conclusions from the Christian belief in God and redemption, intermingling after the Pauline manner paraenesis (note the resumption of the second person of address: see note on 7:8) and exposition. He reaffirms that God loved men and gave them privileges which culminated in the sending of the Son and the promise of the heavenly kingdom. The knowledge of this manifested love fills men with joy and moves them to an answering love which seeks to imitate the goodness of God. A man can copy God when he wills. For true happiness does not consist in domination, wealth, and power; it lies rather in the service of the weak and needy. There is the true *imitatio Dei*. And such a life of well-doing brings in its train new insight and judgment.

1. ταύτην ... τὴν πίστιν. The words, emphatic by position, may refer specifically to the faith in God's goodness enjoined in 9:6. But probably the wider sense of the term, as used in 8:6 ("faith, by which alone it is given to see God") is intended. Here, as there, no object of faith is assigned.

ἐὰν ποθήσῃς, καὶ λάβῃς κτλ. If this, the MS reading, be accepted, the twofold conditional sentence lacks an apodosis. So Krenel, Funk, and Lake. Editorial conjectures show much variety. (1) Otto reads καὶ λήψῃ, regarding it as the apodosis ("you shall also receive," etc.).[143] (2) Gildersleeve suggests καταλάβοις ἄν κτλ. ("you must gain"). (3) Lachmann prefers ἐπιποθήσαις, καὶ λάβοις (optatives expressing a wish, "mayest thou desire ... and gain"). So Bunsen. (4) Gebhardt reads ἐὰν ποθῇς, κατάλαβε, and so Geffcken. (5) Scheibe would emend to κἂν λάβοις.

---

143. See his note in *Epistola ad Diognetum*, 2nd ed., 197–98.

There is no need to depart from the MS reading. The second καί does not necessarily introduce an apodosis; it may well begin another protasis. The loss of apodosis may be due to a lacuna in the text or to the digression of thought in §2. For such aposiopesis, cf. Dan 3:15; Luke 13:9. Moreover, the MS reading brackets "this faith" and "knowledge of the Father" as conditional elements of some unspecified consequences, and this is better than to make (as 4) faith consequent upon gaining knowledge of the Father, a view which reverses the dictum of 8:6, cited above.

For ποθέω cf. 3:1 (with the infinitive); 12:8 (of God).

ἐπίγνωσιν πατρός. Robinson argues that ἐπίγνωσις denotes not "*complete* knowledge," but knowledge directed to (ἐπί) a particular object.[144] πατρός, objective genitive. Cf. 2 Pet 1:2 (θεοῦ). God is here named "Father" (there is no article in the three occurrences of the term) in relation to both the Son or Word (11:2; 12:9) and to man, as §3 implies. See p. 211n101.

Nock, retaining καὶ λάβῃς, would emend to ἐπιγνώσῃ πατέρα.[145]

2. This section is in the nature of a digression (§3 resuming or being correlated to §1; note μὲν ... δέ). But it gives in brief compass a comprehensive survey of God's gifts of love to men in creation, redemption, and sanctification.

ὁ γὰρ θεὸς κτλ. A free recollection of John 3:11, 16. Cf. 1 John 4:9, and see below, 10:3: τὸν οὕτως προαγαπήσαντά σε.

δι' οὓς ἐποίησε τὸν κόσμον, a point frequently stressed by early Christian writers. Cf. Justin Martyr, *1 Apol.* 10: "we have been taught that he in the beginning did, of his goodness, for man's sake [δι' ἀνθρώπους], create all things," etc.

So also *2 Apol.* 4, διὰ τὸ ἀνθρώπειον γένος. Cf. *Dial.* 41. See also *Apology of Aristides* 1 (Syr.); Herm. Mand. 12.4.2. The universalism of this note contrasts with the Jewish view of a chosen race, as, e.g., 2 Esdr. 6:55–56, "O Lord ... thou hast said that for our sakes thou hast created the world. But as for the other nations that are descended from Adam, thou hast said that they are nothing and that they are like spittle" (cf. 7:11). For other references see note by Blakeney,[146] and his edition of the epistle οἷς ὑπέταξε ... γῇ.[147] See note on καὶ ὑποτέτακται (7:2).

λόγον, here = "reason" (see on 7:2). Cf. Epictetus 1.3.3: ὁ λόγος δὲ καὶ ἡ γνώμη κοινὸν πρὸς τοὺς θεούς,[148] Justin Martyr, *2 Apol.* 7: παρὰ λόγον καὶ νοῦν.

---

144. Robinson, *Ephesians*, 248ff.
145. Nock, "Diognetum," 40.
146. Blakeney, "Note," 193ff.
147. Blakeney, *Diognetus*, 74ff.
148. Cited in Sharp, *Epictetus*, 127.

οἷς ... ἐπέτρεψεν. (1) "whom alone he permitted to look upward to him" or (2) "on whom alone he enjoined that they should look upward to him" (Lake). (1) is preferable, and is the prevailing sense of ἐπιτρέπω in the NT.

For αὐτόν Lachmann (so also Lightfoot) conjectures οὐνόν, a contraction of οὐρανόν (cf. Matt 14:19). The thought is akin to that of Col 3:1–2 (the quest of τὰ ἄνω).

It is gratuitous to see here, with Geffcken,[149] a loan from essentially Stoic thought. The passage he cites from Xen., *Mem.* 1.4.11 affords no real parallel. There the regard of the gods for men is seen in the fact that they made man alone, of all animals, of upright posture, and the whole context stresses man's superiority to the animals. More relevant is Cicero, *Nat. d.* 2.56: "He (the Deity) has made us of a stature tall and upright, in order that we might behold the heavens and so arrive at the knowledge of the gods." Lactantius, *Inst.* 2.1.15, cites a passage from Ovid, *Meta.* 1.84ff., enshrining the same idea. On this "upright form" peculiar to man, see Abrahams.[150] See Blakeney for further references.[151]

But the setting in Diognetus makes no such contrast between man and lower creatures, although the insertion of μόνοις in the clause may be significant in that regard. What seems to be more decisive is the meaning of the words "to look upward to him." It is improbable that they refer merely to man's physical stature. The author is recounting the initial blessings man has received at the creation, and these are mental and spiritual in character. A *physical* reference would be an intrusion in the series "reason"—"mind"—"in his own image." The phrase "to look upward to him" is a figurative description of man's capacity for aspiration Godward, being thus in line with the preceding and especially the following words ("whom he made in his own image"). Philo stresses this very point, that man's likeness to the image of God is not bodily: "the resemblance is spoken of with reference to the most important part of the soul, namely, the mind," etc. (*Opif.* 69). Genesis 1:26ff. is a sufficient source for the thought of Diogn. 10:2. Man by divine gift has the ability to look up to God. Hence the frequent exhortations of psalmist (Ps 123:1 *al.*), prophet (Isa 40:26), and apostle (Col 3:1). Athanasius (*Inc.*) associates the upward look with man's knowledge of God. Cf. 12:6; 14:7; 45:3.

ἐκ ... εἰκόνος, "in accordance with [cf. Herodotus, *Hist.* 1.64; John 3:34; 2 Cor 8:11; and the papyri] his own image," for which κατ' εἰκόνα is more usual in the Greek Bible (Gen 1:27; Col 3:10). See the note on εἰκών in Lightfoot, *Colossians*, 142ff.

---

149. Geffcken, *Diognetos*, 26.
150. Abrahams, *Pharisaism*, n7, 164–65.
151. Blakeney, *Diognetus*, 77–78.

ἔπλασε, of God's "forming" (Gen 2:7f, 15; 1 Tim 2:13). πλάσσω, "form" is perhaps a literary variation on ποιέω, "make" (above). The two verbs are interchanged in Rom 9:20–21. Contrast also Gen 1:27 (ποιέω), 2:7 (πλάσσω). The metaphor of the potter applied to God is frequent in the OT (Isa 45:9; 64:8; Jer 18:4ff.). Testament of Naphtali 2:2ff. draws out the comparison between God's creation of man and the work of the potter.

ἀπέστειλε . . . μονογενῆ. From 1 John 4:9. μονογενής, "unique" (1 Clem. 25:2), "only," of children (Tob 3:15). Cf. John 1:14, 18; 3:16, 18. See note on 8:11 (above). On ἀπέστειλε, see 7:2.

τὴν ἐν οὐρανῷ βασιλείαν. In 9:1 τὴν βασιλείαν τοῦ θεοῦ. Our author has virtually both the Matthean (τῶν οὐρανῶν) and the Lukan (τοῦ θεοῦ) equivalents. The passage οἷς τὴν . . . αὐτόν is apparently borrowed from Jas 2:5 (cf. also 1:12). For the idea that Christians receive or inherit the kingdom, cf. Matt 5:3; 1 Pet 1:4; 2 Thess 1:5. For τοῖς ἀγαπήσασιν αὐτόν cf. 12:1, τοῖς ἀγαπῶσιν ὀρθῶς.

3. ἐπιγνοὺς δέ, "and when you have this knowledge," i.e., of the Father (10:1). τίνος . . . σε; for these NT reminiscences see above p. 55. On οὕτως see p. 11. προαγαπήσαντά. The verb is apparently confined to late and ecclesiastical writers (it is not registered in LS⁹). An obvious coinage from 1 John 4:19.

4–6. Here the author reverts to the practical issues of faith. See note on ch. 5 (*init.*). The thought is that if a man loves God he will seek "to imitate his goodness." And this will be seen not in dominance over one's neighbor (how alien is such an attitude from God himself!), but in helpful service to those in need. In a word, love towards God must express itself in love towards man. Here the influence of 1 John (4:11–12, 20–21) is marked.

ἀγαπήσας. Coincident aorist participle, "by loving." On μιμητὴς ἔσῃ . . . γενέσθαι θεοῦ see Additional Note A. For the χρηστότης of God, see 8:8.

δύναται θέλοντος αὐτοῦ. The genitive absolute here only in the epistle, with the possible exception of 3:5. The reference of αὐτοῦ is uncertain. (1) "it is possible when he (ἄνθρωπος) will." (2) "he can, if God wills it," αὐτοῦ referring to θεοῦ. So Lightfoot. Cf. Acts 18:21. This is probably the better view, for, although the context stresses man's own moral effort to imitate God (cf. μιμητὴς γενέσθαι), as in all NT instances, it is the divine grace and initiative that enables men to imitate God.

For δύναμαι used absolutely see 4 Macc 14:17; 1 Cor 3:2; 10:13.

5. A negative definition of happiness (εὐδαιμονεῖν). Geffcken thinks that we have here an echo of familiar Platonic conceptions.[152] But in the

---

152. Geffcken, *Diognetos*, 26.

two passages he cites (*Gorgias* 488B; *Rep.* 349B) Plato is concerned with the concept of justice (τὸ δίκαιον), not happiness.

The precept (οὐ γὰρ τὸ καταδυναστεύειν) is no doubt intended to be of general application. But, since καταδυναστεύω is frequently used of men in authority misusing their power (Wis 15:14; 17:2; Sir 48:12 *al.*), this may be the shade of meaning here. Cf. βιάζεσθαι τοὺς ὑποδεεστέρους (5). It would have special point, if Diognetus held official rank. See pp. 96.

For καταδυναστεύω with the genitive, cf. Diod. Sic. 13.73: καταδυναστεύσειν τῶν πολιτῶν, Jas 2:6; Herm. Mand. 12.5.1. In the LXX it always takes the accusative (Wis 2:10 *al.*). It is practically a Koine word, first found in Xenophon.

βιάζεσθαι. See note on 7:4. τοὺς ὑποδεεστέρους, literally "inferior," i.e., "poorer." Cf. 1 Clem. 19:1: τὸ ὑποδεές, "submissiveness."

τῆς ἐκείνου μεγαλειότητος. For the "majesty" of God cf. Ign. *Rom.* (heading) ἐν μεγαλειότητι πατρὸς ὑψίστου, also Josephus, *C. Ap.* 2.168: πρέποντα τῇ τοῦ θεοῦ φύσει καὶ μεγαλειότητι, and 2 Pet 1:16. The suggestion is that the majesty of God is the majesty of love. Cf. the use of the term in the story of the healing of the demoniac child (Luke 9:43).

6. τὸ ... βάρος. Perhaps there is a sidelong glance at Gal 6:2 (βαστάζω). The thought, however, is familiar. The βάρος is general, "something hard to be borne" (cf. Acts 15:28), though the nuance "financial burden," as in the papyri (P. Giss. 1.7, 117 CE), would fit the sense of ἀναδέχομαι (see on 9:2) and is in keeping with what follows. Cf. 2 Cor 11:9 (ἀβαρής).

κρείσσων ... ἐλαττούμενον. For the spelling see above, p. 11.

ἐθέλει. In the Greek Bible always θέλω (not ἐθέλω). Note θέλει in 11:7.

ὃς ἄ. So van Hengel conjectures for the MS. ὅσα. With τοῖς ἐπιδεομένοις (absolute as in Sir 34:21) cf. τοὺς ὑποδεεστέρους (above). For the communism of the early Christians see Acts 2:44–45; *Apology of Aristides* 15; Justin Martyr, *1 Apol.* 14.

θεὸς γίνεται τῶν λαμβανόντων. See Additional Note B.

7. τότε, "then" (note the repetition in §§7, 8), i.e., in consequence of such well-doing there follows insight into "the mysteries of God" and a new valuation of men and the world. Knowledge waits on doing. Cf. John 7:17. For τυγχάνων see on Diogn. 2:1.

πολιτεύεται. The verb means (*a*) "to live the life of a citizen," (*b*) more generally, "to live" (see note on 5:4, above), (*c*) "to rule," "govern." Cf. Dem. 2.29 (of citizens); 1 Clem. 44:6 (of bishops); and papyri.[153] As here used of God (a rare application) it probably carries the sense of (*b*). Man's lot (τυγχάνων) is on earth; God "lives" in heaven (for the latter thought see Eph

---

153. Moulton and Milligan, *Vocabulary*, 526.

6:9: ὁ κύριός ἐστιν ἐν οὐρανοῖς. Cf. Matt 5:16 al.). But the meaning may well be "God rules in heaven." So Radford ("ruleth").

μυστήρια θεοῦ λαλεῖν. For μυστήριον see on 4:6. Cf. 1 Cor 14:2: πνεύματι δὲ λαλεῖ μυστήρια. The Christian knows God's "secret counsel" (contrast Wis 2:22).

ἐπὶ τῷ μὴ θέλειν, "on the ground of their unwillingness." For the construction see p. 12. For ἀρνήσασθαι θεόν see on 7:7 (τὸν κύριον). θαυμάσεις. Cf. 10:8. In Attic Greek, the future commonly takes the middle form. For the active form of the future cf. Plutarch, *Mor.* 823f; Deut 28:50; for the middle Isa 41:23.

For "the deceit and error of the world" cf. 4:6. ἀπάτη (of the heathen world), 8:4, πλάνη (of the heathen philosophers). See 2 Pet 2:18 (τοὺς ἐν πλάνῃ ἀναστρεφομένους, i.e., the heathen); Herm. *Sim.* 6.3.3; 2 Clem. 6:4.

ἐπιγνῷς. So Lachmann, Bunsen, and others. The MS reads ἐπιγνώσῃ. Cf. 10:8 (*fin.*).

ὅταν ... καταφρονήσῃς. A suggested emendation adopted by Otto (text), τότε ... καταφρονήσεις, relates the clause in sequence to the preceding ὅταν ... ἐπιγνῷς. This, however, would interrupt the succession of ὅταν clauses balancing that of the foregoing τότε clauses.

τοῦ δοκοῦντος ἐνθάδε θανάτου contrasts with τὸν ὄντως θάνατον, perhaps a Platonic touch. Note too the implied double contrast with τὸ ἀληθῶς ἐν οὐρανῷ ζῆν. In heaven life is "true" (ἀληθῶς); here on earth (ἐνθάδε) death is merely "apparent" (δοκοῦντος). Do we have here a reflection of the saying of Jesus (Matt 10:28)? For the use of ὄντως as an attributive adjective cf. 1 Tim 5:3, 5, 16; 6:19 (τῆς ὄντως ζωῆς), Athenagoras, *Suppl.* 7 (τὸ ὄντως θεῖον).

The striking phrase, τοῦ δοκοῦντος ἐνθάδε θανάτου, is probably a reminiscence of Wis 3:2: ἔδοξαν ἐν ὀφθαλμοῖς ἀφρόνων τεθνάναι.

ὃς φυλάσσεται ... αἰώνιον. Cf. 2 Pet 2:9: οἶδεν κύριος ... ἀδίκους δὲ εἰς ἡμέραν κρίσεως κολαζομένους τηρεῖν. For τὸ πῦρ τὸ αἰώνιον cf. 4 Macc 12:12; Matt 18:8; 25:41; Jude 7. αἰώνιος, "perpetual," "of unknown duration," being associated with such terms as βάσανος (4 Macc 9:9), κόλασις (Matt 25:46), gained an eschatological sense, the future punishment of the wicked. See above, p. 41. It is needless to see here "a cryptic reference to Heraclitus."[154] The context and language suggest rather reflections of the NT.

μέχρι τέλους, "up to the end," a semi-technical phrase (Wis 16:5; 19:1; Dan 7:26; Heb 3:14), modifying κολάσει. Eternal fire punishes "up to the end."

It is interesting to notice how §7 takes up three points in Diognetus's first question. Diognetus had asked about (1) the kind of God whom the Christians believe in and worship, their (2) disregard of the world, and (3) contempt

---

154. Blakeney, *Diognetus*, 9, 83.

for death. The author now says in effect: when you are a Christian, Diognetus, you yourself will (1) know that God lives in heaven and be able to "speak his mysteries," (2) understand the Christians' disregard of the world (its "deceit and error"), and (3) love and admire the Christians who endure punishment (i.e., death) rather than deny God (such death is only "apparent").

8. τοὺς ὑπομένοντας ... μακαρίσεις, a virtual repetition of τότε τοὺς κολαζομένους ... θαυμάσεις (7). See pp. 157–58. For the association of the terms ὑπομένω and μακαρίζω cf. Dan 12:12; 4 Macc 7:22; Jas 1:12. For ὑπὲρ δικαιοσύνης see note on τὸν νῦν τῆς δικαιοσύνης (9:1).

θαυμάσεις τὸ πῦρ ... μακαρίσεις. The MS reading is uncertain. Reuss restores it thus: θαυμάσεις τὸ πῦρ τοῦτο καὶ μακαρίσεις.[155] Through scribal disarrangement this becomes τὸ πῦρ τοῦτο θαυμάσεις καὶ μακαρίσεις, which Otto prints. This is the reading of Haus's copy and is adopted by Geffcken (text). On this reading τὸ πῦρ τοῦτο is antithetical to ἐκεῖνο τὸ πῦρ. The emendation τὸ πρόσκαιρον (with the order θαυμάσεις τὸ κτλ) is followed by many editions (Funk, Lightfoot, Lake) and contrasts well with τὸ πῦρ τὸ αἰώνιον (7). Cf. 4 Macc 15:2, 3; 2 Cor 4:18.

The allusion is to the fires endured by Christian martyrs. Otto refers to Justin Martyr, *Dial.* 110: "for it is plain that, though beheaded, and crucified and thrown to wild beasts and chains and fire," etc., and to the letter to the Church at Smyrna (Eusebius, *Hist. eccl.* 4.15), which gives an account of Polycarp's martyrdom at the stake. With the passage cf. Polycarp's words: "you threaten with the fire that burns for a time [πρὸς ὥραν], and is quickly quenched, for you do not know the fire which awaits the wicked in the judgment to come and in everlasting punishment" (αἰωνίου κολάσεως), *Mart. Poly.* 11:2.

ἐκεῖνο τὸ πῦρ. Sc. τὸ αἰώνιον (7).

Chapter 10 is plainly incomplete. The MS shows a lacuna after ἐπιγνῷς and adds a marginal note: καὶ ὧδε ἐγκοπὴν εἶχε τὸ ἀντίγραφον. See p. 63. Blakeney supplies "by way of makeshift": (ὅ ἐστιν ὁ δεύτερος θάνατος). It is probable that the gap is not considerable, since the questions raised in the Preface have been dealt with, and the epistle ends appropriately in ch. 10 on the paraenetic note.

Chapter 11

As a disciple of apostles, I speak and teach with right the truths that have been handed down. These truths the Word has plainly revealed to disciples, who, being deemed faithful, thus gained knowledge of the mysteries of the

---

155. See Otto, *Epistola ad Diognetum*, 2nd ed., 202n19.

Father. The Word was sent to appear to the world; he was dishonored by God's own people, but proclaimed by the apostles, and believed on by the heathen. He is from of old, yet is ever young in the hearts of the saints. This eternal Word is now accounted a Son, and the Church inherits the riches of his grace, grace which works variously in the life of the Church. It also enables the individual to understand the message which the Word speaks through chosen men. For all things which the Word moves us to speak we share with you, out of love for what he has revealed.

1. ξένα, "foreign to" (the apostolic faith). Cf. the διδαχαὶ ξέναι of Heb 13:9. For ὁμιλῶ with the accusative cf. 11:7. Bunsen conjectured ζηλῶ (for ζητῶ).

ἀποστόλων γενόμενος μαθητής. The meaning of the phrase depends on the sense of the term ἀπόστολος. In the NT the term is used in (a) a particularized sense, indicating those who exercised general authority given directly by Christ, and sometimes limited to the Twelve (Acts 1:2ff., 17, 25f.). (b) a wider sense, of one engaged in the service of the gospel, almost a "missionary" (Acts 14:4, 14; Rom 16:7). In our epistle ἀπόστολος is confined to the appended chapters (11:1, 3, 6; 12:5, 9). In 12:5 ὁ ἀπόστολος (= Paul) is clearly used in the narrower sense, and the context favors that reference in the remaining four passages. This limitation of meaning agrees with the general usage of the Apostolic Fathers (1 Clem. 42; Ign. *Rom.* 4), though the Didache (11:3ff.) apparently employs the term in the wider sense. The writer of the appended chapters may indeed be claiming that he was personally a pupil of the apostles, though the phrase in itself need imply nothing more than his acceptance of apostolic teaching.

διδάσκαλος ἐθνῶν (cf. 1 Tim 2:7; 2 Tim 1:11 [אC CD et al.]). He represents the gentiles as believing on the Word (11:3). For the significance of this phrase for the probable connection of chs. 11–12 with the end of Hippolytus's *Philosophumena*, see Connolly.[156] For ἐθνῶν see on 11:3.

τὰ παραδοθέντα. One of several terms (παράδοσις, πίστις, κήρυγμα) denoting the "traditions" about Jesus which became part of the basis of the faith. Cf. the note on μάθημα (5:3) and Additional Note D.[157]

ἀξίως ὑπηρετῶ. So Funk and Lake. Bunsen, Gildersleeve, and Lightfoot read ἀξίως ὑπηρετῶν. Bunsen later read ἀξίοις. The MS has ἀξίοις ὑπηρετῶ. The date γινομένοις κτλ. goes with ὑπηρετῶ rather than (as Lake's translation) with παραδοθέντα.

For ὑπηρετῶ with accusative (τὰ παραδοθέντα) and dative (γινομένοις), cf. Plato, *Symp.* 196C: πᾶς γὰρ ἑκὼν Ἔρωτι πᾶν ὑπηρετεῖ.

---

156. Connolly, "Ad Diognetum xi–xii," 13.
157. See also Harnack, *History of Dogma*, 1:155–56.

With γινομένοις ἀληθείας μαθηταῖς, i.e., presumably catechumens, cf. 1 Tim 2:4: εἰς ἐπίγνωσιν ἀληθεῖς ἐλθεῖν.

2. λόγῳ προσφιλὴς γενηθείς. The MS reads λόγῳ προσφιλεῖ γεννηθείς "begotten by the loving Word." Read (with Bunsen) γενηθείς and (with Prud. M.) προσφιλής.[158] It is improbable that λόγος should be used in such close contiguity in two senses ("word" and "Word"), as Lake's translation implies. The absence of the article is not decisive against this view. See note on θεός (p. 21n101). Read the title "the Word" throughout.

προσφιλής may be taken in either (a) a passive sense "beloved" (of the Word), for which cf. Sir 4:7, 20:13, or, more probably, (b) active, "kindly affectioned" (to the Word). Cf. Thuc. 7.86. It is used absolutely in Phil 4:8.

διὰ λόγου, the Word being the medium of the revelation. But when διά is followed by a *personal* genitive mediate approximates to direct agency (= ὑπό with genitive).[159]

ἐφανέρωσεν. Sc. αὐτά. Cf. John 21:2. φανείς, "on his appearance" (to the world). Cf. § 3. παρρησίᾳ λαλῶν. A Johannine phrase (John 7:26; 16:29; 18:20), except Mark 8:32.

ἀπίστων . . . πιστοί. In the active sense, "unbelieving". . . "believing." Cf. John 20:27. "Faithful" best renders πιστοί as covering both its active and passive signification. Cf. 11:5. διηγούμενος, "expounding." Lachmann and Bunsen conjecture διηχούμενος (passive), "bruited" (by the disciples). But the emphasis lies on the *training* of the disciples.

λογισθέντες, "accounted," almost "found (to be)." Cf. 11:5, and Neh 13:13, πιστοὶ ἐλογίσθησαν. For πατρὸς μυστήρια cf. μυστήρια θεοῦ (10:7). Cf. εἰς ἐπίγνωσιν τοῦ μυστηρίου τοῦ θεοῦ (Col 2:2).

3. οὗ χάριν, "for which cause." Lake takes οὗ as masculine, "for his sake." But who then is meant? It can hardly be the remote τίς ὀρθῶς διδαχθεὶς κτλ. (§2 ad init.), though it is true to the tenor of the epistle to say that the Word was sent for man's sake (cf. 7:3ff.; 10:2). If οὗ refers to God or the Word the sense is difficult. For the neuter ("wherefore") cf. Luke 7:47.

χάριν is placed after its case as generally in classical Greek. So also in the NT except 1 John 3:12. In the LXX and the papyri it generally precedes a Hellenistic use.[160] For ἀπέστειλε see on 7:2.

ὑπὸ λαοῦ ἀτιμασθείς. Cf. John 8:49: καὶ ὑμεῖς ἀτιμάζετέ με. λαοῦ . . . ἐθνῶν. The terms are regularly contrasted in the LXX: "the chosen people (Israel)". . . "the heathen." Cf. also Luke 2:32.[161]

---

158. See Otto's note in *Epistola ad Diognetum*, 2nd ed., 203.
159. See Meecham, *Letter of Aristeas*, 144–45.
160. Blass-Debrunner, *Grammatik*, §216, 1.
161. See Kennedy, *Sources*, 98; Hort, *1 Peter*, at 1 Pet 2:9.

διὰ ἀποστόλων κηρυχθείς. If διά is here differentiated from the two occurrences of ὑπό with the genitive, the apostles are the media of the preaching. But see note on διὰ λόγου (§2).

The last two clauses are perhaps reminiscent of 1 Tim 3:16 (probably a fragment of an early Christian hymn): ἐκηρύχθη ἐν ἔθνεσιν, ἐπιστεύθη ἐν κόσμῳ. Probst suggested that §§3–6 may have a similar origin. See notes (above) on 7:4, 9:2, and also p. 14.

For the thought of §3b cf. Acts 13:46–48.

4. οὗτος ὁ ἀπ' ἀρχῆς. Cf. 1 John 2:13, 14; John 1:1; and Diogn. 11:5 (below) οὗτος ὁ ἀεί. εὑρεθείς, "found to be," "proved." Cf. 1 Cor 4:2 al. On the thought of 11:4–5 see Additional Note C.

καινὸς ... νέος. If the classical distinction is intended, the incarnation of the Son is qualitatively "a new departure in God's ways with men" (Radford), and a recurring new experience in the hearts of men. But the distinction is often blurred in late Greek. For the opposition of καινός and παλαιός see Matt 13:52; Eph 4:22–24.

ἐν ... γεννώμενος. Causal, supplying the reason for νέος. This is preferable to taking νέος closely with γεννώμενος, "being born young," an otiose statement. This mystical note of the indwelling Christ is both Pauline (Rom 8:10; Gal 2:20) and Johannine (John 14:20; 17:26). It is frequently stressed in Ignatius (*Magn.* 12; *Smyrn.* 4:1). The thought is amplified in the following section (5) in the words ἡ ἐκκλησία ... πληθύνεται.[162]

5. ὁ σήμερον υἱὸς λογισθείς. An obscure phrase. Its ultimate source is probably Ps 2:7, interpreted as a messianic prediction by the author of πρὸς Ἑβραίους (1:5; 5:5). Whether or not we can fix our author's σήμερον to denote a feast of the nativity (Lake) or a celebration of Easter Day (Radford; cf. Paul's citation of Ps 2:7 in Acts 13:33), the term obviously refers to the Christian era. So Heb (3:7, 13, 15) seems to interpret the σήμερον of Ps 95:8. For the sense of λογισθείς see on 11:2.

ἡ ἐκκλησία. Stephanus and many editions insert ἡ. Otto thinks that the article is unnecessary and cites ἐκκλησίας χάρις (11:6) and 1 Cor 14:4. See pp. 12–13. χάρις ... πληθύνεται. See above p. 51. This "grace" is unfolded or extended in its influence. ἁπλόω, a late word. Cf. Job 22:3.

διαγγέλλουσα καιρούς. In what sense does grace proclaim seasons? Bunsen thinks the reference is to the direction of the Church by the Spirit on the question of the times of festivals (cf. the collocation of "the Lord's Passover" and "the seasons" in 12:9). More probably the meaning is that

---

162. For parallels in Hippolytus see Connolly, "Ad Diognetum xi–xii," 8–9.

grace proclaims the times of fulfillment of the promises. Cf. the use of διαγγέλλω in Acts 21:26.[163]

χαίρουσα ἐπί, with the dative. Cf. Bar 4:33; Matt 18:13 al. Classical Greek has the simple dative and also ἐπί with the dative. For πιστοῖς see on Diogn. 11:2. Here it is almost a technical term for the Christian brotherhood (cf. 1 Tim 4:3, 10).

ἐπιζητοῦσι δωρουμένη. Cf. 11:2: τίς ... οὐκ ἐπιζητεῖ σαφῶς μαθεῖν, κτλ. The dative of agent (οἷς) is used chiefly with the perfect and pluperfect passive. It occurs, however, with the present passive (as here) in Thuc. Cf. 3:64: τίνες ἂν οὖν ὑμῶν δικαιότερον πᾶσι τοῖς Ἕλλησι μισοῖντο; cf. also 6.87.3: τῶν ἡμῖν ποιουμένων. This usage of the dative is probably an extension of the dative of interest.

ὅρκια πίστεως. If Lachmann's conjecture, accepted by most editions, ὅρκια (for the MS ὅρια) is read, the allusion is to the baptismal vows. πίστις, here and in 11:6, is objective, "the faith," i.e., a defined body of Church doctrine. Cf. Jude 3; the "sound teaching" of 1 Tim 1:10; Titus 2:1; and Justin's "pure and pious faith" (*Dial.* 80). See below, p. 175.

ὅρια πατέρων. The bounds set by the Church Fathers relating to doctrine and discipline. Cf. Clement, *Virg.* 2.15.5: "haec fida sunt, haec vera et recta, hi limites, quos non mutant, qui recte in Domino conversantur."[164]

παρορίζεται. Late word. Cf. P. Tebt. II, 410[4] (16 CE): πρόσεχε χάριν οὗ παρορίζεται ὑπὸ γίτονος, "give heed on account of the encroachments made by a neighbor."[165]

6. For the significance of the question of law and prophecy with the Gospels and apostolic tradition, see above p. 50. Cf. also Theophilus, *Autol.* 3.12: Gospels, Prophets, Law.

Note the series of short rhetorical clauses connected by καί, as also in 12:9. Connolly sees here a further link in the proof that 11–12 derive from a work of Hippolytus.[166]

εἶτα marks the transition to a new point. Cf. Barn. 6:3; Heb 12:9. νόμου, objective genitive. ᾄδεται refers to the chanting of the law in psalm or hymn. For the figure see Ign. *Eph.* 4; *Rom.* 2.

προφητῶν χάρις. See above, p. 51.

εὐαγγελίων πίστις. Note the plural "gospels." The term is here used concretely of *books* (cf. the well-known passage in Justin Martyr, *1 Apol.*

---

163. See Bauer, *Wörterbuch*, 301, and Schniewind, Entry in *Theologische Wörterbuch*, 1:67.

164. See Funk, *Patres Apostolici*, 2:26. See also Radford's note in *Diognetus*, 83.

165. Cited in Moulton and Milligan, *Vocabulary*, 684b.

166. Connolly, "Ad Diognetum xi–xii," 11–12; 39; idem, "Eucharistic Prayer of Hippolytus," 361.

66: ἐν τοῖς γενομένοις ὑπ' αὐτῶν ἀπομνημονεύμασιν, ἃ καλεῖται εὐαγγέλια) aligned with the law and the prophets as sources for Christian instruction. On the other hand, it is the *oral* teaching of the apostles that is mainly in view (ἀποστόλων παράδοσις). See Additional Note D. The πίστις is again objective, as in 11:5. For the phrase cf. Phil 1:29.

ἐκκλησίας χάρις, "grace which works in the Church." Lachmann suggests χαρά (for the MS χάρις), which goes fittingly with σκιρτᾷ (cf. Luke 1:44). χαρά is a *variant* for χάρις in 2 Cor 1:15 (χαράν ℵ^C BLP), and χάρις for χαρά in 3 John 4 (χάρις B, Vg., Cop.). Cf. Clement of Alexandria, *Paed* 1.5.22: μόνη αὕτη (i.e., ἐκκλησία) εἰς τοὺς αἰῶνας μένει χαίρουσα ἀεί. On the other hand, note the following ἥν χάριν (7), and the preceding notion (5) of the "grace of the Church."

7. ἃ λόγος ὁμιλεῖ. Cf. 11:1. δι' ὧν, relative assimilated to the omitted antecedent. For θέλει see on 10:6.

8. The first person plural is used because the author is including himself among the agents of the Word just mentioned (7). They are under a double constraint to impart Christian truth to others: the command laid upon them by the Word, and love of what has been revealed to them.

μετὰ πόνου is best taken with ἐξειπεῖν ("to declare under stress") rather than γινόμεθα. Connolly shows the close kinship of this phrase (and indeed 11:8—12:1) with passages in the *Philosophumena* of Hippolytus.[167]

ἐξ ἀγάπης κτλ. See Connolly.[168]

Chapter 12

Those who love God rightly become "a paradise of delight," a fertile tree rich in varied fruits. Scripture records that God planted in the garden of Eden the tree of knowledge and the tree of life. Both trees were planted together to show the intimate union of knowledge and life. This is the force of the apostle's precept, "knowledge puffs up, but love edifies." Wherefore "let your heart be knowledge, your life the true word received (into the heart)." This true word is a fruitful tree, yielding the harvest of blessings that God desires.

1. ἐντυχόντες, "meet with," hence "to read." Cf. Plato, *Lysis* 214B; Polybius 1.3.10; Justin Martyr, *1 Apol.* 26. For the conjunction of "reading" and "hearing" see 2 Macc 15:39. Note ch. 1 (above) the writer "speaks" and the reader "hears." οἷς, i.e., the preceding ὅσα . . . μετὰ πόνου (11:8). εἴσεσθε. Attic form of the future of οἶδα. Note the second person plural, but the singular (σοί, τρυγήσεις) in 12:7-8. See note on 2:1.

---

167. Connolly, "Ad Diognetum xi–xii," 6–7.
168. Connolly, "Ad Diognetum xi–xii," 6.

ὅσα ... ὀρθῶς recalls the citation in 1 Cor 2:9b.

οἱ γενόμενοι παράδεισος τρυφῆς may refer to (1) τοῖς ἀγαπῶσιν ὀρθῶς. So Lightfoot and Lake, or (2) οἱ ἐντυχόντες καὶ ἀκούσαντες, "you who become thereby," etc. So Otto and Radford. A point that perhaps favors the latter view is that the reader is pictured as a fruitful tree. Hoffmann's conjecture, τρύγης (cf. τρυγήσεις Diogn. 12:8), is improbable, since the phrase is taken from Gen 3:24 (cf. Diogn. 2:15; also Joel 2:3). It is figuratively applied in view of their fertility, to those who love God rightly. Cf. Isa 51:3; Pss of Sol 14:2–3 (ὁ παράδεισος τοῦ κυρίου, τὰ ξύλα τῆς ζωῆς, ὅσιοι αὐτοῦ).

εὐθαλοῦν. Cf. Dan 4:4 (Theod.), P.Oxy. IV, 729[22] (2nd c. CE) τὰ φυτὰ εὐθαλοῦντα.

ἀνατείλαντες. So Stephanus for the MS ἀνατείκατε. Otto reads ἀνετείλατε. For the transitive use, found in Homer, cf. Gen 3:18; Matt 5:45; 1 Clem. 20:4. Lightfoot takes it as intransitive, "growing up in themselves," making πάγκαρπον ξέλον in apposition to παράδεισος.

ἐν ἑαυτοῖς, "in themselves"; if the alternative view (above) of οἱ γενόμενοι κτλ. is taken, "in yourselves."

ποικίλοις καρποῖς κεκοσμημένοι. In Herm. Sim. 9.28.1, believers are likened to δένδρα καρπῶν πλήρη, ἄλλοις καὶ ἄλλοις καρποῖς κεκοσμημένα (cf. 9.1.10).

ποικίλος, as in classical Greek, "variegated," "of diverse hues." Then, "various."

2. ἐν τῷ χωρίῳ (i.e., τῷ παραδείσῳ) ... ζωῆς. Cf. Gen 2:9. See above pp. 52–53. πεφύτευται, "there stands planted" (force of the perfect). So also in § 4. Contrast the aorist ἐφύτευε (§3).

3. οὐδὲ ... ἄσημα. Litotes. "With significance." The phrase perhaps suggests that there is an allegorical meaning behind the Scripture. τὰ γεγραμμένα, i.e., the passage in Gen 2:8–9. The perfect tense denotes the abiding record (in Scripture). ὡς, "how that" (= ὅτι).

ξύλον γνώσεως καί. Rightly inserted by Bunsen. The scribal omission might easily arise from the repetition of ξύλον.

διὰ ... ἐπιδεικνύς. A compressed phrase. The meaning is that man's true life (cf. ζωῆς ἀληθοῦς, 12:4) is to be gained through knowledge. For ἐπιδεικνύς see on 8:6.

ᾗ, i.e., γνώσει. Cf. Gen 3:7. καθαρῶς may refer to physical or moral "purity." If the former the reference is to the physical intercourse of the parents. Probably the latter sense is intended: they did not use their knowledge "rightly."

οἱ ἀπ' ἀρχῆς, "the first parents." This is preferable to taking ἀπ' ἀρχῆς with γεγύμνωνται. Possibly metaphorical, "were deprived of it" (i.e., knowledge or true life). If literal ("were left naked") the author gives a somewhat free interpretation of the Genesis story, which represents Adam and Eve as naked *before* their disobedience (Diogn. 2:25) and as awaking to their condition in consequence of yielding to the serpent.

4. This section is explanatory (note γάρ) of the statement that "life is through knowledge," the connection being momentarily interrupted by the words "but our first parents . . . serpent." There is thus a vital bond between sound knowledge and true life. Harnack says that this "classification is a Hellenistic one, which has certainly penetrated also into Palestinian Jewish theology."[169] It is Johannine in origin (cf. John 17:3) and is richly reflected in later writings. Cf. the eucharistic prayer in Did. 9:3: "we give you thanks, our Father, for the life and knowledge [ὑπὲρ τῆς ζωῆς καὶ γνώσεως] which you make known to us through Jesus your servant."

γνῶσις ἀσφαλής (cf. 1 Clem. 1:2) may mean "knowledge that is safe or secure." But the association of γινώσκω and ἀσφαλής in Acts (2:36; 21:34; 22:30) suggests the sense "certainty." The meaning would then be that knowledge to be "sound" must take account of religion (i.e., the true life).

διό. Here only in the epistle. It is rare in the apologists generally. ἑκάτερον, sc. ξύλον.

ἣν δύναμιν, i.e., "meaning" of both trees being planted together. For δύναμις, "force," "meaning," cf. Plato, Crat. 394B: ἡ τοῦ ὀνόματος δύναμις, 1 Cor 14:11: τὴν δύναμιν τῆς φωνῆς, Polybius 20.9.11: οὐκ εἰδότες τίνα δύναμιν ἔχει τοῦτο.

ὁ ἀπόστολος, i.e., Paul, who is thus included in the apostolate, as in Ign. Rom. 4:3. Cf. also Athanasius, Inc. 25:5, where φησὶν ὁ ἀπόστολος introduces a citation of Eph 2:2. For Paul as "apostle" see Gal 1:1, 17; Acts 9:15. See on Diogn. 11:1 (above).

εἰς ζωήν may be taken with ἀσκουμένην, "knowledge exercised unto life apart from the truth of the commandment."[170] But it yields a better sense to take it as a pregnant phrase connected with προστάγματος "knowledge which is exercised apart from the truth of the commandment which tends unto life."

What is the προστάγματος εἰς ζωήν? If a precise injunction is meant it may be the "commandment" not to eat of the tree of knowledge of good and evil (Gen 2:16f.; 3:11, 17, ἐντέλλομαι). This, however, is negative in character and has no suggestion of εἰς ζωήν. Paul is more explicit in his ἐντολὴ ἡ εἰς ζωήν (Rom 7:10), where, though the immediate reference is to the tenth commandment, he is allegorizing the Genesis story of the fall. The term

---

169. Harnack, *History of Dogma*, 1:170n1.
170. So Bauer, *Wörterbuch*, 194b.

πρόσταγμα may, however, be used here quite generally by our author. Cf. John 12:50 (ἐντολή). With ἀληθεία προστάγματος cf. λόγος ἀληθής (12:7).

6. ὑπὸ τοῦ ὄφεως πλανᾶται. Deception by the serpent (cf. §3) here operates on a wider scale. Any man who lacks knowledge that is true and attested by life is its victim. The allegory of the garden of Eden is present to the author's mind throughout the chapter.

ἐπ᾽ ἐλπίδι ... προσδοκῶν. Cf. the similar spiritual interpretation of "ploughing" and "threshing," ἐπ᾽ ἐλπίδι (1 Cor 9:10). The note of patient waiting for fruit is frequently struck. Cf. Sir 6:19 (ἀναμένω); Jas 5:7; 2 Clem 20:3 (ἐκδέχομαι).

7. A pregnant sentence. The meaning seems to be that the heart should be filled with the knowledge of divine things so that true teaching (λόγος ἀληθής), thus received in the heart, may become effectual in the life. For λόγος = "teaching," cf. 7:2 (above); John 5:24. We may compare ὁ λόγος τῆς ἀληθείας of the NT (Eph 1:13; Col 1:5; 2 Tim 2:15), and ὁ περὶ τὸ θεῖον ἀληθὴς λόγος of Hippolytus, *Philos.* 10:34.

χωρούμενος. A difficult expression. Probably the meaning is "received" (into the heart), i.e., "comprehended." Cf. Aelian, *Var. hist.* 3.9: ὅσον αὐτῷ καὶ ἡ ψυχὴ χωρεῖ. Also Matt 19:11–12; Ign. *Trall.* 5:1. It may, however, mean "being spread abroad," for which cf. Herodotus, *Hist.* 1.122: ἡ φάτις κεχώρηκε. So also John 8:37 (active), "my word makes no headway among you!" (Moffatt).[171] Bunsen prefers to read χορηγούμενος, "offered" (to you), Hollenberg, δωρούμενος, "presented."

8. οὗ, "of it," i.e., λόγος ἀληθής.

καρπὸν αἴρων. The MS has καρπὸν ... ρῶν. See Otto's full note for the various conjectures. Otto reads εὑρών, which (in the 2nd edition) he emended to αἴρων. But in the third edition he adopted Reuss's conjecture, ὁρῶν. Funk, Lightfoot, and Lake prefer αἴρων. τρυφήσεις, "shall fare sumptuously on." παρὰ θεῷ, "with God," i.e., in his judgment. Cf. Rom 2:13; 1 Cor 3:19; Jas 1:27.

οὐδὲ πλάνη ... πιστεύεται. Some editions (Bunsen, Hollenberg, Gildersleeve) read οὐδὲ πλάνη συγχρωτίζεται Εὔα οὐδὲ φθείρεται, "Eve is not defiled with deceit, nor is she corrupted." Ewald would read οὗ ("where") οὐδὲ Εὔα κτλ. See Radford's note.[172]

συγχρωτίζομαι is a rare word found in Diog. Laert. 7.2: ἀποκρίνασθαι τὸν θεόν, εἰ συγχρωτίζοιτο τοῖς νεκροῖς, "the god's response was that he should take on the complexion of the dead" (Hicks's trans.). The context of our passage supports the sense of sexual "taint" found in a later writer

---

171. See Field, *Notes*, 94–95.
172. Radford, *Diognetus*, 87–88.

(Eustathius 1069.1). Cf. also Hermetica (ed. W. Scott) 1.198.19: ἀνέχεσθαι συγχρωτιζόμενον αὐτῇ παθητὸν σῶμα, "to submit to contact with a body defiled by passion" (Scott's trans.).

Eve here probably denotes the Virgin Mary. From the story of the serpent's deceit the author's mind passes swiftly and naturally to "the second Eve." The purity of Eve (i.e., Mary) and the consequent Christian benefits specified in the following clauses ("and salvation is set forth," etc.) form the harvest (desired of God) of "the true word." The parallel between the Eve of Genesis and the Virgin Mary is familiar. Justin Martyr, *Dial.* 100 describes Eve as the mother of disobedience and death, but Mary as the mother of him through whom God destroys the serpent and delivers man from death. Irenaeus, *Haer* 3.22.4 similarly contrasts the Virgin Mary found obedient and Eve disobedient: "for she did not obey, being yet a virgin. As, having indeed a husband, i.e., Adam, yet being still a virgin . . . was made the cause of death . . . So also did Mary . . . by yielding obedience, become the cause of salvation." Irenaeus elaborates the contrast in 5.19.1. This same parallel appears in Tertullian, *Carn. Chr.* 17: "as Eve had believed the serpent, so Mary believed the angel. The delinquency which one caused by believing, the other by believing effaced."

Böhl thinks that the allusion is to the Virgin Mary, but takes πιστεύεται in the active sense, "Mary exercises faith." There would thus be a pointed contrast between Eve's enticement and transgression and Mary's confidence in the divine announcement (Luke 1:26f.). Funk thinks that, while the allusion is to Eve, the author has in mind Mary the Virgin as a second Eve.[173]

The idea that Eve lost her virginity through sexual seduction by Satan and so bequeathed infection to mankind is familiar in rabbinic tradition.[174] While this is not a biblical notion, it may lie behind 2 Cor 11:2–3, the serpent which deceived Eve being regarded as identical with Satan. Cf. 4 Macc 18:8; 2 En. 31:3ff.; Wis 2:24 (possibly). Note the suggested analogy between Eve and Mary in this regard in James or Protoevangelium 13:1.

9. For the stylistic feature of short sentences joined by καί cf. 11:6. See p. 66.

σωτήριον δείκνυται, "salvation is set forth" (in the gospel). For σωτήριον cf. Luke 3:6 (= Isa 40:5); T. Sim. 7:1; T. Dan 5:10.

συνετίζονται. Cf. also Herm. Mand. 4.2.1; T. Levi 4:5; 9:8. All these instances show the active voice and meaning "to give understanding," "instruct." Connolly cites five occurrences of the verb in Hippolytus.[175] For the

---

173. Funk, *Patres Apostolici*, 1:413.
174. See Oesterley and Box, *Religion*, 240; Thackeray, *Relation*, 50ff.
175. Connolly, "Ad Diognetum xi–xii," 11.

passive as here, cf. T. Dan 3:2: οἱ μακάριοι πορφῆται ὑπὸ τοῦ ἁγίου πνεύματος ἀεὶ συνετιζόμενοι. In view of the fairly common use of the word to denote "instruction" by the Spirit or the Lord, it is better to render the present passage "apostles are given understanding." If so, the thought would seem to be that the apostles have special divine enlightenment. Hence their tradition must be "guarded" (11:6). Otto, however, points to the secondary sense of συνετός "intelligible," and renders here "are understood" (*intelliguntur*). Radford prefers "are interpreted" (i.e., the writings of the apostles are read and explained), and points to Justin's reference to the reading of the "memoirs of the apostles" at the Sunday Eucharist.

καὶ τὸ ... προέρχεται. This phrase may denote the time of the year when the passage was written, i.e., shortly before the Passover.

καιροί. So Sylburg for the MS reading κηροί. Otto accepts κηροί ("wax candles" used by Christians at night to avoid persecution); Sylburg thinks that the reference is to the feasts at the three seasons (cf. Exod 34:23, 24; Deut 16:16). Funk thinks that the καιροί denote the seasons of the Christian year.[176] Maran suggests χοροί. So Hefele. Other conjectures are πηροί (Lachmann), κλῆροι (Bunsen. See Otto's note).

μετὰ κόσμου ἁρμόζονται. So Otto, Funk, Lake, Lightfoot (the last-named reads the [πάντα] μετὰ κόσμου ἁρμόζεται of Bunsen's suggestion [1854]). The MS has μετὰ κόσμου ἁρμόζεται. On the spelling ἁρμόζω see p. 11.

καὶ διδάσκων ... ἀμήν. On this passage see Connolly, who shows its close kinship, especially in the form of the doxology, with Hippolytean passages.[177]

δόξα. Cf. 9:6. The word here connotes "visible splendor," "radiance," a non-classical use which came in with the LXX as the translation of כָּבוֹד. Cf. Exod 24:16; Acts 22:11 *al.*[178]

---

176. Funk, *Patres Apostolici*, 1:413.
177. Connolly, "Ad Diognetum xi–xii," 10.
178. See Kennedy, *Sources*, 97; Milligan, *Thessalonians*, 27.

Additional Notes

A. The Imitation of God (10:4–6)

Abrahams shows the dispersion of this religious ideal.[1] In Diognetus it is the imitation of God especially in acts of beneficence that is in view. This aspect we may trace in:

The Letter of Aristeas, where kingly duty is constantly based upon God's benign rule of men. "As God does good to the whole world, so also would you, by imitating him, be void of offence" (210). See also §§190, 205, 281.

Philo, *De Judice* 73: "men never act in a manner more resembling the gods than when they are bestowing benefits; and what can be a greater good than for mortal men to imitate the everlasting God?" (Yonge's translation). Cf. also Philo, *Migr.* 131: "the end is, according to the most holy Moses, to follow God" (l); *De humanitate* 168: "to imitate God (μιμεῖσθαι θεόν) as far as possible."

Dio Chrysostom 2.26: "a kindly disposition . . . and above all, rejoicing in acts of beneficence, which is the nearest approach to the nature of the gods."

Ignatius, *Trall.* 1: "I received your godly benevolence . . . and found you . . . imitators of God" (μιμητὰς ὄντας θεοῦ). Cf. Ignatius, *Eph.* 1:1.

Aristides, *Apol.* 14: "and they (the Jews) imitate God by reason of the love which they have for man" (Syriac text).

Clement of Alexandria, *Paed.* 3.1.1: "and knowing God he will be made like God, not by wearing gold or long robes, but by well-doing."

Longinus, *De Sublimitate* 1.2: "for he answered well who, when asked in what qualities we resmble the gods, declared that we do so in benevolence and truth" (W. Rhys Roberts's translation).

We need not assume here direct borrowing by the author of Diognetus from Hellenistic-Jewish sources as such. It is clear that the idea had long and

---

1. Abrahams, *Pharisaism*, 138ff.

wide currency in popular religious thought.[2] In view of the indebtedness of our epistle to Pauline teaching the immediate source of the passage may be Eph 5:1, where the ethical expression of beneficent acts is "to walk in love." Cf. also the teaching of Jesus (Matt 5:44f., 48; Luke 6:36). In 1 Cor 11:1; 1 Thess 1:6, we have the *imitatio Christi*, a natural extension to the Son of the character faith recognized in the Father. See further in Additional Note B.

B. The Deification of Man

"But whosoever takes upon himself his neighbor's burden . . . supplying to those in what the things which he has received and holds from God becomes a god to those who receive them" (10:6). The meaning is that in virtue of such godlike service he becomes as a god to his beneficiaries, thus being truly an "imitator of God." The thought is akin to 7:4: "He sent him as God." On "the variability and elasticity of the concept 'θεός'" see Harnack's valuable note: "the genius, the hero, the founder of a new school who promises to show the certain way to the *vita beata*, the emperor, the philosopher (numerous Stoic passages might be noted here), finally man, in so far as he is inhabited by νοῦς—could all somehow be considered as θεοί, so elastic was the concept."[3] See also Nock, who thinks that the passage in Diogn. 10:6 is "important as showing how commonplace this mode of expression was at the end of the second century A.D."[4]

Stephanus cites the Greek proverb ἄνθρωπος ἀνθρώπου δαιμόνιον. More apposite is a passage from the Acts of John 27:[5] "but if, next to that God, it be right that the men who have benefited us should be called gods."[6] Note also Clem. Alex., *Paedag.* 3.1.5: "the man with whom the Logos dwells . . . is made like to God . . . and that man becomes God, for God wishes it."[7] Hippolytus, too, has the idea of the deification of man. Note the following from the *Philosophumena* (Legge's translation):

---

2. It was clearly reflected in Stoic teaching. Cf. Epictetus 2.14.13: "he, who would please and obey them (the gods), must try with all his power to be like them" in faithfulness, freedom, beneficence, and magnanimity; Marcus Aurelius 7.31: "love the human race; follow God" (ἀκολούθησον θεῷ).

3. Harnack, *History of Dogma*, 1:119n1.

4. Nock, "Ruler-Cult," 31, see also his note on p. 51 for illustrative references; see also Inge, *Christian Mysticism*, Appendix C.

5. Lipsius and Bonnet, *Acta*, 2:166, 3–4.

6. Cited in the Greek original by Funk, *Patres Apostolici*, 1:408–7.

7. See Butterworth, "Deification," 157ff.

10.33: "but if thou dost wish also to become a God, hearken to the Creator and withstand him not now, so that being found faithful over a little, thou mayest be entrusted with much."

10.34: "thou (wilt) have become God . . . thou hast been made divine, since thou hast been begotten immortal."[8]

10 (end): "having hearkened to whose august precepts, and having become a good imitator of the Good One, thou wilt be like unto and be honored by him. For God asks no alms, and has made thee God for his own glory."

Funk also quotes a saying from Gregory of Nazianzus, *Orat.*, 14.26, 27, of the same tenor:[9]

"Be thou a god to him that is in misfortune, imitating the mercy of God; for man has nothing which is so truly of the nature of God as the doing of good."

Geffcken names similar passages in Pliny, *Nat.* 2.7.18:[10]

"For mortal to aid mortal . . . this is god . . . To enrol such men among the deities is the most ancient method of paying them gratitude for their benefactions" (Rackham's translation of 2.5.18–19 in Loeb ed.).

"Do as the gods, those glorious authors of all things do; they being to give benefits to him who knows them not," etc. (Basore's translation).

The author of our epistle is evidently familiar with this current idea[11] that man may share in the divine nature and stand in the role of God to men.[12] But he has shaped it in the light of Johannine teaching that love and well-doing are integral to faith. Cf. John 13:34; 1 John 3:16–17; 4:21. Note in the two former passages the association of beneficence with the "imitation" of Christ.

---

8. Harnack (*History of Dogma* 3:164n2) shows that the notion of man's deification, as understood by the Greek Church, consisted mainly in imperishableness.

9. Funk, *Patres Apostolici*, 1:409.

10. Geffcken, *Diognetos*, 26.

11. For its prominence in Orphic religion see Harrison, *Prolegomena*, 476f., 662 (θεὸς ἐγένου ἐξ ἀνθρώπου). The theory of Euhemerus (ca. 316 BCE) bore on the question of the deification of Hellenistic kings by showing that even the older gods of Greece had been really no more than deified men.

12. There are hints that even in the strict Jewish monotheism of the Old Testament the term "god" was not rigidly exclusive. John 10:34ff. (citing Ps 82:6) implies an elastic use of the term "god" to include men who were commissioned by God as his representatives. Many scholars think that the "gods" addressed in that psalm (cf. also Ps 58:1 R.V.m.) are not heathen deities or angelic powers, but the rulers and judges of the time, who are given this title of honor as God's vicegerents on earth. Justin Martyr, *Dial.* 124, in his interpretation Ps 82 think that it proves "that all men are deemed worthy of becoming gods, and of having power to become sons of the Highest."

C. The Sonship of the Logos

The Appendix (11:4–5) has the noteworthy statement: "This is he (the Word) who was from the beginning, who appeared as new and was proved to be old . . . he who is the eternal one, who today was accounted a Son (ὁ σήμερον υἱὸς λογισθείς)." Can we trace here the idea of a progressive development from the status of λόγος to that of υἱός or παῖς? Connolly[13] finds here one among many evidences that Diogn. 11–12 came from the hand of Hippolytus, who in one passage (ch. 15, given below) plainly asserts and in several others implies that the pre-incarnate Logos was not yet "perfect Son of God." He cites the following excerpts[14] from the *Contra Noetum*, which we here reproduce in Salmond's translation (*Ante-Nicene Christian Library*, vol. 9)

Ch. 4: "Yet there is the flesh which was presented by the Father's Word as an offering—the flesh that came by the Spirit and the Virgin, (and was) demonstrated to be the perfect Son of God."[15]

Ch. 11: "And the Father is the All, from whom cometh this Power, the Word. And this is the mind (or reason) which came forth into the world, and was manifested as the Son of God."[16]

Ch. 15: "For neither was the Word, prior to incarnation and when by himself, yet perfect Son, although he was perfect Word, only-begotten. Nor could the flesh subsist by itself apart from the Word, because it has its subsistence [τὴν σύστασιν] in the Word. Thus, then, one perfect Son of God was manifested."[17]

Ch. 17: "In the same manner also did he come and manifest himself,[18] being by the Virgin and the Holy Spirit made a new man."

As a further illustration of the idea Connolly cites Hippolytus, *Antichr.* 3, where Hippolytus asks his addressee (Theophilus) to pray "that the things which the Word of God revealed in olden time to the blessed prophets, (the Word) who was again the child of God,[19] being of old the Word, but now also manifested[20] in the world for our sakes as man, these he may make clear to thee through us."

---

13. Connolly, "Ad Diognetum xi–xii," 2ff.; idem, "Eucharistic Prayer of Hippolytus," 357–58.
14. See also *Egyptian Church Order*, 164–65.
15. τέλειος υἱὸς θεοῦ ἀποδεδειγμένος.
16. ἐδείκνυτο παῖς θεοῦ.
17. εἷς υἱὸς τέλειος θεοῦ ἐφανερώθη.
18. ἐφανέρωσεν ἑαυτόν.
19. νῦν αὐτὸς πάλιν ὁ τοῦ θεοῦ παῖς.
20. φανερωθείς.

The notion that the Word "was shown"[21] in the incarnation to be the perfect Son is thus expressly stated in Hippolytus, "His Sonship, therefore, was a growing one, and first attained completion at the incarnation." Diognetus 11:4–5 is briefer and less explicit than the passages cited above. If, however, on other grounds we accept the strong case for the Hippolytean authorship of 11–12, then probably 11:4–5 adumbrates the notion which appears in a developed form in Hippolytus's other writings.

D. Guarded Tradition

The writer of the appended chapters makes the interesting statement: ἀποστόλων παράδοσις φυλάσσεται (11:6). The association of apostolic tradition with the fear of the law, the grace of the prophets, and the faith of the Gospels is significant. Among the Jews, tradition was of major importance. Paul rated highly among his credentials "in time past" his zeal for "the traditions of my fathers" (Gal 1:14). The orally transmitted traditions were strictly observed by the Pharisees, and were the chief means of preserving the teaching of the great rabbis (Mark 7:3–4 = Matt 15:2–3). Josephus[22] speaks of τὰ ἐκ παραδόσεως τῶν πατέρων in contradistinction to νόμιμα τὰ γεγεραμμένα (in the laws of Moses). There are indications that "guarded tradition" played an important part in early Christian history. The need of garnering information about Jesus would be felt by Christians at a fairly early stage and would be intensified as the hope of a speedy parousia began to fade. Some authoritative summary of Christian truth would be necessary for the instruction of converts and the equipment of missionaries, the more so since the earliest Christians had no New Testament in their possession or even within their purview. The following Pauline passages are significant:

2 Thess 2:15: "Stand fast, and hold the traditions [τὰς παραδόσεις] which you were taught, whether by word, or by epistle of ours."

2 Thess 3:6: "That you withdraw yourselves from every brother that walk disorderly, and not after the tradition [τὴν παράδοσιν] which they[23] received of us."

1 Cor 11:2: "Hold fast the traditions [τὰς παραδόσεις], even as I delivered (παρέδωκα) them to you."

Two points of interest emerge here. (*a*) "Paradosis" apparently included both doctrinal instruction and ethical guidance (cf. 1 Thess 4:1; Phil 4:9),

---

21. φανερόω, δείκνυμι, ἀποδείκνυμι (in the Hippolytean passages), φαίνω (in Diogn. 11:2–4).

22. *Ant.* 8.297.

23. Or "you" (*variant*).

the latter perhaps in the form of rules for Christian living.[24] (*b*) The written word begins to be conjoined with oral tradition as authoritative for faith. Paul in 2 Thess 2:15 (cited above) aligns the traditions he had either originated or transmitted to his converts "by word" and what he had since written "by epistle."[25] In 1 Cor 11:2 the tradition is that which Paul has himself received (παραλαμβάνω) either from (ἀπό) the Lord (1 Cor 11:23; cf. 7:10) or from those who have been "in Christ" before him (1 Cor 15:3), and has delivered (παραδίδωμι, cf. Luke 1:2) to others.[26] We may confidently posit an amount of more or less fixed Christian tradition, oral and written. Cf. Paul's τύπον διδαχῆς (Rom 6:17). It is generally agreed that 1 Cor 11:23-24; 15:3-4 show actual examples of such παράδοσις. Hence more generally 2 Tim 1:13-14 bids the reader "hold the pattern of sound words which you have heard from me . . . that good thing which was committed to *you* guard" (τὴν καλὴν παραθήκην φύλαξον).[27] Cf. 1 Tim 6:20. So also the writer of Jude 3 exhorts "to contend earnestly for the faith which was once for all delivered to the saints" (τῇ ἅπαξ παραδοθείσῃ τοῖς ἁγίοις πίστει). See 2 Pet 2:21, and similarly 2 Tim 2:2.[28]

The apologists frequently appeal to the authority of tradition as interpretative of Scripture. So Justin Martyr, *1 Apol.* 10: "We have received by tradition (παρειλήφαμεν) that God does not need," etc. . . . "and we have been taught (δεδιδάγμεθα) . . . and so we have received" (παρειλήφαμεν). Still earlier 1 Clem. 7:2 exhorts the readers to come ἐπὶ τὸν εὐκλεῆ καὶ σεμνὸν τῆς παραδόσεως ἡμῶν κανόνα,[29] while Polycarp, *Phil* 7:2 urges a return "to the word which was delivered to us in the beginning" (ἐπὶ τὸν ἐξ ἀρχῆς ἡμῖν παραδοθέντα λόγον). Didache 4:13 has the more general injunction: φυλάξεις

---

24. In the Thessalonian passages above directions for Christian conduct seem to be in view, and there the nuance of the term παράδοσις is rather "rule" or "instruction" than "tradition."

25. Moffatt, *Thrill*, 176n1, shows that it is the oral associations of παράδοσις, παραδίδωμι that predominated in primitive Christian usage, and cites the present passage (Diogn. 11:6).

26. Dibelius, *From Tradition to Gospel*, 21, shows that these two correlative terms are technical, having their equivalents in Jewish usage, both Palestinian and Hellenistic.

27. The metaphor in the term παραθήκη reflects the custom of depositing valuables for safe custody. The apostles have been entrusted by God with previous "securities," namely, the truth of the gospel tradition. Diogn. 7:1f. insists that the gospel is *God's* trust to men, which they must carefully guard (φυλάσσειν).

28. See Mayor, *Jude*, 23, 61ff.; and Prestige, "Tradition," 8ff.

29. The language here may be metaphorical, the "rule" being the measure of the leap or race, and the "tradition" referring to the example set by the Neronian martyrs.

δὲ ἃ παρέλαβες. At a later time, Clement of Alexandria[30] pays his grateful tribute to tradition, which he further insists is a unity.[31]

E. Diognetus and the Apology of Quadratus

Dom P. Andriessen has recently revived and elaborated an interesting theory.[32] His view is that Diognetus is to be identified with the Apology of Quadratus, which was formerly presumed to be lost apart from a fragment preserved in Eusebius, *Hist. eccl.* 4.3. This apology was presented to the Emperor Hadrian at the beginning of the second century CE, Diognetus, the addressee, being no other than the emperor himself. H. Kihn had examined Dorner's suggestion that Quadratus was the author of Diognetus,[33] but had rejected it in favor of his own view that Aristides was the author of the epistle. Kihn had hazarded the notion that the fragment of the Apology of Quadratus might have occupied one of the lacunae in Diognetus, especially 7:6-7.[34] Andriessen revives this abandoned supposition. He argues (1) that the missing portion (Diogn. 7:6-7) contained references to the miracles wrought by Christ (an inference drawn from a careful examination of the sections following and preceding the lacuna), and (2) that the Quadratus fragment agrees in point of view, contents, and style with the presumed theme of Diogn. 7:6-7.

In support of (1) Andriessen makes the following points:

(*a*) The assumption that earlier apologists, apart from Justin, are relatively silent about the life, miracles, passion, and resurrection of Christ calls for qualification. Andriessen thinks that the early apologetic writings included at least a short conspectus of the chief facts of the life of Christ and cites Aristides and Quadratus as proof. The former touched briefly on the main evangelical facts, the latter on the miracles. Diognetus, he holds,

---

30. "Preserving the true tradition of the blessed teaching derived directly from the holy apostles Peter and James, John and Paul, the son receiving it from the father (though few sons were like their fathers), they [the missioners] came by God's favor to us as well, in order to deposit these ancestral, apostolic seeds. Well do I know that they will rejoice. For, in my opinion, a soul desirous of preserving the blessed tradition unbroken may be described as follows: 'in a man who loves wisdom his father takes delight'" (*Strom.* 1.1.11f., quoted by Moffatt, *Thrill*, 77)

31. μία γὰρ [ἡ] πάντων γέγονε τῶν ἀποστόλων ὥσπερ διδασκαλία, οὕτως δὲ καὶ [ἡ] παράδοσις (*Strom.* 7.17.108). Cf. Plato, *Leg.* 803: διδασκαλία καὶ παράδοσις, where the terms denote oral teaching and exposition.

32. Andriessen, "Quadratus," 5-39, 125-49, 237-60.

33. Kihn, *Ursprung*.

34. Kihn, *Ursprung*, 97.

is to be classed in temper and outlook with the early apologies. It would therefore be strange if the epistle contained no reference to the miracles and the historical events of the Christian tradition.

(*b*) The term παρουσία (Diogn. 7:6–9) is significant in this regard. Its two occurrences in this context carry a different reference: 7:6 = the second coming; 7:9 = the first coming. Andriessen therefore interprets the passage to mean that the fidelity of Christians and their numerical increase under persecution are for the author of Diognetus signs that Christ has already come, and he suggests that other evidences of Christ's first advent originally stood in the lacuna (7:6–7). Similarly, Justin Martyr, *Dial.* 121, 110; *1 Apol.* 39; and Irenaeus, *Haer.* 4.34.3; 4.33.9 consider the constancy and growth of Christians under trial as proofs of the *first* coming of Christ.

(*c*) The staunchness and increase of Christians (Diogn. 7:7–8) are *moral* miracles, attesting indeed Christ's presence and aid, but inferior, as a foundation for faith, to physical miracles. What was needed was some account of actual works wrought by Christ as *direct* testimony to his coming. This is given in Justin and Irenaeus, both of whom refer to the miracles of Christ as direct evidence of his first coming. The presumption is that a similar section dealing with the miracles originally stood in the lacuna (Diogn. 7:6–7), and Andriessen points to the triumphant tone of 7:9 in confirmation.

"It is therefore unquestionable that the missing section is about an issue of some miracles at least, performed by the Lord, which were to prove to Diognetus that Christ was not an ordinary man, but that he was the true Son of God come among men."[35]

(*d*) Andriessen infers from Digon. 7:1–5 the character of the miracles set forth in the lacuna (6–7). They are deeds which exhibit the gentleness and beneficence of Christ (cf. 8:11 μετασχεῖν τῶν εὐεργεσιῶν and 9:5). He points out that Christ himself names such miracles as proofs of his coming (Matt. 11:4ff.).

(*e*) The lacuna must have comprised some complete phrases and probably was of a fairly considerable size. It is suggested that the two lacunae (7:6–7; 10:8) consisted originally of four pages, two for each gap.

In relation to (2) the fragment of the Apology of Quadratus, Andriessen argues:

(*a*) that the content harmonizes with what he supposes was the subject-matter of the hiatus in Diogn. 7:6–7, and that his hypothesis clarifies several phrases in the epistle (7:9; 8:4, 11; 9:6). The term σωτήρ (9:6) gains special point in that Christ heals men from disease. His saviorhood is linked with his miracles of healing. Cf. Irenaeus, *Epid.* 53, Just. Mart., *2 Apol.* 5.

---

35. Andriessen, "Quadratus," 11.

(*b*) that a close examination of the language and style shows that the Apology of Quadratus "has all the characteristics of Diognetus."[36]

The general conclusion is that all the data concerning the person and work of Quadratus favor strongly the identification of his Apology of Quadratus with Diognetus. This view is also acceptable on more general grounds: both documents are apostolic in teaching and temper; both show an admirable style in imitation of the best pagan authors, but are marked by an absence of citations from such writers.

Andriessen then proceeds to discuss the identity of Quadratus and of Diognetus, the inquirer. After assembling the relevant passages in Eusebius and other sources, he concludes that Quadratus, at the time when he presented his Apology to Hadrian, was bishop of Athens.[37] Diognetus he identifies with the Emperor Hadrian.[38] Some passages in the epistle point, he holds, to this conclusion:

The name Diognetus was an honorific title given to princes, and was fittingly applied to Hadrian by the Apologist and by Marcus Aurelius.

Pride in the mutilation of the flesh (4:4) is given point by the fact that Hadrian had published a decree forbidding circumcision.

Emphasis on obedience to the laws (5:10; cf. ἄνομος, ἀνομία 9:2, 4, 5) would appeal to Hadrian with whom honor shown to the laws was of the first importance.

The improvement of the soul through asceticism (6:9) may reflect Hadrian's Spartan self-discipline.

Fidelity to an appointed τάξις (6:10) was entirely appropriate to Hadrian's firm military discipline.

The inquisitiveness of Hadrian ("*curiositatum omnium explorator*," Tertuallian, *Apol.* 5:7) is a further link in the proof of identity.[39] Andriessen sees in the epistle many allusions to the fact that Hadrian had been initiated into the Eleusinian mysteries, and remarks on Diognetus's "curiosity" (see ch. 1 *ad init.*; 3:1; 4:6; 5:3).

καὶ τίς αὐτοῦ τὴν παρουσίαν ὑποστήσεται; (7:6). The emphatic position of αὐτοῦ (contrast 7:9) is, Andriessen thinks, deliberate.[40] It is intended to make a pointed contrast with παρουσία of Hadrian.

Other significant passages are 2:1; 7; 10:4–6.

---

36. Andriessen, "Quadratus," 39.

37. So also Jerome, *Vir. ill.* 19. Note the phrase "discipulus apostolorum" (cf. Diogn. 11:1).

38. Andriessen, "Quadratus," 242.

39. Andriessen, "Quadratus," 244ff.

40. Andriessen, "Quadratus," 244.

Andriessen concludes that in the light of his theory chs. 11–12 of Diognetus, which frequently reflect the Eleusinian mysteries, form an authentic part of the epistle, i.e., the Apology of Quadratus.

The care and thoroughness with which Andriessen propounds his view calls for a more detailed examination than can here be given. Some queries, however, may be raised. While it is agreed that Diogn. 7:6–7 shows a break in sense and sequence as well as in text, it is speculative to assume a lengthy lacuna such as Andriessen's theory seems to posit. The interpretation of Diogn. 7:6–7 seems to hinge on the meaning of παρουσία in v. 9. Andriessen takes it to denote the first "coming" of Christ. We have seen reason to prefer the meaning "(God's) presence." See note *ad loc*. The meaning thus gained seems more natural: the firmness of Christians and their numerical growth under trial are due not to any agency of man but to the power (δύναμις) and presence (παρουσία) of God. Moreover, it is surely straining language to find in the emphatic position of αὐτοῦ (7:6)[41] a pointed contrast between the παρουσία of Christ and the παρουσία of Hadrian. Again, would the actual miracles of Christ prove a more powerful aid to faith than the fidelity and increase of Christians under persecution? Andriessen argues that in the missing section (7:6–7) there must have been a reference to Christ and some of his works and points to the significance of the words ἀρνήσωνται τὸν κύριον (7:7). But if such reference is to be presumed, why only here? The author is throughout consistently silent about the earthly life of Christ. Andriessen suggests that the term σωτήρ (9:6) is linked with the healing miracles of Christ, as in Quadratus, Justin, and Irenaeus. In point of fact in 9:6 the term stands in a context which suggests not Christ's healing works but his power to "save" men impotent in sin. The comparison of the epistle with the fragment of Quadratus suffers from the brevity of the latter. It would seem precarious to deduce so much from so slender an excerpt as Eusebius gives. Nor is it at all certain on chronological grounds that Quadratus, "the disciple of the apostles" and the author of the Apology of Quadratus, is the same person as the Bishop of Athens. Finally, some points which Andriessen finds in favor of the identification of Diognetus with Hadrian seem forced, for example, the reflection in the epistle of the supposed "curiosity" and austerity of the emperor.

---

41. It is doubtful whether the position of the pronoun lends emphasis. Cf. Matt 2:2; John 2:23 (can we differentiate between the force of the first αὐτοῦ and that of the second?). Cf. Diogn. 2:1 (σου); 6:4 (αὐτῶν); 10:4 (αὐτοῦ), all apparently unemphatic.

Bibliography

Aall, Anathon. *Der Logos. Geschichte seiner Entwicklung der griechischen Philosophie und der christlichen Literatur.* Leipzig: O. R. Reisland, 1896–99.
Abbott, Thomas Kingsmill. *A Critical and Exegetical Commentary on the Epistles to the Ephesians and to the Colossians.* International Critical Commentary. Edinburgh: T&T Clark, 1922.
Abrahams, Israel. *Studies in Pharisaism and the Gospels.* Series II. Cambridge: Cambridge University Press, 1924.
Adam, James. *The Religious Teachers of Greece.* Edinburgh: T&T Clark, 1908.
Allen, Alexander V. G. *Continuity of Christian Thought: A Study of Modern Theology in Light of Its History.* Boston and New York: Houghton, Mifflin, 1897.
Altaner, Berthold. *Patrologie.* Freiburg: Herder, 1938.
Andriessen, Dom Paul. "L'Apologie de Quadratus conservée sous le titre d'Épître à Diognète." *Recherches de Théologie ancienne et médiévale* 13 (1946) 5–39, 125–49, 237–60.
Angus, Samuel. *The Religious Quests of the Graeco-Roman World: A Study in the Historical Background of Early Christianity.* London: John Murray, 1929.
Anz, Heinrich *Subsidia ad cognoscendum Graecorum sermonem vulgarem e Pentateuchi versione Alexandrina repetita* . Halis Saxonum: E. Karras, 1894.
Arnold, Edward Vernon. *Roman Stoicism: Being Lectures on the History of the Stoic Philosophy.* Cambridge: Cambridge University Press, 1911.
Aubé, Benjamin. *Saint Justin, Philosophe et Martyr.* Paris: E. Thorin, 1875.
Bardenhewer, Otto. *Geschichte der altkirchlichen Literatur.* Vol. 1. 2nd ed. Freiburg im Breisgau: Herder, 1913.
———. *Patrology: The Lives and Works of the Fathers of the Church.* Freiburg: Herder, 1908.
Bardy, Gustave. *La vie spirituelle d'après les pères des trois premiers siècles.* Paris: Bloud & Gay, 1935.
Batiffol, Pierre. *Anciennes Littératures Chrétiennes. La Littérature Grecque.* Paris: Lecoffre, 1897.
———. *Primitive Catholicism.* London: Longmans, 1911.
Bauer, Walter. *Griechisch-Deutsches Wörterbuch zu den Schriften des Neuen Testaments und der übrigen urchristlichen Literatur.* 3rd ed. Berlin: Alfred Töpelmann, 1937.
Bethune-Baker, James F. *An Introduction to the Early History of Christian Doctrine to the Time of the Council of Chalcedon.* London: Methuen, 1903.

———. *An Introduction to the Early History of Christian Doctrine to the Time of the Council of Chalcedon*. 5th ed. London: Methuen, 1933.
Bevan, Edwyn. Chapter in *Cambridge Ancient History*. Vol. 11. Cambridge: Cambridge University Press, 1936.
———. *Hellenism and Christianity*. London: G. Allen & Unwin, 1930.
———. *Holy Images: An Inquiry into Idolatry and Image-Worship in Ancient Paganism and in Christianity*. London: G. Allen & Unwin, 1940.
———. "Idolatry," *Edinburgh Review* 243.496 (1926) 253-72.
———. *Later Greek Religion*. London: Dent, 1927.
———. "Review of *The Epistle of Diognetus* by E. H. Blakeney," *Hibbert Journal* 42 (1943).
———. *Stoics and Sceptics: Four Lectures Delivered in Oxford*. Oxford: Clarendon, 1913.
Beyschlag, Willibald. *New Testament Theology or Historical Account of the Teaching of Jesus and of Primitive Christianity*. Vol. 2. 2nd ed. Edinburgh: T&T Clark, 1908.
Birks, Edward B. "Epistle to Diognetus." In *Dictionary of Christian Biography, Literature, Sects and Doctrines*, edited by William Smith and Henry Wace, 2:162-67. London: Murray, 1880.
———. "Epistle of Diognetus." In *Dictionary of Christian Biography*, edited by Henry Wace and William Piercy, 2:257ff. 2nd ed. London: Murray, 1911.
Bishop of Gloucester. Article in *Church Quarterly Review* 81 (1940).
Blake, Buchanan. "Contributions and Comments." *Expository Times* 45 (1933) 142.
Blakeney, Edward Henry. *The Epistle to Diognetus*. London: Macmillan, 1943.
———. "A Note on the Epistle to Diognetus, X, §I." *Journal of Theological Studies* 42 (1941) 193-95.
Blass, Friedrich. *Gramamtik des neutestamentlichen Griechisch*. 2nd improved ed. Göttingen: Vandenhoeck & Ruprecht, 1902.
Blass, Friedrich, and Albrecht Debrunner. *Grammatik des neutestamentlichen Griechisch*. 5th ed. Göttingen: Vandenhoeck & Ruprecht, 1921.
———. *Nachträge zur 5. Auflage*. 5th ed. Göttingen: Vandenhoeck & Ruprecht, 1931.
Bonner, Campbell, ed. *The Homily of the Passion by Melito, Bishop of Sardis, and Some Fragments of the Apocryphal Ezekiel*. Studies and Documents 12. London: Christophers, 1940.
Bonwetsch, G. Nathanael. "Der Autor der Schlusskapitel des Briefes an Diognet." *Göttingen Nachricht philologisch-historische Klasse* (1902) 621-34.
———. "Hippolytisches," *Nachrichten von der Königlichen Gesellschaft der Wissenschaften zu Göttingen. Philologisch-historische Klasse* (1923) 27-32.
Bunsen, Christian Karl Josias. *Analecta Ante-Nicaena*. Vol. 1. London: Longman, 1854.
———. *Christianity and Mankind: Their Beginnings and Prospects*. Vol. 1. London: Longman, 1854.
———. *Hippolytus and His Age. Or: The Beginnings and Prospects of Christianity*. Vol. 1. London: Longmans, 1854.
Buonaiuti, Ernesto. *Lettera a Diogneto, testo, traduzione e note*. Scrittori christia-ni antichi 1. Rome: Libreria di Cultura, 1921.
Burkitt, Francis C. "Pagan Philosophy in the Christian Church." In *Cambridge Ancient History*. Vol. 12: 450-75. Cambridge: Cambridge University Press, 1936.
Burton, Ernst. *Galatians*. International Critical Commentary. London and New York: T&T Clark, 1920.
Cadbury, Henry J., et al. *Christian Beginnings*. 4 vols. London: Macmillan, 1933.
———. *The Making of Luke-Acts*. New York: Macmillan, 1927.

Bibliography

Cadoux, Cecil J. *The Early Church and the World: A History of the Christian Attitude to Pagan Society and the State down to the Time of Constantinus*. Edinburgh: T&T Clark, 1925.
Carrington, Philip. *Christian Apologetics of the Second Century in Their Relation to Modern Thought*. London: SPCK, 1921.
Cassels, Walter Richard. *Supernatural Religion*. 3rd ed. Vol. 2. London: Longmans, 1874.
Chambers, C. D. "On a Use of the Aorist Participle in Some Hellenistic Writers." *Journal of Theological Studies* 24 (1923) 183–87.
Chapman, John. "Epistle of Diognetus." In *Catholic Encyclopedia*, edited by Charles G. Herbermann and Edward A. Pace, 5:8–9. New York: Appleton, 1909.
Charles, Robert Henry. *The Greek Versions of the Testament of the Twelve Patriarchs*. Oxford: Clarendon, 1908.
Cohn, Leopold, et al. *Philonis Alexandrini Opera quae supersunt*. Berlin: Reimer, 1896–1930.
Connolly, Richard Hugh. "Ad Diognetum xi–xii." *Journal of Theological Studies* 37 (1936) 2–15.
———. "The Date and Authorship of the Epistle to Diognetus." *Journal of Theological Studies* 36 (1935) 347–53.
———. "The Eucharistic Prayer of Hippolytus." *Journal of Theological Studies* 39 (1938) 357–69.
———. *The So-Called Egyptian Church Order*. Texts and Studies 8. Cambridge: Cambridge University Press, 1916.
Cotterill, Joseph M. "Justin Martyr's Epistle to Diognetus and the Oration to the Gentiles," *Church Quarterly Review* 4 (1877) 42–76.
———. *Peregrinus Proteus. An Investigation into Certain Relations Subsisting between* De Morte Peregrinie, *the Two Epistles of Clement to the Corinthians, the Epistle of Diognetus, the* Bibliotheca *of Photius, and Other Writings*. Edinburgh: T&T Clark, 1879.
Credner, Carl August. *Geschichte des neutestamentlichen Kanon*. Edited by G. Volkmar. Berlin: Georg Reimer, 1860.
Cruttwell, Charles Thomas. *A Literary History of Early Christianity, Including the Fathers and the Chief Heretical Writers of the Ante-Nicene Period*. Vols. 1–2. London: Charles Griffin, 1893.
Cureton, William. *Spicilegium Syriacum. Containing Remains of Bardesan, Meliton, Ambrose, and Mara Bar Serapion*. London: Rivingtons, 1855.
Cuq, Édouard. "De la nature des crimes imputés aux chrétiens, d'après Tacite." *Mélanges d'archéologie et d'histoire* 6 (1886) 115–38.
Dalman, Gustav. *The Words of Jesus Considered in the Light of Post-Biblical Jewish Writings and the Aramaic Language*. Edinburgh: T&T Clark, 1902.
Deissmann, Gustav Adolf. *Bible Studies: Contributions from Papyri and Inscriptions to the History of the Language, the Literature, and the Religion of Hellenistic Judaism and Primitive Christianity*. Translated by Alexander Grieve. Edinburgh: T&T Clark, 1901.
———. *Light from the Ancient East. The New Testament Illustrated by Recently Discovered Texts of the Graeco-Roman World*. Translated by Lionel R. M. Strachan. London and New York: Hodder & Stoughton, 1890.
Dibelius, Martin. *From Tradition to Gospel*. Translated by Bertram Lee Woolf. New York: Scribner, 1935.

Di Pauli, A. von. "Die Schlußkapitel des Diognetbriefs." *Theologisches Quartalschrift* 88 (1906) 28–36.
Dittenberger, W. *Sylloge Inscriptionum Graecarum*. 3rd ed. Leipzig: Hirzel, 1915–24.
Dobschütz, Ernst von. *Christian Life in the Primitive Church*. Edited by William Douglas Morrison. Translated by G. Bremner. London: Williams & Norgate, 1904.
———. *Das Kerygma Petri kritisch untersucht*. Texte und Untersuchungen 11. Leipzig: Hinrichs, 1894.
Dodd, Charles Harold. *The Bible and the Greeks*. London: Hodder & Stoughton, 1935.
———. *The Epistle of Paul to the Romans*. London: Hodder & Stoughton, 1947.
Donaldson, James. *A Critical History of Christian Literature*. Vols. 1–3. London: Macmillan, 1864–66.
Dorner, Isaak August. *History of the Development of the Doctrine of the Person of Christ*. Vol. 1.1. Edinburgh: T&T Clark, 1863.
Doulcet, Henry. "L'Apologie d'Aristide et l'Épître à Diognète." *Revue des Questions Historiques* 28 (1880) 601–12.
Dräseke, Johannes. "Der Brief an Diognetus." *Jahrbücher für protestantische Theologie* 7 (1881) 213–83 and 414–84.
———. "Zur 'Refutatio Omnium Haeresium' des Hippolytos." *Zeitschrift für wissenschaftliche Theologie* 45 (1902) 263–88.
Drummond, James. "Researches on the Epistle to Diognetus," *Academy* 4 (1873) 27–29.
———. *Philo Judaeus*. Vol 1. London: Williams & Norgate, 1888.
Ewald, Heinrich. *History of Israel*. Vols 1–8. London: Longmans, 1869–74.
Fermi, M. "L'apologia di Aristide e la lettera a Diogneto." *Ricerche religiose* 1 (1925) 541–47.
Field, Frederick. *Notes on the Translation of the New Testament*. Cambridge: Cambridge University Press, 1899.
Friedländer, Ludwig. *Roman Life and Manners under the Early Empire*. Vols. 1–3. Translated by Leondard Arthur Magnus et al. London: Routledge, 1913.
Funk, Franz Xaver. *Patres Apostolici*. Vol. 1. 2nd ed. Tübingen: Laupp, 1901.
———. *Patres Apostolici*. Vol. 2. 2nd ed. Tübingen: Laupp, 1901.
———. "Das Schlusskapitel des Diognetus Briefes." *Theologisches Quartalschrift* 85 (1903) 638–39.
Gass, W. "Das patristiche Wort οἰκονομία." *Zeitschrift für wissenschaftliche Theologie* 17 (1874).
Gebhardt, Oskar von, et al. *Patrum Apostolicorum Opera*. Leipzig: Hinrichs, 1878.
Geffcken, Johannes. "Der Brief an Diognetus." In *Neutestamentliche Apokryphen*, edited by Edgar Hennecke, 619–23. 2nd ed. Tübingen: Mohr Siebeck, 1942.
———. *Der Brief an Diognetos*. Heidelberg: C. Winter, 1928.
———. "Der Brief an Diognetos?" *Zeitschrift für Kirchengeschichte* 43; Neue Folge 6 (1924) 348–50.
———. *Zwei griechische Apologeten*. Leipzig: Teubner, 1907.
Gildersleeve, B. L. *The Apologies of Justin Martyr. To Which Is Appended the Epistle to Diognetus*. New York: Harper & Brothers, 1877.
Glover, Terrot Reaveley. *The Conflict of Religions in the Early Roman Empire*. 12th ed. London: Methuen, 1932.
Goodenough, Erwin Ramsdell. *The Theology of Justin Martyr*. Jena: Frommann, 1923.
Goodspeed, Edgar J. *Die ältesten Apologeten. Texte mit kurzen Einleitungen*. Göttingen: Vandenhoeck & Ruprecht, 1914.
———. *Index Apologeticus*. Leipzig: Hinrichs, 1912.

———. *Index Patristicus*. Leipzig: Hinrichs, 1907.
Goodwin, William Watson. *Syntax of the Moods and Tenses*. London: Macmillan, 1929.
Grensted, Laurence William. *A Short History of the Doctrine of the Atonement*. Manchester: Manchester University Press, 1920.
Gwatkin, Henry Melvill. *Early Church History to AD 313*. Vol. 1. London: Macmillan, 1927.
Harnack, Adolf von. *Geschichte der altchristlichen Literatur*. Vol. 1. Leipzig: Hinrichs, 1893.
———. *Geschichte der altchristlichen Literatur*. Vol. 2.1. Leipzig: Hinrichs, 1897.
———. *Geschichte der altchristlichen Literatur*. Vol. 2.2. Leipzig: Hinrichs, 1904.
———. *History of Dogma*. Vol. 1. Translated by Neil Buchanan. London: Williams & Norgate, 1894.
———. *History of Dogma*. Vol. 2. Translated by Neil Buchanan. London: Williams & Norgate, 1896.
———. *The Mission and Expansion of Christianity in the First Three Centuries*. Translated by James Moffatt. 2 vols. 2nd ed. London: Williams & Norgate, 1908.
———. *Patrum Apostolicorum Opera*. Vol. 1.1. Leipzig: Hinrichs, 1877.
———. *Die Quellen der sogenannten apostolischen Kirchenordnung nebst einer Untersuchung über den Ursprung des Lectorats und anderen niederen Weihen*. Texte und Untersuchungen, N. F. 2. Heft 3a. Leipzig: Hinrichs, 1886.
———. "Die Überlieferung der griechischen Apologeten des 2. Jahrhunderts in der alten Kirche und im Mittelalter." In *Texte und Untersuchungen* 1, 1–300. Leipzig: Hinrichs, 1882.
Harris, James Rendel. *Celsus and Aristides*. Cambridge Texts and Studies 1.1. Aberdeen: Aberdeen University Press, 1921.
Harris, James Rendel, and J. Armitage Robinson. *The Apology of Aristides on behalf of the Christians. From a Syriac Ms. Preserved on Mount Sinai*. Cambridge Text and Studies 1.1. Cambridge: Cambridge University Press, 1891.
Harris, James Rendel, and V. Burch. *Testimonies*. Part 2. Cambridge: Cambridge University Press, 1920.
Harrison, Jane Ellen. *Prolegomena to the Study of Greek Religion*. 3rd ed. Cambridge: Cambridge University Press, 1922.
Harrison, Percival Neale. *Polycarp's Two Epistles to the Philippians*. Cambridge: Cambridge University Press, 1936.
Hatch, Edwin. *Essays in Biblical Greek*. Oxford: Clarendon, 1889.
———. *The Influence of Greek Ideas and Usages upon the Christian Church*. 6th ed. London: Williams & Norgate, 1897.
Heinzelmann, Wilhelm. *Der Brief an Diognet, "die Perle des christlichen Altertums."* Erfurt: H. Neumann, 1896.
Hennecke, Edgar, *Die Apologie des Aristides*. Texte und Untersuchungen 4. Leipzig: Hinrichs, 1893.
Herzog, Rabbi I. "The Outlook of Greek Culture upon Judaism." *Hibbert Journal* 29 (1930) 49–60.
Hicks, E. L. "On Some Political Terms Employed in the New Testament." *Classical Review* 1 (1887) 4–8.
Hort, Fenton John Anthony. *1 Peter*. London: Macmillan, 1898.
Howard, Wilbert Francis. *Christianity according to St. John*. London: Duckworth, 1947.
———. "On the Futuristic Use of the Aorist Participle in Hellenistic." *Journal of Theological Studies* 24 (1923) 403–6.

Inge, William Ralph. *Christian Mysticism: Considered in Eight Lectures Delivered before the University of Oxford*. London: Methuen, 1948.
Jacquier, Eugene. *Le Nouveau Testament dans l'Église Chrétienne*. Vol. 1. Paris: Lecoffre, 1913.
James, Montague R. *The Apocryphal New Testament: Being the Apocryphal Gospel, Acts, Epistles, and Apocalypses*. Oxford: Clarendon, 1926.
Jannaris, Antonius N. *An Historical Greek Grammar*. London: Macmillan, 1897.
Jülicher, A. "Diognetos." In *Real-encyclopädie der classischen Altertumswissenschaft*, edited by August Pauly and Georg Wissowa, 5:786. Stuttgart: Metzler, 1905.
Keim, Theodor. *Rom und das Christenthum. Eine Darstellung des Kampfes zwischen dem alten und dem neuen Glauben im römischen Reiche während der beiden ersten Jahrhunderte unsrer Zeitrechnung*. Berlin: G. Reimer, 1881.
———. "Die Zeit der Apologie Justin's des Märtyrers an Kaiser Antonin den Frommen," *Protestantische Kirchenzeitung* 20 (1873) 618–24.
Kennedy, Henry Angus Alexander. *Sources of New Testament Greek. Or, The Influence of the Septuagint on the New Testament*. Edinburgh: T&T Clark, 1895.
Kihn, Heinrich. *Der Ursprung des Briefes an Diognet*. Freiburg im Breisgau: Herder, 1882.
———. "Zum Briefe an Diognet." *Theologisches Quartalschrift* 28 (1880) 601–12.
Kittel, Gerhard [and Otto Bauernfeind], ed. *Theologisches Wörterbuch zum Neuen Testament*. Stuttgart: Kohlhammer, 1933–[79].
Knowling, R. J. *The Epistles of St James*. London: Methuen, 1904.
Krüger, Gustav. *History of Early Christian Literature*. London and New York: Macmillan, 1897.
Lake, Krisopp. *The Apostolic Fathers*. Vol. 2. Loeb Classical Library. Cambridge: Harvard University Press, 1913. Repr. ed. 1930.
Lechler, Gotthard Victor. *Das apostolische und das nachapostolische Zeitalter mit Rücksicht auf Unterschied und Einheit in Leben*. 3rd ed. Karlsruhe: Reuther, 1885.
Legge, F. *Philosophumena or the Refutation of All Heresies*. London and New York: SPCK, 1921.
Lidgett, John Scott. *The Spiritual Principle of Atonement*. London: Charles H. Kelly, 1898.
Lietzmann, Hans. *An die Galater*. Handbuch zum Neuen Testament. 3rd ed. Tübingen: J. C. B. Mohr, 1932.
———. *Beginnings of the Christian Church*. Vol. 2. Translated by Bertram Lee Woolf. London: Lutterworth, 1949.
Lightfoot, John B. *The Apostolic Fathers*. Vol. 1.2. London: Macmillan, 1877.
———. *The Apostolic Fathers*. Vol 2.2, *St. Ignatius and St. Polycarp*. London: Macmillan, 1889.
———. *Biblical Essays*. London: Macmillan, 1904.
———. *Commentary on Colossians and Philemon*. 8th ed. London: Macmillan, 1879.
———. *Historical Essays*. London: Macmillan, 1909.
———. *Philippians*. London: Macmillan, 1913.
Lightfoot, John B., and J. R. Harmer. *Apostolic Fathers*. London: Macmillan, 1891.
Lightfoot, Robert Henry. *Locality and Doctrine in the Gospels*. London: Hodder & Stoughton, 1938.
Lipsius, Richard Adelbert. "Review of *Über den pseudojustinischen Brief an Diognetus* by Franz Overbeck," *Literarisches Centralblatt* 40 (1873) 1250–52.
Lipsius, Richard Adelbert, and Alfred Bonnet. *Acta Apostolorum apocrypha*. Vol. 2. Leipzig: Mendelsohn, 1903.

Little, Vivian Agincourt Spence. *The Christology of the Apologists. Doctrinal.* London: Duckworth, 1934.
Lock, Walter. "1 Corinthians 8:1–8. A Suggestion." *Expositor* 5.6 (1897) 49–65.
Mansel, S. "The Apologists." In *Dictionary of Christian Biography, Literature, Sects and Doctrines*, edited by William Smith and Henry Wace, 1:140–47. London: Murray, 1877.
Manson, Thomas Walter. *The Teaching of Jesus Studies from Its Form and Content.* Cambridge: Cambridge University Press, 1948.
Mayor, Joseph B. *The Epistle of St. James.* London: Macmillan, 1913.
———. *The Epistle of St. Jude and the Second Epistle of St. Peter Jude.* London: Macmillan, 1907.
Mayser, Edwin. *Grammatik der griechischen Papyri aus der Ptolemäerzeit.* Vol. 1. Leipzig: Teubner, 1906.
———. *Grammatik der griechischen Papyri aus der Ptolemäerzeit.* Vol. 2. Leipzig: Teubner, 1938.
McGiffert, Arthur Cushman. *A History of Christian Thought.* New York: Scribner's and Sons, 1932–33.
Meecham, Henry G. *Letter of Aristeas.* Manchester: Manchester University Press, 1935.
———. *The Oldest Version of the Bible. "Aristeas" on Its Traditional Origin. A Study in Early Apologetic.* London: Holborn, 1932.
———. "The Theology of the Epistle to Diognetus." *Expository Times* 54 (1943) 99–100.
Meyer, Eduard. *Ursprung und Anfänge des Christentums.* 3 vols. Stuttgart: Cotta, 1921–23.
Milligan, George. *Selections from the Greek Papyri.* Cambridge: Cambridge University Press, 1910.
———. *St. Paul's Epistles to the Thessalonians.* London: Macmillan, 1908.
Moberly, Robert Campbell. *Atonement and Personality.* London: J. Murray, 1901.
Moffatt, James. *Commentary on Hebrews.* International Critical Commentary. Edinburgh: T&T Clark, 1924.
———. *Introduction to the Literature of the New Testament.* 3rd ed. New York: Charles Scribner's Sons, 1921.
———. *The Thrill of Tradition.* London: Macmillan, 1944.
Molland, Einar. "Die literatur- und dogmengeschichtliche Stellung des Diognetbriefes." *Zeitschrift für die Neutestamentliche Wissenschaft* 33 (1934) 289–312.
Moulton, James Hope. *A Grammar of New Testament Greek.* Vol. 1. 3rd ed. London: Hodder & Stoughton, 1908.
Moulton, James Hope, and George Milligan. *The Vocabulary of the Greek New Testament.* London: Hodder & Stoughton, 1914.
Moulton, James Hope, and Wilbert Francis Howard. *A Grammar of New Testament Greek: Prolegomena.* Edinburgh: T&T Clark, 1906.
Murray, Gilbert. *Stoic, Christian and Humanist.* London: C. A. Watts, 1940.
Nägeli, Theodor. *Der Wortschatz des Apostels Paulus.* Basel: Buchdruckerei zum Basler Berichthaus, 1904.
Neander, August. *General History of the Christian Religion and Church.* Vol. 2. London: H. G. Bohn, 1851.
Neumann, Karl Johannes. "Ueber eine den Brief an Diognet enthaltende Tübinger Handschrift." *Zeitschrift für Kirchengeschichte* 4 (1881) 284–87.
Newman, John Henry. *A Grammar of Assent.* London: Longmans, Green, 1888.
Niese, B. *Flavii Josephi Opera.* 6 vols. Berlin: Weidmann, 1889–95.

Nock, Arthur Darby. *Conversion: The Old and New in Religion from Alexander the Great to Augustine of Hippo*. Oxford: Oxford University Press, 1933.

———. "A Note on Ep. ad Diognetum X §1." *Journal of Theological Studies* 29 (1927/28) 40–41.

———. "Notes on Ruler-Cult, I–IV." *Journal of Hellenistic Studies* 48 (1928) 21–43.

Norden, Eduard. *Die antike Kunstprosa*. Vol. 2. 2nd ed. Leipzig: Teubner, 1909.

Oesterley, William Oscar Emil, and George Herbert Box. *The Religion and Worship of the Synagogue: An Introduction to the Study of Judaism from the New Testament Period*. London: Sir Isaac Pitman and Sons, 1911.

Ottley, Robert L. *Lux Mundi: A Series of Studies in the Religion of the Incarnation*. London: Murray, 1891.

Otto, Johann Carl Theodor von. *Corpus Apologetarum*. Vol. 9. Jena: Prostat apud F. Mauke, 1872.

———. *Corpus Apologetarum Christianorum saeculi secundi*. Vol. 3. 3rd ed. Jena: Prostat apud F. Mauke, 1879.

———. *Epistola ad Diognetum Justini philosophi et martyris nomen prae se ferens*. 1st ed. Leipzig: T. O. Weigel, 1845.

———. *Epistola ad Diognetum Justini philosophi et martyris nomen prae se ferens*. 2nd ed. Leipzig: T. O. Weigel, 1852.

———. *Epistola ad Diognetum Justini philosophi et martyris nomen prae se ferens*. 3rd ed. Leipzig: T. O. Weigel, 1879.

Otto, Rudolf. *The Kingdom of God and the Son of Man: A Study of the History of Religion*. London: Lutterworth, 1943.

Overbeck, Franz. Review of *Der Brief an Diognetus* by Dräseke. *Theologische Literaturzeitung* (1882) 28ff.

———. *Studien zur Geschichte der alten Kirche*. Vol. 1. Schloss-Chemitz: Schmeitzner, 1875.

———. *Über den pseudojustinischen Brief an Diognet. Programm für die Rectoratsfeier der Universität Basel*. Basel: Universitätsbuchdruckerei, 1872.

Oxford Society of Historical Knowledge. *The New Testament in the Apostolic Fathers*. Oxford: Oxford University Press, 1905.

Pfleiderer, Otto. *Primitive Christianity: Its Writings and Teachings in Their Historical Connections*. Vol. 4. London: Williams & Norgate, 1911.

Prestige, Leonard. "Tradition." *Theology* 13 (1926) 8–14.

Puech, Aimé. *Les apologistes grecs du IIe siècle de notre ère*. Paris: Librairie Hachette, 1912.

———. *Histoire de la littérature qrecque chrétienne*. Vol. 2. Paris: Belles Lettres, 1928.

Raabe, Richard. *Die Apologie des Aristides. Aus dem Syrischen übersetzt und mit Beiträgen zur Textvergleichung und Anmerkungen herausgegeben*. Texte und Untersuchungen 9. Leipzig: Hinrichs, 1893.

Radermacher, L. *Neutestamentliche Grammatik: Das Griechisch des Neuen Testaments im Zusammenhang mit der Volkssprache*. 2nd ed. Tübingen: Mohr, 1925.

Radford, Lewis Bostock. *The Epistle to Diognetus*. London: SPCK, 1908.

Ramsay, William Mitchell. *The Church in the Roman Empire before AD 170*. London: Hodder & Stoughton, 1893.

Rashdall, Hastings. *The Idea of Atonement in Christian Theology*. London: Macmillan, 1925.

Rauschen, Gerhard. *Frühchristliche Apologeten und Märtyrerakten*. Vol. 1. München: Kösel, 1913.

Reagan, Joseph Nicholas. *The Preaching of Peter: The Beginning of Christian Apologetic.* Chicago: University of Chicago Press, 1923.

Renan, Ernest. *Marc-Aurèle et le fin du monde antique.* Paris: Calmann-Lévy, 1922.

Reuss, Eduard. *History of the Sacred Scriptures of the New Testament.* Translated by Edward Lovell Houghton. Boston: Houghton Mifflin, 1884.

Richardson, E. C. "Bibliographical Synopsis." In *Ante-Nicene Fathers*, 10:5–7. Buffalo, NY: Christian Literature, 1887; repr. ed. 1917.

Rivière, Jean. *St. Justin et les apologistes du second siècle.* Paris: Bloud, 1907.

Roberts, Alexander, et al. *The Epistle to Diognetus.* Ante-Nicene Christian Library. Buffalo, NY: Christian Literature, 1867.

Robertson, Archibald Thomas. *A Grammar of the Greek New Testament in the Light of Historical Research.* New York: Hodder & Stoughton, 1914.

Robinson, J. Armitage. *St. Paul's Epistle to the Ephesians.* London: J. Clarke, 1928.

Routh, Martin Joseph. *Reliquiae Sacrae.* Vol. 1. Oxford: E Typographeo Academico, 1846.

Rutherford, William Gunion. *St. Paul's Epistle to the Romans.* London: Macmillan, 1900.

Sanday, William. *Christologies, Ancient and Modern.* Oxford: Clarendon, 1910.

Sanday, William, and Arthur Headlam. *The Epistle to the Romans.* Edinburgh: T&T Clark, 1901.

Sanders, Joseph Newbould. *The Fourth Gospel in the Early Church: Its Origin, and Influence on Christian Theology up to Irenaeus.* Cambridge: Cambridge University Press, 1943.

Scheibe, C. "Zur Kritik der Epistola ad Diognetum." *Theologische Studien und Kritiken* 35 (1862) 576–88.

Schmidt, Karl Ludwig. "ἐκκλησία." *TDNT* 3, 501–36. Grand Rapids: Eerdmans, 1965.

Schniewind, Julius. "ἀγγελία, ἀγγέλλω, ἀν-, ἀπ-, δι-, ἐξ-, κατ-, προκαταγγέλλω, καταγγελεύς." In *Theologische Wörterbuch* 1. Stuttgart: Kohlhammer, 1933.

Schürer, Emil. *History of the Jewish People in the Time of Christ.* Vol. 2.3. Edinburgh: T&T Clark, 1890.

Schwartz, Eduard. *Griechische Apologeten.* Texte und Untersuchungen 4. Leipzig: Hinrichs, 1888–93.

Scott, Ernest Findlay. *The Apologetic of the New Testament.* London and New York: Williams & Norgate, 1907.

———. *The Fourth Gospel: Its Purpose and Theology.* London: J. Murray, 1923.

Scullard, Herbert Hayes. *Early Christian Ethics in the West: From Clement to Ambrose.* London: Williams & Norgate, 1907.

Seeberg, R. "Die Apologie des Aristides." *Forschungen zur Geschichte des neutestamentlichen Kanons und der altkirchlichen Literatur* 5 (1893) 239–43.

Sharp, Douglas Simmonds. *Epictetus and the New Testament.* London: C. H. Kelly, 1914.

Sidgwick, Henry. *Outlines of the History of Ethics for English Readers.* London: Macmillan, 1888.

Stählin, Otto. "Christliche Schriftsteller." In *Geschichte der griechischen Literatur*, edited by Wihelm von Christ, 2.2:907–1244. 5th ed. München: C. H. Beck, 1913.

———. *Clemens Alexandrinus.* 4 vols. Berlin: Akademie Verlag, 1905–36. München: C. H. Beck, 1913.

Strack, Hermann, and Paul Billerbeck. *Kommentar zum Neuen Testament aus Talmud und Midrash.* Vol. 4. München: C. H. Beck, 1929.

Streeter, B. H., et al. *Cambridge Ancient History.* Vol. 11. Cambridge: Cambridge University Press, 1936.

Streeter, B. H., et al. *Cambridge Ancient History*. Vol. 12. Cambridge: Cambridge University Press, 1939.
Swete, Henry Barclay. *The Gospel according to St. Mark*. London: Macmillan, 1920.
Taylor, Vincent. *The Atonement in New Testament Teaching*. London: Epworth, 1941.
———. *Jesus and His Sacrifice*. London: Macmillan, 1943.
Telfer, William. "Review of *The Epistle to Diognetus* by E. H. Blakeney." *Journal of Theological Studies* 45 (1944) 220–25.
Tennant, Frederick Robert. *The Nature of Belief*. London: Centenary, 1943.
Thackeray, Henry. *A Grammar of the Old Testament in Greek according to the Septuagint*. Vol. 1. Cambridge: Cambridge University Press, 1909.
———. *The Letter of Aristeas*. Appendix to Henry Barclay Swete, *An Introduction to the Old Testament in Greek*. 2nd ed. Cambridge: Cambridge University Press, 1902.
———. *The Relation of St. Paul to Contemporary Jewish Thought*. London: Macmillan, 1900.
Thomsen. "Review of *Der Brief an Diognetus* by J. Geffcken," *Philologische Wochenschrift* (1930) 561–63.
Tixeront, Joseph. *A Handbook of Patrology*. London: Herder, 1920.
Trench, Richard. *Synonyms of the New Testament*. 7th edition. London: Macmillian, 1871.
Turner, Cuthbert H. "ho huios mou ho agapetos." *Journal of Theological Studies* 27 (1925–26) 113–29.
Uhlhorn, Gerhard. "Der Brief an Diognet." In *Realenzyklopädie für protestantische Theologie und Kirche*, edited by Johann Jakob Herzog et al., 4:675ff. Leipzig: Hinrichs, 1898.
Walford, Walter Shirley. *Epistle to Diognetus: The Greek Text, with Introduction, Notes, and Translation*. London: James Nisbet, 1908.
Weiss, Johann. *The History of Primitive Christianity*. 2 vols. New York: Wilson-Erickson, 1937.
Wendland, Paul. *Die hellenistisch-römische Kultur in ihren Beziehungen zum Judentum und Christentum: Die urchristlichen Literaturformen*. Handbuch zum Neuen Testament 1. Tübingen: Mohr, 1912.
———. *Hippolytus Werke*. Vol. 3, *Refutatio omnium Haeresium*. Die Grieschischen Schriftseteller der ersten drei Jahrhunderte. Leipzig: Hinrichs, 1916.
Westcott, Brooke Foss. *The Canon of the New Testament*. 5th ed. Cambridge and London: Macmillan, 1881.
———. *Gospel of St. John*. London: Macmillan, 1886.
———. *The Epistle to the Hebrews. An Experiment in Conservative Revision*. Cambridge: Cambridge University Press, 1912.
———. *Introduction to the Study of the Gospels: With Historical and Explanatory Notes*. London: Macmillan, 1895.
Westcott, Brooke Foss, and Fenton John Anthony Hort. *The New Testament in the Original Greek*. 2nd ed. New York: Macmillan, 1946.
Whitehouse, Owen C. "Demon, Devil." In *A Dictionary of the Bible*. Vol. 1. Edited by James Hastings, 590–94. New York: Scribner's, 1911.
Wilamowitz-Moellendorff, U. von. *Griechisches Lesebuch*. Vol. 1.2. 3rd ed. Berlin: Weidmann, 1906.
———. *Griechisches Lesebuch*. Vol. 2.2. 2nd ed. Berlin: Weidmann, 1906.
Wilcken, Ulrich. *Grundzüge Chrestomathie der Papyruskunde*. Leipzig: Teubner, 1912.
Workman, Herbert B. *Persecution in the Early Church*. London: Epworth, 1923.
Zeller, Eduard. *Outlines of the History of Greek Philosophy*. 2nd ed. London: Longmans, 1892.

Index of Subjects

allegorization, xv, 35, 50, 52–53, 64, 121, 165–66
alliteration, 13
almsgiving, 40, 172
angels, xv, 26, 36–37, 39, 57, 59, 85, 110, 134–35, 168
anti-Semitism, 2
Apelles, 17
apodosis, omitted, 153
Apollonius Molon, 2
Apologists, xiv, xvi, 1, 3–5, 13, 19–20, 22, 26–29, 32–34, 36–37, 46–50, 55–61, 97, 124, 130, 142, 166, 175–76
Apostolic Fathers, ix–x, xiv, 1, 4, 18, 41, 55, 73, 142, 144, 152, 160
appendix (of Diognetus), 5–6, 19, 25, 50, 52, 134, 147, 173
Artapanus, 2
article, 9, 11–13, 21, 66, 98, 101, 104, 106, 109, 114–16, 129, 136–37, 150, 152, 154, 161–62
asyndeton, 14, 121
atheism, 3, 98, 126
atonement, xv, 22, 24–26, 115–16, 150, 153
augment, omitted, 11, 149

Bar-Kokhba, 38, 126

canon of NT, 1, 3, 36, 56
chiasmus, 13, 114
children, exposure of, 122

Christianity
 a revealed religion, 6, 33–34, 44–45, 47, 52, 132
 newness, 5, 23
 relation to its period, 1
 relation to State, 37–39, 43–44, 123
 supernatural character, 28, 48, 117
 timeliness of, 100, 146–47
Christians
 a "new race," 5, 18, 77, 95, 102
 as "seed," 129, 131–32
 charges against, 3–4, 37–39, 42, 54, 96, 122, 126
 grades of, 50–51
 ignorance concerning, 3, 124–25
 love for all men, 5, 30, 96, 99, 124
 otherwordliness, 5, 40, 118, 123, 129
 purity, 40
church, 48, 50, 63–64
circumcision, 35, 63, 81, 112–14, 116, 119, 178
Codex Alexandrinus, 1
Codex Argentoratensis, xiv, 5, 18, 60, 63, 67–68
Codex Graec. Voss., 67
Codex Misc. Tübing. M.b., 67
Codex Sinaiticus, 1
Commodus, 138
compounds, 10, 15, 101, 120, 147
conjunctions, 64
crasis, 11, 109

Index of Subjects

dative
  advantage, 137
  agent, 12, 105, 137, 163
  instrument, 136–37, 147
  interest, 163
  person, 133
  possession, 119
  respect, 131
  thing, 148
death, despised, 5, 95–97
dedication (of epistle), 8,
deification (of man), 45, 171–72
Demetrius, 2
demons, 22, 29, 32, 38, 60, 124, 135, 157
diminutives, 15
dittography, 134, 140

elision, 11
epanastrophe, 13, 126
epigrams, 13
Euhemerus, 172
Eupolemus, 2
Eve, 93, 165, 167–68

faith, 39, 51, 64, 153, 163
fasting, 40, 81, 112–13, 131
food
  feasts, Jewish, 35, 37, 81, 116
  taboos, 122
future tense for present, 12, 103

genitive
  absolute, 13, 156
  agent, 12, 161
  comparison, 103, 106
  objective, 30, 115, 154, 163
  personal, 148, 161
  source, 100
glosses, suspected, 138, 149, 152
gods, 22, 31–32, 38, 42–43, 46, 60–62, 77, 79, 95, 98, 103–10, 126, 128, 144, 155, 170–72
grace, 49–51

Hecataeus of Abdera, 2
Heraclitus, 34, 44, 60, 141, 151
hiatus, 15, 128, 177
hymn, fragment of, 14, 138, 149, 161

imitatio dei, 5–6, 29, 153
immortality, 28, 40–41, 45, 85, 89, 98, 130, 172
infinitive
  absolute, 12
  articular, 12
  epexegetic, 12
  future, 12, 142

Jews
  Alexandrian, 1, 48
  angel worship, 57, 59, 110
  charges against, 30, 36
  fasting, 113
  Law of, 35–36, 113
  monotheism, 16, 20–21, 36–37, 43, 109
  sacrifices, 6, 35, 81, 109
  superstition, 5, 35, 77, 95
  political toleration, 2

judgment, 41, 85, 139, 159, 167

lacunae, xvii, 63, 68, 84–85, 89–90, 116, 124, 139, 153, 159, 176–77, 179
Law, *see* Jews
litotes, 13, 165
logos, 19, 21, 27, 33, 44, 47, 49–50, 55, 60, 133, 135–36, 141, 144, 171, 173

Manetho, 2
Marcion, 3, 16, 37, 56
marriage, 16, 40, 123
Mary, the Virgin, 167–68
miracles, 5, 20, 33., 87, 176–77, 179
moon, new, 36–37, 81, 85, 112–13, 115, 136
note, marginal, 63, 84, 120, 139, 146, 159

Pantaenus, 65
parataxis, 14
paronomasia, 13, 62, 113, 123
particles, 11–12, 15, 64, 100, 112
participles
  aorist, 66, 104, 156
  future, 12, 104, 139
  perfect, 12, 97, 105, 139
  present, 12, 102–3, 107

Index of Subjects

Paul
    Greek of, 7, 10
    letters of, xiii–xiv, 7
perfect, periphrastic, 12, 118–19
Photius, 3
Platonism, 28, 33–34, 43, 46, 48, 156, 158
pleonasm, 13
plural, alternates with sg., 102
Posidonius, 2
prayer, 40, 100–101, 143, 166
prepositions, 10–13, 137, 150
present, historic, 18
prophecy, argument from, 5, 20, 53, 58, 60, 64
prophets, 63
providence, xv, 21, 34, 44–45
punishment, eternal, 28, 41, 83, 87, 107–8, 126, 140, 158–59

Quadratus, 1, 16, 176–79

repentance, 39

Sabbath, 35, 37, 63, 81, 98, 112–15, 119
sent (title), 23, 26
Septuagint, 2, 73
singular alternates with plural, 103
Son, titles of, 25–26
soul *v.* body, 34, 40, 43, 127–30

soul
    immortal, 130
    invisible, 128
speech, figures of, 13
Spirit, Holy, 19, 50–51
Stoicism, 27, 33–34, 42–46, 49, 120, 155, 171
subordination (of Christ), 26
syncretism, 42
synonyms, 10, 65

tenses, use of, 15
testimonia, 53
Thales, 141
Therapeutae, 3
Tillemont, 60
tradition, 174–76

voice, middle, 12, 99–100, 107, 129, 138, 150, 158

world
    created by God, 26–28, 81
    created for man, 28, 45, 57, 81
    scorn of, 5, 95, 98,
    sustained by Christians, 126
    world-soul, 43
    world-state, 43

yezer hara, 28

zeugma, 13, 102

Index of Authors

Abbott, Thomas, 107, 150
Abrahams, Israel, 37, 155, 170
Allen, Alexander, 4, 26, 44, 113, 145
Altaner, Berthold, 69
Andriessen, Dom, 74, 176–79
Anz, Heinrich, 125
Arnold, Edward, 46
Aubé, Benjamin, 17, 48

Bardenhewer, Otto, 19, 69
Bardy, Gustave, 16
Batiffol, Pierre, 7, 65, 69
Bauer, Walter, 69, 110, 163, 166
Bethune-Baker, James, 69
Bevan, Edwyn, 31–32, 36, 41–42, 45, 47, 98, 144
Beyschlag, Willibald, 26,
Billerbeck, Paul, 28
Birks, Edward, 8, 17, 63, 70
Bishop of Gloucester, 22
Blake, Buchanan, 24, 31,
Blakeney, Edward, 31, 36, 41, 44–45, 63, 68–69, 99–100, 107, 110, 112, 116, 121–22, 130, 142–43, 154–55, 158–59
Blass, Friedrich, 70, 99, 125, 127, 139, 142, 149, 151–52, 161
Bonwetsch, G., 65–66
Bonner, Campbell, 14, 65–67, 70
Box, George, 168
Brannan, Rick, xiv
Brooke, Eberhard, 73

Bunsen, Christian, 3, 16, 18–19, 38, 65, 68, 80, 84, 90, 92, 97, 100, 105–6, 110, 116, 121–22, 134, 136, 139, 142, 145–46, 153, 158, 160–62, 165, 167, 169
Buonaiuti, Ernesto, 16, 73
Burch, V., 53
Burkitt, Francis, 47, 72, 99

Cadbury, Henry, 8, 70, 97–98, 145
Cadoux, Cecil, 1
Carrington, Philip, 70
Cassels, Walter, 10
Chambers, C. D., 104
Chapman, John, 17, 70
Charles, Robert, 70, 73, 114
Cohn, Leopold, 73
Connolly, Richard, 17–19, 65, 70, 138–39, 160, 162–64, 168–69, 173
Cotterill, Joseph, 18,
Credner, Carl, 63
Cruttwell, Charles, 18, 30, 50, 70
Cureton, William, 17

Debrunner, Albrecht, 70, 99, 127, 139, 142, 149, 151–52, 161
Deissmann, Gustav, 7, 70, 117, 122, 139
Di Pauli, A., 65
Dittenberger, W., 70
Dobschütz, Ernst von, 29, 57
Dodd, Charles, 41, 151
Donaldson, James, 17–18, 26, 31, 42, 47, 69–70
Dorner, Isaak, 17–18, 52, 63, 176

Index of Authors

Doulcet, Henry, 17, 19, 58, 70
Dräseke, Johannes, 17, 19, 62, 65, 70, 72, 96
Drummond, James, 17, 35

Ehrman, Bart, xiv
Estienne, Henri, xiv
Ewald, Heinrich, 8, 18, 55, 65, 70, 167

Fermi, M., 74
Field, Frederick, 71, 98, 130, 149, 167
Friedländer, Ludwig, 33
Funk, Franz, 71, 104, 106, 110, 112, 115–16, 140, 153, 159–60, 163, 167–69, 171–72

Gallandi, Andrea, xiv
Gass, W., 115
Gebhardt, Oskar, 67–69, 80, 88, 106, 110, 112–13, 116, 153
Geffcken, Johannes, 17–18, 31, 34, 41, 58–59, 61–63, 68–69, 95, 99, 101–7, 110–11, 120, 123, 125–26, 135, 139, 153, 155–56, 159, 172
Gildersleeve, B., 98, 100, 102, 105, 108–9, 111–12, 116, 121, 129, 133, 136–37, 142, 145, 147, 149, 153, 160, 167
Glover, Terrot, 71
Goodenough, Erwin, 71
Goodspeed, Edgar, 66, 71, 139
Goodwin, William, 152
Grensted, Laurence, 25

Harmer, J. R., 68–69, 116, 133, 138, 143
Harnack, Adolf, 4, 18–19, 29, 33, 35, 37, 46, 49, 61, 67–69, 71, 99, 126–27, 135, 138, 160, 166, 171–72
Harris, James, 20, 53, 57–59, 71
Harrison, Jane, 172
Harrison, Percival, 64
Hatch, Edwin, 97–98, 126
Headlam, Arthur, 53, 151
Heinzelmann, Wilhelm, 69
Hennecke, Edgar, 58
Herzog, Rabbi, 2
Hicks, E. L., 128

Holmes, Michael, xiv
Hort, Fenton, 10, 73, 131, 161
Howard, W. F., xvii, 10–11, 23, 27, 71–72, 99, 104, 132, 137, 148–49

Jacquier, Eugene, 56
James, Montague, 57
Jannaris, Antonius, 71
Jefford, Clayton N. xiii
Jülicher, A., 71

Keim, Theodor, 13, 18, 138
Kennedy, Henry, 71, 121, 161, 169
Kihn, Heinrich, 17, 58, 63, 67, 71, 96, 176
Kittel, Gerhard, 71
Knowling, R. J., 115
Krenkel,
Krüger, Gustav, 1

Lachmann, 18, 26, 68, 76, 78, 80, 84, 86, 88, 90, 97, 103, 105–6, 109, 116, 132, 138, 146–47, 149, 153–55, 158, 161, 163
Lake, Krisopp, 64, 68–70, 73, 98, 100, 105–6, 110, 112, 115–16, 129, 132, 137–38, 152–54, 159–62, 165, 167, 169
Lechler, Gotthard, 71
Legge, F., 71, 171
Lidgett, John, 24
Lietzmann, Hans, 72, 115, 121, 136
Lightfoot, J. B., 3, 18–19, 25, 46, 65, 68–69, 98, 105–6, 108, 110, 112, 115–16, 120, 128, 133, 135, 137–38, 141, 143, 146, 155, 159, 165, 167
Lipsius, Richard, 62, 171
Little, Vivian, 26
Lock, Walter, 32
Lona, H. E. xiii

Mansel, S., 71
Manson, T. W., xvii, 21
Marrou, H. I., xiii
Mayor, Joseph, 97, 100, 115, 140, 150, 175
Mayser, Edwin, 10
McKechnie, H. M., xviii

Index of Authors

Meecham, Henry, 7, 72, 128, 149, 161
McLachlan, H., xvii
McGiffert, Arthur, 72
Meyer, Ed, 72, 97
Moberly, Robert, 151
Moffatt, James, 8, 26, 71, 121, 135, 139, 150, 167, 175–76
Molland, Einar, 7, 16, 34, 58–59, 62, 72, 96
Moulton, James H., xv, 10–11, 15, , 23, 99–100, 102, 113, 117, 121, 130, 132, 136, 138–39, 142, 144, 148–49, 157, 163
Murray, Gilbert, 43, 45

Nägeli, Theodor, 151
Neander, August, 3
Neumann, Karl, 67, 69, 72
Newman, John, 151
Niese, B., 73
Nock, Arthur, 47, 124, 154, 171
Norden, Eduard, 13, 72

Oesterley, William 168
Otto, Johann, 11, 18, 60, 64, 66–69, 92, 96–101, 103–4, 106–11, 113–16, 118–22, 126–28, 130–34, 136–43, 146–50, 152–53, 158–61, 165, 169
Overbeck, Franz, 17,–18, 62, 72, 124
Oxford Society, 55

Piercy, William, 17, 70
Pfleiderer, Otto, 60
Puech, Aimé, 14, 19, 30, 34, 59, 72, 100, 122

Raabe, Richard, 58
Radermacher, I., 72
Radford, Lewis B., xiii, 18, 27, 49–50, 69, 107, 119, 122, 126, 133, 146–47, 157, 162–63, 165, 167, 169
Ramsay, William, 30,
Rashdall, Hastings, 24
Rauschen, Gerhard, 69
Raymond George, A., xviii
Reagen, Joseph, 3, 57
Renan, Ernest, 18, 29, 96, 118

Reuss, Eduard, 56, 68, 159, 167
Richardson, E. C., 68, 72
Rivière, Jean, 72
Roberts, Alexander, 69
Robertson, Archibald, 102
Robinson, J. A., 57–58
Routh, Martin, 50, 66, 109
Rutherford, William, 7

Sanday, William, 20, 53, 151
Scott, Ernest, 2, 39, 133, 152
Scullard, Herbert, 4
Schwartz, Eduard, 73
Scheibe, C., 72, 100–101, 116, 153
Schürer, Emil, 2
Seeberg, R., 72
Sharp, Douglas, 154
Sidgwick, Henry, 46
Stählin, Otto, 55, 61, 72–73, 101
Stephanus, Henricus, xiv, 17, 63, 67–68, 76, 80, 82, 84, 86, 97, 101, 104–5, 107, 111, 113, 116, 128, 131, 139–40, 142–43, 145
Strack, Hermann, 27
Streeter, B. H., 72

Taylor, Vincent, 24, 26, 72
Telfer, William, 8, 42, 47
Tennant, Frederick, 39
Thackeray, Henry, 10, 72–73, 112, 128, 132, 149, 168
Tixeront, Joseph, 72
Trench, Richard, 97

Uhlhorn, Gerhard, 72

Wace, Henry, 17, 70–71
Walford, Walter, 69
Weiss, Johann, 7, 73
Wendland, Paul, 73
Wescott, Brooke, 10, 18, 46, 50, 65, 73, 137, 151
Whitehouse, Owen, 31
Wilamowitz-Moellendorff, U., 18, 63, 69
Wilcken, Ulrich, 109
Workman, Herbert, 29

Zeller, Eduard, 43–44

Index of Ancient Sources

OLD TESTAMENT

Genesis

1:1	27
1:10	113
1:12	113
1:15	149
1:18	113
1:26ff	155
1:26f	52
1:26	137, 144
1:27	156
2:7f	156
2:7	156
2:8–9	19, 52, 56, 165
2:8	52
2:9	52–53, 165
2:15	156
2:16f	166
2:22	144
3:7	165
3:10	151
3:11	166
3:13	102
3:17	166
3:18	165
3:23f	52
3:24	165
4:15	104
9:2	137
11:3	142
12:4	102
13:10	52
14:19	125
14:23	125
17:13–14	114
17:13	112
21:15	122
22:2	146
24:26	106
25:38	112
26:5	99
31:28	148
37:1	130
37:7	109
37:10	137
39:20	130
39:22	148

Exodus

1:12	140
1:19	105
12:25	109
20:8	112
20:11	53, 111
24:15	151
24:16	169
34:6	144
34:23	169
34:24	169

Leviticus

3:12	110
6:22	111
10:9	112
14:36	102

Numbers

6:3	112
10:10	113
10:32	125
15:22	110

Deuteronomy

1:31	152
10:17	110
16:16	169
28:50	158
32:12	114
32:17	32

Judges

19:6	101

1 Samuel

6:2	143

1 Kings

25:26	114

2 Chronicles

5:7	125
16:2	136

Nehemiah

13:13	161

Job

5:8	110
5:9	151
6:11	148
8:20	150
9:10	151
16:7	103
22:3	162
26:10	136
38:8	136

Esther

3:1	125
6:4	97

Psalms

2:7	52, 162
8:6	137, 152
31:1	150
33:6	27
34:17	131
34:19	126
44	146
47:13	116
49:1	110
50:15	151
58:1	172
65.4	151
68:5	126
82	172
82:6	172
84:3	150
93:14	149
95:8	162
104:9	136
115:5ff	30
115:8	106
118:16	106
123:1	155
134:18	106
135:15f	31
144:7	144
145:6	53, 111

Proverbs

1:21	114
3:34	129
5:29	136
6:8a	116
8:3	114
8:22ff	27
8:22	113
8:27ff	136

13:8	139
24:57	131
28:20	141
30:8	116
30:22	131

Isaiah

9:5	145
9:6	145
11:2–3	152
12:2	152
22:7	114
24:6	106
37:24	114
37:26	143
40:5	168
40:18–20	30
40:26	155
41:23	158
42:1	145
43:25	149
44	31
44:9–20	30
44:20	31
45:9	156
45:18	137
51:3	165
52:13	145
53	24
53:2–3	103
53:4	150
53:11	150
53:12	150
58	131
64:8	156
64:11	148
69:18	102

Jeremiah

5:22	136
6:26	146
6:29	104
10:1–16	30
11:19	150
18:4ff	156
31:34	149

Ezekiel

20:44	99
31:8f	52

Daniel

3:15	154
4:4	165
7:26	158
8:23	149
12:12	159

Joel

2:3	52, 165

Habakkuk

1:8	152
2:18	105

Zechariah

9:9	138

Malachi

3:1	53
3:2	52, 139

DEUTEROCANONICAL WORKS

Tobit

3:15	156
5:14	103
12:12	110

Judith

6:3	139

Wisdom of Solomon

1:3	102
1:5	102
1:11	114
2:13	145
2:16	114, 145

Wisdom of Solomon (cont.)

2:18	145
2:22	158
2:23	137
2:24	168
3:2	53, 158
3:4	140
6:7	110, 143
7:17	142
7:18	115
9:1–2	27
9:3	135
9:15	130
10:8	100
11:10	21
11:15	97, 102
11:23	23, 39
12:10–19	31
12:15	135
12:19	145
12:20–21	145
12:24	31
13:1	135
13:2	98
13:11	13
13:11b	104
13:17	105
14:1–11	33
14:17	97
14:18	111
14:21	100
14:29	105
15:7	104
15:14	157
16:5	158
17:2	157
17:15	128
19:1	158
19:13	117
19:21	99
28:5	122
33:16	30

Sirach

Prologue	7
1:25	97
1:26	100
3:10	125
4:7	161
15:14	28, 102
20:9	132
20:13	161
21:11	28
24:8	133
32:24	97
34:21	157
48:12	157

Baruch

3:16	135
4:7	32
4:8	152
4:33	162
6:4–22	31

Epistle of Jeremiah

19	107
23	107
45	105
57ff	103

1 Maccabees

1:57	148
1:62	122
2:64	125
3:59	11
5:61	111
7:5	151
13:5	11
14:22	11
14:46	128

2 Maccabees

1:11	102
1:24	133
2:19–32	7
2:30	119
2:31	113
3:16	119
4:11	144
4:16	106
4:19	12

4:21	148
4:40	11
5:5	11
6:5	113
7:11	97
7:23	97
7:37	110
8:12	139
8:18	133
8:21	121
8:36	150
9:12	108
11:25	120
11:31	12
12:4	102
12:43	97
12:44	141
13:3	113
13:14	121
14:20	145
14:23	123
14:25	121
14:35	110
15:39	164

1 Esdras

4:34	136
4:56	127
8:16	111

3 Maccabees

1:19	147
1:22	106
2:26	120
2:29	119
3:2	147
5:17	111
9:2	110

2 Esdras

3:3	137
6:55–56	154
7:62–68	144
12	139

4 Maccabees

1:8	106
2:6	142
2:8	139
5:23	129, 147
5:24	107
7:22	159
9:9	158
11:27	119
12:12	158
14:6	130
14:17	156
15:2	159
15:3	159
15:6	99
15:9	99
17:5	115
17:14	100
18:8	168

OLD TESTAMENT PSEUDEPIGRAPHA

Ascension of Isaiah

1.4	146

1 Enoch

99:7	32

2 Enoch

31:3ff	168

Jubilees

1:9–11	30
15:26f	114

Letter of Aristeas

1	96
5	96
18	115
31	120
36	144
43	11
81	114

Letter of Aristeas (cont.)

87	151		
100	168		
108	28		
122	152		
135	30, 105		
137	37		
147	148		
151	35		
161	35		
168	35		
175	120		
185	113, 133		
190	170		
205	170		
208	144		
210	170		
211	110		
224	112		
227	111		
229	112		
236	109		
242	125		
254	144		
277	28, 129		
281	170		
322	7, 96		

Psalms of Solomon

14:2–3	165

Sibylline Oracles

3.15	143
5.77ff	30
5.84	105
8.391	108

Testament of Dan

3:2	169
5:10	169

Testament of Judah

22:2	140

Testament of Levi

4:5	168
8:15	145
9:8	168

Testament of Naphtali

2:2ff.	156
3:3	31

Testament of Simeon

7:1	168

PHILO

Cherub

127	136

Conf.

77f	121

Contempl.

6	114

De humanitate

168	170

De Judice

73	170

Decal.

7ff	30

Det.

10	10

Deus

10	116
57	110, 136

Leg. Alleg.

3.96	27

Index of Ancient Sources

Legat.

71	114

Mig. Abr.

6	27
9	130
89ff	35
131	170

Mut.

15	10
29–31	136

Opif.

16	148
53	126
69	155
103	138

Post.

2	100

Sacerdot

42	131
81	27, 136
117	111
315	142

JOSEPHUS

Ant.

1.8	96
1.31	136
3.6–12	18
3.237	112
8.297	127, 174
10.25	111
10.42	98
14.264	115
15.69	97
20.183	132

Contra Apion

1.1ff	29
1.1	2
1.183–205	2
1.73ff	2
1.227ff	2
2.1	96
2.43	2
2.168	157

Jewish War

7.346	133

NEW TESTAMENT

Matthew

1:18	105
1:21	143
2:2	179
5:3	156
5:13ff	129
5:16	158
5:17–18	124
5:44f	171
5:44	54, 129
5:45	165
5:48	171
6:25	54, 153
6:28	54, 153
6:31	54, 153
8:13	163
8:25	152
10:26	151
10:33	140
11:2	163
11:4ff	177
11:7	104
11:10	53
11:12	139
11:19	125
12:12	114
12:18	145
12:28	40
13:47	99
14:19	155
15:2–3	174

Matthew (cont.)

15:17	142
17:17	148
18:8	158
18:13	162
19:11–12	167
19:17	54, 144
19:26	148
20:23	146
20:25	135
20:28	150
21:35	104
23:32	149
24:9f	140
25:34	146
25:41	158
25:46	140, 158

Mark

1:2	53
1:11	146
3:4	114
5:28	109
7:3–4	174
7:26	98
8:32	161
9:7	146
9:32	124
9:37	23
9:43–47	149
10:17	149
10:18	54, 144
10:20	99
10:24	149
10:25	149
10:27	54, 148
10:45	150
13:19	113
13:52	162
14:24	150
14:30	105
14:44	11
14:58	30
15:35	103
16:8	108

Luke

1:1–4	7
1:2	175
1:3	97
1:13	128
1:26f	168
1:44	164
2:13	147
2:29	143
2:32	161
3:6	168
4:14	127
4:18	23
4:23–24	121
5:26	120
6:9	114, 125
6:23	109
6:25	144
6:26	109
6:27–28	129
6:27	54
6:33	125
6:35	125
6:36	171
7:27	53
7:47	161
9:37	109
9:43	157
10:1	142
11:48	148
12:19	131
13:9	154
15:19	54
16:16	139
17	54
17:11	54
17:14	54
17:16	54
17:20	115
18:14	129
18:19	54, 144
18:27	148
21:11	13
22:37	150
22:63	130
28:27	152

John

1:1ff	27
1:1	162
1:3	27, 136
1:10	27, 124, 136
1:11–12	120
1:14	27, 156
1:18	141, 143, 156
2:13	55
2:14	55
2:23	179
2:24	133
3:5	54, 148
3:11	124, 154
3:16	54, 154, 156
3:17	54
3:18	156
3:22	123
3:34	155
4:2	142
4:21–22	99
4:23	106
4:32	112
4:46	145
4:47	145
4:50	145
4:51	145
4:53	145
5:16	106
5:19	26
5:24	167
5:30	26
5:37	103
5:38	23
5:44	110
6:38	26
6:64	102
7:2	27
7:16	26
7:17	157
7:22	112
7:26	161
8:7	27
8:37	167
8:49	161
8:59	151
10:2	27
10:34ff	172
10:36	26
12:28	125
12:47	54, 99
12:50	166
13:31	55
13:34	172
14:6	133
14:13	55
14:17	127
14:20	162
15:13	151
15:18–19	54, 126
15:19	54, 127
15:25	126
16:2	104
16:24	149
16:29	161
17:3	151, 166
17:11	127
17:14	54, 127
17:16	127
17:17	134
17:26	162
18:20	161
20:27	161
21:1	143
21:2	161
21:25	109

Acts

1:1	7
1:2ff	160
1:7	148
1:17	160
1:19	117
1:25f	160
2:36	166
2:41	141
2:44–45	157
2:47	131
3:13	145
3:14	150
3:26	125, 139, 145
4:26–28	135
4:27	145
4:30	145

Acts (cont.)

5:15	109
7:12	131
7:21	122
7:52	150
8:1	127
8:27	104
8:30	137
9:15	114, 166
9:31	127
10:14	122
10:23	147
10:28	113
10:42	41
12:19	148
13:14	112
13:18	152
13:33	162
13:46–48	162
14:1	98
14:4	160
14:14	160
14:15	53, 111
14:17	53, 142
15:27	139
15:28	157
16:6	129
16:34	122
17:18	146
17:22	98
17:23	141
17:24	127
17:30	23, 39, 97, 147
18:21	156
19:24	104
20:35	143
21:15	102
21:26	163
21:34	166
22:11	169
22:14	150
22:30	166
23:1	120
23:20	97
23:26	96
24:3	96, 100
25:10	98
25:19	98
26:2	98
26:25	96
27:20	149
28:11	119

Romans

1:18ff	30
1:25	104
2:4	23, 39, 144, 148
2:5	51
2:7	152
2:10	152
2:13	167
3:2	133
3:8	125
3:21–26	54, 147
3:25f	23, 148
3:25	143
3:26	148, 151
3:30	151
4:5	151
4:6	102
4:18	55, 137
5:2	55
5:12ff	151
5:15	151
5:18	151
5:20	147
6:17	175
7:10	166
7:18	123
7:22–23	130
8:3	137, 152
8:4	123
8:9ff	41
8:10	162
8:12f	53
8:18	148
8:20	55
8:28	149
8:30	151
8:32	146, 153
8:33	151
9:4	109
9:20–21	156
9:21	104

10:4	35	10:3	53
11:1–2	149	10:13	156
11:22	103, 144	10:19–20	32
11:28	53, 114	10:30	125
11:33	151	10:32	99
12:2	105	11:1	171
12:3	51	11:2	174–75
12:6	51	11:3	26
12:10	99	11:23–24	175
12:13ff	14	11:23	175
12:14	125	12:2	105, 127, 148
13	125	13:1	56
13:1ff	38, 123	14:2	54, 158
13:2	129	14:4	162
13:10	123	14:11	166
14:8	140	14:40	144
16:7	160	15:3–4	175
16:25–26	117, 146	15:3	175
		15:27f	26
		15:27	137
		15:41	115
		15:53f	54
		15:53	130–31
		15:58	125

1 Corinthians

1:4	51
1:21	126
1:25	152
2:1–7	54
2:6–8	135
2:7–10	146
2:9	146
2:9b	165
3:2	156
3:19	167
4:2	162
4:4–5	41
4:10	125
4:12	53, 125, 148
7:10	175
7:28	121
8	122
8:1	55, 64
8:4	32
8:5–6	110
8:6	27
8:7	102
8:8	125
9:10	55, 167
9:13	114
9:17	54, 133
10	122

2 Corinthians

1:14	102
1:15	164
2:2	148
4:10	124
4:15	51
4:18	159
5:1–4	130
5:1	130
5:10	41
5:14	130
5:17	101
6:8	125
6:9–10	53, 124
6:10	53, 122–26
6:18	133
8:1	55
8:8	152
8:11	155
9:1	109
9:6	137
9:8	51

2 Corinthians (cont.)

9:10	100
10:1	138
10:3	123
10:4	102
10:7	97
10:10	139
11:2–3	168
11:2	11
11:7	157
11:9	157
11:16	124
11:29	55
11:32	127

Galatians

1:1	166
1:12	117, 120
1:14	174
1:17	166
1:22	124
2:7	133
2:20	162
3:8	151
3:23ff	35
3:23	128
3:28	98
4:4–5	114
4:4	26, 147
4:10	115
5:13	137
5:17	54, 128
5:19ff	123
5:23	124
5:25–26	41
6:2	54, 157
6:5	54
6:14	127
6:15	101

Ephesians

1:7	150
1:9	143, 149
1:10	115
1:13	167
1:15	148
2:2	166
2:10	137
2:19	121
3:2	115
3:4f	146
3:8	51, 151
3:17	143
4:5	140
4:22–24	53, 101, 162
4:22	102
4:24	101
4:30	49
5:1	171
5:6	102
5:11	107
5:23	152
6:9	54, 157–58

Philippians

1:9	125
1:17	111
1:22	143
1:27	120
1:29	164
2:9	26
2:12	139
3:6	50
3:19	132
3:20	53, 123, 152
4:6	143
4:7	127
4:8	161
4:9	174
4:12	125

1 Thessalonians

1:4	114
1:6	171
2:14–16	126
2:19	139
3:12	131
4:1	174
4:7	137

2 Thessalonians

1:5	156

1:7ff	41	*2 Timothy*	
1:11	148	1:11	160
2:15	174–75	1:13–14	175
3:6	174	2:2	175
		2:15	167
Colossians		2:20	104
1:5	167	3:13	142
1:13	40	4:3	108
1:15	133		
1:16	27, 127, 135	*Titus*	
1:18	50	2:1	163
1:24	50, 126	2:14	150
1:26f	146	3:2	125
1:26	117	3:3–7	147
2:2	161	3:3	129, 147
2:16	112–13	3:4–5	54, 149
3:1–2	155	3:4	144
3:1	155	3:8	119
3:10	155	3:14	119
3:11	98, 120		
		Philemon	
1 Timothy		13	150
1:9	124		
1:10	163	*Hebrews*	
1:17	133	1:2	26–27, 136
2:3	142	1:3	103
2:4	161	1:6	26
2:6	150	2:8	137
2:7	160	3:3	148
2:10	97	3:7	162
2:13	156	3:13	162
3:16	55, 117, 120, 162	3:14	158
4:3	114, 163	3:15	162
4:4	113	4:2	102
4:5	122	4:12	145
4:7	113	5:5	26
4:8	55	6:5	40
4:10	163	6:13	109
5:3	158	6:17	143
5:4	142	7:8	18
5:5	158	7:23	129
5:14	122	7:26	150
5:16	158	9:6	111
6:17	146	10:13	149
6:19	158	11:10	135
6:20	175	11:13–14	120–21

Hebrews (cont.)

11:27	133, 143
11:37	125
12:9	107, 163
12:16	150
13:2-4	122
13:20	26

James

1:7	109
1:12	156, 159
1:17	115
1:26f	97
1:27	126, 167
2:5	156
2:6	157
3:15	132
4:2	128
4:3-4	100
4:13	101
5:1	101
5:2	103
5:3	104
5:6	36
5:7	167
5:20	150

1 Peter

1:2	51
1:4	156
1:5	131
1:7	104
1:10	51
2:3	144
2:9f	99
2:9	99, 146, 161
2:11	121, 128
2:13	38
2:15	126
2:20	126
3:9	53, 125
3:17	126
3:18	125, 150
4:3	113
4:8	150
4:13	126
4:19	133

2 Peter

1:2	51, 154
1:8	131
1:13-14	130
1:16	107, 157
2:1-3	14
2:1	143
2:9	158
2:18	158
2:21	175
3:3	117
3:9	39
3:10	136
3:12	136
3:16	117
3:18	54

1 John

1:4	54
1:5	152
1:7	152
1:8	134
1:10	134
2:1	150
2:8	40
2:13	162
2:14	134, 162
2:15ff	98
3:4	151
3:12	161
3:13	129
3:16-17	172
4:4	127
4:9	54, 137, 154, 156
4:11-12	156
4:14	137
4:19	24, 56, 156
4:20-21	156
4:21	172
5:19	98

2 John

12	54

3 John

4	164
11	126

Jude

3	163, 175
7	158

Revelation

1:8–9	133
2:9	36
2:11	148
9:20	32
10:10	121
14:8	38
18:21	38
19:15	133

GRECO-ROMAN LITERATURE

Acts of Apollonius

25–28	98

Aelian
N.A.

3.24	107

Var. hist.

3.9	167

Aeschylus
Agamemnon

368	151

Aristophanes
Nub.

318	142

Aristotle
Ath. pol.

42.1	120

Eth. nic.

2.7.12	112
3.6.2	126

Mundo

399a	133

Pol.

3.9.5	126

Rhet.

1.2.7	112
2.2.24	112
2.5.11	112
3.6.7	15

Cicero
Nat. d.

2.56	155

Sen.

73	132

Somn. Scip.

3	130

Tusc.

1.74	132

Cornutus
Nat. d.

6	134

Demosthenes
De Corona

work	100
2.29	157

Dio Chrysostom

2.26	170

Diodorus Siculus

1.37.4	119
4.44.1	99
13.73	157

Diogenes Laertius
Lives

7.2	167

Dion Halicarnassus
Ant. or.

proem.	96
4.19	116

Epictetus
Diss.

1.2.18	106
1.3.3	154
1.14.7	135
2.8	45
2.11	45
2.14.13	171
3.24.64	150

Eustathius

1069.1	168

Herodotus
Hist.

1.64	155
1.112	122
1.122	167
2.63	111

Homer
Od.

5.92	122

Horace
Satires

1:8	105

Lucian of Samosata
Alex.

4	141

Hermotimus

22–24	118

The Passing of Peregrinus

13	98

Marcus Aurelius

2.3	120
2.16	46
3.11	46
4.21	45
4.40	43
5.8	43
6.9	43
7.31	171
10.7	45
11.3	98
12.36	46

Menander
Sam.

4	97

Ovid
Meta.

1.84ff	155

Pausanias

4.32.4	130

Plato
Apol.

23B	109
29A	132

Crat.

394B	166

Index of Ancient Sources

Gorgias
488B	157
514E	101
515C	150

	Leg.
2.660B	147
803	176
832D	120

Lysis
214B	164

Phaed.
62B	130, 132
82E	130
257D	112

Prot.
323A	108
328C	108

Rep.
349B	157
592B	123

Symp.
196C	160
202E	22

Theat.
176	48
178A	110

Tim.
32C	142
44B	130

Xen.
work	145

Pliny

Nat.
2.5.18–19	172
2.7.18	172

Trajan
10.96	127

Plutarch
Def. orac.
13	22
29	128

Lib. ed.
7.5A	147

Mor.
74E	104
85C	131
101B	128
363B	115
823f	158
823B	119
830E	104
1008A	134

Nic.
2	112

Polybius
1.3.10	164
1.7.3	104
2.17.6	142
2.26.2	102
2.29.1	119
3.16	11
3.19.7	127
3.55.1	119
4.1–2	7
4.67.9	147
9.43.5	114
20.9.11	166

Pseudo-Phocylides

185	122

Pseudo-Plato
Ax.

365E	128

Seneca
Ep.

41:2	46
102	45

Otio

4.1	46
12.36	46

Sophocles
Antig.

164	136

Oed. tyr.

719	122

Strabo
Georg.

8.1.2	119
16.2.24	132

Tacitus
Annals

15.44	30, 127

Thucydides

1.22	116
1.34	116
2.70	112
2.97	120
3.64	163
6.87.3	163
6.90	120
7.25.9	139
7.70	139
7.72	139
7.86	161

Xenophon
Anab.

1.2.3	142
1.5.5	104
3.1	103
3.3	103
6.4.27	136
7.1.33	131
7.4.9	150

Cyr.

1.4.3	99

Hell.

4.5.18	148

Mem.

1.1	98
1.1.10	112
1.4.11	155
1.7.2	107
1.7.5	114
4.4.19	107

Oec.

8:4	128

APOSTOLIC FATHERS

Barnabas

work	8, 35
1:6	120
3	131
5:5	144
5:6	41
6:1	145
6:3	163
9:2	145
9:4	35
9:7	120
10	35

15:9	41	17:7	140
16:7ff	30	20:3	167
16:10	109	20:5	133, 152
19:8	130		

Didache

2:2	122
4:13	175
6:3	109
8	36
8:1	113, 131
9:2f	145
9:3	166
10:5	40
11:3ff	160
11:3	120
16:3–8	140

1 Clement

1:2	166
2:3	133
2:8	123
7:2	175
8	51
9:1	144
19:1	157
19:3	144, 146
20:1	135
20:2ff	115
20:4	165
20:5	130, 151
20:6–7	136
20:6	151
20:10	148
20:11	143
24:1	41
25:1	120
25:2	156
26:1	136
29:1	114
33:3	136
35:5f	40
35:5	136
38:3	148
40:4	110
41:2	18
42	160
42:3	41
44:6	157
54:4	123
59:2	136, 145, 147
60:2	135
61:1–2	135

Diognetus

1–10	9, 16–17, 19, 27, 30, 49, 51, 63–65
1	6, 29, 35, 38, 63, 164
1:1–2	xiv
1:1	5, 8, 10–12, 15, 18, 22, 38, 40, 42, 59, 102–3, 106–7, 109, 178
1:2	8
1:5	162
1:6	96
2–5	60
2–4	xv, 96
2	6, 8, 15, 30
2:1	10, 12–13, 31, 42, 53, 61, 64, 97–99, 101–3, 108, 110, 116, 123, 134, 157, 164, 178–79
2:2ff	13, 62
2:2–3	103
2:2	11–12, 15, 33, 58, 61, 101, 103–4, 108, 113, 119, 142
2:3–4	103–5
2:3	10–13, 15, 58, 103, 113, 141

2 Clement

work	8
6:4	158
6:6	130
16:4	40

Diognetus (cont.)

2:4	10–12, 15, 61, 104–5, 107, 142
2:5ff	43
2:5–6	38, 103
2:5	10, 14, 31–32, 62, 103, 105–6
2:6	98, 106, 126
2:7–8	106–7
2:7	10–11, 61–62, 103, 110, 130, 136–37, 178
2:8	10, 32, 61, 97, 107–8, 111, 126, 131, 148, 152
2:9	10–15, 102, 106–8, 121, 133
2:10	8, 11–12, 33, 38, 46, 58, 98, 105, 117, 126
2:15	165
2:25	166
3–4	6
3:1	6, 10–12, 37, 43, 97–98, 103, 109, 117, 154, 178
3:2–3	10
3:2	10, 12, 14, 16, 21, 35–36, 97–98, 107, 109, 132, 143
3:3ff	21
3:3	10–11, 44, 98, 102, 105–6, 110–11, 116
3:4–6	14
3:4	10, 14, 21, 44, 52–53, 58, 100, 110–13, 153
3:5	13, 101, 105, 107–8, 111, 120, 156
4	64
4:1	10–11, 22, 43, 98, 102, 112–14, 117, 131
4:2ff	13
4:2	9, 12–13, 16, 22, 44, 58, 103–4, 113, 132, 136, 142
4:3	12–13, 114, 129
4:4	10, 13, 22, 113, 114, 178
4:5	10, 12–13, 21, 44, 58, 104, 106, 110, 113–15, 133, 137, 141, 147
4:6	6, 10–12, 15, 28, 36, 41, 43, 46, 59, 97–98, 101, 113–14, 116–17, 119–21, 132–33, 157–58, 178
5–10	6
5–7	6, 25
5–6	xv, 29, 96
5	29, 40, 99, 117–19, 126, 140
5:1	11–12, 118–19
5:2	100, 117–20
5:3	6, 11–12, 28, 43, 46, 59, 97, 116–20, 132, 160, 178
5:4–5	38
5:4	12–15, 38, 41, 100, 119–20, 123, 127, 137
5:5—6:9	14
5:5	11, 13, 38, 44, 117, 120–21, 127, 162
5:6	11, 14, 16, 29, 120–22, 128
5:7–8	38, 40
5:7	13, 62, 122–23
5:8	28, 53, 103, 114, 123, 128
5:9–10	44
5:9	41, 53, 117, 120, 123, 131, 137
5:10–15	14
5:10	38, 117, 123–24, 178
5:11ff	38
5:11–16	123–24
5:11–12	14

Index of Ancient Sources

5:11	30, 96, 99, 124, 139	7	15, 24, 50, 140
5:12f	53	7:1ff	6, 117
5:12–13	53, 124	7:1f	8, 43, 175
5:12	3, 13–14, 41, 45, 126, 130–31	7:1–5	17, 140, 177
		7:1	11, 14, 16, 28, 54, 59, 115, 117, 119, 134–35
5:13	13, 40		
5:14–16	14	7:2	10–16, 21, 23, 25–27, 39, 44, 47, 59, 102, 107, 111, 113, 115, 117, 130, 132–37, 140, 143, 145, 150, 154, 156, 161, 167
5:14	125		
5:15	53, 125		
5:16	13–14, 45, 53, 107, 124–26, 130–31		
5:17	14, 38, 42, 98, 106, 109, 120, 126, 128–29		
		7:3ff	161
6	29, 34, 40, 43–44, 48, 117–18, 126, 132	7:3	12, 15, 23, 132, 134, 137
		7:4ff	25
6:1ff	15	7:4–6	14
6:1	12, 15, 44, 126–27	7:4–5	14, 54, 137
6:2–9	14	7:4	11, 14, 16, 18, 23, 26, 28, 41, 54, 58, 62, 137–39, 141, 150, 157, 162, 171
6:2f	14		
6:2	12, 15, 43, 120, 127, 129, 132		
6:3	44, 54, 121, 127–28	7:5	12, 14, 2, 114, 138–39
6:4	13, 43, 48, 97, 129–30, 179	7:6–9	177
		7:6–7	124, 176–77, 179
6:5–6	128	7:6	12, 14, 27, 41, 52–53, 68, 139–40, 177–79
6:5	11–12, 15, 38, 41, 54, 106, 114, 126, 129, 147		
		7:7–9	98
6:6	15, 30, 54, 96, 99, 124, 129	7:7–8	177
		7:7	25, 38, 139–40, 157, 179
6:7	14–15, 43, 62, 107, 128–30, 132, 136	7:8	38, 97, 107, 124, 126, 131, 139–40, 149, 153
6:8	14–15, 28, 40–41, 45, 54, 59, 119, 121, 123, 130–31, 137		
		7:9	13–14, 24, 41, 106, 139–40, 177–79
6:9	10, 15, 38, 40, 107, 120, 124, 126, 131, 140, 178	7:11	154
		7:12	13
		8–9	6
6:10	12, 15, 30, 113, 130, 178	8	140
		8:1	11–12, 21, 27, 29, 57, 60, 105, 137, 140–41, 153
7ff	96		
7–10	63		
7–9	XV, 19, 22	8:2–4	33

Diognetus (cont.)

8:2–3	14
8:2	12–16, 21, 23, 34, 44, 102–3, 113, 141–42
8:3	11–13, 102, 142
8:4	62, 142, 158, 177
8:5–8	62, 142–44
8:5–6	13–14
8:5	10, 137, 142–43
8:6	10, 15, 21, 28, 39, 43, 59, 62, 64, 118, 143, 154, 165
8:7–9	96
8:7	16, 22–23, 26, 28, 44, 110, 113, 136, 143–44
8:8	13, 22, 41, 54, 142, 144, 148
8:9	9, 23, 25, 44, 144–47, 152
8:10–11	23, 54, 146
8:10	23, 60, 117
8:11	10, 12, 14–15, 22–23, 25–26, 28, 64, 102, 136, 145–46, 151, 156, 177
9–12	62
9	24, 46, 50, 99, 141, 143, 147
9:1–2	21, 39
9:1	4, 11–15, 18, 22–26, 28, 40, 54, 115, 129, 140, 145, 147–48, 150–52, 156, 159
9:2–6	25
9:2–5	24
9:2	11–15, 20–25, 28, 41, 47, 54, 62, 114, 121, 133, 138, 140, 144, 146, 148–49, 151, 157, 162, 178
9:2b	14
9:3	8–9, 11–12, 25, 54, 150
9:4	13, 24–25, 125, 143, 148, 151, 178
9:5	xv, 12–14, 23–24, 29, 146, 148–51, 177–78
9:6	11–14, 25, 44, 54, 107, 110, 118, 144, 147, 150–53, 169, 177, 179
10	xv, 6
10:1	21, 25, 29, 39, 49, 57, 68, 118, 140, 153–54
10:2	16, 22, 25, 28, 40, 45, 49, 52, 54, 102, 104, 113–14, 127, 130, 137, 146, 153–56, 161
10:3–4	24
10:3	11, 23–24, 29, 47, 51, 54, 56, 114, 124, 140, 154, 156
10:4–7	118
10:4–6	45, 156, 170–71, 178
10:4	11, 13, 34, 140, 144, 179
10:5–6	40
10:5	10, 13–14, 22, 39–40, 139
10:6	11, 13–15, 40, 54, 124, 137, 150, 157, 171
10:7	11–12, 14, 38, 41, 47, 53–54, 96, 98, 107, 116–17, 123–24, 126–27, 137, 139–42, 157–59, 161
10:8	7, 38, 47, 68, 140–42, 148, 157–59, 177
11–12	xv, 6, 9, 17, 19, 40, 49, 51, 55–56, 63–65, 103, 160, 163, 173–74, 179
11	5, 34

Index of Ancient Sources

11:1	11, 16, 51, 63, 109, 119, 160, 164, 166, 178	12:8	13, 49, 165, 167–68
11:2–3	50	12:9	11, 14, 21, 25, 49, 51, 55, 66, 102, 127, 134, 136, 140, 147, 154, 160, 162–63, 168–69
11:2	11, 21, 25, 39, 49, 51, 55, 66, 102, 117, 134, 136, 146, 154, 160–63		
11:3–6	162	**Ignatius**	
11:3	11, 14, 21, 25–26, 49, 55, 66, 102, 134, 137, 149, 160–62	*Eph.*	
		1:1	170
		4	163
11:4–5	162, 173–74	15:3	30
11:4	49, 51, 55, 64, 66, 102, 162	16:2	142
11:5–7	49, 51	*Magn.*	
11:5–6	50	12	162
11:5	11, 15, 25, 39, 50–52, 66, 136, 161–63, 163–64	13	120
		Phil	
11:6	14, 19, 39, 49, 51, 56, 64, 66, 160, 162–63, 169, 174	2	141
		9:2	140
11:7–8	56		
11:7	25, 49–51, 102–3, 134, 160, 164	*Poly.*	
		3:2	127
11:8—12:1	164		
11:8	50, 63, 103, 147, 164	*Rom.*	
		heading	157
12:1–2	51	2	163
12:1	49, 52, 103, 147, 164–65	4	160
		4:3	166
12:2ff	49		
12:2–8	52	*Smyrn.*	
12:2–3	52	3	98
12:2	15, 51, 165	4:1	162
12:3–7	64	7:2	114
12:3	12–13, 19, 49, 56, 64, 143, 165, 167	*Trall.*	
12:4	12, 51, 166	1	170
12:5	11, 55, 64, 160	5:1	167
12:6	11, 55, 147, 167	5:2	127
12:7–8	103, 164	10	114
12:7	102, 142, 166–67		

Martyrdom of Polycarp

2.4	107
7.2	175
11.2	159
14.1	146
14.3	146
20	146

Polycarp
Phil.

7	131
11:2	55

Shepherd of Hermas
Mandates

4.1	110
4.2	110
4.2.1	168
9.1.10	165
9.28.1	165
12.4.2	154
12.5.1	157

Similitudes

1.1ff	121
5.1ff	131
6.3.3	158
8.11.1	144
9.1	49
9.11	40
9.12.2	144
9.12.5–8	25
9.22.2	111
9.23.4	149

NEW TESTAMENT APOCRYPHA AND PSEUDEPIGRAPHA

Acts of John

27	171

Acts of Paul and Thecla

5–16	40

EARLY CHRISTIAN LITERATURE

Apostolic Constitutions

8.5	146
8.14	146
8.39	146
8.40	146
8.41	146

Aristides
Apology

work	20, 29
1	58, 144, 154
2	37, 99, 101
3	34, 58, 104
3.2	103
4ff	141
4	58
5	58
7	58
10	58
13	58
14	35–37, 58–59, 113
15–17	5
15	40, 58–59, 118, 124–25, 157
16	40, 59, 129
16.4	99
17	41, 57

Arnobius

2.9–10	33
2.69	99
2.75	23, 100

Athanasius
Inc.

12:6	155
14:7	155
19:3	141

25:5	166
31:2	141
45:3	155

Athenaeus
Deipn.

400a	103

Athenagoras
Petition

work	67

Res.

work	67
12	40
19	39
21	121

Suppl.

2	3
3	38, 122
4	98
7	158
9	20, 102
10	135
16	104
21	144
27	134
30	143
32	123
33	121
34	123
35	122

Clement of Alexandria
Paed.

1.1.1	131
1.5.20	102
1.5.22	164
1.24	145
3.1.1	170
3.1.5	171
3.8.1	121

Philosophumena

10.33	172
10.34	172

Protrepticus

1.10.8ff	61
1.10.15	62
2.7.11f	61
2.12.18f	62
2.13.13	62
2.29.13	62
4.39.19ff	61
4.48.3–4	62, 106
5	55
9.62.11	62
9.63.2	61
10.68.9	62

Quis dives salv.

35	151
36	129

Strom.

1.1.11f	176
1.2	34
1.4–5	34
1.13	34
1.17	34
1.19	34
1.29.182	57, 133–34
2.5.20	115
5.13	34
6.5.39ff	32, 57, 109, 113
6.5.39	33, 99, 115
6.5.41	36, 99
6.8	34
6.17	34
7.17.108	176

Virg.

2.15.5	163

Cyprian
Donatum
work	8
1	100

Eusebius
Dem. Ev.
1.6.62–63	98

Hist. eccl.
2.3	127
2.25	130
4.3	17, 176
4.7	127
4.15	159
4.26	96
5.10	65

Praep. ev.
63	142
132	142

Gregory of Nazianzus
Orat.
14.26	172
14.27	172

Hippolytus
Anti.
2	101
3	173

Contra Noetum
4	173
11	173
15	173
17	173
18	66

Dan.
3.9	145

Philos.
work	65
10.33	17, 139
10.34	167

Irenaeus
Epid.
53	177

Haer.
3.11.8	127
3.22.4	168
4.20.6	143
4.20.11	143
4.33.9	177
4.33.11	145
4.34.3	177
4.59	138
5.1.1	138
5.19.1	168

Jerome
Vir. ill.
19	178

Justin
1 Apol.
1	127
2	125
3	119
4	100
5	38, 120, 125
6	50, 98, 106
7	120
8	41
9	30, 32, 61
10	28, 111, 154, 175
11–12	98
12	26, 41
13	26, 50, 98
14–15	118
14	5, 40, 122, 124, 157

15	40	22	36
17	38, 41	27	114
20	33	30	22
23	27, 105	32	140
26	164	34	122
27	122	35	103
28	39	39	140
29	40, 106, 121	40–43	60
30	20, 60, 105	41	154
31	126	54	133
32	133	55	110
36	126, 144	56	145
37	37	76	145
39	98, 177	80	163
44	143	83	27
45	41, 129	105	120
46	60, 120	110	131, 139–40, 159, 177
52	140		
53	60	117	150
59	98	119	98, 120
62	106	121	139, 177
63	37, 135	124	172
66	163–64	127	145
68	41	128	145
		133	126
		140	144

2 Apol.

1	38–39
2	122
4	154
5	136–37, 177
7	129, 154
9	41
10	60, 132
11–12	98
13	26, 33, 60
14	125
15	33

Lactantius
Div. Inst.

6.23	123

Inst.

5.19	132

Longinus
Subl.

1.2	170
32	147

Dial.

5	130
8	33
10	118
14	140
15	131
16	37, 126
19	126

Melito
Homily on the Passion

work	65–66
16	66
59	14
68–71	66

Melito (cont.)

75	66
82–86	66
87	66
91	14
93	14
104	66

Minucius Felix
Oct.

5	43
9.2	99
12	129
27	31
30	122

Origen
C. Cels.

1.26	99
2.31	19
4.2	19
4.7	100
4.24	28
4.99	28
6.66	95
6.78	23, 100
7.9	145
7.10	145
7.26	132
8.35	22
8.60	22
8.70	129

Pseudo-Clement
Epistles

	1.12.2455

Homilies

7.8	97

Recognitions

5.15–16	58
5.15	103, 106–7

Pseudo-Justin
Cohort. ad Gent.

8	43, 132

Tatian
Or. Graec.

2	33
3	33
4	110
11	40
13	45
15	45
19	39
31	29

Tertullian
Adv. Jud.

4	114
5	36

Apol.

1	123, 125
5	178
7	122
9	122
12	106
24	98
31ff	125
32	129
38	129
39	30, 122, 129
41	123
42	118, 121
46–47	33
47	33
50	131

Carn. Chr.

17	168

Marc.

1.29	16
4.34	16

Scap.
5	132

Theophilus
Autol.
work	8
1.2	95
1.3	134, 144, 152
1.4	136
1.11	133
2.1	96
2.3.36	143
2.4	33
2.9	20
2.10	49, 110, 133
2.15	50
2.18	144
2.27	130
3.12	163
3.20ff	29

PAPYRI

B. G. U.
1011.2.15
120916	137

P.Giss.
1.7	157

P.Magd.
2	114

P.Oxy.
II, 275	150
IV, 70559	100
IV, 72922	165
IV, 744	122
VI, 9252	144
VI, 930	97
VII, 107018	103
VIII, 115316	111
IX, 118718	136
IX, 12134	121
XII, 14645	107
XIII, 1600	66

P.Par
1566	120
26	102

P. S. I.
II, 120	138

P.Tebt.
1.6.48	111
2.27830	124
2.4104	163

www.ingramcontent.com/pod-product-compliance
Lightning Source LLC
Chambersburg PA
CBHW051055230426
43667CB00013B/2313